SEA

HAMGYŎNG

To Vladivostok

Yalu R.

P'YŎNGAN

Ŭiju

Pukch'ŏng

Taedong R.

Yŏnghŭng

Port Lazareff

Munch'ŏn

Tŏgwŏn

Bay of Yŏnghŭng

Wŏnsan

P'yŏngyang

HWANGHAE

Kaesŏng

Kanghwa City

Kanghwa Island

Tŏngjin

Ch'oji

SEOUL

Yŏngjong Is.

Inch'ŏn

KYŎNGGI

ANGWŎN

Ullŭng Island

Taebu Is.

Suwŏn

Bay of Asan

Namyang

P'ung Is.

Tangjinp'o

Han R.

Haemi

Andong

CH'UNGCH'ŎNG

Naktong R.

Kunsan

Okku

Taegu

Puan

KYŎNGSANG

CHŎLLA

Tongnae

Pusan

Mokp'o

Tsushima

Chin Island

Shimonoseki

Kŏmun Island

Soan Island

Port Hamilton

KYŪSHŪ

Sasebo

Cheju Island

Nagasaki

D1029041

PUBLISHED FOR THE ROYAL ASIATIC SOCIETY
KOREA BRANCH
BY THE UNIVERSITY OF WASHINGTON PRESS

CONFUCIAN GENTLEMEN
AND
BARBARIAN ENVOYS

The Opening of Korea, 1875–1885

MARTINA DEUCHLER

UNIVERSITY OF WASHINGTON PRESS
SEATTLE AND LONDON

Library of Congress Cataloging in Publication Data

Deuchler, Martina, 1935-
    Confucian gentlemen and barbarian envoys.

    Bibliography: p.
    Includes index.
    1. Korea—History—1864–1910. 2. Korea—Foreign
relations. I. Title.
DS915.D48   1976   951.9'02   76-57228
ISBN 0–295–95552–X

To the memory of Ching Young Choe

CONTENTS

Photographs
    Sin Hŏn, Kuroda Kiyotaka
    Min T'ae-ho, Min Yong-ik, Kim Hong-jip, Kim Ok-kyun
    Inoue Kaoru, Li Hung-chang, Paul Georg von Moellendorff, Lucius H. Foote
    The Korean Foreign Office, King Kojong

PREFACE

The decade that began with the conclusion of Korea's first modern treaty in 1876 and ended with the Convention of Tientsin in 1885 was important for two reasons. The international situation in the Far East changed drastically which stimulated unprecedented developments on the peninsula. The impulses Korea received from abroad and a new predisposition for change heralded an era of gradual socio-political and economic development. Korea had to give up her isolation and her seclusion policy. She was forced to establish her identity in a world situation that was no longer determined by unilateral dependence on China, but by a new network of multilateral relations. Korea did not easily take up these complicated new responsibilities. Although she had had a long history of adapting foreign values to her socio-political system, in the nineteenth century she was a thoroughly Confucianized state. It was the Confucian heritige as well as her age-old reliance on her tributary relations with China that conditioned Korea's response to the outside world. Korea had to resolve the problem of preserving the traditional order and also devise a way of adjusting herself to the exigencies of the modern world.

This study has two focal points. First, it analyzes the inception of Korea's treaty relations with Japan and the West and the establishment of treaty ports and international trade. Second, it explores the repercussions caused by the entry of foreign ideas and goods into the peninsula. Although this study is primarily a diplomatic history of the decade, attention is also given to internal problems—those that can best be understood within the diplomatic framework. Korea's attitude and behavior toward the outside world, her "diplomacy," can not be comprehended without reference to the traditional forces that conditioned the country's response, as well as to the new forces that attempted to shape this response according to models that were adopted from outside the country. Especially after 1882, when the first round of treaties was finished, the intellectual debate on the country's course of modernization determined Korea's orientation toward the outside world. Intellectual history became inseparable from foreign policy.

Foreign policy is shaped not only by external factors that converge upon a country and intellectual issues that stimulate debate within, but also by economic problems. Therefore, in this study the relevant aspects of the traditional economy and the new features that developed because of the treaty ports are described. Modernization presupposes intellectual and psychological motivation, but it takes place on an economic and technological level. Korea's economic history just prior to the opening of the ports has received less attention than that of earlier and later periods. Although this gap in research is partly because of the scarcity of relevant source material, Korea's total response to the outside world can not be evaluated without analyzing post-1876 economic policy in the light of the country's traditional economic situation.

The decade 1875 to 1885 is viewed from different angles: it is seen as the final stage of the old order or the beginning of a "new age." It is often considered the period during which Western-style capitalism first penetrated the country, one during which the Japanese tried out their fledgling imperialist policy. Causal relationships are forged with subsequent events. The periodization of Korea's modern history is still debated among Korean historians and gives rise to polemical discussions about the specific value of certain dates in Korea's modern history. These discussions generally try to answer two major questions: when did Korea's modernization begin, and what was the course and nature of Japanese imperialism on the Korean peninsula?

In answer to the first question some scholars insist that there is more reason to designate 1894, the year of the Kabo reforms, as the starting-point of Korea's modernization because those reforms introduced genuine modern features into Korea. The reforms of 1894 were, however, only possible because the groundwork had been laid during the preceding decade by the development of "enlightened thought." Other scholars stress one of the most important concomitants of modernization—nationalism—and see the years 1896 to 1898, when the movement for national independence got under way, as the formative period of Korea's modernization.

As for the second question concerning the nature of Japanese imperialism, 1876 is often construed as the point of departure for an undeviating, inevitable process that climaxed in Japan's annexation of Korea in 1910. In explaining such traumatic events, hindsight at times replaces factual analysis, and therefore it is easy for events and personalities to appear in a distorted light.

An examination of these two questions falls within the area of this study. One can not be considered without the other; both must be studied in the light of Korea's whole tradition. The history of the decade 1875 to 1885 thus contributes to an understanding of the forces that inhibited Korea's response to the outside world as well as of the new elements that made the decade qualitatively different from the previous one. It also outlines the basis for the factors that shaped Korea's modern history beyond 1885.

⋈⋈⋈⋈⋈⋈⋈⋈⋈⋈⋈⋈⋈⋈⋈⋈⋈⋈⋈⋈⋈⋈⋈⋈⋈⋈⋈⋈⋈⋈⋈⋈⋈⋈

This study was originally undertaken as a Harvard doctoral dissertation at a time when most of the relevant Korean primary sources were not available outside Korea. Later, research was continued during a two-year period in the former royal archives, the Kyujanggak Archives (Seoul National University). This broadened the scope of the topic and added detail to the original version. I owe a special debt to Mr. Yi Sang-ŭn and his staff for providing me with the facilities of the Kyujanggak over a long period of time. In the search for documents in the vast holdings of the former royal archives, Prof. Chŏn Hae-jong's *Han'guk kŭnse taeoe kwan'gye munhŏn piyo* (Manual of Korean foreign relations, 1876–1910) was an invaluable guide. Whereas this investigation yielded rich dividends as far as the political aspects of the period were concerned, the economic information remained sketchy because most documents dated from the late 1880s and the early 1890s. Many gaps, however, could be filled by using Chinese, Japanese, and Western sources.

Archival research in Western sources bearing on Korea's foreign relations during the period under consideration started in Houghton Library (Harvard University). It was also done in the Auswärtiges Amt, Bonn, and in the Public Record Office, London. I wish to thank both institutions for patiently tracking down seldom-used materials. With special permission I studied the Korea correspondence of Jardine, Matheson & Company in the

Library of Cambridge University, England.

In the dissertation stage I greatly profited from the advice and guidance I received from Prof. John K. Fairbank (Harvard University). My appointment as research fellow in East Asian studies by Harvard from 1967 to 1969 enabled me to go to Korea to conduct further research and to revise and expand the original thesis. I am grateful to Prof. Fairbank for his encouragement and the counsel he generously gave me over many years. I also wish to thank Prof. Lee Kwang-rin (Sogang University, Seoul), Prof. James B. Palais (University of Washington, Seattle), and Dr. Susan Shin for reading earlier versions of this book and for making many helpful comments and suggestions for its improvement. Dr. Edward R. Wright, Jr. (Fulbright Commission, Seoul) and the Council of the Royal Asiatic Society, Korea Branch (Seoul) encouraged the preparation of the manuscript for publication. Mr. Ch'oe Yŏng-hŭi, chairman of the National History Compilation Committee (Seoul), kindly provided photographic materials. My indebtedness to Karl Moskowitz (Harvard University) is especially great. With his editorial criticism and unsparing suggestions he contributed significantly to the preparation of the final version. This book would not have become publishable without the assistance I received from Sandra Mattielli (Seoul) who edited, prepared the layout and the art work, and saw the book through the various stages of production. Her expertise and dedication have helped me to endure the rigors of authorship.

KOREA
ON THE EVE OF HER OPENING

During the first half of the nineteenth century the Western powers set in motion the forces that were to bring East Asian societies into the modern world. While China and then Japan were coping with these outside forces, Korea remained a "hermit nation,"[1] maintaining relations only with China and, to an insignificant extent, with Japan. When Korea emerged from isolation in the 1870s, her image was that of a country stifled intellectually by orthodox Confucianism, stagnant economically, and politically bound to the decaying Chinese empire.

Westerners used the word "secluded" to describe a country that lacked foreign relations in the modern sense. The word had a negative and anti-foreign connotation which implied an unenlightened view of the outside world. Nineteenth century Korea, to Western eyes, was an example of a secluded, backward country with little civilization. Charles Gutzlaff in the early 1830s wrote of Korea that "we cannot think the interior is as thickly inhabited as the maritime provinces of China. Their state of barbarism, cherished by the odious system of exclusion, which had nowhere, by a maritime nation, been carried further than in Corea, does not admit a numerous and flourishing population; nor do we think there are any large cities to be found."[2] Gutzlaff drew these conclusions after only a brief glimpse of Korea's coastal areas; he did not and could not evaluate the significance seclusion had for the Koreans.

The Koreans became a racially and linguistically homogenous people during United Silla (668–935). They lived in a well-defined territory administered by a centralized bureaucracy. Their shared traditions and cultural values made them well aware of their special position toward China and Japan. To the Koreans, China as a political entity and China as the source of Chinese culture were two different concepts. The Koreans thought of themselves as members of a universal system, the so-called Sinic Zone. They identified their country with geographically-oriented names: *tongguk* (eastern country), *haedong* (east of the sea), *chwahae* (left of the sea), or *tongbang* (east side). Within the Sinic Zone[3] the guardianship over Chinese culture could shift. This was especially so when the barbarian Ch'ing took control of China in the middle of the seventeenth century; the Koreans thought they should act as caretakers of Chinese culture. This assumed cultural role, however, stood in great contrast to Korea's political status vis-à-vis China.

Before United Silla, during the Three Kingdoms (Koguryǒ, Paekche, and Silla) Sino-Korean relations were shaped into a unique pattern. Strategic as well as economic and cultural considerations dictated a more regulated relationship with their powerful northern neighbor. This was especially true for Koguryǒ, the northernmost kingdom. From the early fourth century A.D., the basic features of tributary relations began to emerge.[4] Within the next two centuries the characteristics that later marked Sino-Korean relations during the Ming and Ch'ing dynasties crystallized.

The Sino-Korean tributary relationship entered its "classic" period after the Ming wrested power from the Mongols and established a new Chinese dynasty. In Korea, the founder of the Yi dynasty (1392–1910), Yi Sǒng-gye, and his successors reaffirmed Korea's allegiance to the Ming emperor.[5] In time, Yi-Ming relations were put to an unprecedented test. At the end of the sixteenth century the hordes of Hideyoshi's armies twice cut through the peninsula. China was called upon to fulfill her part in the relationship: the defense of her tributary against foreign aggression.[6] Ming forces came to Korea's rescue and took an important part in forcing the Japanese intruders back to their home islands. Although Ming help in those dark years was not motivated by pure altruism, the Koreans came to remember it with special gratitude.

The Koreans' allegiance to the Ming brought them into conflict with the Manchu who conquered China and established the Ch'ing dynasty in 1644. The Manchu invaded Korea twice—in 1627 and again in 1636—and eventually forced the Koreans to accept their terms.[7] The Korean king became a vassal of the Manchu khan. Henceforth, whenever a new king ascended the throne in Korea, envoys were sent to Peking to request an imperial mandate from the Ch'ing, and an imperial patent of appointment was bestowed on the new king, the queen, and the crown prince. From 1645 to 1894 the kings of Korea sent to Peking an average of about two missions per year in addition to the annual winter solstice mission (*tongjisa*).[8] These missions, headed by an envoy (*chŏngsa*) and, in most cases, accompanied by an associate envoy (*pusa*), were usually made up of two to three hundred members. They followed a fixed, 750 mile overland route which led to Peking. The trip took about fifty days, and five months passed before they were back in Seoul.[9] On the Chinese side, Korean-Ch'ing relations were put under the management of the Reception Department (Chu K'o Ssu) which in turn was part of the Board of Rites. The Chinese emperor usually sent one command (*choch'ik*) a year to Korea. In most cases it was transmitted by an imperial envoy.[10] The relationship was called *sadae*, literally "serving a superior."

In contrast to the *sadae* relationship Korea maintained with China, her attitude toward Japan was cast in the formula of *kyorin*, literally "dealing with a neighbor." Korea's relations with Japan are based on geographic proximity and an historical tradition which reaches back as far as Early Silla and Paekche. During the early Yi dynasty an increasing number of Japanese pirates (*Wakō*) swarmed over the Korean coast in search of food and booty. The Korean government devised a plan to control the troublesome raiders: a pacification policy that transformed the pirates into traders. The program was so successful that before long the number of traders had increased to the point where the government had to adopt measure to restrain them. Surrounded on three sides by the sea, the Koreans kept the intruding foreigners in check by confining them to a few selected ports along the southern coast.[11] The rigid lines along which Korean-Japanese relations moved for the next centuries, however, were laid down after the Hideyoshi invasions in the 1590s. These invasions brought disaster to the peninsula and put a halt to trade. They also instilled in the minds of the Koreans a distrust and apprehension toward their insular neighbors. The settlement of 1609 granted the daimyo of Tsushima the monopoly on Korean trade. An elaborate scheme of regulations kept trade under tight control. Only ships carrying a certificate stamped with special seals which Tsushima had received from the Korean authorities were allowed to cast anchor in Pusan, the only port open to the Japanese after 1609. Korean embassies were dispatched to Edo even more rarely than before.[12]

Pusan thus became the only point of contact that Korea maintained with Japan from 1609 until the late nineteenth century. It was the station where the Japanese missions were received, and it was, in a limited sense, a trading place. The center of these diplomatic and commercial activities in Pusan was the Japan House (Waegwan) which was first established in 1408 when the Japanese traders were being confined to designated ports. This compound was designed to keep the Japanese under close surveillance and reduce their contact with the Korean populace. Anyone who wanted to enter or leave the Japan House had to undergo a thorough search at one of the two (after 1709, three) gates which were staffed by soldiers and interpreters. Outside the walls, six military checkpoints further discouraged smuggling and spying. The only permanent inhabitants of the compound were the head of the Japan House (*kwansu;* Jap. *kansu*) whose tour of duty was limited to two years, a judicial official, a number of trade officers (*taegwan;* Jap. *taikan*), a doctor, and a staff of interpreters, secretaries, and artisans. All of them were appointed and sent to Pusan by the daimyo of Tsushima. On the Korean side routine matters were handled by the language officer (*hundo*) and the assistant language officer (*hundo pyŏlch'a*) who were directly responsible to the prefect of Tongnae, the naval commander of the Left Navy Headquarters of Kyŏngsang, and the commander of Pusan Fort. They were assisted by a large number of minor officials. The governor of Kyŏngsang was the key figure for transmitting the reports between Pusan and Seoul. The exchange of diplomatic communications was impeded by the long distance between the two cities and by the cumbersome administrative procedures. The arrangement that developed at Pusan clearly stunted "neighborly relations" with Japan.[13]

Korea's traditional "foreign relations" thus were characterized by tributary relations with China and restricted neighborly relations with Japan. The Sino-Korean relationship was dominated by China; the Korean-Japanese relationship was dominated by Korea. For Korea, the tributary relationship with China had a strong self-protective quality. Her initially difficult relations with the Manchu made a minimization of contact politically desirable. To avoid provoking the Ch'ing, the Koreans imposed restrictions upon themselves. From the early eighteenth century, their fishermen were not allowed to fish on the high seas.[14] Korean law prohibited the disclosure of any information about the country to outsiders.[15] The sending of tribute to China was a defensive measure. It was the political side of a policy of minimal interaction with the outside world. Such a policy of national preservation is generally subsumed under the term "seclusion." This policy was also directed against Japan. Seclusion was thus a positive concept as far as the Koreans were concerned. It was the expression of a self-sufficient system that excluded the raison d'être of relations with countries outside this system. It was instrumental in preserving the stability of the Far Eastern balance of power. Up to the nineteenth century, seclusion was a tradition that fitted Korea's particular status within the Far Eastern world.

During the nineteenth century, Western ships appeared more frequently off Korea's shores to back up the Western demands to open trade relations. But the Koreans were not receptive. They had no reason to admit into their well-balanced world those countries that threatened to undermine the system with their "heterodox ideas." The intrusion of the West forced the Koreans to restate the principles that had guided their "foreign policy" for the past two hundred years. This restatement of the seclusion policy has become associated with the name of the Taewŏn'gun, who reigned for his son, King Kojong (r. 1864–1907), during the decade 1864 to 1873. Under the Taewŏn'gun the seclusion policy underwent a definite escalation. From the claim that a vassal state (*sin*) did not have foreign relations, the policy was broadened to include an active component: repulsion. Korea's world view narrowed to two dimensions: the "celestial court" of China on the one side, and the foreign "barbarians" or "wild animals" on the other.[16] Formal relations with the latter was unthinkable. The Taewŏn'gun defended Korea's morality and righteousness militarily. His successful repulsion of the French in 1866 and the Americans in 1871 proved to the Koreans that the seclusion policy was effective and gave them a false sense of security and preparedness. The Taewŏn'gun's seclusion policy thus preserved the peninsula's isolation and retarded Korea's response to the outside world after 1874.[17]

When the first Western nations came into contact and subsequently into conflict with Korea, they turned to Peking to find redress for their grievances. In the late 1860s and the early 1870s the Chinese government was called upon to restate the nature of the Chinese-Korean relationship. The Chinese, however, failed to perceive that the Confucian concept of suzerain-state vis-à-vis vassal-state could not be equated with state sovereignty as set forth by modern international law. The Chinese, although not oblivious to the changing circumstances of the time, found it difficult to adapt their relations with Korea to the exigencies of the modern world; they were unable to discard a system that had outlived its usefulness.[18] Instead, China was content to refer to the fact that although Korea was subordinate to China, she was solely responsible for matters such as her trade with foreign lands, the propagation of alien religions, and her own laws. Furthermore, there was no responsible government organ in Peking which specialized in Korean affairs. The traditional agency, the Board of Rites, fulfilled the purely ceremonial function of transmitting correspondence to and from Korea. The Tsungli Yamen, although not nominally in charge of Korean affairs, came to assume the role of interpreting Chinese-Korean relations to the outside world. Since it was preoccupied with problems of more immediate concern to China, however, its pronouncements on the Korean case lacked determination and firmness. China's inattention to the full proportions of the Korea problem irreparably damaged her influence over her vassal.

In contrast to China's slow absorption of the West's new ideas concerning international relations, Japan was quick to realize the advantage international law brought to herself and to her relations with her neighboring countries. The Meiji Restoration in 1868 deeply reformed Japanese thinking and institutions. Demands to change the stagnating relationship with Korea became strong and irreversible. The daimyo of Tsushima was no longer satisfied with his traditional, virtually tributary relationship with the Koreans and urged economic and ceremonial reforms that would improve his status vis-à-vis Korea. The most revolutionary of his proposals was that demanding the replacement of the Korean seals of authority with Japanese seals. Because of the special nature of Korean-Japanese relations, the newly established Foreign Office left the initiative of renewing contact with Korea to the daimyo. Late in 1868 he dispatched a mission to Korea to announce the Meiji Restoration. This attempt to open an era of "reformed formality" came to naught. The Koreans protested that the Japanese violated the treaty relationship by sending an "irregular envoy" through Tsushima. They also protested the abolition of the Korean seal and the use of a number of Chinese characters that were reserved only for their correspondence with China. Korea's stubborn rejection of subsequent missions, and her refusal to acknowledge the announcement that the Japanese Foreign Office had taken charge of Korean affairs (on September 8, 1871) created a sense of frustration in Japanese government circles that eventually gave rise to demands for "armed diplomacy." The Japanese moved to abolish the Japan House, the very embodiment of an outdated relationship. In June 1873, continued disputes and exchanges of protest climaxed in a warning issued by the prefect of Tongnae. The prefect bluntly attacked Japan's adoption of institutions "from other countries" and called her a "land of no law." This document prompted some segments within the Japanese government to formulate the *seikanron*, the "debate about the punishment of Korea."[19]

Japan's active post-1868 diplomacy led to the conclusion of a treaty between Japan and China on September 13, 1871. Article one contained a non-aggression clause.[20] It vaguely referred to the "nations and territories belonging to either of the contracting parties." It was a grave oversight on the part of the Chinese chief negotiator, Li Hung-chang, not to insist on a more precise formulation in terms of geography and boundaries. Li memorialized to the throne that the non-aggression clause tacitly protected Korea from a possible Japanese attack.[21] Therefore, when the Japanese asked for China's mediation in their growing frustration over the Korea issue, the Tsungli Yamen disclaimed any responsibility in the question and referred to article one of the treaty of 1871. The ambiguous meaning of this document and the Tsungli Yamen's lukewarm stand led Japan to interpret the treaty clause according to her own will.[22]

Korea's complete failure to communicate with Japan was also an expression of the general consternation and alarm the Koreans felt about Japan's rapid Westernization. The adoption of Western ways meant to many tradition-minded Koreans a breach with tradition that revealed the unstable and fickle nature of the Japanese people. The Koreans feared that Japan might conspire with the West against Korea.[23] During their long period of minimal contact, Korea and Japan had lost the substance of "neighborly relations" and, thrust into the turmoil of nineteenth century international politics, they did not easily find the ways and means for a rapprochement.

When King Kojong assumed the full responsibilities of government in 1874, he inherited his father's "restored" government. His kingship seemed securer than those of his predecessors because the Taewŏn'gun had made great efforts to restore to the royal house the prestige and the glory it had had in the early days of the dynasty. The Taewŏn'gun had moved against the powerful clans which, through their marriage connections with the royal house, had come to threaten the royal prerogatives. King Kojong was assisted by an elaborate, centralized bureaucracy. Access to the ranks of officialdom was still determined by success in the civil service examinations; by the nineteenth century, kinship ties became an additional criterion for official success. The Taewŏn'gun had also restored to the Council of State (Ŭijŏngbu) its old status as the supreme administrative organ of the state. King Kojong came to rely on the cooperation of those who held the three top posts: the chief state councillor, the left state councillor, and the right state councillor. For the implementation of his post-Taewŏn'gun policies, the selection of these three men was crucial.[24]

In the economic sphere the Taewŏn'gun had reformed the "three systems" (the land tax, the military tax, and the grain-loan system), but his economic program had been basically conservative.[25] Korea was an agrarian country. Most of the daily necessities were produced in the home, and there were few markets. From the beginning of the dynasty, guild-like associations of merchants in Seoul obtained goods for the government and disposed of surpluses from the government storehouses. During the seventeenth century and especially during the eighteenth century, private merchants who operated outside government restrictions and supervision emerged. Although this development is often interpreted as a sign of economic dynamism, there is little evidence from the nineteenth century that shows a sustained growth of commercialism. The Korean economy remained basically non-commercial.[26]

Korea engaged in very little trade with her neighbors. On the occasion of the official missions to China, the Korean mission members and Chinese government authorities exchanged a limited amount of goods. The Chinese especially valued Korean ginseng.[27] After the middle of the seventeenth century, some trade towns were opened along Korea's northern border where Korean merchants periodically traded with Chinese merchants under strict governmental control.[28] More important in terms of value was the illegal border trade which came to flourish in the eighteenth century. Most of the merchants involved in this illegal trade came from Kaesŏng and Ŭiju.[29] Korea's northern border with China was difficult to close effectively to illegal trade and traffic. Her contact with Japan, maintained across a channel of water, was more easily kept under control. Commercial exchanges at Pusan were made, under government supervision, only when an official Japanese embassy arrived in the port.[30]

Under the Taewŏn'gun there was no change in the government's policy on trade. No measures were taken to stimulate domestic or foreign trade. Korea's limited trade relations with China and Japan before 1876 served the particular purpose of securing her position within the traditional Far Eastern framework: vis-à-vis China, trade was a duty forced upon her as a tributary; vis-à-vis Japan, trade had a strong defensive quality. In both cases, trade was government controlled. Trade outside this control was considered alien to the country's interests and was therefore suppressed by administrative as well as legal measures. The government feared that opened borders would lead to an unrestrained outflow of the goods that were necessary to sustain the life of the people.

King Kojong thus inherited a politically and economically self-sufficient country. The king and his officials had confidence in the country's strength. The seclusion policy had been successful, and the moral superiority of the Confucian state had been demonstrated. There was no reason for King Kojong to give up this inheritance when the Japanese returned to Korea in 1874 with their renewed determination to open Korea to Japanese diplomacy and trade.

SIN HŎN (above) and KURODA KIYOTAKA were the chief negotiators of the 1876 Korean-Japanese treaty, Korea's first modern treaty. Sin Hŏn had had a brilliant military career under the Taewŏn'gun. He was sixty-one years old when this portrait was painted, five years before his historic diplomatic assignment. Kuroda was a lieutenant-general in the Japanese army.

Protagonists of Min power: MIN T'AE-HO (upper left) and his son, MIN YŎNG-IK (upper right)
Min Tae-ho's photograph probably was taken by the Japanese photographer who opened the firs
photo studio in Seoul in 1883. In Min Yŏng-ik's photograph, the crown of his Korean hat is missing
KIM HONG-JIP (lower left) was sent on an official mission to Japan in the summer of 1880, an
this photograph was taken in Tokyo. The box contained his official seal. KIM OK-KYUN (lowe
right) first visited Japan in the spring of 1882. This photograph was taken in Nagasaki.

Formulators of Japan's and China's policies toward Korea during most of the decade: Foreign Minister INOUE KAORU (upper left) and the Governor-General of Chihli, LI HUNG-CHANG (upper right). Both photographs were probably taken in the 1890s.

PAUL GEORG VON MOELLENDORFF (lower left) was the first Western adviser in Korean service. LUCIUS H. FOOTE (lower right) was the first envoy extraordinary and minister plenipotentiary of the United States in Korea. He took office in Seoul in May 1883.

The above photograph of several members of the Korean Foreign Office was taken on February 18, 1884. Seated in the front row, from left to right: Yi Kyo-yŏng, Yi Cho-yŏn, Min Yŏng-mok, Kim Hong-jip, Hong Yŏng-sik, and Pyŏn Wŏn-gyu.

KING KOJONG, surrounded by his bodyguard, carried in procession from Tŏksu Palace.

OVERTURES TO CHANGE

The Taewŏn'gun's forced retirement in December 1873 did not bring about a rapid modification of Korea's seclusionist policy. His withdrawal from power, however, ushered in a period during which the Koreans could reconsider their attitude toward the outside world. Ascending a throne his father had greatly strengthened, Kojong had the prerogative to reevaluate Korea's most pressing foreign policy issue: her relations with Japan. Kojong's assumption of power coincided with Japan's formulation of the post-*seikan* policy. These two events helped to set the stage for a rapprochement between the two countries.

King Kojong's Search for a New Political Rationale

The shift of power from the Taewŏn'gun to King Kojong was brought about by an interplay of ideological and political factors. It is an oversimplification to attribute this shift, as earlier works have done, to a plot by members of the Yŏhŭng Min clan.[1] Some scholars argue that the Min established direct access to power through Queen Min, a clan member who had been chosen as King Kojong's consort. The Min supposedly used her as the pivot of their power and, as a "faction," grew so influential that they were able to force the Taewŏn'gun into retirement and then bring about a drastic change in foreign policy.[2] This theory can not be maintained without serious qualifications. The personal relationship between King Kojong and his in-law clan may never be uncovered in full detail, especially since little is known about the young king until 1874. Documentary evidence shows that at least during the first years of his reign King Kojong was not a mere puppet manipulated by the Min. He chose his highest advisers independently of Min influence and also set out on a foreign policy course that does not reflect direct Min interference.

All of the high ministers retired on December 30, 1873. On January 1, 1874, King Kojong appointed Yi Yu-wŏn chief state councillor. Yi served in this capacity until May 26, 1875. On January 24, 1875, Yi Ch'oe-ŭng filled the post of left state councillor; he was elevated to chief state councillor on December 17 of that same year. The post of right state councillor was given to Pak Kyu-su on January 19, 1874. He was succeeded a year later by Kim Pyŏng-guk. Yi Yu-wŏn and Pak Kyu-su continued in government as ministers-without-portfolio.[3] If the Min plot theory were true, these important appointments should reflect the tendency to recruit individuals who were known for their opposition to the Taewŏn'gun. The records of the officials concerned, with the exception of Yi Yu-wŏn, do not warrant such an assumption. Yi Yu-wŏn (1814–1888), a member of the Kyŏngju Yi clan, had had a long political career before he served a short term as left state councillor under the Taewŏn'gun from the summer of 1864 to early 1865. He had gone to Peking as secretary of the winter solstice mission as early as 1845.[4] Although generally described as a Min partisan, he evidently enjoyed King Kojong's trust. He was criticized several times for bad management of state affairs, but his outspoken critics were punished, not he.[5]

Yi Ch'oe-ŭng (1815–1882), the Taewŏn'gun's older brother, held minor appointments during the Taewŏn'gun period, but he seems to have been a well-known advocate of the abolition of his brother's seclusion policy.[6] After Yi Yu-wŏn's retirement in May 1875,[7] Yi Ch'oe-ŭng shared the administrative responsibilities with Pak Kyu-su. Pak Kyu-su (1807–1877) can not be easily put into any category. As the grandson of the Sirhak scholar Pak Chi-wŏn, he was educated in an atmosphere free of heavy Confucian orthodoxy. He went to Peking in 1860 as vice-envoy, and in 1872 he went again as mission head. Although he became famous as governor of P'yŏngan in 1866 for ordering the burning of the *General Sherman*—an act that epitomized the Taewŏn'gun's seclusion policy—he later approached the problem of foreign relations with a pragmatic view.

He was never close to the Min.[8] Kim Pyŏng-guk (1825–1904), who succeeded Pak as right state councillor on January 24, 1875, held several
posts, including that of minister of rites, under the Taewŏn'gun.[9] These
appointments do not reflect Min instigated reaction against the Taewŏn-
gun.[10] In fact, people such as Kim Pyŏng-hak, Hong Sun-mok, and Kang
No—all very prominent in the Taewŏn'gun era—were recalled to serve
again as high ranking officials under King Kojong.[11] The young king thus
began his rule with a slate of officials that showed a continuity of personnel
rather than a sharp break with the past.

It is true that the Min began occupying posts in the higher echelons
of the government during the last years of the Taewŏn'gun. They did not,
however, immediately climb to top positions after his retirement.[12] Their
political fortunes undoubtedly suffered a setback with the untimely
death of Min Sŭng-ho (1830–1875) on January 5, 1875. Min Sŭng-ho, the
natural uncle of King Kojong, began his political career under the Taewŏn'gun and died when he was the minister of war. He was the most prominent member of his clan at the time of his death.[13] His father, Min
Ch'i-gu (1795–1875), died three weeks later. Min Kyu-ho (1836–1878)
then emerged as the clan's leading spokesman and continued to hold a
variety of posts. He advanced to the position of right state councillor only
a few weeks before his early death in 1878.[14] It is obvious, then, that the
Min were omnipresent in the government, but they did not hold offices
high enough to exert the important influence on government affairs, and
especially on foreign policy, that has often been ascribed to them. Much more
manifest is the fact that King Kojong tried to surround himself with men
of proven ability in government, regardless of their factional affiliation.
He put special trust in Yi Yu-wŏn and Pak Kyu-su. Both had experienced the world outside Korea's boundaries, and they were well known as
advocates of a reasonable alternative to the seclusion policy.

The Taewŏn'gun had been an ambivalent ruler in that he had broken with tradition in certain fields of domestic policy but had been rigidly
traditional in other areas, especially in Korea's foreign relations. The
common denominator underlying all his policies had been his indomitable
will to enhance the prestige and the power of the royal house. If, after the
Taewŏn'gun's retirement, the Min had emerged as the ruling faction,
surely they would have forced Kojong to reverse his father's policies and
follow their political ambitions.[15] This, however, was not the case. An
analysis of the internal policies implemented by King Kojong during the
period between 1874 and 1876, for example the abolition of the Ch'ing

cash and the eventual reestablishment of the Mandongmyo (shrine to the Ming), shows that the king was able to act quite independently and actually did so.[16] His policies cut across partisan lines. This was true in the domestic area. It becomes clear later that it was also true in the realm of foreign policy. It is possible to advance the hypothesis that the eventual opening of the country to the outside world was less the result of factional victory than the culmination of a pragmatic course of action initiated by the young King Kojong himself.

If Kojong was setting the stage for a more realistic foreign policy, it is pertinent to look for the roots of his concern with the world outside Korea. One of the most important channels through which he received information about events in China, and to some degree in Japan and even the West, was the reports brought back by the Korean missions which were sent to Peking on various occasions. Even during his father's rule, King Kojong showed great interest in these missions and turned the audiences for the returning envoys into veritable question and answer sessions. His curiosity was not easily satisfied, and the discussions ranged over a variety of topics: China's attitude toward the West, activities of the Western barbarians in Peking, China's foreign trade, Japan's Westernization, the conclusion of the Sino-Japanese treaty, the influence of Christianity, and the internal state of affairs in China and its comparison to conditions in Korea. These reports from abroad undoubtedly had a marked influence upon the young king, as his ever more detailed questions reveal. He was eager to broaden his knowledge about foreign matters and widen his perspective on Korea.[17]

King Kojong found that Yi Yu-wŏn and Pak Kyu-su observed the Peking scene with more perception than the average mission member. Both had serious reservations about contact with the West. When Pak Kyu-su returned from Peking in January 1873, he reported that the Western powers wanted trade, but that the Chinese had found out that Western goods were only dazzling the people's eyes and had no real usefulness. China herself, Pak continued, had begun producing arms on the Western model and even had built her own steamship in order to become less dependent on foreign trade.[18]

When King Kojong received the chief envoy of the winter solstice mission, Chŏng Kŏn-jo, on May 15, 1874, he heard about some surprising changes in Peking's diplomatic world. Kojong was startled to learn that the Japanese envoy was received in audience by the Chinese emperor on the same footing as his Western colleagues and that the Japanese were even opening a legation in the Chinese capital. Since her defeat by the Western powers in 1860, Chŏng explained, China was following a conciliatory course by allowing some trade and establishment of foreign legations in Peking. King Kojong mused about the decline of China's political status and interpreted it as a show of weakness toward foreigners.[19]

The reports about China's reactions to the West undoubtedly made King Kojong and his advisers realize that China's preoccupation with the West could affect her commitments to Korea. They began to doubt China's role as suzerain when they received a secret communication sent by the Tsungli Yamen via the Board of Rites in August 1874. The message warned that Japan, after finishing the Formosa expedition, might turn her troops against Korea. In such a case, the Tsungli Yamen speculated, France and the United States, still smarting from expeditionary defeats at Korean hands, might support Japan. Korea would be unable to stand up against three adversaries. Korea, the Chinese explained, would therefore be well advised to meet the Westerners' demands for trade and conclude trade treaties with them to secure their friendship and avert the danger of their attack.[20]

This secret warning was received with anything but gratitude. Yi Yu-wŏn and Pak Kyu-su shared the opinion that China had invited the West's incursions through her unguarded show of weakness. Yi angrily exclaimed that the Chinese advice did not go beyond words and that China apparently was totally unaware of Korea's high level of military preparedness. Pak's argumentation was somewhat broader: trouble had arisen in the past because Korea alone rejected trade with the West. Japan had been trading with the Western countries for a long time, although she strongly objected to Christianity, which seemed the usual concommitant to Western trade. Now Japan was demanding trade relations with China on the Western model. Trade, in Pak's view, was not objectionable, but since the Westerners were so cunning and unfathomable, it was doubtful that all they wanted was trade.[21]

Korea's highest officials, who had seen China retreat in the face of Western demands, were reluctant to take the message from the Tsungli Yamen as sincere advice. Their reaction discloses that their confidence in China was somewhat shaken. They did not underestimate the magnitude of the danger Korea was facing, but they could not believe that commerical treaties with the West were a guarantee against disaster. Yet, with Kojong's cooperation, they developed a new foreign policy that combined armed precaution and diplomatic circumspection. This new formula, which contained a choice between these two alternatives, seems to be indicative of the subtle change of tone and argumentation that differentiates Kojong's foreign policy from that of his father. Whereas the Taewŏn'gun had based his seclusion policy almost exclusively upon the maintenance of military power, his successor acquired a wider political perspective that called for a flexible approach to foreign policy issues. It was, however, one thing to obtain this new perspective; it was another to translate it into action. Tradition, whether at the home front or in the field of foreign relations, was not easily broken.

The tenacity of tradition was revealed in King Kojong's first foreign policy task: a reevaluation of relations with neighboring Japan. In his attempt to steer a new course, the king faced the formidable obstacle of a basically conservative officialdom. The king and his highest advisers had developed a new outlook on Korea and her neighbors, but the large majority of officials did not accept the new philosophy easily. Some were ambivalent in their support of Kojong's ideas while others were completely opposed to a new understanding with Japan. The rest were indifferent to the growing debate.

Initially, it was easy enough to remove from office those who were held directly responsible for the deadlocked relations with Japan. The governor of Kyŏngsang, Kim Se-ho, and the prefect of Tongnae, Chŏng Hyŏn-dŏk, were found guilty of having neglected their duties. The main target of royal displeasure was the language officer, An Tong-jun, who, as faithful executor of the Taewŏn'gun's seclusion policy, was held responsible for the stalemated relations. An's words and actions had put the situation into the wrong light and had helped strengthen the negative attitude toward Japan. Kim Se-ho was reprimanded and dismissed from office; Chŏng Hyŏn-dŏk was banished to the Munch'ŏn district in Hamgyŏng; An Tong-jun was decapitated and his head displayed on April 9, 1875.[22] The king then chose Yu Ch'i-sŏn as the new governor of Kyŏngsang and Pak Che-gwan as the new prefect of Tongnae. Receiving them in audience, he emphasized that he had chosen them as men of special ability to fill the posts so close to "another country." Hyŏn Sŏg-un and Hyŏn Che-sun were appointed to the posts of language officer (*hundo*) and assistant language officer (*pyŏlch'a*), respectively.[23] This changing of the guard in diplomatically strategic posts did not, however, signify a basic change of mind in the higher officialdom. King Kojong still needed official consensus to normalize Korean-Japanese relations. The king had first to win the battle against official lethargy and adherence to tradition at home before he could hope to resolve the deadlock with Japan. Despite the king's initiative, the legacy of the Taewŏn'gun's seclusion policy was to linger on for some years to come.

Obstacles to a Korean-Japanese Rapprochement

After 1873, the Korean problem lost some of its topical interest for the Japanese leadership. Issues of more immediate relevance to the internal and external strengthening of Japan preoccupied the minds of those in power. But rumors about the restoration of the king's rule in Korea and his punishment of the officials who were held responsible for the impasse of Japanese-Korean relations suggested the feasibility of renewing efforts to normalize relations with Korea. Such efforts would be the first test of the moderate course of action Iwakura Tomomi, Ōkubo Toshimichi, and their colleagues of the "peace party" had vowed to take after they had renounced war against Korea.[24] This moderation was expressed in two ways. First, the Japanese were willing to approach Korea again through the daimyo of Tsushima, although he had been relieved from his traditional duties in September 1871. Second, they recognized that a special relationship between Korea and China existed. The exact nature of this relationship was not clear to them, but they thought that they had to take it into consideration in reevaluating their own attitude toward Korea. Conciliatory as the tone of this new commitment to a diplomacy of moderation was, the Japanese were firm in their desire to exact a Korean apology for Korea's stubborn resistance to their overtures during the past seven years. Moderation therefore was susceptible to provocation.

Early in 1874, Foreign Minister Terashima Munenori, who had become the executor of the post-*seikan* policy, approved Moriyama Shigeru's suggestion to renew diplomatic contact with Korea through the daimyo of Tsushima. Moriyama, who had accompanied earlier missions to Korea and was considered a Korea specialist, was sent unofficially to Korea in September of the same year to test the new political climate. At Pusan he met the new language officer, Hyŏn Sŏg-un, and the assistant language officer, Hyŏn Che-sun. Moriyama sounded out the prospects of submitting a diplomatic note in which Japan would announce the dismissal of the daimyo of Tsushima, Sō Shigemasa, from his traditional duty as intermediary. If Korea were to refuse this note because its language style was unacceptable to the Korean government, Moriyama gave assurances of Japanese willingness to revise it. As a last possibility he suggested that Korea draw up its own version of the note and send it to Japan.[25]

Moriyama's probing of the political mood in Korea coincided with the Koreans' own reevaluation of their relations with their insular neighbors. Pak Kyu-su came out in favor of attaching less importance to the vocabulary and style the Japanese chose in their correspondence with Korea. Unmistakably, Pak called for peace with Japan. Chief State Councillor Yi Yu-wŏn, examining the reasons for the stalemated relations with Japan, indignantly remarked on August 11, 1874, that complete confidence in the words of a single language officer (he referred to An Tong-jun) had led to the abrupt deterioration of relations after three hundred years of smooth and peaceful intercourse.[26] Yi memorialized on September 19 that the Korean government should accept Moriyama's suggestions. With promising speed, the new prefect of Tongnae, Pak Che-gwan, was instructed to accept the Japanese letters in the future. The king also sent a secret letter to Moriyama that affirmed the complete change of political atmosphere within Korea.[27]

Favorably impressed by this turn of events, Moriyama Shigeru returned to Tokyo to report personally to his government. Foreign Minister Terashima felt that Moriyama's report warranted the dispatch of an official mission that would demand a formal apology and would explore Korea's status vis-à-vis China. To avoid antagonizing the Koreans, Terashima followed tradition and had the letters the envoy was to carry to Korea written in the name of the lord of Tsushima, Sō Shigemasa.[28] On January 10, 1875, Moriyama was appointed commissioner (*rijikan*) and Hirotsu Hironobu, who at one time had been the head of the Japan House in Pusan and who was regarded as a Korea expert, was made his deputy.[29]

Moriyama Shigeru left Tokyo aboard a steamship on February 10, 1875, and arrived at Ch'oryang on the 24th. During the negotiations, which started on the following day, Moriyama told Language Officer Hyŏn Sŏg-un that he intended to go to Tongnae to present the letters he carried directly to the prefect at a formal reception. He planned to arrange for formal negotiations according to the Korean government's promise of September 1874. Hyŏn asked to be allowed to take a first look at the letters. According to old practice, the language officer was authorized to examine letters for form and content and decide whether to send them back for revision or forward them to the government in Seoul. Moriyama initially rejected Hyŏn's request on the grounds that he would present them to no one but the negotiating official. But a short time later he handed copies to the language officer upon the latter's assurance of speedy action.[30] The local Korean officials felt, however, that the arrangement of a formal reception for the Japanese did not lay within their competence. They asked for a decision from the Korean government; it was promised within twenty-five days. When the twenty-fifth day passed by, Hyŏn offered the excuse that bad weather had delayed an answer from Seoul and that he was recalled to the capital for oral consultations. The Japanese took a dim view of the situation and threatened to leave their compound with one hundred men and march on Tongnae. Intimidated, the language officer then revealed what he had obstinately withheld: Seoul had indeed instructed the prefect of Tongnae to accept the Japanese letters at a formal reception. Although the date of April 1 apparently was set for the reception, it did not take place because Hyŏn had to leave for Seoul.[31]

Hwang Chŏng-yŏn, the prefect of Tongnae, sent a memorial summarizing the encounter with Moriyama. The Korean government's first reaction was consternation and indecision. This is evident from the March 12 reprimand King Kojong gave his ministers for hesitating to formulate a recommendation. Annoyed, Kojong demanded that his instructions to receive the Japanese and to examine their letters be delivered promptly to Tongnae. Obviously the king and the majority of the officialdom were at cross purposes. The encouragement relayed to Moriyama in the fall of 1874 apparently had been given by the king without his putting the issue to debate among his officials. In the spring of 1875, when Moriyama came back on the formal mission, the king could no longer ignore his ministers' opinions. It became clear that Kojong's course of action was seriously hampered by a conservative officialdom. This conservatism was nurtured by the deep distrust and continued apprehension about Japan's real motives and was founded on rigid adherence to traditional diplomatic convention and usage. In contrast, the king was neither alarmed at the reported differences between the Chinese and Japanese versions of the letters nor disturbed by the continued use of some hitherto unacceptable characters. Under royal pressure, the Council of State sent instructions to the prefect of Tongnae to arrange a reception for the Japanese and to take a close look at the original texts of their letters.[32]

The formal reception of the Japanese mission was thus in principle sanctioned by the Korean government and nothing, it seemed, could prevent it from taking place in due time. A few days after the Council of State begrudgingly recommended the reception of the Japanese, however, it decided that Moriyama's desire to return the old seals and alter the travel permits, which the Japanese had originally received from the Korean government, undermined the basis for discussion about renewing the friendship. It ordered the prefect of Tongnae to reprimand the Japanese for their rash action on these points.[33] Moreover, the Korean government refused to grant the Japanese request that the rules of the reception be fixed in advance and that the Japanese envoy be allowed to wear Western-style clothes.[34] In addition, it made a new list of conditions for the arrangement of the formal reception. Honorific characters such as *kō* (imperial), *choku* (imperial order), and *dai* (great) were terms which could only be used in reference to China. The Japanese should not refer to themselves in these terms. They were further advised to use the Chinese calendar in their official papers.[35]

His mission stalled, Moriyama concluded that Japan should adopt a bolder policy by taking advantage of Korean irresolution to achieve the Japanese objectives.[36] He thought his government should not insist upon using the characters objectionable to the Koreans, but considered the Korean request to use a Chinese reign-title instead of a Korean date as indicative of Korea's dependent status. Moriyama's deputy, Hirotsu, who was in Tokyo for consultations with the Foreign Ministry in April, used rumors about a reversal of the political situation in Seoul as a means of changing tactics. He urged Terashima to dispatch one or two warships as an indirect show of support for those forces within the Korean government that supposedly favored the opening of the country to the Japanese. The additional instructions Terashima sent to Moriyama, however, demanded patience. If the Korean government found it difficult to renew the old friendship with Japan, Moriyama should be satisfied with trying to persuade the Koreans to send an envoy to Japan to convey Korea's congratulations for the Meiji Restoration.[37]

The positions of both sides were summarized in a report from the prefect of Tongnae which was received in Seoul on June 13. On the same day, Hwang's appeal for guidance to break the deadlock gave rise to the largest debate yet on the issue (insofar as attendance of officials was concerned). Despite the king's repeated exhortations, the tone of the debate remained vague and hesitant. All agreed that the matter was delicate and could be reduced to the question of whether it was opportune to accept the Japanese letters or to reject them. Yi Yu-wŏn, who opened the debate, did not commit himself to a definite opinion. Yi Ch'oe-ŭng censured the Japanese for their one-sided change of diplomatic etiquette and the improper use of language in their correspondence, but he thought that Korea could not insist on a revision without grave consequences. Kim Pyŏng-hak rallied the opponents of rapprochement. They thought that the acceptance of the documents would demonstrate Korea's patience and her determination not to be the first to start a conflict; but such an attitude would be interpreted as weakness and would harm the "national polity" (*kukch'e*). This was an oblique call for resistance.

Only Pak Kyu-su favored the acceptance of the Japanese letters. Although his words in public were not as unequivocal as in his private correspondence, he unmistakably took issue with his colleagues' wavering. He also feared that the young king would be unable to manage the conflicts within the officialdom or present his own views forcefully. Although the wording of the Japanese documents was presumptuous, Pak said, the Koreans could hardly expect modest and polite language from rude "island barbarians." Since the Japanese themselves had announced that they had been changing their political system and were revising their neighborly relations, it would be provocative not to receive them. Pak, who evidently feared war, insisted that the acceptance or rejection of the Japanese documents could be interpreted as neither weakness nor as strength. If the Koreans received the Japanese with politeness and propriety, they would manifest strength despite their country's weakness. A renewed rebuff, Pak warned, would force the Japanese into a violent reaction.

The debate revealed that the first decision, in March 1875, to grant the Japanese a formal reception had been reached through royal pressure and over the heads of the opposition. The debate of June 13 offered no new points of view and led Yi Yu-wŏn to express his fears that news about the indecision and lack of a consensus within the Korean government might reach the ears of the Japanese. He urged the king to cut the knot with a royal decision. The king, however, ordered his ministers to rethink the whole complex of problems and to submit their recommendations in writing. From the memorial which the Council of State submitted in the late afternoon of the same day it is clear that Yi Yu-wŏn and Yi Ch'oe-ŭng were unable to round up enough supporters for their views which contained the ingredients for a compromise formula. Right State Councillor Kim Pyŏng-guk, backed by the majority, seems to have dictated the text of the memorial. It stated that the Council of State decided against permitting the submission of the documents drawn up by the Japanese Foreign Ministry, against tolerating their overbearing and arrogant wording, and against changing the old rules on the occasion of the formal reception.

The conciliatory tone was gone. Subsequent instructions to the prefect of Tongnae, however, were less determined. They repeated the ambiguous formula: "reject what must be rejected, and accept what must be accepted."[38]

One of the government's most able language officers, Kim Kyu-un, was dispatched to explain the official Korean viewpoint and work out a compromise with the waiting Japanese. Before Kim reached Tongnae, Language Officer Hyŏn Sŏg-un, presumably upon the prefect's order, told Moriyama on June 24 that the Korean government was not willing to arrange a formal reception for the Japanese envoy as long as the Japanese letters contained unacceptable terms and the Japanese insisted upon wearing Western-style clothes. Moriyama concluded that there was no hope for a successful outcome of his mission. He sent Hirotsu back to Tokyo to request that his government recall the mission.[39] When Kim Kyu-un finally saw Moriyama in the Japan House on July 19, the latter refused to discuss the issues again. Moriyama's uncompromising language shocked the Korean government, and some officials took it as corroboration of their views that the Japanese might start an armed conflict.

During all this confusion Pak Kyu-su continued his one-man campaign for a rapprochement with Japan. He castigated some of his colleagues for not speaking up even though they had made up their minds to accept the Japanese documents. Pak ridiculed the government's rigid attitude toward Moriyama. The use of a steamship did not mean that the Japanese were harboring belligerent intentions, and their style of clothes was of absolutely no concern to the Koreans. In a letter to Yi Ch'oe-ŭng, Pak criticized the Council of State for again entrusting the final decision to a single Pusan language officer.

The intensity of Pak's reasoning, the king's continuous remonstrance, and Moriyama's adamant attitude finally seem to have had an effect on those who hitherto had lacked the motivation or the courage to support the compromise plan. Only in this light is the unexpected change of mind that was revealed within the Council of State three weeks later understandable. On August 9 the Council instructed the prefect of Tongnae to arrange the formal reception promptly, to accept the Japanese notes even if they contained some unacceptable terms, and to send copies to Seoul. Hwang Chŏng-yŏn, the man ordered to implement the new policy, balked. He could not, he felt, act in the face of continued Japanese insistence upon wearing Western clothes and entering and leaving through the main gate of his prefecture. Hwang's "extremely rash and careless" attitude earned him official wrath and dismissal from office. Moriyama, unable to realize the full significance of these events, gladly left Pusan on September 21, 1875. For him the normalization of Japanese-Korean relations was a long way off.[40]

The Unyōkan Incident

Moriyama Shigeru's rebuff in Korea tested the oligarchy's patience and made it more receptive to the envoy's plea for a show of military force off Korea's coast. In May 1875, the warship *Unyōkan* had been maneuvering in Korean waters to expedite negotiations with the Korean officials.[41] In September, about the same time Moriyama was preparing to leave Pusan, the commander of the *Unyōkan*, Inoue Yoshika, was ordered to survey the ship route from the southwestern coast of Korea to Newchwang (on the Gulf of Liaotung). His instructions do not seem to have included permission to open military action against the Koreans.

According to Japanese sources, on September 20 the *Unyōkan* was steaming along the shore of the military district of Ch'oji on the southern part of Kanghwa Island. With the intention of getting some fresh water, a small boat was lowered from the *Unyōkan*. When it approached the coast, shore batteries fired on it in violation of the Japanese flag. Caught by the enemy attack and a rough sea, the small boat signaled for help, and the *Unyōkan* began to shell the Korean batteries. After this exchange of fire the warship retreated. In the meantime, it lowered another small boat, and a group of about thirty soldiers was set ashore on Yŏngjong Island, south of Kanghwa Island. The commander of the military district of Yŏngjong, Yi Min-dŏk, fled in panic. Fighting ensued, and thirty-five Korean soldiers were killed. The Japanese attackers looted and set fire to the district town and captured large quantities of weapons and gunpowder. After this clash the *Unyōkan* returned to Japan.[42]

The Korean version of the encounter became known much later. Kanghwa Island occupied a foremost position in the Korean defense system because it was not only the "door to the national capital," but also the traditional haven of Korean kings in times of emergency. It was securely guarded by defense batteries to ward off "peeping strangers." When the coastal guards at the southern tip of the island spotted the strange ship flying a yellow flag, they fired a few warning shots. They did not hit the boat, nor did they kill a single man. The Japanese, however, fell into a rage and retaliated by razing the city of Yŏngjong. The Koreans did not know until much later that they had engaged in battle with a Japanese warship.[43]

The Koreans had always been suspicious of Japanese intentions, and the *Unyōkan* incident (also called the Kanghwa incident) shocked them into realizing that their country's defenses were not impenetrable after all. Yi Min-dŏk, the military commander of Yŏngjong, set an example for this deplorable state of affairs. He was negligent in preparing adequate coastal defenses, and he failed to report the encounter. Thus when the Council of State belatedly learned of the incident, its first concern was to strengthen national defense.[44] Those within the government who opposed a new agreement with Japan saw their position vindicated. Right State Councillor Kim Pyŏng-guk was again their spokesman. He carried the day with policy suggestions that combined Confucian values with seclusionist tenets. He insisted that "to put the country in order internally and to repel the foreigners externally" (*naesu oeyang*) was the foremost need of the moment. He proposed strengthening the coastal defenses and urged the government to keep finances under tight control. He further admonished the government to establish internal order, to punish greedy officials, and to prohibit extravagance. The basis for this whole program, he emphasized, was the wisdom of the classics.[45]

The *Unyōkan* incident was welcome news in Tokyo and a call for immediate action. By telegram, Terashima ordered Moriyama Shigeru, who was in Nagasaki on his way to Tokyo, to return to Pusan to take care of the Japanese residents there. He furthermore instructed Moriyama to refer to Tokyo any inquiry about the incident that the Korean government might address to him. This precautionary directive proved to be unnecessary. When Moriyama got back to Pusan on October 3, 1875, he was surprised not to hear a single word about the *Unyōkan* incident. The news of the clash evidently had not yet reached the southern part of the country.[46]

The incident was also conveniently used to draw international attention to Japan's diplomatic and military involvement with Korea. In the first days of October, Terashima informed the foreign envoys about the details of the event off Kanghwa Island. In mid-October the foreign minister relayed the news to the Japanese ministers abroad. On October 13, the Tsungli Yamen learned of the *Unyōkan* incident through a letter from the Japanese chargé d'affaires, Tei Einei. Terashima reminded Tei that since the degree of Korea's dependence on China was unknown, the Japanese government did not feel obliged to disclose all the details of the case to the Chinese government.[47]

The news did not fail to have its impact. All observers grasped the significance of the event and the serious situation it created in the Far East. The American minister, John A. Bingham, reported to Washington that "war may be declared by Japan against Corea," and recommended to his government that "considering the relations of Corea and China, ... in the event of war between Japan and Corea, [it] would be proper to declare a strict neutrality."[48] To Admiral Enomoto Takeaki, the Japanese ambassador in Russia, the military value of the incident was clear at once. He labeled it casus belli which would give Japan an excuse to urge her terms on Korea. Convinced that neither Russia nor China would intervene, Enomoto's strategy called for the occupation of an island opposite Tsushima where the Japanese would deal with the high Korean ministers. Or, if Tokyo were prepared for bolder steps, he advocated capturing Korea's capital for a quick subjugation of the whole country. He also urged that several warships occupy Port Lazareff, just north of Wŏnsan, to weaken Korea further.[49]

The Tsungli Yamen did not immediately respond to the news about the *Unyōkan* incident. While the Chinese ministers were reconsidering China's policy toward Korea, the Japanese representative, Tei, tried to convince the foreign representatives in Peking to accept the Japanese version of the incident. Presumably with considerable satisfaction, he reported to Terashima that all the foreign representatives shared the opinion that Korea was the attacker and all blame should be put on her. He gathered from their statements that the Western powers would welcome Japanese efforts to open Korea since their own attempts at persuading the Chinese government to use its influence to get the Korean ports opened for Western trade had come to naught.[50]

Japan's Challenge to China's Assertions

Moriyama Shigeru's mission to Korea in 1875 was a failure. It not only fell short of making a new start in the normalization of Korean-Japanese relations, but it did not contribute significantly to a clarification of Sino-Korean relations. For Japan, the Korea problem remained unsolved; it

even threatened to grow once more into a source of major frustration. Although there is no indication that the Japanese government intended to
substitute military action for its basic policy of moderation toward Korea,
the *Unyōkan* incident created the tense atmosphere in which Japan could
capitalize on the fears of Korea and China. It was an opportunity to assume
a bolder posture without taking great risks. In October 1875, State Councillor Kido Kōin, who at the time of the *seikanron* had initially advocated
"armed diplomacy" against Korea, but who had eventually moved into
Iwakura Tomomi's moderate camp, proposed a peaceful solution to the
impasse in Korea. Kido was supported by Iwakura, Ōkubo Toshimichi,
and Sanjō Sanetomi. They formulated a policy that contained two simultaneous approaches. One led directly to Korea: the demand for the conclusion of a peace treaty (see Chapter 3). The other was the exploration of
China's attitude toward her vassal.

Although the Japanese had their doubts about the validity of Korean
and Chinese claims that Korea was dependent on China, the Japanese
government decided to inform the Chinese government about the failure
of Japanese overtures in Korea since the Meiji Restoration and notify it
of Japan's determination to approach the Korea problem with greater
forwardness. For this purpose the Japanese government sent a new
ambassador to Peking.

On November 10, 1875, Mori Arinori, a youthful but experienced
diplomat, was appointed ambassador plenipotentiary. He was to transmit
the Japanese government's decision to send a special envoy to Korea to
inquire into the Kanghwa incident and demand indemnities, and to negotiate the renewal of old ties between Japan and Korea. The unofficial
purpose of his mission was to continue the exploration into the nature of
the Chinese-Korean relationship. When Mori arrived in Peking on January
4, 1876, some foreign observers, such as the German minister Max von
Brandt, assumed that his arrival signified that the Japanese intended a
more determined course of action, perhaps even war, against Korea.[51]

Before contacting the Chinese government, Mori visited the British
ambassador, Sir Thomas Wade, who had become a mentor to the Chinese
government and who exercised considerable influence on the formulation
of its foreign policy. Mori evidently hoped to get firsthand information
from him about the attitudes of the leading officials in the Peking government toward the Sino-Korean relationship. He briefed Wade about recent
developments in Korea and asserted Japan's peaceful intentions there. He
then asked for Wade's good offices in influencing the Chinese ministers

toward a favorable reaction to the Japanese demands. Wade, however, was reluctant to commit himself, and he also distrusted Mori. "The minister's manner, rather than his language, made me distrustful. I fancy that an expedition on Corea is determined on, and that the object of his confidential communication to me was to ascertain whether objection to the expedition would be taken by England, or any other foreign country."[52]

Without the backing he had hoped to receive from Wade, Mori went to the Tsungli Yamen on January 10 and met Shen Pao-chen, Mao Ch'ang-hsi, Tung Hsün, Ch'ung-hou, Kuo Sung-tao, and Chou Chia-mei. After handing over a memorandum that summarized the latest state of Japanese-Korean relations and reiterated Japan's peaceful intentions toward Korea, Mori did not lose much time in reaching the topic he had come to clarify: the quality and nature of the Sino-Korean relationship.[53] Demanding a comment on recent rumors that Korea had asked China for military help, Mori prompted Shen Pao-chen, who acted as the Yamen's spokesman, to restate in rather blunt words the policy China had been pursuing since the 1860s. Korea, Shen asserted, was a dependent of China and subject to the control of the Board of Rites. The Tsungli Yamen therefore had no knowledge of Korea's request for military help. Urged to define *shu-kuo* or *shu-pang* (dependent country), Shen stated that Korea was left to her own devices in internal matters (*cheng-chiao chin-ling*, lit., "government exhortations and restrictions"), and that she also possessed complete power of decision in the field of foreign affairs. The term *shu-kuo*, Shen emphasized, denoted a country that at times sent tribute to the Ch'ing court and received the Chinese investiture and calendar. Mori must have been more than satisfied to hear the additional affirmation that the Chinese government had no control over its dependent countries' foreign relations. In Mori's opinion the relationship between China and her dependent countries was so loose that there was hardly any reason why the latter should be called "dependent." Shen emphasized, however, that in case Korea got into a conflict with foreign countries (presumably meaning Japan), China would discuss the matter only within the framework of the Sino-Japanese treaty of 1871. Although he had to admit that that treaty did not contain a clear passage on the dependent countries, Shen categorically pronounced the invasion of a dependent country by another power a cause for war. In reply, Mori found it utterly impossible and pointless to relate the invasion or occupation of Korea to the question of Korea's status vis-à-vis China. Shen was apparently unable to refute this contention.[54]

The concern that Mori's statements caused among the ministers of the Tsungli Yamen is reflected in their memorial to the throne reporting Mori's visit. Japan's hostility toward Korea, they were certain, was motivated by Korea's disrespect for Japan. The ministers also considered the possibility that the Western powers, which had been unsuccessful in Korea in recent years, were encouraging Japan. The ministers made no secret of their deep distrust of their aggressive and incomprehensible neighbor. Japan's Westernization had made her more unpredictable than ever before.[55]

If the discussions with Mori left the Chinese rather apprehensive and nervous, they did not satisfy Mori either. He was under the impression that the Chinese government was preoccupied with more urgent foreign matters than the Korea problem. After Tei Einei, sent to the Tsungli Yamen for further deliberations on the following day, reported only a fruitless repetition of familiar arguments, Mori drew his preliminary conclusion: the Chinese term "dependent country" was devoid of any meaning because it did not represent reality. A country which was in full possession of the management of its internal and external affairs deserved, in his eyes, the name of "independent country." This assumption, he was confident, would be supported by all other countries.[56]

Meetings in the Tsungli Yamen were followed by an exchange of communications between Mori and Prince Kung. Mori refuted the claim that Korea was China's dependent country. He insisted that the Sino-Korean treaty would have no binding power in case of conflict between Korea and Japan, nor would the conclusion of a treaty between the two countries be of any concern to China. Prince Kung replied that since the word *li* (lit., "to control," "to rule") was synonymous with *shu* (lit., "belonging to"), Korea belonged to the category of dependent countries and territories (*shu-pang-t'u*) defined in the treaty. This assertion, as Mori interpreted it, meant that if a conflict arose between Korea and Japan the Chinese government would take upon itself the responsibility for Korea. Prince Kung acknowledged this. Mori then complained that the factual evidence of China's assertion was still not clear to him. Prince Kung thereupon tried once more to elucidate the "actual basis" (*shih*) of the dependent country: Korea fulfilled her role vis-à-vis China by presenting tribute and accepting the Chinese calendar; she acted autonomously in the collection of taxes and the management of governmental affairs. China discharged her obligations vis-à-vis Korea by granting relief during times of stress and by restoring order during times of war. Prince Kung thought the Sino-Japanese treaty would prevent Japan from attacking China's "dependent countries and territories," and he was indignant about Japan's pretense of peaceful intentions toward Korea while she was at the same time speculating about the possibility of conflict with Korea. In his last communication to Prince Kung, Mori impatiently wrote that Japan would deal with Korea as an independent country and that any connection between China and Korea would be of no concern to Japan.[57]

Neither a subtle argument nor a cleverly twisted sentence could reconcile the divergent views on Korea's international status. Although Mori was undoubtedly aware of this, he nevertheless decided to exhaust all possibilities for resolving the confused matter by visiting Li Hung-chang. He also wanted to convince the "grand old man" of Chinese foreign policy of Japan's sincerity toward Korea.[58]

Mori Arinori and Li Hung-chang

After the conclusion of the Sino-Japanese treaty of 1871, Li Hung-chang continued to be concerned with the Korea problem. In 1874 he expressed his fear to the Tsungli Yamen that although Japan had launched an expeditionary force against Formosa, her real aim was Korea. He warned that because Korea was a protective fence for the three Eastern Provinces, a Japanese attack on Korea would threaten the homeland of the Manchu.[59] In spite of his interest in Korea, Li evidently did not have the opportunity to present his thinking on the problem to any leading Korean official until 1875. In the latter part of that year, Yi Yu-wŏn visited Peking.[60] During his visit, Yi sent a letter and some gifts to Li Hung-chang and expressed regret that he was unable to visit Li and listen to his advice. In answer to this, Li sent a note to Yi Yu-wŏn in which "he expounded about the meaning of foreign relations." He described Korea's vital position in China's defense posture and expressed his hope that the Korean government would prepare for any eventuality. Speaking about China, but undoubtedly hinting at the Korean situation, Li stressed that the seclusion policy could no longer be justified in terms of geographical circumstance and that the prerequisite for the opening of the country was an adequate defense system.[61]

When Li Hung-chang received news of Mori Arinori's intended visit, he guessed the topic of the impending discussion immediately. To define his standpoint in advance, he outlined his latest concept concerning Korea in a letter to the Tsungli Yamen. Humiliated a short time ago, Korea, he conjectured, would refuse to receive a Japanese envoy in a peaceful way. The hostile attitude of the Koreans could easily provoke an armed conflict between the two countries. Since she was weak and poor, Korea would not be able to hold out against Japan and, remembering the precedent of the Ming time, would presumably call on China for help against her attacker. Invoking the first article of the Sino-Japanese treaty, Li warned, would not restrain Japan. He reminded the Yamen of Korea's strategic position and pointed to the catastrophic consequences the loss of Korea would have for China. Trusting in Japan's good faith, he recommended that the Yamen draft a letter to the Korean government exhorting it to "bear the small anger," receive the Japanese envoy with courtesy, or send a mission to Japan for an explanation of the *Unyōkan* incident. If Korea heeded this advice, Li was confident, tension between the two countries could certainly be lessened.[62]

Li Hung-chang received his Japanese guest in Paotingfu on January 24, 1876.[63] He seated Mori and his companion, Tei Einei, at a conference table and treated them to food and wine. He apprehensively noticed Mori's proud and haughty behavior and ascribed it to Mori's long sojourn in the West. After reminiscing for a while about his experiences abroad, Mori asked Li what he thought about the practical results of the treaty concluded between China and Japan. Without hesitation, Li cited the first article which guarded against the invasion of each other's dependent countries. Seemingly annoyed that Li, too, was referring to that treaty clause, the Japanese stated bluntly that he considered treaties useless and that the relations between two countries were based solely on power. On the contrary, Li impressed upon Mori that China would honor the treaty and that he thought the treaty was "good and complete."

Mori then changed the topic. In Japan's view, he stated, it was incomprehensible that Korea was called a "dependent country" by the Tsungli Yamen when Korea was in full possession of the administration of her internal and external affairs. Undoubtedly aware of the deficiency of the Chinese argumentation, Li betrayed some uneasiness at Mori's words and could only admit that according to Mori's definition Korea was an independent country. He hastened to add, however, that he supported the Yamen's standpoint in all respects. "Everybody," he maintained, knew that Korea had been one of China's dependent countries for centuries. He tried again to define the term *shu-pang-t'u*, without, however, visibly impressing Mori. He thereupon attempted to cut Mori's "chattering" short by referring again to the treaty. Mori countered by stating that the boundaries of the tributary states were not fixed in the treaty, a fact which certainly made a revision of the first clause necessary. Taking advantage of Li's noticeable discomfort about this remark, Mori continued in an "imposing speech" to refute Li's accusation that Japan really had provoked the *Unyōkan* incident by violating Korea's territorial waters. He argued that Korea, which had never concluded treaties with other nations, had no right to international law as a defense against Japan. Li explained that Korea's refusal to intensify her contact with Japan was caused by her suspicion of Japan's recent Westernization and her fear that other countries would penetrate Korea in Japan's wake. Korea, Mori answered, would not have to be concerned about this if she took care of shipwrecked foreigners, opened her country to foreign trade, and allowed surveys along her coast.

The hours passed by and, growing tired of debate, Mori complained about China's lack of cooperation. Li reproached him and charged that Japan had acted too rashly toward Korea and that the conquest of such a poor country would certainly bring no advantage to Japan. Mori could only urge his partner to ask Korea to fulfill Japan's two simple demands: receive the Japanese envoy with due courtesy and protect Japanese sailors shipwrecked along the Korean coast. Li promised to relay this request to the Chinese government, but he asked Mori to abstain from putting too much pressure upon the Yamen.

The debate between Li Hung-chang and Mori Arinori ended in an atmosphere of mutual admonition. After a short second meeting, Mori left Paotingfu for Peking on January 27, 1876. He had found no more satisfaction in Paotingfu than he had in his previous meetings with the Tsungli Yamen. He had not succeeded in bringing the Chinese viewpoint any closer to that of the Japanese. Despite this failure, he sent Tei again to the Tsungli Yamen two weeks later. However, Tei's consultations did not result in any last-minute reconciliations.[64]

The meetings with Mori left Li Hung-chang no happier. More than ever before the fragility, and therefore the uselessness, of the first treaty clause was obvious. To be sure, Li Hung-chang realized that the Sino-Japanese treaty gave no assurance that Korea, as China's dependent, would stay politically and territorially within the sphere of Chinese interests. He dissociated himself openly from the Tsungli Yamen's unerring trust in the letter of the treaty, thus making it very easy for Mori to discern a discrepancy of attitude and commitment between Li and the Yamen. His talks with Mori evidently convinced Li that only a consistent policy could stand up under Japanese pressure. He advised the ministers at Peking to refer to the earlier communications between Prince Kung and Mori in their future contacts with the Japanese. In addition, he urged again that Korea be fully informed about the latest Sino-Japanese contacts concerning the peninsula.[65]

The years 1873 and 1874 were a trial period. In Korea, young King Kojong began his rule. He separated himself from his authoritative father by searching for an alternative to the seclusion policy. He also showed his independence from his in-law clan, the Min, by trying to set the country's internal and external affairs on a course mapped out according to his own plan. He was encouraged in these endeavors by his chief advisers, Yi Yu-wŏn, Yi Ch'oe-ŭng, and Pak Kyu-su. The latter, especially, did not lose time in disavowing the seclusion policy. Yi Yu-wŏn and Yi Ch'oe-ŭng acted with less forcefulness and courage when their convictions were put to the test. The seclusion policy had become so much a part of Korean tradition that it was not easily altered. The retarding influence of this carefully guarded tradition was clearly shown in the reaction of the general officialdom to Kojong's call for a more realistic Japan policy. The majority of the officials remained unenlightened and seclusionist despite their king's considerable awareness of international realities. Ironically, this was even more true of the officials who were to implement the new policies on the local level. Kojong's ensuing conflict with his officialdom resulted in the erratic course that the negotiations with the Japanese took. Procrastination and sudden changes of mind provided a poor basis for negotiations; the chance for a speedy rapprochement with Japan was lost.

Japan's objectives in Korea following the *seikan* controversy were limited, and the oligarchy was determined to pursue them with circumspection and moderation. The Koreans' lack of responsiveness or outright resistance gradually stiffened Japan's attitude and motivated her to quicken the pace with which she wanted things done in Korea. Moreover, her explorations into the nature of the Sino-Korean relationship, part of the policy of moderation, were fruitless. Korea presented herself as a country dependent on China, and China described her tributary ties with a formula that no longer carried any authority. Preoccupied with matters of more importance to her immediate survival, China had yet to rethink her role vis-à-vis Korea in the light of contemporary events. The clash of opinions between Mori Arinori and the Chinese ministers in Peking at the beginning of 1876 contained the seeds of China's future conflicts with Japan over the Korean peninsula. At the same time, Japan took Korea's indecision as a chance for bolder action and interpreted China's vagueness and uneasiness as an indication that traditional commitments had no longer to be taken seriously. Japan could hope to prove herself in Korea without major risks.

THE BREAK WITH THE PAST

After the *Unyōkan* incident the Japanese oligarchs formulated two policies which they planned to execute simultaneously. One of them, Mori Arinori's mission to Peking, turned out to be of less importance. The more significant policy was the conclusion of a new treaty with Korea. Hoping for a breakthrough, Tokyo concentrated on sending a successful mission to Korea.

Kuroda Kiyotaka's Mission to Korea

Supported by his intimates—Moriyama Shigeru and Hirotsu Hironobu—Kido Kōin asked to be sent to Korea, but illness prevented him from serving.[1] On December 9, 1875, Kuroda Kiyotaka, an army lieutenant general, vice-minister, and director of the Development Agency of Hokkaido, was appointed ambassador plenipotentiary to Korea. Inoue Kaoru, a member of the Genrōin, was made the vice-envoy.[2] Kuroda's primary duty was the conclusion of a normalization treaty with Korea. He was instructed to be flexible in his dealings with the Koreans since the degree to which their government was involved in the *Unyōkan* affair was unknown. Korea's consent to conclude a treaty would be regarded as compensation for the violence Japan suffered in the incident. Kuroda was told to include the following stipulations in the treaty: the nationals of both countries should be allowed to conduct trade at places designated for this purpose by the two governments; the Korean government should allow the Japanese merchants free trade at Pusan and select for them a convenient place on Kanghwa Island or near the capital for trade and residence; Japanese warships as well as merchant ships should be permitted to conduct surveys along the Korean coast, and castaways of both countries should be properly cared for and sent back to their home countries; envoys should be stationed in both capitals and consuls in the trading places to preserve the mutual friendship. Furthermore, the treaty should treat both countries on the basis of equality.[3]

The confidential instructions to Kuroda were somewhat different. They reveal that although the Japanese government would hold Korea responsible for past actions and would negotiate only with Korea, it recognized that under certain circumstances Korea's claim of being one of China's vassals had to be taken into consideration. Kuroda was instructed that if Korea thought it vital to seek China's consent for her negotiations with Japan, he should station Japanese soldiers in Seoul at the expense of the Korean government until Korea received Chinese counsel.[4]

In view of the uncertainty of Korea's response, the Japanese government was anxious to convince foreign representatives of the mission's peaceful nature. In a conversation with American Minister Bingham on December 9, Terashima compared the Japanese mission to Commodore Perry's expedition to Japan. French worries about Russian and Chinese attitudes were dispelled with the argument that Russia presented no danger, and that China had nothing to say in this matter since Korea was not regarded by Japan as one of China's subject-states. This statement was made before Mori Arinori's discussions in Peking. The German minister, Eisendecher, reflected on the military implications. The major concern of the British ambassador, Sir Harry S. Parkes, was trade. The only representative who came out in support of the Japanese action was the Russian minister. He thought the expedition would help open Korea's doors to Russia.[5]

Traditionally, a mission to Korea was preceded by a special messenger who announced it to the Korean government, a task that this time was entrusted to Hirotsu Hironobu.[6] Hirotsu left Tokyo on December 1, 1875, and reached the Japan House on the 17th. Two days later he met the language officer, Hyŏn Sŏg-un, to whom he gave a letter that briefly outlined the past history of the Korean-Japanese relations and contained the details of Kuroda's appointment. At first Hyŏn was reluctant to accept the letter, but recognizing the seriousness of its contents he promised to send it on to the prefect of Tongnae with the request that it be forwarded to Seoul. After Hirotsu was assured that this promise had been carried out, he left Pusan on December 23.[7] Hyŏn considered Hirotsu's announcement so important that he went to Seoul to personally inform the government of Kuroda's mission.[8]

Kuroda's imposing expeditionary force consisted of two warships, the *Nisshinmaru* and the *Mōshunmaru*, for the protection of the envoy, and four transportation ships. Kuroda sailed with his suite aboard the *Genbumaru* from Shinagawa on January 6, 1876, arriving in Pusan on January 15. He immediately sent Yamanoshiro, the deputy chief of the Japan House, to notify the language officer of his arrival and of his intention to sail to Kanghwa Island to meet Korean negotiators.[9] The advance of Kuroda's ships, however, was greatly hampered by the necessity of surveying the route to Kanghwa before leaving Pusan, and Kuroda was detained in Pusan until January 23.

The Koreans first spotted the survey ships sometime before January 22 off the coast of Kyŏnggi. The excited prefect of Namyang, Kang Yun, reported almost every day about the movement of "strange ships" along the coast. Although the Korean government knew through Hyŏn Sŏg-un's personal report about Kuroda's appointment and the impending mission, no arrival date had been announced. On January 22 the members of the Council of State, obviously taken by surprise, hurried the Pusan language officer and his colleagues to the coast to conduct a detailed investigation into the case of the ships of "unknown origin." At the same time, the defenses along the Han River were reinforced.[10]

The Japanese ships slowly headed northward, searching their way through the countless islands and inlets along Korea's western coast. Several times they were approached by Korean junks which carried inquiring local officials. On January 27 the *Nisshinmaru*, which Kuroda had boarded at Pusan, anchored at Tangjinp'o in the southern part of the Bay of Namyang. Two Korean junks pulled alongside, and an official presented a letter and gifts from the prefect of Namyang, Kang Yun. Kuroda then sent Miyamoto Koichi and the interpreter, Urase Yutaka, to invite the prefect to the ship. The Japanese urged Kang to transmit a report to Seoul revealing the ship's identity and explaining Kuroda's intentions.[11] When the *Mōshunmaru* reached the southern tip of Kanghwa Island during her surveying mission, her crew was warned by the local official that it was against the law for foreign ships to intrude into Korean waters. The senior language officer, O Kyŏng-sŏk,[12] and the Pusan language officer, Hyŏn

Sŏg-un, arrived soon after and conducted a thorough inquiry. They, too, promised to report the intention of Kuroda's mission to the capital.[13] On January 30, O and Hyŏn went aboard the *Nisshinmaru*, which had moved up near Taebu Island, to meet Miyamoto Koichi and Moriyama Shigeru. The Koreans were told that the Japanese ships were awaiting the return of the survey vessels before proceeding to Kanghwa Island.[14]

Korean Debate and First Treaty Negotiations

The *Unyōkan* incident had vindicated the fear of Japan's aggressiveness and, for a while, strengthened the position of those who upheld the tradition of *naesu oeyang* and who were thus opposed to a rapprochement with Japan. The Council of State's decision of August 9, 1875, had all but become a useless piece of paper. The government's attention had shifted away from diplomatic matters to the urgent problems of national defense. Between mid-August and early December nobody dared mention the Japanese communications again. Left State Councillor Yi Ch'oe-ŭng broke the moratorium with a memorial on December 12 in which he sought a reaffirmation of the decision of August 9. Echoing Pak Kyu-su's point of view, Yi maintained that the Japanese, by using unsuitable language in their documents, were only disclosing their own impropriety rather than really harming Korea. Yi requested that the prefect of Tongnae be ordered to accept the Japanese letters in the future and promptly forward them to Seoul. Yi's request was immediately approved by the king.[15]

It is not clear what activated the debate again. It may have been a newspaper article in the *Wankuo kungpao* (*Chinese Globe Magazine*) brought back to Seoul by a Korean envoy in early November. Although the indignant envoy called the content of the article false and misleading, he feared that "all the nations of the world" would take it as the truth. The article described the Korean situation vis-à-vis a rapacious Japan as most precarious. It stated that if Korea continued to insist upon the many petty demands with which she intended to restrict the Japanese, she would bring disaster upon herself.[16]

In any case, Yi Ch'oe-ŭng's overture was followed by unexpectedly rapid action. In late December 1875 or early January 1876, the Korean government learned about Kuroda Kiyotaka's mission through Hyŏn Sŏg-un's personal report. Shortly afterward, Yi Yu-wŏn came back from Peking and was received in audience on January 12. Yi may have transmitted some of Li Hung-chang's thoughts about the desirability of Korea's opening to the outside world.[17] But before the communication from the Chinese Board of Rites reached the king and officially informed him of Mori Arinori's presence in Peking and Japan's intention to conclude a treaty with Korea—it did not reach Seoul until the first days of February[18]—Kuroda Kiyotaka's squadron had already sailed almost to the gates of the kingdom. The ships were not identified because of the procrastination of the prefect of Tongnae whose report about Kuroda's arrival in Pusan was received only on January 27.[19]

The Korean government had not expected Kuroda's arrival so soon and so unprecedentedly close to Seoul. Clouds of crisis formed over the capital. Fast action was demanded. Yi Ch'oe-ŭng had reopened the debate with his call for conciliation, and the approach of the Japanese ships emphasized the seriousness of Japanese intentions. The opposition within the government was subdued for the moment. On January 30, without preceding debate, the Council of State recommended compliance with Japanese demands to meet with high Korean officials. Sin Hŏn and Yun Cha-sŭng were appointed high reception officer (*chŏpkyŏn taesin*) and deputy reception officer (*pugwan*), respectively. The selection of these two men, in particular of Sin Hŏn, indicated that the government no longer wanted to put off the Japanese with mere language officers. Sin Hŏn (Sin Kwan-ho; 1810–1888) had made a brilliant career during the period of the Taewŏn-gun by introducing a number of military reforms, and his appointment presumably was thought to match Kuroda's military background. Sin was then the commander of the Ŏyŏng Regiment, but he was temporarily elevated to the office of vice-president of the Board of Officials-without-Portfolio to equal Kuroda's rank.[20]

The appointment of reception officers on the occasion of a Japanese mission was, to be sure, nothing new. Sin Hŏn's appointment, however, was the first since the Meiji Restoration. It was a breakthrough of sorts. In January 1876 the Koreans no longer took issue with Japanese deviations from traditional etiquette. They demonstrated a degree of flexibility that had been lacking in the Taewŏn'gun's response to Japanese overtures. They failed, however, to grasp the full significance of Kuroda's appearance. Kojong and his ministers did not anticipate Kuroda's demand for a new treaty. They sent Sin to meet the Japanese envoys with innocent instructions to renew "the old friendship." Sin and Yun were not empowered to make important decisions, and their sole function was to receive the Japanese and to report back to the government. The appointments of Sin Hŏn and Yun Cha-sŭng were relayed to the Japanese on February 2.[21]

Procedural details of the impending meeting between the Korean delegates and the Japanese envoys were discussed during the first days of February. The main problem, which had to be settled in advance, was the selection of a meeting place. The Japanese insisted upon Kanghwa City because it was close to the capital and therefore was a vantage point from which to exert pressure on the Korean government. Kanghwa's strategic position, however, made the Koreans reluctant to open the island to the Japanese. This opposition was finally broken by a joint memorial by Sin Hŏn and Yun Cha-sŭng who convincingly argued that the important reason for the meeting with the Japanese—the resumption of good relations—surpassed the strategic significance of Kanghwa City. A royal order allowed them to choose their own place.[22]

The first formal meeting between Sin Hŏn and Kuroda Kiyotaka took place on February 10, 1876, at Kanghwa City. The Japanese landed at nearby Kapkwanjin. Escorted by four detachments of marines in full regalia, they marched to their headquarters in Kanghwa City. After an exchange of calling cards, the envoys greeted each other formally, and the Japanese and Korean representatives took seats around a table according to a carefully arranged seating plan. Some refreshments were served. Shortly afterward the Japanese retired. Later in the day, the Korean reception officers, accompanied by a detachment of military buglers and drummers, repaid the visit.[23]

Grand ceremony was followed on February 11 and 12 by working conferences. Without a long introduction, Kuroda showed Sin a draft treaty of thirteen articles which had been drawn up in Tokyo. The Japanese warned that another conflict could be prevented only by the conclusion of a new treaty that would replace the old argeements and would rebuild the relationship on the basis of international law. The treaty would assert Korea's independence and treat her on the same basis as Japan. Sin reminded Kuroda that Korea was not familiar with the diplomatic laws of the world and could not quite understand why Japan, with whom Korea had been conducting trade for the last three hundred years, especially insisted upon trade. Korea, he argued, was a poor country with a limited number of products. Expanding trade, Sin feared, would lure the common people into profit-making business and would tempt them to violate the laws. Sin's final remark that he would have to report the contents of the draft treaty to Seoul and wait for instructions raised the question of his competence to negotiate with the Japanese. Fearing drawn-out negotiations, Kuroda demanded that the Korean government send someone with the authority to discuss and reconcile the different views about the treaty stipulations. When Sin said that such a demand would be difficult to meet within the framework of Korea's governmental structure, Kuroda thought the Koreans were simply delaying, and he quickly threatened military intervention if the Korean government did not reach a decision within a reasonable period of time. Although the Japanese agreed to a ten-day waiting period, they left no doubt in the minds of their counterparts that this time they would use force rather than yield.[24]

Even before Sin's first report reached the capital, the state councillors met almost daily. On February 14, 1876, the king called his ministers to audience in order to deliberate on the situation and formulate a policy. The roster of the highest attending officials was the same as on June 13 of the preceding year, although Yi Ch'oe-ŭng had become chief state councillor in the meantime. The deliberations were vague and inconclusive. The tradition of *naesu oeyang* still lingered on, although the voices of opposition softened under the threat of the moment. Yi Yu-wŏn and Hong Sun-mok uttered surprise about the arrogance of the Japanese who still resisted Korea's superior morality. Kim Pyŏng-hak suspected that the Japanese had not come to renew the old friendship, but rather to begin conflict. Pak Kyu-su countered this by arguing that since the Japanese had come, as they said, to restore good relations, Korea should not rebuff them again. Arms should be used only if something unexpected happened. Yi Ch'oe-ŭng remarked that the Council of State should continue its consultations. Kim Pyŏng-guk, who again questioned Japanese intentions, seconded Yi and demanded that they wait for Sin's report before drawing up a policy. Nobody mentioned the conclusion of a treaty.[25]

Sin Hŏn's report about his meetings with Kuroda and a copy of the Japanese draft treaty were received in Seoul on the next day. Although King Kojong and the state councillors had not anticipated a new treaty, they reacted to the draft with surprising promptness. Under the pressure of Kuroda's presence and vociferous opposition from outside the government, they apparently had to deliberate the document in secret sessions. Despite certain reservations about a few specific points in the Japanese draft, on February 18 the Council of State reached the momentous decision that the "time has come for a continuation of the good relations with Japan, and it is no longer necessary to reject their trade treaty."[26] One day later, the ministers memorialized that during the settlement of the treaty details it would be too burdensome for the negotiators to have to submit each new subject one by one to the deliberations of the Council of State. They suggested that if the items of the treaty "were benefiting the people and profitable to the country," the negotiators should be allowed to make a decision without prior consultation with Seoul. Sin Hŏn was subsequently empowered to continue the negotiations in this way.[27] A few days later, however, Sin Hŏn declined to accept these special powers. The king was adamant: Sin's profound knowledge and competence in both civil and military affairs, he insisted, were urgently needed at a time when the safety of the country was endangered by the Japanese. The Council of State shared the king's confidence in Sin's ability to use the special powers for the benefit of the country. Sin reluctantly accepted his assignment.[28] The last procedural hurdles were removed on the Korean side, and the stage was set for the actual treaty negotiations with Kuroda and Inoue.

Voices of Protest

The impending rapprochement with Japan was savagely contested in various quarters outside the government. The Taewŏn'gun broke the silence of his retirement to voice his disdain for the government's decision. He caught the state councillors' attention with a letter denouncing their action in a fulminant tone. In this document dated February 12, 1876, he censured the "preposterous" language of the Japanese communications, condemned the Japanese adoption of Western ways, and accused the Council of State of being weak toward the foreign intruders and of having given in to their demands without serious opposition. The Taewŏn'gun's letter climaxed with the declaration that the acceptance or rejection of the Japanese letters was up to the Council, but that the preservation of the country was solely his own matter. The Taewŏn'gun then threatened to lead his adherents to sacrifice themselves in a war against the Japanese. These words, thundering as they were, seem to have had little effect on the government, but they did raise the problem of Japanese security. The language officer, Hyŏn Sŏg-un, repeatedly warned the Japanese that followers of the Taewŏn'gun were assembling a number of comrades to jeopardize the peace negotiations. Kuroda had apparently expected that his coming to Korea could lead to serious clashes with the local population. He issued strict orders to the mission members not to disclose any information about the negotiations to the Koreans.[29]

Not so surprisingly, those Confucian literati who had raised their voices against some of King Kojong's internal policies also were against the king's Japan policy. A former assistant inspector (*chip'yŏng*) of the Inspectorate, Yi Hang-nyŏn, demanded that the king mobilize troops to throw the foreign villains out of the country.[30] Yi's harsh demand was supported by a former vice-censor general of the Censorate, Chang Ho-gŭn, who admonished the government to undertake an all-out moral effort to keep the Japanese at bay. "The most pressing task of the moment is to tighten the military system, to fortify strategic points, and to mobilize the army and the people."[31]

The most vociferous adversary of government policy undoubtedly was Ch'oe Ik-hyŏn, who had been an outspoken advocate of the Taewŏn'gun's retirement. In a lengthy memorial written on February 17 he accused the government of lacking a determined policy and of seeking an easy peace with the enemy. Ch'oe thought nobody could object if peace resulted from Japan's desire for good neighborly relations and Korea's strength kept the Japanese in check. But, he urged, this was not the case. He presented five reasons that explained why a rapprochement with Japan would surely lead to disaster: (1) If peace were asked for out of fear and without preparing deterrents, rapprochement would only be a temporary solution. How could Japan's limitless greed be checked in the future? (2) Exchanging Korean goods needed for daily life for Japanese luxury items would lead before long to a loss of the country. (3) On the heels of the Japanese, Christianity would penetrate the country. (4) After the conclusion of a treaty, there would be no way to stop the Japanese from going back and forth, building houses, and getting themselves involved with Korean women. (5) Those who propagate the treaty like to use the treaty of 1636 (with the Manchu) as an example, but they are terribly mistaken because the Japanese resemble wild animals that only crave material goods and are totally ignorant of human morality. To conclude a treaty with wild animals is an utterly impossible thing. Ch'oe went on to caution the king not to take the present Japanese for those of earlier times. "The Japanese who come today are wearing Western clothes, are using Western cannons, and are sailing upon Western ships: this indeed is clear proof that the Japanese and the Westerners are one and the same." Ch'oe ended his tirade with the ominous demand that the compromisers within the officialdom be severely punished. Carrying an axe and leading a group of some fifty literati to the main gate of Kyŏngbok Palace, Ch'oe submitted his memorial with the vow that he would be willing to accept death if his demands were not heard within the palace.[32]

A minor official, O Sang-hyŏn, touched upon a similar theme. He reminded the king of the time when there were stone tablets on every busy road with the warning: "Foreign barbarians are invading; those who insist upon peace are selling out the country." He, too, said that the Japanese, who now dressed in Western clothes and rode Western boats, were indistinguishable from Westerners. Trade in Western goods, he maintained, would open the door to Christianity.[33]

The government's reaction to these voices of dissent was prompt and harsh. Chang Ho-gŭn's and Ch'oe Ik-hyŏn's memorials were returned, and Ch'oe was arrested. The leading officials requested in a joint memorial that a special tribunal be set up to judge Ch'oe's case. Before the treaty with Japan was signed, he was convicted and sent into exile on an island off Chŏlla.[34] The literati's outrage reflected the general mood of the populace. The bold Japanese advance to Kanghwa Island, the hitherto impenetrable sanctum of the Korean kings, terrified the people and whipped up a wave of antiforeignism. Some people took advantage of the general unrest of the times and slipped through "the meshes of the law" and forgot their "right place in society." They swarmed over the countryside and harassed the villagers. News about the growing number of robbers and thieves alarmed the government, and strict measures were ordered to apprehend and punish the evildoers.[35]

While Ch'oe Ik-hyŏn stood trial, the government received support in the form of a memorial sent in by the fourth aide-de-camp, Yun Ch'i-hyŏn. Echoing some of the "official" lines, Yun maintained that the present uproar within and without the government was rooted in the unfortunate fact that the people associated the Japanese with Westerners and unhappily mixed up the issues of peace and war. It was possible, Yun exclaimed, to reject trade with the West and even go to war with it, but it would be impossible to reject Japan's request for a treaty since the treaty was simply the continuation of a three hundred year old relationship. Everything depended on receiving the Japanese with courtesy. If strict regulations guided trade with Japan and all Western goods were banned from Korea, this would not harm good neighborly relations. Thus, while continuing her relations with Japan, Korea could ward off the evil influence of Christianity. Yun's argumentation was well received by the government.[36]

The Korean-Japanese Treaty

The Korean government began the final treaty settlement with Japan on February 18, 1876. It greatly objected to some passages in the draft treaty. When O Kyŏng-sŏk returned to Kanghwa City from Seoul the next day, he asked Kuroda to send Miyamoto Koichi and Nomura Yasui to the Korean headquarters to discuss these objectionable points. The Council of State took offense at the preamble of the treaty which designated Japan as *Dai-Nippon* and in a derogatory way called Korea *Chosŏn'guk*. The Japanese compromised on this point by adding the character "great" (*tae*) to *Chosŏn'guk*. The Koreans also successfully demanded the rephrasing of article 2 in such a way that a Japanese envoy sent to Korea in the future would be received by the president of the Department of Rites, and not by "the high officials in power." In the same article they contested the necessity of stationing a permanent envoy at Seoul. Although they seem to have gotten Miyamoto's approval to revise this passage, the final versions clearly differed. The Chinese text stipulated a temporary sojourn; the Japanese text kept the original wording that allowed the envoy to stay on or to return to Japan upon the completion of his mission. In article 4 the Koreans withdrew their request to fix in advance the limits within which the Japanese would be allowed to move in the ports which were to be newly opened. In article 5 the Japanese relinquished their intention of making Yŏnghŭng in Hamgyŏng, in the vicinity of which there was a dynastic ancestor shrine, an open port. The Koreans no longer insisted on confining the search for additional ports to the area of Kyŏngsang. Article 12 granted the Koreans the right to engage in trade in those Japanese ports open to foreigners. In return, the Japanese would enjoy most-favored-nation treatment in case Korea should conclude a treaty with a Western nation. The Koreans successfully convinced the Japanese that such a formulation would imply that Korea intended to conclude treaties with Western nations—an impossible thought! The Japanese negotiators dropped this article from the draft.[37]

The Koreans did not confine themselves merely to commenting on the Japanese draft. Sin presented to Miyamoto six points which the Koreans insisted had to be included in the treaty: (1) copper cash (*sangp'yŏng t'ongbo*) should not be used; (2) trade in rice should be forbidden; (3) all trade should be carried out on the basis of barter, and in commercial dealings between Koreans and Japanese, lending and borrowing money and charging interest should not be permitted; (4) no foreign traders other than Japanese should be allowed to enter Korean ports; (5) opium and the propagation of Western religion should be banned; (6) new regulations should deal with shipwrecks. Although generally sympathetic to the Korean point of view, Miyamoto maintained that time did not allow for a thorough consideration of Sin's proposals and demanded their withdrawal. Sin refused, and the two parties agreed to put points four and five, which had more general significance than the others, on record in a memorandum.[38]

The treaty text was finalized only after both sides made concessions. Now the question of how the treaty was to be ratified unexpectedly brought the negotiations to the brink of failure. During the conference on the evening of February 20, Sin Hŏn conveyed to Kuroda the Korean government's objection to the king's having to personally sign and seal the treaty. Kuroda, who evidently had not expected a last-minute obstacle, threatened to break off the negotiations if there were no signature from the king. Finally, Sin proposed that the king write "granted" (*yun*) under the text of the memorial in which the Council of State recommended the ratification of the treaty to the king. Kuroda could not agree to this and, two days after the stalemated conference, warned the Korean negotiators that he was about to return to Japan. Allowing five days for an answer from Seoul, Kuroda dramatically returned to his ship to wait but left Inoue, accompanied by Miyamoto, Nomura, and an interpreter, in the Japanese headquarters. Sin immediately sent O Kyŏng-sŏk and Hyŏn Sŏg-un to the capital with a copy of the formal treaty text to report about the precarious situation.[39]

The Japanese chief negotiator's dramatic gesture was effective. On February 24, an edict ordered the Council of State to return the texts of the treaty and of the ratification to Kanghwa City. A new seal with the words "the seal of the King of Great Korea" was cast to be affixed to the text of the ratification in place of the king's personal signature.[40] O and Hyŏn hastened back to Kanghwa and on the next day announced the king's compliance with the Japanese demands. They also handed over the various treaty documents.[41] Before Kuroda left Chŏngsan Island, where he had waited for a favorable answer, he dispatched an army captain to Tokyo to report to Sanjō and Yamagata about the successful course of events at Kanghwa. In the afternoon of February 26, Kuroda set out with his escorts and honor guard to Kanghwa City. He arrived there on the same day.

On the morning of February 27, 1876, Kuroda and Inoue, accompanied by their staff and escorted by an honor guard, all in formal uniform, left their headquarters and proceeded toward the Yŏnmu Hall where the Korean plenipotentiaries awaited them. In a brief ceremony, both parties signed, sealed, and exchanged the treaty. Sin Hŏn thereupon presented the Korean king's ratification, a letter from the Council of State, and gifts to the Japanese envoys. In return, Kuroda sent the king a cannon with two thousand rounds of ammunition, pistols, a gold watch, a thermometer, a compass, and other gifts. After the event was duly celebrated at a banquet, Kuroda returned to his ship leaving Nomura Yasui and Miyamoto Koichi behind to take care of the remaining business.[42] His historic mission completed, Kuroda left for Japan the next day, and on March 5, 1876, he arrived in Tokyo where he was enthusiastically welcomed. On the same day he was honored with an audience by the Emperor Meiji.[43]

The treaty of twelve articles, called the Kanghwa Treaty (dated February 26, 1876, but exchanged on the 27th), recognized Korea in article 1 as an independent state enjoying the same sovereign rights as Japan. Article 2 provided for the mutual exchange of envoys after fifteen months from the date of the signature of the treaty. The Japanese envoy was to confer with the president of the Department of Rites; the Korean envoy was to be received by the Foreign Office. Article 3 stipulated that the Japanese were to use the Japanese and Chinese languages in their official communications, whereas the Koreans were to use Chinese. All the old agreements existing between Korea and Tsushima were abolished by article 4, and trade at Pusan was henceforth to be carried out according to the provisions of the treaty. Moreover, the government of Korea agreed to open two additional ports for commercial intercourse with Japan. Article 5 permitted the search for suitable ports in Kyŏngsang, Kyŏnggi, Ch'ungch'ŏng, Chŏlla, and Hamgyŏng, and their opening in October 1877. Article 6 secured assistance and support for ships stranded or wrecked along the Korean or Japanese coasts. Any Japanese mariner was allowed, according to article 7, to conduct surveys of the Korean coast. Article 8 permitted the government of Japan to appoint an officer for each of the open ports of Korea for the protection of Japanese merchants residing there. Freedom to carry on business without interference from the authorities of either government and trade without restrictions and prohibitions were guaranteed by article 9. Article 10 stipulated extraterritorial jurisdiction. For the benefit of the merchants of the respective countries, article 11 arranged for the conclusion of trade regulations. They were to be agreed upon at the capital of Korea or at Kanghwa within six months from the conclusion of the treaty.

Article 12 affirmed that the above eleven articles were to mark the beginning of mutual trust and would be unchangeable.[44]

ผผผผผผผผผผผผผผผผผผผผผผผผผผผผผผ

The peaceful outcome of the negotiations with Japan was a victory for King Kojong and his highest ministers, Yi Yu-wŏn, Pak Kyu-su, and Yi Ch'oe-ŭng. Within two years after coming to power, the young king, inspired and supported by these advisers, succeeded in transforming the rationale behind Korea's Japan policy from uncompromising rejection to guarded flexibility. This process was not connected with the workings of partisan politics. Rather, the king seems to have spoken the decisive word despite fierce attacks on his Japan policy as well as on the quality of his leadership. The king faced opposition from within as well as from without the government. Although the opponents' tones differed, the charge was the same: a rapprochement with the Japanese, who had Westernized to the point where they were indistinguishable from the barbarian Westerners, would undermine the moral and political foundations of the state. Resistance was the only possible response to Japanese overtures. This was a persuasive battlecry for the opponents outside the government. Within the government, Kim Pyŏng-hak and Kim Pyŏng-guk rallied tradition-bound officials around them to give their seclusion policy a last defense. But the king's admonitions, the pressure of Kuroda's presence, and perhaps doubts about the strength of the country's defenses finally eroded the vigor of their arguments and muted their opposition.

Even at the last, a consensus within the government was not reached. Two days after the signing of the treaty the principal ministers, led by Chief State Councillor Yi Ch'oe-ŭng, handed in their resignations after stating that they had no other course of action than the one they had taken vis-à-vis Japan. Such a collective resignation was an act customarily taken after a national crisis had been settled without the usual consensus; it was a gesture to appease the outmaneuvered opposition. King Kojong reinstated his ministers immediately afterward in a show of royal confidence.[45]

The Korean-Japanese treaty was the first modern treaty Korea entered into with any country. Far from having only bilateral significance, it laid the basis for more far-reaching changes in the old Far Eastern order than was realized at the time of its conclusion. The Koreans saw the treaty in a narrow perspective. They rationalized the peaceful continuation of the "three hundred year old friendship" with Japan as the natural response of a morally superior country toward the challenge of a neighbor that had lost all sense of propriety and etiquette by its hasty adoption of Western ways. The Koreans had no intention of altering the quality of the relationship and therefore envisaged the new agreement as one of local significance, dealing with trade and safeguarding against Western intrusion. Kojong's flexibility was directed only at a normalization with Japan. At this time it contained neither the psychological nor the political preconditions for ending seclusion.[46]

Significantly, during the entire negotiations, Sino-Korean relations were not discussed. There is no documentary evidence that Korea sought Chinese counsel. When the Korean government sent the treaty text to Peking, it apparently omitted the preamble and the first article. This was consistent with Korea's traditional behavior toward China (*sadae*) and Japan (*kyorin*). Korea had always acted autonomously vis-à-vis Japan. Korean-Japanese relations were not "diplomacy"–that was the exclusive right of China. Korea used the respectful "great" (*tae*) only toward Ch'ing China, but to emphasize her own superiority to Japan, she demanded Japan add it to Chosŏn'guk. In the same sense, she accepted in the first article the expression "independent" or "sovereign" (*chaju*) as being congruous with tradition. Thus Korea did not attach the same meaning to the first article that the Japanese did. The Koreans considered it a mere reaffirmation of a tradition-sanctioned reality. The Japanese intended to use it as a means of isolating Korea from the Chinese tributary system.[47]

Forced to sign the treaty, Korea committed herself to a set of obligations that she interpreted on the basis of hitherto accepted standards of neighborly relations with Japan. She even accepted extraterritorial jurisdiction: criminal cases involving Japanese had always been judged by the local Japanese officials. Having become treaty stipulations, however, these obligations took on, in a modern context unfamiliar to Korea, the ominous characteristics of the stipulations embodied in the "unequal treaties." Not yet aware of the full proportions of her new commitments, Korea vigorously resisted the two unprecedented Japanese demands: the opening of two more ports and the exchange and (temporary) stationing of Japanese envoys in the Korean capital. It took many more years of negotiations before Korea finally gave in to these demands. In early 1876, Korea's seclusion was not ended.[48]

No official comments reveal China's immediate reaction to the

Kanghwa Treaty. There can be no doubt, however, that when China finally learned about the first article it realized the full significance at once.
Japan's declaration of Korea's independence would undermine one of the
most dependable pillars of Chinese world order.[49] But China herself had
contributed to this by her weak and unconvincing interpretation of her
role toward her vassal. Fears that Japan would take up arms against
Korea and thus endanger the security of the Celestial Empire had led her
to recommend the conclusion of the treaty. This treaty, however, maneuvered the peninsula into a diplomatic isolation that did not alleviate Chinese fears of an armed conflict. Rumors of Russian troop movements
along China's northeastern border further complicated an assessment of
the situation for the Chinese.[50] On the positive side, Prince Kung apparently believed that the treaty had at last extinguished antiforeign opposition in Korea and consequently would strengthen China's influence
there.[51] By 1876, however, China had not yet developed a policy that
exerted much influence on the developments in Korea.

By putting his signature to the treaty, Kuroda Kiyotaka successfully
ended his mission. He had more than fulfilled the Japanese government's
objectives as outlined in his instructions. He had signed a document that
revolutionized Korean-Japanese relations and ended Korea's centuries-
old domination of this relationship. Japan became the new master by re-
establishing the relationship with Korea on the model of the humiliating
treaties she herself had been forced to sign with the West only a quarter of
a century before.

Kuroda granted a few points to Korea. Without much opposition he
withdrew the most-favored-nation clause. At this time, Japan actually
welcomed Korea's repeated insistence that it would not conclude treaties
with Western nations. Japan was anxious to keep the peninsula out of the
reach of Western competition.

The peaceful negotiation of the treaty vindicated the opponents of
seikanron. After 1873, the oligarchy had consistently followed a course of
moderation. This was not unqualified moderation, however. The oligarchs had renounced war, but within the next three years they changed
the focus of their Korea policy. In 1873 they recognized Korea as a part of
the traditional political order in the Far East; in 1876 they denied the Sino-
Korean relationship its special quality and justification. By forcing the
Kanghwa Treaty upon Korea, Japan initiated a reorientation of the traditional balance of power and assured herself a wide field for future action.

VICTORY OF DIPLOMACY

The Kanghwa Treaty of 1876 was the first in a series of agreements that Korea and Japan were to conclude during the remaining years of the decade. It broadly outlined the new relationship between the two countries, but the details remained to be worked out in subsequent negotiations. Diplomatic gains were invariably followed by demands for trade concessions. The Japanese continued to maintain the diplomatic initiative. Taking the new treaty as a justification for further action, the Japanese strove to consolidate their position in the peninsula. Their major concern at this stage was to find additional ports that would be suitable for concessions and trade. Surveying along the Korean coast, therefore, was the most urgent task. In pursuing their course in Korea, the Japanese encountered determined Korean resistance. The Koreans, whose adaptability to Japanese demands had been strained to the utmost in 1876, were opposed to granting concessions they felt were not founded on precedent. By procrastinating, they hoped to contain the Japanese. But containment was no longer effective. The Koreans had to give in to the Japanese step by step. Against their will, a new era had started.

Kim Ki-su's Mission to Japan

The conclusion of the Kanghwa Treaty was followed by a traditional diplomatic ritual: the dispatch of an official Korean mission to Tokyo. The

Japanese envoys first suggested that an observation of each other's "laws and customs" would benefit the friendship between the two countries. An initially reluctant Sin Hŏn finally agreed that such a mission would indeed help build mutual trust and confidence.[1] Upon his recommendation, the Council of State proposed the appointment of the *ŭnggyo* (official with the rank of senior fourth grade in the Academy of Literature), Kim Ki-su, as envoy (*susinsa*) to head the mission. Kim was well known for his profound learning in classics and literature. To give the appointment more weight, Kim's rank was elevated to *tangsang* (official with the rank above upper senior third grade). He was to carry state papers attesting to the restoration of the old friendship between the two countries.[2]

Preparations for the mission were entrusted to the language officer, Hyŏn Sŏg-un, and the temporary head of the Japan House, Yamanoshiro Sukenaga. They met at Tongnae during the first days of April. In general, the Koreans were happy to leave the travel arrangements to the Japanese since they had had no experience in sending a mission to Japan since 1810. But the Japanese offer to pay the expenses and provide the steamship *Kōryūmaru* to transport the mission was accepted with reluctance.[3] Kim Ki-su took leave of the king on April 27, 1876. Kim's suite included Hyŏn Sŏg-un (who held the same rank as Kim), a language specialist, a number of interpreters, military people, language officials, and some clerks and a painter. On May 19 the mission arrived in Pusan where the Japanese steamer lay at anchor. After sacrificing to the God of the Sea and entertaining the local officials, Kim went aboard. In his diary he confessed that even in his dreams he had never seen anything like this ship with its two sails and a chimney. The ship left Pusan on May 22 and arrived at Yokohama on May 29. From Yokohama, Kim traveled to Tokyo by train.[4]

Upon his arrival in Tokyo, Kim Ki-su's official program included a visit to the Foreign Ministry where he was received by Foreign Minister Terashima, Miyamoto Koichi, Moriyama Shigeru, and others. He also had an audience with the emperor.[5] Kim Ki-su stuck to his duty which, he repeatedly emphasized, consisted of nothing more than conveying Korea's thanks for Kuroda Kiyotaka's mission. He was extremely reluctant to take the opportunity offered by his hosts to acquaint himself with Japanese life and institutions. He could not, however, hide his surprise at such novelties as photography, trains, and the telegraph. He entrusted some of his casual discoveries to his diary. In Kobe he had his first glimpse of Westerners. He was amazed at their long noses, their deep eyes, and their yellow hair. The "dull eyes" of the Westerners seemed incongruous with their intelligence.

He observed that Westerners lived all over the country, built houses, had official Japanese positions, and even married Japanese women.[6]

Kim also reflected on the issue of *fukyō* (*fukoku kyōhei*, "to enrich the nation and to strengthen the army") which was explained to him as the magic formula behind Japan's modernization. *Fukyō* was based, Kim surmised, on foreign trade, but he was convinced that Japan's production had not risen enough to supply all the buyers from abroad. Surely prices would rise, and the increased issue of money would lead to the danger of "cheap money and expensive commodities." He concluded that foreign trade was the surest way to calamity.[7]

Kim's official visit ended on June 18. When he departed from Japan, Terashima gave him a polite return letter to the minister of rites, Kim Sang-hyŏn, which expressed the Japanese government's gratitude for the mission. Kim returned to Pusan on June 28, 1876.[8]

On July 21, Kim was received by the king to give a report on his mission to Japan. The king was eager to hear a firsthand account. He asked about Japan's armament and agricultural tools and its government organization and imitation of things Western. The king's curiosity surely was disappointed by Kim's evasive and inexact answers. Instead of personal insights, Kim presented to the king two Chinese works, the *Hai-kuo t'u-chih* and *Ying-huan chih-lüeh*, which he had acquired in Japan. He mentioned that Inoue Kaoru, with whom he had had his only political discussion, was concerned about Korea's unpreparedness for a Russian attack. Kim finally acquitted himself of his task as *susinsa*, which he had fulfilled with such a punctilious sense of duty, by delivering a note in which Terashima announced the coming of Miyamoto Koichi to Korea to carry out the treaty stipulations.[9]

Kim Ki-su's mission resumed the long tradition of diplomatic exchanges between Korea and Japan. Seen in the light of the changing circumstances brought about by the Kanghwa Treaty, however, the mission seems oddly antiquated. Kim Ki-su, the traditional Confucian scholar-official, was confronted in Japan with a modernized world that evoked his curiosity, but that apparently seemed to him to have no relevance to his own country's situation. Rather than building mutual trust and confidence, Kim's experiences in Japan tended to confirm the Korean officialdom's general apprehension about Japanese designs. Kim's report thus contained no incentive for the ensuing negotiations between the two countries.

The Conclusion of the Supplementary Treaty and the Trade Regulations

Japan achieved a diplomatic breakthrough in 1876, but this was not her ultimate goal. The Tokyo government envisaged close coordination between its diplomatic and commercial activities in Korea. In its search for markets and raw materials outside Japan, the government was prepared to support the initial phase of Japanese-Korean trade with government subsidies. Previous expectations about Korea's commercial potential, however, were not realistic. The observations collected by the Japanese chief negotiators caused the Japanese government to reduce the speed with which it planned to pursue its new course in Korea. Kuroda and Inoue gave Sanjō a gloomy picture of the prospects for trade with Korea. They complained that there was no money and not a single important product in the peninsula. They considered it too early to commence full-scale commercial and diplomatic activities. They suggested that Japan should follow the limited objective of revising trade practices at Pusan and draft simple trade provisions to facilitate Pusan's trade with Tsushima and Japan. In the meantime, the Korean government's attitude toward such matters as the extension and modernization of trade could be studied.[10]

Action to conclude additional agreements was not taken until June. On the 8th of June, Miyamoto Koichi was appointed commissioner (*riji-kan*) and entrusted with the negotiation of the supplementary treaty and the trade regulations. Miyamoto's impending mission was announced to the Korean government by Kim Ki-su upon his return to Korea, and preparations for receiving the Japanese envoy were undertaken immediately.[11] A building in the military headquarters of Kyŏnggi was repaired, and on July 22 Cho In-hŭi was appointed treaty negotiator (*kangsugwan*), Hwang Chong-hyŏn protocol officer (*panjŏpkwan*), and Yi Hŭi-wŏn reception officer (*yŏnjŏpkwan*) on the recommendation of the Council of State. One day later an elaborate procedure for the reception of the Japanese mission was approved by the king.[12] Miyamoto arrived in the Korean capital on July 30, 1876. The presentation of the ratification document of the Korean-Japanese treaty was followed by a royal audience on August 1. Four days later the formal negotiations began.[13]

In working out the provisions of the supplementary treaty, the Japanese and Korean negotiators, who were sometimes joined by Sin Hŏn and Yun Cha-sŭng, argued about the freedom of movement of the Japanese at Pusan and the stationing of a Japanese envoy at Seoul. Since the Japanese did not demand the immediate opening of two more Korean ports, as provided for by articles 4 and 5 of the treaty, they wanted to secure a wider area of activity at Pusan. Basing himself on the draft treaty which he had brought with him, Miyamoto proposed that the watch gates which had been set up around the Japan House be removed as a first step toward free movement in and out of the Japanese compound. Also, the Japanese placed high priority on procuring a zone around Pusan with a radius of ten Japanese *ri* (approximately 25 miles) within which the Japanese merchants would be free to travel and engage in trade with the Koreans. Furthermore, they requested that Taegu and other important cities be opened to Japanese trade several times a year. Sin opposed these proposals because he feared that their enactment would lead to clashes between Koreans and the Japanese traders. It was only after long bargaining that the Koreans were ready to meet the Japanese part way: the travel limit was to be set at ten Korean *i* (one Japanese *ri*), and the Japanese merchants were to be granted the right of free travel between Pusan and Tongnae.

Of much greater complexity was the problem of stationing a Japanese envoy in Seoul. Article 2 of the treaty called for an exchange of envoys fifteen months after the date of the treaty conclusion. The slightly different wording of the Japanese and Chinese treaty texts gave rise to different interpretations. The Japanese insisted that the treaty clause provided for the permanent residence of their envoy in the Korean capital. The Koreans read it as meaning a temporary sojourn. Sin Hŏn made it clear that the Korean government would insist on separating trade from diplomacy. All matters concerned with trade should be handled by Japanese trade superintendents (*kanrikan*) stationed in the ports, and diplomatic problems should be settled by envoys sent to the respective capitals on a temporary basis.[14]

Miyamoto recognized that there was a wide gap between Japanese and Korean views on the interaction of trade and diplomacy and dropped the issue of the establishment of a permanent Japanese legation in Seoul from the agenda. The trade regulations were agreed upon without causing a major controversy, and Cho In-hŭi and Miyamoto signed and affixed their seals to the eleven *Additional Articles Appended to the Treaty of Kanghwa* and the *Trade Regulations* on August 24, 1876.[15]

According to article 4 of the Additional Articles, the range of Japanese movement and activities was widened to ten Korean *i* (approximately

2.5 miles). Within this limit the Japanese were free to buy local articles and sell Japanese goods. In the open ports the Japanese were allowed to lease land for the purpose of erecting residences. Article 7 gave both nationalities the right to use Korean and Japanese coins in their transactions.

The Trade Regulations laid down the procedure for import and export trade to and from Korea. The tasks involved in the registration of ships were assigned to the Korean government. Regulation 4 assured that all goods for export would be recorded at the Korean government office before they were placed on shipboard. Regulation 9 provided against smuggling, and regulation 10 prohibited the sale of opium.[16]

Miyamoto sent two important communications to Cho In-hŭi in an effort to further clarify some points in the agreements. The first communication expressed the resolution of the Japanese government to abstain from levying any import and export duties on trade between Japan and Korea. New emphasis was placed on freeing Korean-Japanese trade from the old restrictions and prohibitions which had existed during the Tokugawa period. Furthermore, the document tried to strengthen the legal basis of trade to protect it against official extortions and exactions. Miyamoto impressed upon Cho that "the above rules should be regarded as part of the Appendix to the Treaty and be given due publicity as having the same effect as the stipulations contained therein." The second communication dealt with the treatment of shipwrecked people. On the same day, August 24, Cho In-hŭi replied to Miyamoto that the Korean government regarded the new proposals as relevant and would put them into force and observe them permanently.[17]

Although the Korean government was cooperative as far as the details of trade were concerned, it clung to its basic stand that diplomacy and trade were separate. It tried once again to get its viewpoint anchored in a treaty clause. In a letter dated September 3, 1876, the president of the Korean Department of Rites, Kim Sang-hyŏn, proposed directly to Foreign Minister Terashima that two more provisions be added to the supplementary treaty. First, Japan should send an envoy only for diplomatic dealings (*kyobing*), and all commercial matters should be managed solely by the trade superintendent in the open ports. Second, the route the envoy would take to Seoul should be fixed so that he could be received and escorted. Kim proposed the road leading from T'ongjin to Seoul.[18] There was no immediate echo to the Korean proposals in Tokyo. Miyamoto seems to have been the only one who was sympathetic to the Korean point of view.[19] The Japanese government could not commit itself to a set of rules that endorsed past practices. The incompatibility of Japanese and Korean views on trade and diplomacy made an easy understanding impossible. Hard bargaining between the two countries lay ahead.

The Opening of Additional Ports: The First Phase

One of the most important provisions for furthering Japanese interests in the Korean peninsula was article 5 of the Treaty of Kanghwa. It reads: "On the coast of five provinces, viz., Kyŏnggi, Ch'ungch'ŏng, Chŏlla, Kyŏngsang, and Hamgyŏng, two ports suitable for commercial purposes shall be selected, and the time for opening these two ports shall be in the twentieth month from the second month of the ninth year of Meiji, i.e., October 1877." Yet, as late as the early spring of 1877, the Japanese government had taken no steps toward claiming these privileges. It was preoccupied with more urgent matters, notably the suppression of the Satsuma Rebellion. The opening of additional ports in Korea made detailed surveys of the Korean coast necessary, but no navy ship could be spared for this purpose. In May 1877, Foreign Minister Terashima argued in a letter to Iwakura Tomomi that a delay on the part of the Japanese government in carrying out the terms of the treaty might have an adverse effect on the opening of other ports. He therefore urged the resumption of survey missions.[20]

Surveys of the Korean coast by Japanese ships had been conducted sporadically ever since Japan had set her aim at opening Korean ports for trade. Korean officials along the coast were advised to treat the Japanese survey crews cordially.[21] Since the northeastern coastline of Hamgyŏng had been mapped out by the two Japanese ships *Unyōkan* and *Ryūjōkan*, in 1877 the Japanese Foreign Office was mainly interested in gathering information about suitable ports on the west coast. At Terashima's suggestion, Hanabusa Yoshitada was assigned to accompany the ships as chargé d'affaires (*dairi kōshi*). He was a career man in the Foreign Office with experience in Korea. Highly recommended by Enomoto as a person capable of expanding Japanese influence in Korea, his presence was to lend the mission additional diplomatic importance.[22] Hanabusa's main task was to determine which one of four places—Okku and Mokp'o in Chŏlla and Kanghwa and Inch'ŏn in Kyŏnggi—would be the most satisfactory port on the west coast. On the east coast, the Bay of Yŏnghŭng was considered the best choice.[23]

In October 1877, Hanabusa left Nagasaki for the one-day trip to Pusan aboard the *Takaomaru*. He was well aware of the delicacy of his mission. He did not expect quick results and apparently was resolved to yield rather than use force if faced with Korean opposition. Ill-fate marred his expedition from the outset. An outbreak of cholera aboard his ship detained him a full month in Pusan. When he finally left port on November 3, bad weather seriously hampered the surveying. He slowly advanced via the islands of Kŏmun and Soan to the larger island of Chin. From there he explored Mokp'o, which he found inappropriate as a port because the waterway leading to it was dangerous and because there was no large market town in its neighborhood. After surveying Okku and Puan, he anchored on November 13 off the tiny island of P'ung, just outside the bay of Inch'ŏn. From there he inspected the Bay of Asan. Disappointed with his findings and jeopardized by bad weather, he completed the first part of his mission with a brief investigation of Kanghwa and Inch'ŏn.[24]

Ill-prepared for his scheduled negotiations with the Koreans, Hanabusa entered Seoul on November 25, 1877. He found the Korean government very reluctant to receive him. The state councillors were unhappy about the repeated appearance of Japanese envoys in the capital and were dispirited about the impotence of their own "strong words and reprimands," which did not seem to impress the Japanese. They concluded, however, that they had no alternative but to receive the emissary with courtesy. Hong U-ch'ang, who then was vice-minister of the Department of Rites, was appointed reception officer. He was to conduct the negotiations with Hanabusa. Hong insisted that the opening of Pukch'ŏng in Hamgyŏng had been agreed upon earlier, but Hanabusa countered with his demand for the opening of Munch'ŏn, on the Bay of Yŏnghŭng, instead. Hong objected to this choice because it was the site of royal tombs. Although Hanabusa and Hong failed to agree on this issue, both realized the necessity of renewed surveys. To facilitate the refueling of survey ships, they concluded the *Agreement on the Establishment of Coal Depots* on December 20, 1877. According to the agreement, from April 1878 the Japanese were allowed to store coal for twelve months in two places in Chŏlla: at Pyŏkp'ajŏng on Chin Island and on Kŏmun Island. In addition, the Japanese could utilize the village of Songjŏn in the district of Munch'ŏn in Hamgyŏng for six months.[25]

In 1878, after this initial contact with the Korean government, the Japanese stepped up their surveying efforts. Principal attention was paid to the northeastern coast of Korea because the Japanese government believed that the communication line between Nagasaki and Vladivostok should be strengthened for the protection of the Japan Sea and also for the promotion of trade. Wŏnsan and Pukch'ŏng had priority. On the west coast, Hŭngdŏk and Okku in Chŏlla and Haemi and Kyŏlsŏng in Ch'ung-ch'ŏng were scheduled for survey.[26]

The surveying started late in April 1878. The *Tenjōmaru*, under the command of Captain Matsumura Yasushige, sailed to the Bay of Yŏng-hŭng, and, as routine practice, the mission's plans were made known to the prefect of Tongnae. The survey along the coast of the prefecture of Tŏg-wŏn provoked protests from the local officials because of the royal tombs located at Munch'ŏn. Wherever the ship cast anchor to get fresh water and provisions, the sailors were met by nervous officials who made minute inquiries into the identity and motives of the intruders. A language student sent up from Tongnae acted as interpreter. The Koreans were apprehensive about the Japanese survey flags placed on nearby hilltops. Although the Koreans provided food and drink (and often refused to accept money in return), clashes between armed Japanese and panic-stricken Koreans were frequent. Every move the Japanese made was recorded in detail, and a torrent of lengthy reports poured into Seoul. Bad weather again hampered the progress of the Japanese ship, and after Matsumura decided that Pukch'ŏng did not possess the same qualities as Wŏnsan, the ship started back to Pusan during the first days of August. The survey along the west coast in September was cut short by the outbreak of an epidemic aboard the *Tenjōmaru*. In the middle of October the mission was terminated.[27]

The Opening of Additional Ports: The Second Phase

The time limit stipulated by treaty for the opening of two additional trading ports had long passed, yet neither surveys nor negotiations were successful in finalizing the choice of ports. Moreover, the Korean government's decision in the fall of 1878 to tax trade at Pusan, and a clash between Japanese and Koreans near Tongnae in the spring of the following year (for both incidents, see Chapter 5) poisoned the diplomatic atmosphere further and complicated an agreement on the ports.

The Japanese still preferred Wŏnsan on the east coast, and they con-

sidered Inch'ŏn the best temporary choice on the west coast until a suitable
port in its vicinity could be found.[28] On this premise, Hanabusa Yoshitada
set out for Korea again in the late spring of 1879. On his way to Seoul,
Hanabusa surveyed the coast of Ch'ungch'ŏng and Kyŏnggi and investigated such places as Kunsan, Piin, Sŏch'ŏn, the Bay of Asan, Tangjin,
and the coastal area of Namyang. Along the route he was met by concerned local officials who were very reluctant to answer his many questions
about weather conditions, local products, and nearby markets, but who
hospitably provided the ships with food and fresh water. During the first
days of June, Hanabusa sailed along the coast of Kyŏnggi and found that
only Inch'ŏn (Chemulp'o) offered the prospect of becoming a prosperous
harbor. With this conviction, Hanabusa, accompanied by Kondō Masuki,
entered the Korean capital on June 13, 1879. Before Hanabusa sat down
at the conference table, he became entangled in a minor controversy with
local officials over his orders to a group of his entourage. He had directed
the group to take the unauthorized land route from Koonp'o (Namyang)
to Seoul to survey the land and explore the feasibility of opening Suwŏn.
This antagonized Seoul and unnecessarily stiffened the resistance of Hanabusa's Korean counterpart.[29]

The ensuing negotiations between Hanabusa and Hong U-ch'ang,
who once again acted as reception officer, were as tough as before. The
surveys showed that Wŏnsan was superior to the other possible ports on the
east coast. In 1877 the Koreans themselves had suggested Wŏnsan as a
substitute for Songjŏn, and in November 1878 the Japanese foreign
minister had reminded the Koreans of their suggestion and had asserted
that the proximity of royal tombs at neighboring Munch'ŏn was no reason
to exclude Wŏnsan from consideration.[30] The Koreans now opposed the
choice of Wŏnsan because of its dynastic significance. It was not without
justification that Hanabusa, confronted by Hong's tenacious denial of the
previous understanding, accused the Korean government of lacking an
overall policy. When negotiations on Wŏnsan became hopelessly deadlocked, Hanabusa surprised Hong with the unexpected renewal of his
demand that Inch'ŏn (Chemulp'o) be opened to Japanese trade. He argued that Inch'ŏn was conveniently situated near the capital, and since the
Japanese envoys had disembarked there for the last few years, the populace
had become used to the sight of foreigners. The Japanese tried to force
quick compliance with this demand by building some provisional barracks
on the shore of Inch'ŏn. This action, which the protests of the local officials
were unable to forestall, further antagonized the Korean government.

Consequently, the Koreans not only rejected the opening of Inch'ŏn but also refused to consider opening any other port in Kyŏnggi. Inch'ŏn was strategically important for the capital and its opening would not only divert much of the commercial activities from Seoul to the port, but it would also disturb the populace. For the same reasons, the Koreans objected to the opening of Kanghwa, Suwŏn, Namyang, and T'ongjin. Hanabusa's protest that the Koreans had thus eliminated Kyŏnggi as one of the five provinces designated by the treaty was to no avail. Even Hanabusa's offer to postpone Inch'ŏn's opening for some time could not move the Koreans to reconsider the matter.[31]

This fruitless debate continued day after day in the heavy atmosphere of a hot summer. The debate grew even more unpleasant when a Korean crowd, defying government orders, threw stones at members of the Japanese party. By early July there was still no government decision on Wŏnsan. Then, on July 8, 1879, Hong surprised Hanabusa with the news that his government had agreed to designate Wŏnsan an open port. Before reaching this decision, the government had had to silence vociferous outside opposition.[32]

When Hong disclosed his government's decision, he emphasized that the arrangements at Wŏnsan had to follow in all details the rules operative at Pusan. Hanabusa gave Hong a draft agreement, but the final document was delayed by other issues. Hong U-ch'ang wished to add four points to the Wŏnsan agreement: the levying of duties on merchandise, the prohibition of rice exports, the extradition of criminals, and a ban on Westerners entering Korean ports on Japanese ships. Since the scope of these demands far surpassed Hanabusa's more limited aim, he refused to include them in the agreement.[33] Hong U-ch'ang and Hanabusa then concluded the *Convention Regarding the Opening of the Port of Wŏnsan* in seven articles on August 30, 1879. The convention provided for the opening of the port on May 1, 1880.[34]

The negotiations on Wŏnsan were finally successful, but those on Inch'ŏn remained stalemated. Hanabusa reported Korea's adamant opposition to the opening of that port to Tokyo. While he was awaiting further instructions, he planned to sail to Wŏnsan to set the stage for the execution of the convention. He left Seoul on September 3. An outbreak of beriberi aboard his ship foiled his travel plans, and he had to return first to Nagasaki before sailing to Wŏnsan.[35]

The Opening of Inch'ŏn

Inch'ŏn occupied a unique position in the minds of the Koreans. Being the "gate to the capital," its strategic importance had at all times been emphasized by heavy fortifications. Even after the conclusion of the Korean-Japanese treaty of 1876, the construction of fortifications continued, and as recently as August 1879 new batteries around Inch'ŏn and nearby Pup'yŏng were completed. Inch'ŏn continued to be a bastion that would not be given up without resistance.[36]

It is therefore not surprising that Hanabusa's demand for Inch'ŏn's opening gave rise to immediate controversy inside and outside the Korean government and caused an air of crisis in the capital. The responsibility for having allowed the Japanese to display such audacity was passed back and forth. The president of the Board of Officials-without-Portfolio, Yi Yu-wŏn, submitted a memorial on August 4, 1879, in which he denounced the insatiability of the Japanese. Yi was alarmed by the popular unrest that the proposed opening of Inch'ŏn was causing, and he was afraid that government indecision would encourage the Japanese to make even bolder demands. He conceded that under the present circumstances it would be well-nigh impossible to ward off the "foreign robbers," but he warned the king that easy compliance with Japanese demands would bring about unending misery and earn the scorn of future generations.[37] Yi's memorial aroused the joint response of former and incumbent state councillors, including Kim Pyŏng-hak, Hong Sun-mok, and Kim Pyŏng-guk, who vehemently refuted Yi Yu-wŏn's implication that some members of the government were seeking an easy understanding with the Japanese. They firmly stated that they never had disagreed with one another on the Inch'ŏn policy, whether at official or private meetings. In protest, they all tendered their resignations. Regretting his words, Yi Yu-wŏn, too, retired from his position, and even Chief State Councillor Yi Ch'oe-ŭng, on the pretext of illness, presented his resignation. Unable to resolve the dilemma, Yi Ch'oe-ŭng argued that the treaty of 1876 should be used as the basis for further dealings with the Japanese, but he urged that the most important consideration at the moment was containing the Japanese. The king refused to accept the resignations. Once more, under the pressure of Japanese demands, the government faced a crisis of opinion which indicated the fragility of the previous consensus on Wŏnsan. Yi Yu-wŏn's memorial surprisingly revealed that Yi himself was wavering and, for reasons that are not quite clear, was reversing his earlier plea for a reasonable understanding with the Japanese.[38]

The Japanese government was not oblivious of the Korean opposition to Inch'ŏn's opening. In the early summer of 1880, Hanabusa was about to leave for Seoul for the third time, but his departure was postponed until December because a Korean envoy who had been sent to Tokyo hinted that the controversy over the opening of the port still raged in the Korean government.[39] Hanabusa, escorted by a heavy military guard, finally arrived in the Korean capital on December 17, 1880. Once in Seoul, he made it clear that he would not tolerate any further delays. Instructed to coordinate the opening of Inch'ŏn with the question of a Japanese envoy's permanent residence in Seoul, Hanabusa shocked the president of the Department of Rites, Yun Cha-sŭng, with his demand to present his credentials directly to the king. Although such an act was not provided for in the treaty, the Department of Rites hastily prepared the protocol on royal orders. On December 27, chosen as a propitious day, Hanabusa was received by King Kojong in Ch'angdŏk Palace—the first Japanese envoy to be received by a Korean king.[40]

Hanabusa's forceful insistence on taking up residence in Seoul did not expedite the decision on Inch'ŏn. When Hanabusa met his negotiation partner, Kim Hong-jip,[41] on January 4, 1881, no solution to the stalled negotiations was in sight. Kim Hong-jip's evasiveness reflected the indecision of the Korean government. However, Kim reported that his government would continue demanding a postponement of Inch'ŏn's opening for the next five to seven years. This, at least, indicated that the issue was still debated. Hanabusa warned that he would not accept a prolonged postponement. He was prepared to offer only fifteen months. He was also reluctant to agree to the proposition that Inch'ŏn would be opened on the condition that the Japanese minister take up residence there instead of in Seoul.[42]

None of the documents reveal how the Korean government reached its final decision on the opening of Inch'ŏn. Because of extra-governmental opposition, the deliberations must have been held in complete secrecy. Although Hanabusa had been informed about a gradual change of opinion in government circles, he was surprised when Kim Hong-jip transmitted to him on January 28 the Korean government's decision to open Inch'ŏn to Japanese trade. The Korean decision, however, was not unqualified. The government still opposed an early opening of the port for at least two reasons: it would overstrain government finances, and it would add fuel to popular unrest. As a concession, Hanabusa offered a postponement of twenty months. With the goal of his mission in sight, Hanabusa grew impatient when the negotiations were interrupted by New Year's celebrations. He repeatedly expressed his anger at Kim's superiors for their tardiness in reaching the ultimate decision. On February 28, both parties finally agreed that Inch'ŏn would open in September 1882. The laying out of the settlement was left for later negotiations.[43] The disturbances in the summer of 1882 forced a further postponement, and the official date was then set for January 1, 1883.[44]

The opening of Inch'ŏn not only rearoused determined opposition within the government, but it also fanned smoldering unrest within the capital and in the provinces. It was rumored that people in the southern provinces massed together by the thousands intending to march on Seoul, and dissidents from Andong (Kyŏngsang) attracted hundreds of like-minded followers on their march north to protest the port's opening. Although none of the protesters seems to have reached the capital, officials were sent out from Seoul to investigate these threatening developments.[45]

⋈⋈

With the opening of Inch'ŏn, the Korean-Japanese treaty finally reached its full political proportions. The bitter struggle over the opening of the ports, which lasted for almost half a decade, epitomized Korea's general unpreparedness to sanction demands that, although laid down by treaty, went beyond tradition-rooted precedent. In the aftermath of the Kanghwa Treaty the Koreans failed to develop a new Japan policy. On the contrary, they futilely attempted to make the policy of containment work once again. The Koreans' reluctance to accommodate the Japanese conflicted with their new commitment to the treaty stipulations. Therefore, decisions were reached only in reaction to Japanese demands. These decisions were usually preceded by bitter arguments in which the officials accused each other of allowing the Japanese to win further diplomatic advantages. While the government was trying to reach a compromise, it was loudly opposed from without by a conservative opposition. This opposition continued to brand as traitors the government officials who dealt with the Japanese. The government's lack of a policy on the one hand, and its fear of the Confucian opposition on the other, account for the secrecy of its deliberations and the resulting abruptness with which the decisions were made known to the Japanese.

The Koreans accepted foreign trade as long as it was confined to the opened ports and could be controlled by traditional means, but they thought of diplomacy only in terms of ceremonial matters that could be settled on an ad hoc basis. The general change in outlook toward the Western world that was to characterize the early 1880s did not influence Korea's attitude toward Japan, and thus it did not help expedite the decision on the opening of Inch'ŏn. Korean-Japanese relations continued to be guided by criteria that differed from those Korea eventually developed in her relationship with the West. Although at the turn of the decade Korea's policy of containment toward Japan was eroded, the Koreans could find no new formula for dealing with Japan.

In the years after the conclusion of the Kanghwa Treaty the Japanese did not continue to pursue the vigorous course of action that had led to the establishment of their domination of Korean-Japanese relations. One reason for this was the realization that Korean commercial prospects were not as bright as they had anticipated. Another reason was the growing sense of frustration over Korean intransigence. Furthermore, with the suppression of the Satsuma Rebellion, the Japanese dissenters who had conceived of a Korean expedition as a means of venting their frustration were silenced. The oligarchs were no longer under pressure to pursue a Korea policy that ignored realities; the government could steer a quieter course. Up to the early 1880s, Japan contented herself in seeking the fulfillment of the treaty terms. Diplomacy had been given a chance, and diplomacy had won out.

TRADE AND THE OPENED PORTS

Korea's economic life was based on community self-sufficiency. By the second half of the nineteenth century Korea had attained neither a market economy nor a money economy. Domestic trade was limited and conducted under tight government supervision. Foreign trade, regarded as a danger to the domestic economy, was even more restricted. Trade was not considered a source of state revenue, and it suffered from the traditional Confucian contempt for unessential economic activities. Korea lacked the resources as well as the experience and motivation to conduct international trade. The conclusion of the Kanghwa Treaty did not change the Koreans' basic outlook on trade, but it forced them to take practical measures to accommodate the Japanese traders in the opened treaty ports. Until 1880, when Wŏnsan was selected as the second trading port, Pusan was the only place in Korea where the stipulations of the Korean-Japanese treaty were applicable. The southern port therefore became a barometer of Korean-Japanese relations. Plunges in the local atmosphere were more often registered than were tendencies toward stabilization.

Korean Debate on Foreign Trade

The state of Korea's general economy in the latter part of the 1870s was depressed and held little promise for development. As if to underline the seriousness of the time, nature did not cooperate. The documents are full of references to natural disasters. Particularly during 1877 and 1878, Korea was hard hit by droughts which led to wide-spread famine and an upsurge of banditry. Floods devastated the southern provinces in 1879 leaving hundreds of people homeless. In the same year epidemics broke out around Pusan and the capital.[1]

The financial plight of the central government gave rise to a continuous debate on economic issues throughout the second half of the 1870s. When King Kojong assumed power in 1874, he did not inherit a sound fiscal structure. He made things worse by withdrawing Ch'ing cash from circulation, which brought the central as well as the local governments to the brink of bankruptcy.[2] Because of the natural disasters, the manifold taxes and levies owed to the government could not be paid, and finances became even tighter. The government coffers were depleted, and the government warehouses were empty, the officials' salaries could not be paid, and the soldiers' daily rations could not be distributed.[3] This state of general economic disaster gravely affected the government's attitude toward its new trade commitments to Japan.

Searching for a way to alleviate the economic situation, memorialists throughout the 1870s were unanimous in their proposals: the government must curtail its expenditures. The memorialists demanded frugality not only for government operations, but also for the royal court and all the yangban. The concerned officials, almost without exception, rearticulated a concept that had claimed attention before: the financial impasse was created by the use of "extravagant and luxurious" foreign goods which were paid for with daily essentials such as rice and cloth. The importation of foreign goods, they claimed, was undermining the economic life of the country and had to be stopped. Why should the Korean people, who produce everything necessary for their lives, seek "strange and unusable things" from abroad, especially when all the profits flow into the pockets of the foreigners? The Japanese load their steamships and big boats with Korean goods and, the memorialists warned, "the day is not far away when our people will go hungry because they have nothing left to eat, and they will be cold because they have nothing left with which to clothe themselves."[4]

Ten years before, in 1866, the same kind of reasoning culminated in the Taewŏn'gun's ban of Western goods. In 1876 such a ban would have brought the country into military conflict with Japan. Attempting to check the outflow of foodstuffs, the Korean government instructed Sin Hŏn to incorporate a prohibition on rice trade into the text of the Kanghwa

Treaty. Sin's efforts were in vain. Regulation 6 of the Trade Regulations signed in August 1876 provided that "the exportation and importation of rice and other grain shall hereafter be allowed at any of the open ports of Korea."[5] The government's dilemma was expressed in its repeated emphasis on agriculture as the basis of the country's economy and its tendency to discourage foreign trade by belittling the value and usefulness of Korean goods to the Japanese.[6]

Because of the economic problems it was facing, the Korean government's attitude toward trade with Japan was defensive. Moreover, it continued to emphasize the traditional sharp distinction between diplomacy and trade. This viewpoint was stated in a memorial by the state councillors on December 7, 1876. Since the new Japanese representative was to concern himself with commercial matters, the prefect of Tongnae could not be allowed direct day-to-day contact with him. A middleman had to be appointed for regular dealings with the Japanese representative. The councillors recommended that for this role the language officer (*hundo*) should be renamed treaty port inspector (*p'anch'algwan*). The incumbent language officer, Hyŏn Sŏg-un, who had earned special merit during the treaty negotiations, was the obvious choice for continuing a traditional post in a new guise. Although the Koreans explained the appointment in terms of "harmonizing the mutual relationship,"[7] it was a veiled attempt to restrict trade through official supervision.

The Development of the Japanese Settlement at Pusan

Strictly speaking, the Korean-Japanese treaty did not provide for the opening of Pusan harbor, but reconfirmed the right of the Japanese to continue trade in their traditional foothold, Ch'oryang,[8] where the Japan House was located. The Japan House,[9] a large compound of approximately fifty acres, was surrounded landward by a high stone wall with several watch towers. Seaward it opened onto a walled-in anchorage. From the Japan House, a narrow path passed a few tiled houses that were the quarters of the language officer (*hundo*) and his assistant (*hundo pyŏlch'a*) and continued some two miles to the walled town of Pusanjin. Lying on the north side of the harbor, Pusanjin belonged to the larger administrative unit of the prefecture of Tongnae. It was the seat of a naval garrison. Reportedly, two thousand Korean merchants lived there at the end of the

1870s. The main products of the region were fish, edible frogs, seaweeds, pomegranates, pottery, bamboo arrows, and salt. Six miles to the north lay the old town of Tongnae, the prefectural seat. At the end of the nineteenth century, Tongnae had a population of approximately five thousand households. Special trade fairs were held there twice a year, during the second and the tenth months.[10]

After the conclusion of the Kanghwa Treaty, the Japanese government was advised by its returning representatives, who had taken a close look at Korea's commercial potential, to concentrate first on normalizing trade at Pusan. For this purpose, the government decided to send a trade superintendent (*kanrikan*) to the port to protect Japan's commercial interests and promote trade. He was to be vested with the full authority to communicate with the prefect of Tongnae as an equal. Because there was no diplomatic representative in Korea, the trade superintendent was to look after his country's diplomatic interests as well.[11]

A Foreign Office official, Kondō Masuki, was appointed as the first trade superintendent on October 31, 1876, and he arrived in Pusan some three weeks later.[12] A number of topics awaited clarification. Kondō met with the prefect of Tongnae, Hong U-ch'ang, for their initial formal discussions on December 12 and 13. Although the supplementary articles had been concluded, many problems concerning their execution had not been touched upon. The questions of the removal of the watch gates around the former Japan House, the rental fee for the Japanese settlement, and the travel limit of the Japanese merchants were still outstanding.

The preparation of a settlement for the Japanese community was the most urgent task. Kondō pressed for the removal of the two landward watch gates, but Hong feared that without these gates the Koreans would lose all control over the Japanese traders. Therefore, Kondō and Hong decided that one of the gates would remain until the Korean government chose the site for the Customs House. They further agreed that as long as the Koreans were unfamiliar with the management of the customs duties, the Japanese trade superintendent would take care of all customs affairs. The most intractable problem proved to be the zone of free movement. Article 4 of the supplementary articles provided that "the limits within which Japanese subjects may travel from the port of Fusan shall be comprised within a radius of ten *li* [sic], Korean measurement, the landing-place at that port being taken as a centre...." The two parties disagreed about how to measure these ten *i*. The Japanese insisted upon measuring in a direct line that would include Pusanjin within the zone, whereas the

Koreans demanded that the measurement follow the road. No agreement could be reached.[13]

The division of duties between the Korean government and the Japanese government concerning the administration of the settlement was laid down in the *Agreement Concerning the Japanese Settlement at Pusan* signed by Kondō Masuki and the prefect of Tongnae, Hong U-ch'ang, on January 30, 1877. In contrast to the later foreign settlements in Korea, the Japanese government, and not individuals, rented the site of the Pusan settlement. The rent was fixed at fifty yen per year, the payments starting from the first day of the eleventh month (i.e., December 16). The jurisdiction over the buildings within the former Japan House was newly established. Maintenance of roads, sewers, and drainage was placed in charge of the Japanese government. Repairs connected with the breakwater frontage were the responsibility of the Korean government.[14]

The promotion of trade at Pusan seems to have been one of Home Minister Ōkubo Toshimichi's special concerns. To launch the Korea trade, he personally appealed to enterprising Ōkura Kihachirō.[15] As soon as the Trade Regulations were concluded, Ōkura followed this call, packed up some Japanese and foreign products, and sailed to Pusan late in August 1876. Near Tongnae, he displayed foreign-made goods such as woolen cloth, shirtings, and Indian cotton cloth. Most important among the Japanese-made goods were several kinds of silk and daily necessities. Each article on display had a price tag, an innovation that surprised the Korean buyers. Ōkura's initiative proved to be a success. Within a few days the whole shipment was sold out.[16]

After Ōkura's successful venture in Pusan, Sanjō Sanetomi officially opened trade with Korea on October 14, 1876. Any Japanese subject could engage in trade provided he obtained a passport. The Japanese government was prepared to facilitate trade with Korea. It announced that it would consider the import and export of merchandise from and to Korea in the same light as the transport of goods between different places in Japan. This meant that the Korea trade was not subject to the same taxes as Japan's trade with other foreign countries.[17] Still another incentive was the grant, in November 1876, of an annual government subsidy of 5,000 yen to Mitsubishi to open a steamship line to Pusan. A ship was scheduled to run between Nagasaki and Pusan once a month.[18]

The government's encouragement and Ōkura's repeated call to merchants in all parts of Japan to participate in the Korea trade stimulated a growing number of traders to try their luck at Pusan. In February 1876,

Kuroda Kiyotaka estimated the number of Japanese traders, who all came from Tsushima, at around seventy. In November of the same year Kondō Masuki put their number at over one hundred. Kondō found twelve ships anchored at Pusan harbor. In the following months, Japanese ships visited Ch'oryang in increasing numbers.[19] By the middle of 1877, about two hundred Japanese trading establishments were settled in the port. Among these were Ōkura's branch establishment, which had been opened in December of the preceding year, and that of Tomiya of Tokyo. Reportedly, there were also some branch houses from the neighborhood of Nagasaki and Hakata. The greatest share of the Korea trade, however, was still in the hands of Tsushima merchants.[20]

The Japanese settlement, which initially covered the area of the old Japan House,[21] was almost entirely a business colony. Construction was hastily begun to accommodate the growing number of Japanese traders. Streets were laid out and divided into two main sections, Benten-dori and Honcho-dori. Godowns were built along the shore side of the settlement. The office of the trade superintendent (*kanrikan*) was situated in Honcho-dori, facing the harbor.[22] A post office was opened in November 1876,[23] and in the following spring a small hospital, which was staffed by a navy doctor and some medical personnel, opened its doors to Japanese as well as to Korean patients.[24] Early in 1878 a court house was built.[25] The small and unobtrusive customs building in the old Japan House was moved to the northern part of the harbor in 1878 and functioned as the place where the harbor dues of the Japanese ships were collected.[26] The public concerns of the settlement were taken care of by a self-governing council made up of a number of business representatives under the supervision of the trade superintendent.[27]

Rapid expansion of the settlement population, due to the influx of merchants' families, became a matter of grave concern to the local Korean officials. Protests against this influx were carried all the way to Tokyo, but no avail. The trade superintendent was forced to put a close watch on his settlers and curtail their movements. The Korean government stationed inspectors (*kyugŏm kamgwan*) just outside the boundary of the Japanese settlement to observe the traffic.[28] Despite these mutual precautions, there were so many incidents between the Japanese settlers and the Korean population that the Council of State received permission to collect the many reports from Pusan and to present them to the throne once a month.[29] In the summer of 1877 the series of incidents culminated in an affair which had grave consequences. Three Korean women were found guilty of secretly entering the Japanese settlement. All three were decapitated. The local officials, in particular the prefect of Tongnae, Hong U-ch'ang, and the military commander of the Pusan Fort, Im Paek-hyŏn, were held responsible for this case because they had failed to issue strict orders to prevent such happenings. Both were dismissed from office. On June 22, Yun Ch'i-hwa was appointed the new prefect of Tongnae and sent off to his post with the grave admonition that the conclusion of the treaties did not allow for a relaxation of firm government.[30]

From the beginning, the Japanese were aware of Korea's precarious monetary situation. They urged the Korean government to mint new coins. The Koreans, however, disliked the "light treasure which corrupt underlings embezzle, and greedy officials hoard." Moreover, the government lacked the resources to mint large amounts of new coins. For this reason, article 7 of the Additional Articles allowed the Japanese to pay the Koreans in Japanese coin. The Koreans likewise were free to pay either in Korean or Japanese currency.[31]

For the development of trade at Pusan, it was important to establish a Japanese bank. Ōkura Kihachirō, the pioneer and the most enthusiatic promoter of Japanese-Korean trade, was aware that the lack of an adequate banking system would retard the expansion of commercial activities. He appealed to Shibusawa Eiichi, who was then the president of the Dai-ichi Ginkō, to set up a branch office at Pusan to support the weak capital of the small retail merchants. Since the bank's policy was strongly influenced by men who considered the establishment of a branch at Pusan premature, Ōkura and Shibusawa decided to set up a Pusan banking firm at their own risk. In August 1877, they presented a petition to this effect to the Finance Ministry and applied for a government loan of 100,000 yen. The time was ill chosen. The Japanese government needed all of its financial resources to suppress the Satsuma Rebellion. The loan was not forthcoming. Shibusawa revised his plan and decided to undertake the venture alone. Finally, in the spring of 1878, he received the approval of the Finance Ministry and a loan of 50,000 yen. In March he founded a branch office of the Daiichi Kokuritsu Ginkō at Pusan and commenced business on June 8.

The banking establishment proved to be a success. It performed a variety of services: bills of exchange, documentary drafts, loans, deposits, and even a kind of commissioned selling and buying of import and export goods as well as an exchange of Korean and Japanese money. Winning the confidence of the government, it received the remaining 50,000 yen of the loan originally asked for and an additional 10,000 yen as floating capital, and it branched out into still other activities. In the latter part of 1878, it was authorized to sell postage and revenue stamps. It was also in charge of managing the financial transactions of the Japanese trade superintendent (and later of the consul) and became the representative of the Tokio Marine Insurance Company (*Tōkyo Kaijō-hoken kaisha*).[32]

The establishment of a Japanese bank in Pusan principally aided the Japanese traders and was instrumental in circulating Japanese money in the port. The only Korean coin in use, the *sangp'yŏng t'ongbo*, was bulky and heavy, and a Korean dealer needed a number of servants to carry the strings of cash necessary to make even the smallest purchase. The Koreans disliked the Japanese coins, and therefore transactions of any magnitude were carried out by barter. Furthermore, the exchange rate between Korean and Japanese currency fluctuated greatly according to the time of year and the value of the products offered for sale. In 1879 the Japanese government made another major effort to change the financial pattern at Pusan. It suggested that the Korean government should open mines and put a new system of coinage into operation. This appeal had no results.[33]

While the Japanese traders who came to Pusan were encouraged and subsidized by their government, the Korean traders could not count on their government for support. It was difficult for the Japanese to find suitable trading partners. After two watch towers of the former Japan House were removed and official surveillance was slackened, the settlement attracted a growing number of Koreans. Peddlers came to sell rice-gruel soup and a coarse rice wine (*makkŏli*); others began to exhibit simple wares such as tobacco and pipes along the roads. Some Koreans entered Japanese service. In the fall of 1877 the Japanese trade superintendent arranged with Korean officials for the opening of a trade fair to demonstrate the beginning of a new era of unrestricted trade and to promote mutal appreciation of each other's products. The fair was held throughout the month of October and was to be repeated every year.[34]

The peddlers who entered the Japanese settlement, however, were not able to supply enough merchandise to satisfy the Japanese. Since the Japanese were not allowed by treaty to go into the interior, they had to rely entirely on Koreans to bring goods to the port. As a port, Pusan had a particularly advantageous position near the mouth of the Naktong River. The river was the key to the rich hinterland of Kyŏngsang, and at the same time it was a convenient waterway on which goods could be easily transported to the seacoast. To tap these resources, the Japanese traders came to depend on the innkeepers (*kaekchu* and *yŏgak*) who were active along the river and the coast. Their traditional functions as commission agents, brokers, money lenders, and storehouse keepers made them suitable partners for the Japanese traders. Having some financial experience, they played a key role as middlemen. They procured goods from the local producers, transported them to the Japanese settlement, and exchanged them for imported products that were eventually carried further inland to the local fairs by itinerant merchants (*pobusang*).

One of the major obstacles to the smooth functioning of this system of close interdependence was the Koreans' financial weakness. To remedy this, the Japanese began to subsidize the activities of their partners with advance loans. This practice, however, led to many difficulties. Loan recipients were often robbed, and the brokers often embezzled funds. Moreover, due to the lack of adequate funds, the Korean merchants were unable to purchase large quantities of goods. The increasing number of insolvent Koreans led to the general decline of trade in the early 1880s.[35]

The majority of the Korean traders who dealt with the Japanese at Pusan seem to have come from the Kyŏngsang region, but some were lured to the port from as far away as the capital. The latter presumably were licensed merchants (*kongin*).[36] The Kaesŏng and Suwŏn merchants played a surprisingly insignificant role in the Pusan trade. These private merchants who came to Pusan soon faced competition from agents who were employed by local government officials. It seems to have been the officials' practice to have their agents buy from Koreans at extraordinarily low prices and sell to the Japanese for their own profit. By 1882, this abuse of office as well as the monopolies granted to certain officials seem to have hampered trade seriously. The Japanese frequently complained about official corruption. Also, because of the laxity and even the cooperation of officials, smuggling remained a profitable business.[37]

Taxation of Korean Trade at Pusan

In 1878, relations between Japan and Korea were encumbered not only by the debate on the selection of additional treaty ports, but also by the decision of the Korean government to levy taxes on all goods bought or sold by Koreans in the Japanese settlement. This step was not a new policy for collecting additional revenue but rather a measure for controlling trade. Restrictive taxation had been practiced in pre-treaty days and was still in force at the border town of Ŭiju. Duty-free trade at Pusan, the state councillors reasoned, was not only irregular, but also harmed trade at Ŭiju. What undoubtedly precipitated their tax recommendation to the king on September 6, however, was a secret inspector's report which revealed that illegal dealings in rice and other grains had reached catastrophic proportions in Pusan. Taxation was intended to stop "the evil of secret dealings and smuggling." For the execution of the new customs policy, a tax booklet was compiled and sent to the prefect of Tongnae who was ordered to enact the new measures immediately and to punish everyone guilty of smuggling goods out of the country.[38]

Barriers for the collection of taxes were established at Tumojin, near the quarters of the inspector of the treaty port (*p'anch'algwan*). The collection began on September 28, 1878. Taxes varied between fifteen and twenty percent of the value of the goods. The effect of the new policy was immediate: Korean merchants, unable to pay such large sums, stopped bringing their merchandise to the Japanese settlement. Trade came to a standstill. Occasional dealings were carried out clandestinely. The trade superintendent, Yamanoshiro, protested that these taxes were in violation of the treaty and demanded their removal. The prefect of Tongnae, Yun Ch'i-hwa, answered that he was acting on government orders, that only the Korean merchants were taxed, and that this was therefore outside the concern of the treaty.[39]

On October 9, groups of angry Japanese merchants marched to the barriers at Tumojin and threatened to go to Tongnae the next day to remonstrate with the prefect. The result of this protest march was the conclusion of an agreement that the Korean authorities would not tax goods that had been ordered in previous contracts. Yun Ch'i-hwa, who reported posthaste about the incident to Seoul, was ordered to continue the collection.[40]

News about the incident was brought to Tokyo by the surveying ship *Tenjōmaru*, which had been forced to return home at about this time. Protest and speculation arose in the newspapers voicing the opinion that trouble between Japan and Korea was imminent because the arbitrary Koreans had once more given evidence of their hatred of foreigners. Others held Japan responsible for the clash because of her irresolution in fulfilling the treaty stipulations and her inability to establish herself firmly in Korea. Rumors of military and naval preparations against Korea circulated.[41]

The Japanese Foreign Office was more cautious in assessing the situation. Terashima thought the press accounts about a Japanese-Korean collision were an exaggeration. He could not completely deny Korea the right to impose taxes on her own merchants.[42] The Japanese government, however, considered the affair a violation of the treaty and dispatched Hanabusa Yoshitada once more to Pusan where he arrived on November 29, 1878. When the strongly worded notes which Hanabusa sent to the prefect of Tongnae did not achieve the desired result, two small groups of soldiers were landed and stationed in the vicinity of Tumojin on December 4. Hanabusa's determination to reject any compromise was demonstrated. The Koreans had to yield. On December 23, Yun Ch'i-hwa sent a note to Hanabusa saying that he had obtained orders from Seoul to stop the collection of taxes for the time being. Hanabusa then addressed a letter to the president of the Department of Rites, Yun Cha-sŭng, stating that Korea's violation of the treaty and the compensation for the damage done to Japanese trade would be discussed at a later date when a Japanese plenipotentiary would go to the Korean capital. With trade restored, Hanabusa departed from Pusan on December 28, 1878.[43]

Normalization was not easily reestablished, however. This was vividly illustrated by another incident in April 1879. A group of Japanese sailors, accompanied by two members of the permanent Japanese staff, went on a rampage in Tongnae and were stoned by an angry Korean mob. The furious trade superintendent, Yamanoshiro, followed by a band of heavily armed sailors, stormed into the prefect's office and demanded an explanation. Yun Ch'i-hwa's cautious statement could not placate the Japanese who drew their swords and injured the prefect and the inspector of the treaty port, Hyŏn Sŏg-un. Outside the prefect's office, the sailors went on a shooting spree. Yun finally gained control over the situation and took the Japanese to task for their unruly behavior. Yamanoshiro showed signs of regret, and before the intruders retreated Yun convinced him to consent to a few rules that restricted the movement of the Japanese.[44] It was shortly after this unfortunate incident that Hanabusa Yoshitada returned to Korea in Japan's quest for the opening of additional treaty ports. He also was ordered to seek redress of the damage done to trade by taxation in 1878. The atmosphere at Pusan still determined the tenor of Korean-Japanese relations.

The Opening of Wŏnsan to Japanese Trade

In accordance with the *Convention Regarding the Opening of the Port of Wŏnsan,*
concluded in August 1879 after months of tedious debate, Wŏnsan was
opened to Japanese trade on May 1, 1880. This event inspired Japanese
policymakers to new action. Wŏnsan was not only another foothold on
Korean soil, it also was expected to become an important base for supporting the infant trade with Vladivostok. Because of these significant
developments, the trade superintendents (*kanrikan*) in the opened Korean
ports were upgraded to the status of consul on February 28, 1880. Ac-
cordingly, Kondō Masuki was appointed to the post of consul at Pusan
and Maeda Kenkichi to that of consul-general at Wŏnsan.[45]

On the Korean side, even before the convention was signed, the Council of State recommended upgrading the prefectural post at Tŏgwŏn by
appointing a civil official with the rank of *tangsang*. Kim Ki-su, who was
regarded as an expert in foreign affairs, was appointed the new prefect on
August 17, 1879. The king received him in a farewell audience a few days
later and stressed the point that Tŏgwŏn had become a "frontier area"
where matters would not be smooth and predictable. The rules designed
to guide the new prefect were safely patterned after those of Tongnae.
Since his post was so far from the capital, he was permitted to take his
family. His staff consisted of a language officer (*hundo*), a language student,
and several interpreters sent provisionally from Tongnae.[46]

In the fall of 1879, Hanabusa Yoshitada led an exploratory expedition
to Wŏnsan. He arrived on October 3 aboard the *Takaomaru* accompanied
by Kondō Masuki (then trade superintendent at Pusan), Maeda Kenkichi,
two secretaries, and a large military guard. Fourteen venturesome Japanese
merchants had joined Hanabusa's party. Among them was a representative
of the Pusan branch of the Daiichi Ginkō who had been ordered to investigate the conditions at the port and collect impressions about the region
and its inhabitants. Hanabusa had Kondō and Maeda discuss with Kim
Ki-su the responsibilities for the laying out of the Japanese settlement, the
improvement of the roads inside and outside the settlement, and the construction of jetties. The port was not scheduled to open until spring of the
following year, so Hanabusa and his retinue left Wŏnsan on October
11, 1879, without making major decisions.[47]

Wŏnsan lies on the southwestern shore of the Bay of Yŏnghŭng

(Broughton Bay) in the southern corner of the province of Hamgyŏng, approximately halfway between Pusan and Vladivostok. Sheltered from the sea by the peninsula of Kalma, it is considered one of the best harbors in the Far East. It has a suitable depth, adequate holding ground, an easy entrance, and it is ice-free. At the time of the port's opening, Wŏnsan was a sizable town of about two thousand straw-thatched houses. Its inhabitants engaged in farming, fishing, trading, and the manufacturing of liquors, straw sandals, and cloth. Administratively, it belonged to the prefecture of Tŏgwŏn. Communication with the capital, some 135 miles distant, was by a footpath.[48]

The ground for the Japanese settlement at Wŏnsan was broken in the spring of 1880. Maeda Kenkichi, the newly appointed consul general, sailed into the harbor on May 20 aboard the *Akitsushimamaru*. He had found a surprisingly large number of Japanese merchants waiting in the ports of Kobe and Osaka and later in Pusan to accompany him. Heavily loaded with the quantities of lumber and food necessary to start life at the newly opened port, his ship could accommodate only a few of the aspirants.[49] Maeda took up his office as consul general and concurrently as postmaster on the 23rd. He was assisted by student interpreters and protected by military personnel. Several days later he met with the prefect of Tŏgwŏn, Kim Ki-su, to discuss the construction of the settlement.[50]

The size of the settlement had to correspond to that of the Pusan settlement. Despite the opposition of some local Confucianists, construction of the consulate and a few houses began on eighty-five acres of marshy ground some two miles northwest of Wŏnsan. The area had been marked off in the previous fall. The Japanese, who at first lived in temporary quarters, built most of their houses in a Japanese adaptation of the European style with lumber brought from Japan. By the middle of September there were more than one hundred houses and a coal storage shed. The laying out of the streets was the responsibility of the Japanese settlers; the Korean government constructed the quay and the jetties. As agreed, the Japanese were permitted to move around at will within a radius of ten *i*. The town of Tŏgwŏn was open to them according to the example of Tongnae. To forestall incidents with the local population, the prefect strictly enforced rules that prohibited entry into the settlement by unauthorized persons.[51]

The launching of commercial activities as Wŏnsan presented some difficulties. The new settlers were discouraged by the large amount of capital needed to start business. As was the case in Pusan, the Japanese government came to their rescue by making the sum of 10,000 yen avail-

able for long-term credit.[52] Another obstacle was the problem of transportation. Concerned about the losses that the opening of a steamship
line to Wŏnsan would cause to Mitsubishi, Iwasaki Yatarō proposed that
the government provide a subsidy of at least 2,000 yen per round trip for
a period of five years. Later, the government agreed to advance a subsidy
of 10,000 yen a year for running a steamer once every other month. The
commercial representatives soon complained about this arrangement and
demanded a steamer every month.[53] From early 1881, a steamer ran between Japan and Wŏnsan once a month. At the request of Shibusawa Eiichi, the government further granted a loan of 10,000 yen to stimulate the
circulation of money in the newly opened port.[54]

The Japanese community grew rapidly. The small group of merchants
that had set ashore with Maeda was soon joined by others seeking to share
the profits of an untapped market. In the summer of 1880, their number
had already risen to between 200 and 250, including the soldiers and
policemen who were stationed in the port for the protection of their coun-
trymen. An American observer who visited the port in 1883 concluded
from the superior appearance of the houses and from the more active trading that the settlers at Wŏnsan were of a better class than those at Pusan.[55]

Among the principal merchants who settled at Wŏnsan were the
representatives of Mitsubishi, Sumitomo, Ikeda, and Daiichi Ginkō. The
agent of the latter was, as at Pusan, commissioned to transact the finances
of the consul general. Business dealings with the Koreans were begun with
great restraint. Maeda first wanted to test the attitude of the local inhabitants toward the new settlers. To his satisfaction, he observed little opposition. On the contrary, Korean merchants encouraged the Japanese to buy
their goods. Maeda ascribed this to the fact that Wŏnsan did not have a
past marred by friction between the two people. Wŏnsan had always been
busy as a local market town. The marketplace, which had the appearance
of a wide street, was lined on market days by booths in which were displayed goods brought in from near and far. Each booth sold a variety of articles: hemp cloth, pipes, tobacco bags, brushes, ink, needles, and foodstuffs.
Some fancy articles came from China. Cereals, fish, vegetables, pottery,
metalwares, and cattle were exhibited along the road. Grains and beans
were measured out in small cloth bags. Buyers, mostly men (women were
rarely seen in public), crowded the market on every market day, but they
purchased only very small quantities of goods.[56] The Japanese, wishing to
introduce imported goods, followed the Pusan pattern and opened an
exhibit of both Japanese and foreign merchandise to appraise the taste and

needs of the prospective Korean buyers. This was a great success as far as the number of visitors was concerned. Hundreds of Koreans crowded the exhibition field. Curiosity, however, was evidently stronger than the will to purchase the novelties. Prices were asked and the articles scrutinized, but apparently nobody came to buy.[57]

In its general development, Wŏnsan followed the pattern established earlier at Pusan. Both the Koreans and the Japanese had profited from their earlier experiences, however, and the opening of this northern port was without major incident. Wŏnsan's importance as a Japanese trading center in Korea was overshadowed by the much larger foothold at Pusan, but its opening was a significant event in Japan's diplomatic advance in the peninsula.

The Trend of Trade, 1876-1883

An analysis of the trend of the Korean-Japanese trade during the period of 1876 to 1883 in terms of the value of the trade has hitherto been difficult because of the many disparities in the available statistical information. The following discussion is based on a large and coherent set of recently published data.[58] Taking 1878 as the base year, the total value of the trade increased in absolute terms six-and-a-half fold from 1878 to 1883. The growth of trade was steady, with the exception of a slight decrease in 1882. Imports from Japan increased almost eightfold, with a particularly steep increase between 1880 and 1881, and peaked in 1883. In contrast, exports to Japan increased only fivefold. They showed a noteworthy increase in 1880 and declined afterward.[59] Seen from the point of view of Japan's total foreign trade, Korea's share grew from 0.5 percent in 1877 to 4.6 percent in 1883.[60] The center of these transactions was at Pusan. Only about one-eighth of the Korean-Japanese trade was handled at Wŏnsan.[61]

During the first three years of the period, Korea had a great demand for foodstuffs. More than one-fifth of her imports from Japan therefore consisted of grains. After 1878, grain imports fell off, and textiles became the preponderant import. In 1881, for example, textiles were 84.3 percent of the total import. Only a small quantity of these textiles was Japanese-made. The greater part consisted of British-made calicos, shirtings, and lustrings which were reexported from Japan. Japanese-made goods, which between 1879 and 1882 constituted a mere 10 percent of the total imports, were mainly dyes, tin, copper, lacquerware, silk, and small articles such as matches, colored pictures, and photographs. Surprisingly, Korean buyers showed a rapidly increasing interest in modern merchandise such as watches, clocks, music boxes, toys, carpets, and needles. These items reportedly bore Chinese markings to circumvent the Koreans' professed dislike of European-made goods. Throughout the late 1870s and the early 1880s, European goods accounted for a high proportion of Korea's imports. This caused concern within and without the Japanese government about the future of Japanese-made goods. In 1883 the disproportion was briefly reversed when Korea imported an unusually large amount of Japanese copper for minting.[62]

More than 90 percent of the Korean exports to Japan were natural products and raw materials, such as gold dust, gold ore, ginseng, ox hides, dried fish, seaweed, medicines, oils, and some textiles. After 1878, grain exports made up the largest percentage, reaching 75.4 percent in 1879 and 68.2 percent in 1880. The rate levelled off in the early 1880s. Rice constituted by far the largest amount of these grains. It was followed by smaller quantities of beans and wheat. The few manufactured goods, for example cotton cloth and fans, apparently were too crudely made to satisfy Japanese tastes.[63]

The picture of Korean-Japanese trade between 1877 and 1883 has a few rather puzzling aspects. While the trade balance in 1877 and 1878 was in favor of Japan, it turned to Korea's favor in 1879 and 1880, and then back again to Japan's favor from 1881 to 1883. Korea's brief show of strength was due to the large amounts of rice which were exported during that two-year period. Until 1881, Korea was Japan's largest foreign rice supplier. Compared to rice from other foreign sources, Korean rice was cheap for the Japanese. The rice trade was very lucrative; rice bought cheaply in Korea was sold at a profit in the Japanese markets. Therefore, when the rice exports in the first years of the 1880s declined, many Japanese traders at Pusan had to close their shops. This decrease in the grain business at Pusan paradoxically coincided with the turn of the trade balance back to Japan's favor. There seems to be only one explanation for this fact: the rice trade and the textile trade were not in the hands of the same Japanese merchants. The rice trade attracted to the ports individual Japanese traders who hoped to reap quick profits. The import of foreign textiles into Japan and their reexport to Korea was conducted by large merchant houses. These houses were not affected by the decline of the rice trade.[64] Rice, however, continued to be an important smuggling item. Consequently, its price fluctuated greatly and reportedly reached exorbitant heights, particularly in urban centers.[65] There is also evidence that Japanese traders reaped high profits by buying Korean gold dust, hides, and seaweed at Pusan and selling them at a profit in the Osaka market.[66] Finally, it should be noted that the imports of foreign-made textiles into Korea remained at a high level throughout the period. This was partly due to the fact that foreign textiles were cheaper than home-made cotton cloth, and the finer quality seems to have pleased the Korean consumers.[67]

In conclusion, then, Japan held the initiative during the early phase of Korean-Japanese trade. Japanese ships carried the import and export goods back and forth. Japanese money circulated in the ports and was advanced to the Koreans to get merchandise into the ports. Moreover, the Japanese did business without paying any import or export duties. Undoubtedly, the Japanese were the principal beneficiaries of this trade.

><><><><><><><><><><><><><><><><><><><><><><

With the consolidation of Japanese settlements at Pusan and Wŏnsan, Korea's future course was set on the presence of foreigners on Korean soil and on the expansion of foreign trade. The Koreans, however, resisted both of these developments, and the official reaction to Japanese activities in the ports was largely negative. Because there are few studies on Korea's economic history during the second half of the nineteenth century, the impact of Japanese trade on the Korean economy is difficult to assess. Burdened by financial difficulties, the Korean government continued to see trade with Japan as a threat to the people's livelihood, and it made several unsuccessful attempts to stop the outflow of rice. The large grain exports in 1879 and 1880 presumably were possible because of exceptionally good harvests in the southern provinces and not because of an incipient commercialization of the agrarian sector. Since the export trade was mainly in natural goods, it did not stimulate native production of manufactured goods. On the contrary, the finer quality of imported textiles may have had an adverse influence on native production. Korea's problem was that she did not have a single manufactured product that could have been easily developed into an export item. At this stage, the Korean government was as little interested in modernizing the Korean economy as it was in encouraging foreign trade.

The building up of the settlements in the opened ports accomplished Japan's first policy objective. Japanese government subsidies were instrumental for starting trade with Korea, but these investments were relatively small. If the Japanese government had been convinced that Korea's commercial potential could have been developed easily and profitably, and if it had needed new markets for its domestic production, it would have pushed the opening of additional ports more aggressively. On balance, then, political rather than economic factors seem to have determined Japan's policy in the Korean peninsula from 1876 to 1883.[68]

KOREA ON THE THRESHOLD OF A NEW AGE: REFORM AND REACTION

At the beginning of the 1880s Korea was still isolated from the West. She refused to accept the principles of international relations and consequently neglected to take adequate measures to strengthen her position vis-à-vis the outside world. Although she concluded treaties with Japan, she was hesitant to fulfill all her obligations. Her tributary ties with China were loose. Her weakness and backwardness began to be of serious concern to her neighbors. In the Far Eastern context, Korea represented a power vacuum that might attract forces outside Japan's and China's control. This apprehensiveness was not without justification. Countries unrelated to Korea by geography and tradition began to put out their feelers toward the peninsula. The United States of America's first letter of contact was delivered in Pusan during the first days of May 1880 by Commodore Robert W. Shufeldt. Russia loomed large in the northern part of the Far East. Her moves in southern Siberia were interpreted as ominous signs of her intentions against weak and undefended Korea. Fear of Russia led China and Japan to see the Korea problem within a wider context and compelled them to transmit advice to Korea. Thrust into the whirl of Far Eastern power politics, Korea could no longer maintain her seclusionist position. Following outside counsel, she launched a moderate course of self-strengthening and eventually concluded treaties with Western powers.

China Reconsiders the Korea Problem

In the Chinese view, Korea's security was guaranteed by the traditional formula of Korea's tributary relationship to the "superior country" (*shang-kuo*). Even after the Kanghwa Treaty of 1876, China upheld this concept, although it was seriously challenged by Japan's advances in the peninsula. Whenever necessary, the Tsungli Yamen repeated its ambiguous pronouncement that the whole world was aware of the fact that Korea was dependent on China and at the same time independent as far as her internal and external affairs were concerned.[1] Korea herself helped preserve the fragile facade of her dependent relationship by continuing, after 1876, to send to China tributary missions and detailed reports on her dealings and negotiations with Japan.

In the late 1870s, China had to reevaluate her stand on the Korea problem. Japan's ruthless annexation of the Ryūkyū Islands in 1879 showed the Chinese that no region within Japanese reach was inviolable. The possibility that Japan would seek a quick military solution to the opening of additional Korean ports could not be ruled out. Russia's presence in the Far East was of even more concern. Russian infringement upon China's territory in the Amur region, legalized by the Treaty of Peking in 1860, made a deep impression on China and changed her attitude toward Russia's eastward advance. The troubles in Chinese Turkestan in the 1870s brought China again into direct confrontation with Russian expansionism. Turkey's defeat by Russia and the subsequent settlement of the Turkish problem in the late 1870s added yet another dimension to China's fear of a concentrated Russian effort in the Far East.

Above all else, however, Japan's annexation of the Ryūkyū Islands shocked the Tsungli Yamen into reexamining its stand on Korea and made it receptive to new ideas.[2] A man whose opinions were highly respected in the Yamen was the British ambassador in Peking, Sir Thomas F. Wade. In the summer of 1879, Wade went to Prince Kung and expressed his fear that Korea was in immediate danger of being swallowed up by her neighbors. He emphatically repeated his view that countries like Korea could only be saved by opening themselves to all nations. Wade's viewpoint was eloquently argued on the Chinese side by the experienced Ting Jih-ch'ang. In a treatise on maritime defense, Ting wrote that Korea had been forced to conclude a treaty with Japan, and that China would be well-advised to encourage Korea to conclude treaties with the Western nations. Then, he reasoned, if Japan directed her aggressive intentions against Korea, all the countries bound to Korea by treaty would stand up in Korea's defense and expose Japan's sinister motives. Ting recommended that Korea be secretly advised to send observers abroad and yield whenever Western nations requested the conclusion of treaties. Ting's suggestion was received by the Tsungli Yamen with the comment that it was indeed a timely argument.[3]

The Tsungli Yamen did not hesitate to collect these suggestions and to act upon them immediately. At this point, the Yamen ministers happily remembered the contact that Li Hung-chang had maintained on and off with Yi Yu-wŏn since 1875. Emphasizing that they did not intend to interfere unduly with Korea's affairs, they recommended in a memorial dated August 21, 1879, that Li Hung-chang should again take advantage of this channel to transmit to Korea the ideas expounded by Ting Jih-ch'ang. Korea then would be able to weigh the seriousness of her situation. An edict of the same date endorsed the Yamen's recommendation and gave the initiative in the Korea question to Li Hung-chang.[4]

Li Hung-chang carefully reviewed the problem and considerably expanded Ting Jih-ch'ang's line of reasoning. To Li it seemed a proven fact that the Japanese were Korea's principal enemy and that they were pursuing the policy of "gaining one pace, advancing one pace." Japan's recent experiment with "enriching the nation and strengthening the army" (*fukoku kyōhei*) left her destitute and would force her into new adventures abroad as a means of freeing herself from her onerous debts. Therefore, a Ryūkyū-like attack on Korea was not out of the question, and Russia, on Korea's northern border, seemed to be waiting for a good opportunity to push southward into Korea.[5] This assessment of Korea's situation led Li Hung-chang to believe that only one strategy could lead Korea out of her isolation and give her security against stronger neighbors: the conclusion of treaties with the Western nations. Surely, this was the strategy of "attacking one poison with another poison or controlling one enemy with another enemy." Yet, Li thought, it had the advantage of putting a check on Japan as well as on Russia. The Western representatives in Peking had repeatedly told the Yamen of their intentions to form trade relationships with Korea. Li reasoned that since relations between the Western countries were guided by international law, and the countries' geographical distances from Korea made anything else but trade infeasible, England, Germany, France, and the United States were a comparatively small risk.

If Korea concluded treaties with these nations at a peaceful time, they certainly would not put forward unreasonable demands. For China, the settlement of the Korea problem was of purely practical interest: since Korea was the "screen of the Three Eastern Provinces," she should avoid any attack that would, in turn, endanger China's security.[6]

An expansion of the theme Li Hung-chang had developed with so much circumspection was Huang Tsun-hsien's *Chao-hsien ts'e-lüeh* (A policy for Korea).[7] The viceroy read it with approval and considered it a solid plan that one day could become the basis of Korea's self-strengthening. Huang's treatise was by far the most elaborate and eloquent Korea policy formulation. The main danger in the Far East, Huang maintained, was Russia's expansionist tendencies directed against the strategic peninsula of Korea. Japan, Huang felt, was economically too weak to be a serious challenge to Korea's security. Based on his analysis of the Far Eastern situation, Huang's recommendations for Korea were summed up in the simple formula: *ch'in Chung-kuo, chieh Jih-pen, lien Mei-kuo,* intimate relations with China, association with Japan, and alliance with America. Huang reminded Korea of China's very special attitude toward Korea. Not only did China show great affection for her dependent country, but her geographical position predestined her to keep a check on Russia. Once Russia was convinced of the fact that China and Korea really formed one and the same family, Russia would respect Korea's integrity, and Japan would join them in peace. Japan and Korea, because of their close geographical and historical ties, were interdependent in the face of the common threat. Korea, therefore, should free herself of her "small dislikes" and conceive a grand policy. She should renew her ancient relations of amity, and she should find allies abroad. America, Huang continued, was a country which could be trusted. It not only entertained relations with both China and Japan, but it also had been helpful in Japan's commercial and military development. Respected by all other nations, the United States was interested in preserving peace in the Pacific area, and for that purpose it wanted to conclude a treaty with Korea and send an envoy there. The European countries would surely follow America's example. Treaties with these nations, furthermore, would establish a balance of power in the Far East which would ensure the preservation of Korea's integrity. No country on the globe, Huang warned, could permanently seclude itself and refuse contact with foreigners. Now the opportunity had come for Korea to enter into relationships with the outside world and, by launching a self-strengthening program, establish herself as a useful ally.[8]

To Li Hung-chang it was clear that China should assume the task, in a guarded way, of providing Korea with the necessary knowledge for opening the country and concluding treaties. This duty was, in Li's eyes, most important because Korea was still totally ignorant of the management of foreign affairs.[9]

A channel of communication between China and Korea had been opened in 1875 when Li Hung-chang wrote a note to Yi Yu-wŏn in which he expressed for the first time his views on the necessity of opening foreign relations. Afterward, Li and Yi had not lost contact with each other and had exchanged occasional letters. It was only natural that the Tsungli Yamen remembered this connection in the fall of 1879 when the result of the latest thinking on the opening of the country to foreign powers was to be communicated to Korea. Li Hung-chang, too, considered his contact with Yi Yu-wŏn convenient since Yi continued to exercise considerable influence in official circles. Yi, Li thought, also showed an open mind toward contemporary affairs.[10] In the latter part of August 1879, Li Hung-chang resumed his correspondence with Yi Yu-wŏn, in compliance with the imperial edict, by dispatching a secret letter to Korea. In this document, Li gave Yi his detailed analysis of the Far Eastern situation and added his recommendation that Korea should enter into treaty relations with Western nations. Korea, he continued, should also start secret military preparations. Diplomatically she should strictly adhere to the existing agreements in order not to give Japan even the slightest motive for action.[11]

Korea's Response to Outside Exhortations

Li Hung-chang's secret letter arrived in Seoul at an unfortunate time. The Korean government was resigned to Wŏnsan's opening, but was outraged at Hanabusa's continued insistence on selecting Inch'ŏn on the west coast. The responsibility for the government crisis was put squarely on Yi Yu-wŏn, and he was forced into retirement in the countryside. While "staying among his native mountains," he received Li Hung-chang's letter. Yi was discouraged with the government and well aware that the time was not right for transmitting outside counsel to Seoul. In his reply to Li Hung-chang, therefore, he avoided direct comment on Li's suggestions, but he sent a secret note to Li in which he explained himself more clearly. Li's tactic of holding off one barbarian with another barbarian, Yi thought, might not be applicable to a country like Korea that was not only weak but had no relations with Western countries. Self-strengthening, furthermore, might bring Korea into the same financial troubles as Japan. Since Korea had nothing to offer, foreign trade might turn out to be as unprofitable to foreign merchants as to the Koreans themselves. Yi Yu-wŏn had clearly reversed his earlier, more realistic views, and he may have represented general resistance within the government against any further involvement with the outside world beyond Japan. In a second official letter written two months later, Yi expressed his distaste for "Western learning" and repeated his argument that Korea, being poor and weak, would not be able to allow many merchant ships to enter Korean ports. Despite his generally negative reaction to Li's secret letter, Yi passed it on to the king.[12]

While the government's energies were absorbed in preserving the country's "morality and righteousness" in the face of Japan's diplomatic initiative, there were unmistakable signs that some of the leading men, among them King Kojong, were very much aware of developments throughout the Far East. Listening to reports his envoys brought back from Peking, the king was well informed about the West's activities in China. Moreover, the discovery and imprisonment of a French Catholic missionary in Ch'ungch'ŏng and the subsequent correspondence between Seoul and Peking about his release were clear indications that the Westerners would one day seek official relations with Korea. Furthermore, the king noted with concern that the Ryūkyū Islands gradually had shifted out of China's orbit and were annexed by Japan. Although he highly respected Li Hung-chang, the king was baffled at Li's inability to uphold China's suzerain rights. Despite his keen awareness of Korea's weak and isolated position, the king found it inopportune to disclose Li Hung-chang's secret advice. A year later, in the fall of 1880, after the diplomatic storm caused by the opening of Wŏnsan had blown over, the king staged a full debate on Korea's foreign policy. The impulse for this debate was given by Huang Tsun-hsien's *Chao-hsien ts'e-lüeh*.[13]

On October 2, 1880, Kim Hong-jip reported back from his mission to Japan and presented Huang Tsun-hsien's booklet to King Kojong. The king immediately grasped the urgency of Huang's argumentation and called the chief state councillor, Yi Ch'oe-ŭng, for a private exchange of opinions. Yi's reaction to Huang's treatise was enthusiastic. He conceded that he became fully aware of the danger from Russia only after reading Huang's booklet. He had always doubted the credibility of similar warnings given by Japan. Yi was alarmed at the prospect of Russia's expansion into

Korea and had no confidence in Korea's military preparations. He climaxed his argument with a demand for the establishment of a self-strengthening program. His analysis of Huang's propositions led him a step further. Yi regretted his harsh rejection of the American letter in the summer of that year and recommended that if the Americans should again present a letter, the prefect of Tongnae or the Department of Rites should accept it. No undue fear of "heterodox teachings" (i.e., Christianity), Yi insisted, should jeopardize future contact with the West. He came to the second major point of his argument and demanded the conclusion of treaties with the Western powers. The king was impressed by Yi's forceful exposition and requested the opinions of the other high ministers.[14]

On October 11, the incumbent and former state councillors (including the president of the Board of Officials-without-Portfolio, Yi Yu-wŏn; the president of the Office of Royal Kinsmen, Hong Sun-mok; the vice-president of the Board of Officials-without-Portfolio, Han Kye-wŏn; the chief state councillor, Yi Ch'oe-ŭng; and the left state councillor, Kim Pyŏng-guk) submitted their judgment on Huang Tsun-hsien's treatise. They all acknowledged that Huang's contribution was by far the most detailed exposition of Korea's international situation and a cogent warning of the potential danger from Russia. Then they scrutinized Huang's formula of "intimate relations with China, association with Japan, and alliance with America." The first part they dismissed as irrelevant. Korea had been cherishing close and friendly bonds with China for the last two hundred years. As for an association with Japan, this they found problematic. They maintained that Korea certainly strained her good will to the utmost in granting most of the demands the Japanese put forward, but they did not want a Japanese envoy in Seoul. Since they thought an envoy's presence was contingent on the opening of Inch'ŏn, they could allow neither one. The third point, the alliance with America, they regarded with more favor. America and all the other nations of the world were making common cause against Russia. How much more advisable it would be for Korea, isolated in a strategic position so close to Russia, to enter into an alliance with America. The difference of culture and the great geographical distance might exclude America as an ally. Yet, should the Americans come again, the ministers agreed, they should be well received.[15]

The debates of October 1880 signaled a turning-point as important as that reached in January 1876. Again, the principal advocates of a revised policy toward the outside world were King Kojong and Yi Ch'oe-ŭng. There was, however, a difference. Cooperation from the higher officialdom was much more spontaneous than in 1876. The realization of the dangers Korea was facing was fairly widespread. One danger was Russia's expansion into eastern Asia, the other was the continued pressure of Japan's demands. Everybody agreed that Japan's concern for Korea's security against Russia was nothing but veiled self-interest. The impact of Japan's advice, therefore, was dulled, and association with Japan seemed a questionable policy. The officials realized that even China was not prepared to hold off an attack from Russia, and thus they came to view their own country's military weakness with greater alarm. Because of this sense of insecurity, they acknowledged that the conclusion of relations with the West was the only feasible policy alternative.[16]

This consensus in the fall of 1880 gave King Kojong the necessary momentum to break his country's international isolation and start Korea on a moderate course of modernization. Kojong's commitment to such a policy, in fact, antedated his ministers' turn of mind by at least a year. But the king, although more progressive than his advisers, had not been able to act without official support. He had had to wait for this moment to initiate the policy that was to usher Korea into the modern world.

The Launching of Korea's Self-Strengthening Program: The Establishment of the T'ongnigimu Amun

In the Korean view, self-strengthening was only loosely coupled with the issue of concluding treaties with Western nations. It was principally conceived as an instrument to defend the country against Japan and Russia, and therefore it won approval even from those who opposed a further involvement with the outside world. Nobody in the government was still unrealistic enough to believe that Korea could keep her adversaries at bay by the sheer force of her moral superiority. The security of the state depended henceforth on technological and military innovations. These innovations required a fundamental government reorganization. This was the origin of the T'ongnigimu Amun.

Long before self-strengthening became a general topic of debate, King Kojong realized that if Korea wanted to master the secrets of the modern world the first step had to be the training of appropriate personnel. In the fall of 1879, he sent a secret request to China asking for support in this first step. China's positive reaction to his request gave King

Kojong a basis for extensive action. On January 4, 1881, the king announced to his ministers that China approved his idea of sending trainees. He proposed that a special office be established for handling not only the dispatch of the trainees, but also Korea's relations with China and Japan, her military matters, and her border affairs. He ordered all the incumbent and former state councillors and the senior executive officers to deliberate upon this proposition and prepare and present organizational rules. On January 19, 1881, in compliance with an edict of January 16 which repeated this order, the senior ministers formally presented the rules governing the formation and function of the new government body. The establishment of this new office was the most important institutional innovation of the late Yi dynasty. The members of this office presided over the execution of Korea's self-strengthening program and the conclusion of her treaties with Western nations. In addition, it became a means to power for some of the Yŏhŭng Min and their partisans.[17]

The new office was given the name of T'ongnigimu Amun, Office for the Management of State Affairs. The inspiration for this name was undoubtedly the Chinese Tsungli Yamen. In contrast to the Chinese office, the T'ongnigimu Amun had a much wider scope of functions and responsibilities. It not only took over the Military Council (Samgunbu),[18] which it replaced, but also usurped some of the tasks hitherto fulfilled by other government agencies. This is evident from its organizational structure. The work was done by twelve departments: (1) Department of Relations with China (Sadaesa) which handled the correspondence with China, received her envoys, and dispatched military and frontier officials; (2) Department of Neighborly Relations (Kyorinsa) which took care of the correspondence between Korea and her neighbors other than China, and welcomed and escorted their envoys; (3) Department of Military Matters (Kunmusa); (4) Department of Border Administration (Pyŏnjŏngsa) which managed all border affairs and collected intelligence about movements in neighboring countries; (5) Department of Foreign Trade (T'ongsangsa); (6) Department of Military Ordnance (Kunmulsa) which, among other things, controlled the production of arms; (7) Department of Machinery (Kigyesa) which supervised the production of all kinds of machinery; (8) Department of Ships (Sŏnhamsa) which took care of the production and the management of all ships; (9) Department of Coastal Surveillance (Kiyŏnsa); (10) Department of Language Study (Ŏhaksa) which organized the translating and learning of foreign languages; (11) Department of Recruitment (Chŏnsŏnsa) which selected talented people for duty in the various departments of the new office; (12) Department of Supply (Iyongsa) which supplied the departments with whatever material each one needed.

Because the new office was in charge of all military affairs and was also entrusted with diplomatic and political matters, its importance was underlined by the decision to staff it with officials of the first rank. Thus it was accorded the same status as the Council of State (Ŭijŏngbu). Its personnel consisted of a president (*ch'ongni taesin*), who was appointed from among the state councillors; a number of directors (*kyŏngni tangsang*), who had to be officials with the rank of senior 3a grade and above (*tang-sang*); and a number of secretaries (*nangch'ŏng*), who were appointed from among civil or military examination passers or protection appointees (*ŭm*). In mid-January the number of directors was fixed at ten (soon afterward increased to twelve), and the number of secretaries at eighteen. All incumbent and former state councillors belonged concurrently to the new body as commissioners (*tojejo*). A number of clerks completed the roster of the new office's personnel. The T'ongnigimu Amun was housed in the office of the abolished Military Council, and the Department of Rites was ordered to cast a new seal for it.[19]

After the directors (*kyŏngni tangsang*) were selected on January 21, they were assigned to the various departments on February 14 as follows: Yi Ch'oe-ŭng, the chief state councillor, was made president (*ch'ongni tae-sin*); Cho Yŏng-ha (first aide-de-camp of the palace guards, *sanghogun*) and Chŏng Pŏm-jo (second aide-de-camp of the palace guards, *taehogun*) jointly headed the Department of Relations with China and the Department of Neighborly Relations; Min Kyŏm-ho (assistant president of the Board of Officials-without-Portfolio) and Yun Cha-dŏk (first aide-de-camp of the palace guards) jointly headed the Department of Military Matters, the Department of Border Administration, and the Department of Coastal Surveillance; Kim Po-hyŏn (governor of Kyŏnggi) and Kim Hong-jip (vice-minister of the Department of Rites) jointly managed the Department of Foreign Trade; Kim Pyŏng-dŏk (first aide-de-camp of the palace guards) and Min Yŏng-ik (third aide-de-camp of the palace guards) jointly controlled the Department of Supply; Sim Sun-t'aek (vice-president of the Council of the Royal Kinsmen) and Sin Chŏng-hŭi (second aide-de-camp of the palace guards) jointly headed the Department of Machinery, the Department of Military Ordnance, and the Department of Ships; Min Ch'i-sang (minister of the Department of Punishment) and Yi Chae-gŭng (associate vice-president of the Council of the Royal Kinsmen) jointly supervised the Department of Recruitment and the Department of

Language Study.[20]

The T'ongnigimu Amun was in charge of matters paramount to national security. To facilitate its work as a supervisory and coordinating body, the government agencies and military installations within the capital and in the provinces were directed to report all matters pertaining to any one of the twelve departments directly to the Amun. All the directors were to attend the royal audiences together. If an urgent matter demanded attention, the directors of the department concerned were authorized to request an extraordinary audience. Interpreters for Chinese and Japanese were attached to the new office to take care of the translation work.[21] The personnel and the division of work among the various departments underwent many significant changes until the abolition of the office in the summer of 1882. On February 26, 1881, the presidency was split between two men, the chief state councillor and the left state councillor. Besides Yi Ch'oe-ŭng, Left State Councillor Kim Pyŏng-guk was appointed to the new post. Both carried the new title of *ch'ongni t'ongnigimu amunsa*. A few days later, on March 4, the heads of the various departments were renamed *kyŏngni t'ongnigimu amunsa*. Their number did not change, and, with only one exception, the personnel remained the same. A major reorganization took place on January 10, 1882. The work of the various departments was reshuffled and their number reduced to seven: (1) Department of Diplomatic Affairs (Tongmunsa); (2) Department of Military Matters (Kunmusa); (3) Department of Foreign Trade (T'ongsangsa); (4) Department of Supply (Iyongsa); (5) Department of Recruitment (Chŏnsŏnsa); (6) Department of Statutes and Laws (Yullyesa); (7) Department of Works (Kamgongsa). The number of *kyŏngni tangsang* was increased from twelve to nineteen, and a few fresh faces were called in to fill the new posts.[22]

The T'ongnigimu Amun had many characteristics of the former Board of Defense (Pibyŏnsa), which was established in 1517 to devise policies for the pacification of the rising Manchu tribes and the Japanese pirates.[23] Like the Pibyŏnsa, it was superimposed on the conventional government structure at a time when extraordinary policies had to be developed to meet the challenge from the outside world. Having the character of an emergency body, at least in the beginning, the Amun enjoyed unusual authority and thus absorbed many of the main functions of traditional government. It was designed as the supreme organ for planning and executing the self-strengthening program and, at the same time, for guiding and coordinating Korea's foreign policy. Although the institutional plan was strikingly new, the concept of foreign affairs did not deviate from the traditional categories of "subservient relations" with China (*sadae*) and "neighborly relations" with Japan (*kyorin*). The incongruities created by the demands of a new, outward-looking policy and the dictates of a centuries-old value system significantly influenced the workings of the new office. This was also reflected in its personnel policy.

The T'ongnigimu Amun became the stepping stone to power for some members of the Yŏhŭng Min clan. The Min's power was not consolidated in the first half of the 1870s, but a survey of Min careers between 1876 and 1882 shows that the clan's strength grew as its members advanced into the higher echelons of the government. After the deaths of Min Sŭng-ho in 1875 and Min Kyu-ho in 1878, the clan's fortunes were principally linked to the careers of Min T'ae-ho (1834–1884) and Min Kyŏm-ho (1839–1882). Min T'ae-ho, Kyu-ho's elder brother, was governor of Hwanghae and Kyŏnggi during the mid-1870s. He climbed to the post of minister (*p'ansŏ*) in various departments during the last two years of the decade, and he was appointed right assistant state councillor (*uch'amch'an*, senior second grade) on October 11, 1880. Min T'ae-ho's position as a key figure in the clan was further strengthened by several family ties with the royal house. On January 18, 1875, his son, Min Yŏng-ik (1860–1914), was adopted as heir to Min Sŭng-ho, King Kojong's natural uncle, who himself had been adopted to continue the line of Min Ch'i-rok, Queen Min's father. Min Sŭng-ho was posthumously honored with an appointment as chief state councillor on May 14, 1879. Min T'ae-ho's daughter was designated as the bride of the heir apparent on March 15, 1882. Equally rapid was the rise of Min Kyŏm-ho, who was Min Sŭng-ho's younger brother and heir of Min Ch'i-gu's line. From 1877 he held the post of minister (*p'ansŏ*) in various departments and once was commissioner of Seoul. Min Ch'i-sang (1826–1881) belonged to the same generation as Min T'ae-ho's and Min Kyŏm-ho's fathers and had risen to high office (minister of war, revenue, rites, etc.) under the Taewŏn'gun. Whereas Min Kyŏm-ho, Min T'ae-ho, and Min Ch'i-sang were in high office when they were concurrently appointed to posts in the T'ongnigimu Amun, Min Yŏng-ik was young, had passed the higher civil service examination only in 1877, and had no particular distinction when he became a member of the new office. He owed his brief career prior to 1881 to family connections. His appointment to the T'ongnigimu Amun was indeed his first step to power.[24]

The Min's power should not be overemphasized, however, even at this stage. The pace of their advancement within and without the government evidently quickened in the late 1870s,[25] but it is difficult to determine the extent of their influence. Min T'ae-ho was the only Min in the Council of State at the turn of the decade. He became left vice-councillor (*chwach'ansŏng*), which carried a junior first rank, on March 1, 1882. The Min's relationship to King Kojong was close in terms of family, but what this meant in concrete political terms is not clear. The king acted independently and not under the Min's pressure. King Kojong, and not the Min, launched the self-strengthening movement. That the T'ongnigimu Amun eventually turned into the Min's power base is an irony of history.

Throughout the second half of the 1870s, with a brief interruption, Yi Ch'oe-ŭng occupied the office of chief state councillor. From 1878 he was assisted by Kim Pyŏng-guk as left state councillor. This amazing continuity of tenure stands in sharp contrast to the mad frequency with which the higher civil and military posts changed hands: sometimes the term of office was only a few days. Yi Ch'oe-ŭng's allegiance to the Min is usually explained by his supposed enmity toward his younger brother, the Taewŏn-gun, but it is difficult to see him as the executor of "Min policy." Yi did not follow a predetermined course of action. This is illustrated by his enthusiastic acceptance of Huang Tsun-hsien's arguments, which stands in stark contrast to his negative attitude toward the American overture of the previous summer. His change of mind was an individual act and not the reflection of long-term policy. Yi Ch'oe-ŭng's partner was Kim Pyŏng-guk, a Taewŏn'gun holdover. The relationship between the Andong Kim and the Yŏhŭng Min reportedly was not close. Both Yi Ch'oe-ŭng and Kim Pyŏng-guk were appointed to the T'ongnigimu Amun ex officio.

An examination of the backgrounds of the other new appointees leads to the same conclusion: the Min's hold on the new office was not yet complete. Cho Yŏng-ha (1845–1884), nephew of Queen Dowager Cho, joined the Taewŏn'gun's opponents in 1873. Under King Kojong he rose to minister of rites in 1877 and held several high posts afterward. Another member of the Andong Kim clan was Kim Pyŏng-dŏk (1825–1892) who started his career as minister (*p'ansŏ*) of various departments under King Kojong. Kim Po-hyŏn (1826–1882) was not an Andong Kim. Having been purged under the Taewŏn'gun, he climbed to high office in the latter part of the 1870s. Kim Hong-jip (1842–1896), a Kyŏngju Kim, stepped into higher office only in the early 1880s. Yun Cha-dŏk (1827–1890) had a minor career under the Taewŏn'gun and became minister of appointment in 1879. Sim Sun-t'aek (b. 1824) also held minor posts in the 1860s and rose to prominence in the latter part of the 1870s. Sin Chŏng-hŭi (1833–1895), Sin Hŏn's son, had a distinguished military career in the late 1870s before he entered the T'ongnigimu Amun as a military expert. Chŏng Pŏm-jo (1833–1898) was appointed minister of works in 1879. Yi Chae-myŏn (1845–1912) was the Taewŏn'gun's eldest son. He held several minor posts before becoming minister of punishment in 1878.[26] On the basis of the available documents, then, most of these appointees advanced to high office under King Kojong. Cho Yŏng-ha, Kim Po-hyŏn, and Yi Chae-myŏn may have had personal reasons for joining the Min camp, but the others did not emerge as a core group unconditionally loyal to the Min. Rather, there was in all of these appointments a remarkable degree of continuity. There was no radical change in personnel or career patterns.

The second group of men appointed to the T'ongnigimu Amun on January 10, 1882, differed from the first in a few respects. Four of the appointees, Yi Wŏn-hoe, Pak Chŏng-yang (1841–1904), Cho Chun-yŏng (1833–1886), and Ŏm Se-yŏng (1831–1899), had been to Japan as members of an inspection tour (*sinsa yuramdan*) and undoubtedly had close contact with King Kojong. The others were individuals whose backgrounds were not very distinctive. Yi Chae-wŏn (1831–1891) was a nephew of the Taewŏn'gun and held high posts under his uncle. Nothing is known about Cho Hŭi-sun prior to 1881, except that he served as military commissioner to Hamgyŏng. Yi Kŭn-p'il (1816–1882) had been to China and served as governor of several provinces. Common to all of them, except Yi Kŭn-p'il, was relative youth and, except for Yi Chae-wŏn and Yi Kŭn-p'il, inexperience in high office. It is equally difficult to put a general label on this group of officials. Although it may be assumed that some of them owed their appointments to the T'ongnigimu Amun to their connections with the Min, there is no documentary evidence for this.[27]

The impact of the T'ongnigimu Amun as the coordinator of Korea's fledgling self-strengthening movement can not be easily assessed. Its life span was relatively short, only eighteen months. Until its abolition in the wake of the 1882 incident, much time was spent in organizing and reorganizing its elaborate structure. In March 1881 it was put in charge of supervising and arranging the sending of students to China. One of the new office's most important contributions seems to have been the reorganization of the outdated and inefficient military system. Also, members of the T'ongnigimu Amun signed Korea's first treaties with Western powers. The establishment of the T'ongnigimu Amun was Korea's first serious attempt to prepare herself to face the modern world from a strengthened position, but it proved difficult to put substance into this effort.

The Dispatch of Korean Students and Artisans to China

The beginning of Korea's self-strengthening movement can be traced to King Kojong's own initiative. He asked for and received Chinese and Japanese advice about sending students abroad for training in military and industrial skills.[28] In the fall of 1879, Kojong secretly sent Yi Yong-suk to the prefect of Yung-p'ing, Yü Chih-k'ai, to inquire into China's attitude toward accepting Korean students and artisans for training in China. Yi also delivered a secret letter from Yi Yu-wŏn to Li Hung-chang which contained a similar cautious inquiry. Li Hung-chang supported these requests without reservation. Thus assured of Chinese backing, the king ordered a full-scale discussion of the subject among the highest government officials. He received their report on June 7, 1880. The king's initiative did not meet with enthusiasm. It was some months before the debate on Huang Tsun-hsien's treatise changed the government's outlook on the world. The president of the Board of Officials-without-Portfolio, Yi Yu-wŏn, supported the scheme, but thought it wise to select the candidates and secure the finances before the official request to China was submitted. Yi Ch'oe-ŭng and Kim Pyŏng-guk, supported by other high officials, pleaded for extreme caution in the matter and insisted that every step should be minutely planned. The king was not deterred. A month later he issued an edict which ordered all government agencies within and without the capital to recommend suitable candidates on the basis of certain qualifications.[29]

The king's reason for sending students and artisans to China was clearly stated in his first official communication on the subject which was dispatched to China on August 14, 1880. Korea's weaponry, he wrote, was old and useless. Frequently warned of Korea's strong neighbors, he was concerned about the country's military unpreparedness. Therefore he was asking for China's assistance in either accepting Korean artisans as students in the Tientsin arsenal or sending Chinese instructors to Korea. This message was sent to Peking by the special courier, Pyŏn Wŏn-gyu.[30]

When the royal letter was delivered in Peking on September 29, 1880, Li Hung-chang was ordered by edict to study the matter immediately. Li endorsed the project. A strengthened Korea, he thought, would mean more security for China herself. However, he cautioned the Chinese government that assistance at this moment would permanently engage

China in Korea's modernization. Li discussed the whole complex of problems with Pyŏn Wŏn-gyu when the latter arrived in Tientsin on October 19. The only practical way to carry out the Korean plan, Li told Pyŏn, was to train the Koreans in China. Chinese instructors in Korea would not have the necessary equipment and therefore would be ineffective. In preparation for the student mission, four rules were devised by Li and Pyŏn in cooperation with the Tientsin Customs Taotai Cheng Tsao-ju, Yü Chih-k'ai, and the two managers of the Tientsin Arsenal, Hsü Chi-kuang and Liu Han-fang. The number of participants, including artisans, soldiers, interpreters, and attendants, was limited to eighty-seven. The Koreans themselves had to provide the money, the tools, the fuel, and the food for the group; China would provide living quarters. The Koreans, who would receive Chinese identification passes, would be permitted to travel to China by the sea route. In addition, all communications concerning the Korean artisans would be sent to the Board of Rites and directly to Li Hung-chang.[31]

Pyŏn returned to Seoul in January 1881, and preparations got under way. On March 3, the T'ongnigimu Amun was put in charge of all arrangements. The plan for sending soldiers for training to China was dropped. Full attention was given to the selection of apprentices and students, who would be accompanied by an adviser (*yŏngsŏnsa*), two high officials of the Bureau for the Study of Military Arts (Hullyŏnwŏn), an interpreter, a medical doctor, and a number of additional personnel. The dispatch of the group, however, was delayed by the death of the *yŏngsŏnsa*-designate. The prefect of Sunch'ŏn, Kim Yun-sik, was then appointed *yŏngsŏnsa*. He took leave of the king on November 17, 1881.[32]

Kim Yun-sik arrived in Tientsin during the second half of January 1882 with his group of 69 students, artisans, officials, and attendants.[33] The Koreans were assigned to the east and south machine factories of the arsenal compound. The experiment, however, seems to have been ill-fated from the beginning. The North Chinese winter climate did not suit the Korean students. They became ill and were soon unable to pursue their studies and training. There were also language difficulties. Two of the students left for home as early as February. Another serious problem was the project's financing. After the little money which the Koreans had earned from selling ginseng was used up, their financial situation became very precarious, and they had to borrow money. They seem to have obtained a sum of 16,000 tael from the China Merchants' Steam Navigation Company. When news about the 1882 incident reached Tientsin, the few remaining Koreans became worried about their families and expressed the desire to return home. In the middle of November, the king asked that the Korean students and artisans be permitted to return to Korea. With the repatriation of the last trainees, the project to seek industrial skills outside the country came to a premature end.[34]

The training of students was short-lived. The usefulness of the experiment was diminished not only by its shortness but by the fact that, upon their return, the students could not be usefully employed. No preparations for the establishment of an arsenal had been made. The political turmoil of the summer of 1882 delayed efforts to provide the returned students and artisans with a proper working basis. In sum, the sending of students for training abroad was well-intended, but premature; it added very little to Korea's early self-strengthening.

The Dispatch of a Secret Inspection Mission to Japan

Simultaneously with the preparations for sending trainees to China, King Kojong considered a plan for dispatching a secret inspection mission to Japan. The Japanese had made frequent efforts to convince the Korean government to accept Japanese help in planning and executing Korea's self-strengthening program. Always suspicious of the Japanese, King Kojong had not wanted their assistance. At last he was won over to the plan of a mission by the arguments of a mysterious man named Yi Tong-in. The arguments presumably were transmitted to Kojong by Kim Hong-jip. Yi developed a grand scheme for "opening the country and changing the spirit of the time," and insisted that it was necessary for the Koreans to get a firsthand view of Japan's industrial and military superiority.[35]

The preparations for the inspection mission, which came to be known as "the gentlemen's sightseeing group" (*sinsa yuramdan*), were shrouded in so much secrecy that only a very few facts about it are known. Without direct prior consultations with the Japanese government, the order for the mission was handed down on February 9, 1881. It specified that the purpose of the mission should be a detailed and careful investigation of the opinions prevailing in the Japanese government, of the general situation of the country, of the customs, and of Japanese foreign trade. Twelve mission members were appointed: Cho Chun-yŏng, Pak Chŏng-yang, Ŏm Se-yŏng, Kang Mun-hyŏng, Cho Pyŏng-jik, Min Chong-muk, Yi Hŏn-yŏng,

Sim Sang-hak, Hong Yŏng-sik, Ŏ Yun-jung, Yi Wŏn-hoe, and Kim Yong-wŏn. Each member was accompanied by at least two assistants, one interpreter, and one servant. The total number of mission members was sixty-two. The average age of the members was about forty, and all except one held the rank of third grade. Each was assigned one particular government organ or institution for special investigation.[36]

The inspection mission left Seoul at the end of February 1881 in the guise of secret inspectors. The newly appointed prefect of Tongnae, Kim Sŏn-gŭn, evidently gave the Japanese consul at Pusan, Kondō Masuki, advance knowledge of the mission. When the mission arrived at the port, a Japanese ship took it aboard. It arrived in Nagasaki on May 8. The itinerary in Japan included Kobe, Osaka, Yokohama, and Tokyo. The Koreans were welcomed by two old Korea-hands, Miyamoto Koichi and Moriyama Shigeru. While in the Japanese capital they had frequent contact with Inoue Kaoru, who introduced them to Sanjō Sanetomi, Terashima Munenori, and other high ministers. Inoue paved the way for extensive sightseeing and for the inspection of shipyards, schools, industries, mines, arsenals, mints, hospitals, and prisons. After spending almost four months in Japan, the inspection mission returned to Pusan on August 26, 1881.[37]

The mission members collected and reported their experiences and impressions from their journey in Japan in individual books entitled *Sich'algi* (Dairy of an inspection tour) or *Mun'gyŏn sakŏn* (Facts heard and seen).[38] The mission members were received in royal audience in three groups on October 22, 23, and 24 to report directly to the king. The Koreans drew conclusions that turned out to be more against than in favor of Japan. Despite the acknowledged hospitality with which they were received in Japan, they found the Japanese nature fickle and untrustworthy. The general effort for *fukyō* did not fail to impress the Koreans, but Japan's military and industrial achievements seemed to them less than what they had expected. They weighed the dangers of a forced modernization program that would cause staggering debts and eventual financial ruin. The most important result of the inspection tour was the insight that only a strong Korea would be safe from Japanese ambitions, a perception which may have benefited the self-strengthening movement in a way the Japanese had not anticipated. The king made practical use of the accumulated knowledge by appointing four of the mission members to the T'ongnigimu Amun when it was reorganized on January 10, 1882. Others became active in the military reorganization effort.[39]

Military Reforms

The decrepit state of the Korean military was no secret. Military reform had to be an integral part of self-strengthening. It had two aims: institutional reorganization and the training of new army units. Pyŏn Wŏn-gyu received Chinese ideas for Korea's military reorganization from Li Hung-chang when he was at Tientsin in the fall of 1880. Li thought that the 30,000 troops stationed around the Korean capital should be reorganized into infantry, artillery, and cavalry and equipped with modern arms. He urged that the best way to train a modern elite troop would be to send several thousand bright and healthy soldiers to Tientsin for training. After returning to Korea, they would train the remaining troops.[40] The Koreans did not adopt this Chinese plan. Undoubtedly because of Hanabusa's repeated insistence, they accepted Japanese help instead. In May 1881, a Japanese army instructor, Horimoto Reizō, was engaged to train a newly formed military unit (*pyŏlgigun*). Horimoto Reizō's elite unit became the most prestigious military outfit in the country. It was better equipped and better paid than the traditional units. This preferential treatment soon became the source of serious discontent within the military.

Institutionally, the abolition of the Military Council (Samgunbu) and the incorporation of military affairs into the newly established T'ongnigimu Amun were the first attempts at streamlining the military administration. In March 1881, Yi Wŏn-hoe was appointed planner (*ch'amhoekkwan*) and Yi Tong-in adviser (*ch'ammogwan*). They departed for Japan to observe that country's military establishment.[41] Their reports and those later submitted by members of the secret inspection mission to Japan did not fail to have an impact. In the middle of January 1882, a royal edict ordered the head of the Department of Military Matters, Min Yŏng-ik, to work out a sweeping program of military reorganization. Consequently, the department was subdivided into three sections: the Office of General Affairs (Ch'ongmuguk) headed by Min Yŏng-ik and Hong Yŏng-sik; the Office of Planning (Ch'ammoguk) headed by Sin Chŏng-hŭi and Cho Hŭi-sun; and the Office of Training (Kyoryŏn'guk) headed by Yi Chae-wŏn and Yi Wŏn-hoe. The Five Armies were subsequently abolished and two larger units, the *muwiyŏng* and the *changŏyŏng*, were established. Yi Kyŏng-ha[42] was appointed commander (*taejang*) of the former, Sin Chŏng-hŭi commander of the latter.[43]

The planning and execution of the Korean military reorganization was thus heavily influenced by the Japanese. Emphasis was put on trimming down the inefficient and cumbersome traditional military organization and on centralizing the command structure. The new elite unit was naturally favored with special treatment, but it proved to be unprepared and powerless to defend the leaders of the self-strengthening movement against the onslaught of the regular army units during the disturbances of the summer of 1882. The results of the reform efforts seem to have been less striking than the seriousness with which they were pursued.

Confucian Reaction: The Literati Movement of 1881

In Confucian eyes, the events of the early 1880s signaled the imminent collapse of the Confucian state. The government had not resisted Japanese demands for more ports, and it even allowed the Japanese envoy to come and go at will. To make things worse, the government was launching reforms that were threatening to destroy the old order and that were tying the country to the outside world. The main targets of the nation-wide Confucian wrath were high officials in the government who "were advocating peace and protecting heterodox doctrines." Yi Yu-wŏn was castigated for corresponding with Li Hung-chang, and Kim Hong-jip was labeled a traitor for presenting Huang Tsun-hsien's treatise to the throne.[44]

The protest movement started in the fall of 1880 with a memorial by Yu Wŏn-sik who bluntly accused Huang Tsun-hsien of betraying his Confucian heritage and making himself the spokesman for heretic Christian thoughts.[45] Hŏ Wŏn-sik was equally outspoken in his criticism against Huang's suggested strategy of an alliance with America against Russia. Hŏ considered such an alliance utterly impractical and displayed high confidence in Korea's military strength and preparedness. The dispatch of trainees to China, he claimed, would simply convince the Russians that Korea was militarily unprepared and would turn the strategy of "opposing the robbers into a plan for inviting the robbers." For Hŏ, the essence of victory and success lay in the right use of the soldiers and not in technology.[46] The protest movement widened in the spring of 1881 when the *Yŏngnam maninso* (Memorial of the ten thousand people of Yŏngnam) was submitted. Its principal author was a Confucianist of Kyŏngsang, Yi Man-son. In sharp terms he accused the government of abandoning the centuries-old policy of "rejecting heretical thought and repelling the foreign barbarians." He also rebuffed Huang's recommendation of an alliance with Japan and an association with America against Russia; all of these powers were the same kind of barbarian without the slightest difference. Huang, Yi maintained, was really talking in Japan's favor. Yi resolutely demanded the immediate punishment of Kim Hong-jip, who had brought that insulting document to Seoul.[47]

Yi Man-son's memorial ignited a chain reaction in most southern provinces. Memorialists warned that the government's recent policies portended the financial and moral downfall of the country and suggested that Korea should build a strong defense system, restrict its contact with the outside world, and levy high customs duties to ward off the immediate danger. Memorial followed memorial in rapid succession. In the early fall of 1881, Hong Chae-hak, a Kangwŏn Confucianist, Cho Kye-ha, a Ch'ungch'ŏng Confucianist, and Ko Chŏng-ju, a Chŏlla Confucianist, joined the movement "to defend the right learning and to reject heterodoxy" (*wijŏng ch'ŏksa*). They presented their protests in lengthy memorials. Hong Chae-hak, who belonged to the school of Hwasŏ Yi Hang-no, deplored in an extensive memorial that bad influences from abroad had spread all over the country and had even affected the highest level of the government. Japan and the Western countries, he charged, were really one and the same. Yet the government not only received the Japanese, it even rewarded them. Under these circumstances the teachings of the great Confucian masters, Confucius and Mencius, were steadily declining, and the right relations between the people were falling into disorder. The best way to block the entrance of Christian ideas and concepts of international law into the country, Hong maintained, was the abolition of the T'ongnigimu Amun and the reestablishment of the Five Armies. Similar thoughts were put forward by Kyŏnggi Confucianist Sin Sŏp, who argued that trade relations with a Christian country like America would lead to the slow penetration of alien doctrines into the country. He directed his most energetic attacks against Kim Hong-jip and Yi Yu-wŏn and demanded heavy punishment for their role in undermining the foundation of the nation.[48]

The Confucianists' stiffly worded memorials naturally disturbed the government and put it in a very delicate situation. Its credibility as the protector of Confucian values was at stake. It first attempted to invalidate the arguments of its critics by asserting that it did not need their verbal assistance to "defend the right learning and to reject heterodoxy" and that "the privately submitted opinions of a foreigner" (Huang Tsun-hsien's treatise) were not worth deep investigation. Moreover, Min T'ae-ho apparently succeeded in getting Yi Man-son to amend the most offensive passages of his memorial. However, neither soothing words nor behind-the-scenes maneuvers were able to persuade the Confucianists to stop their protest movement voluntarily. The government then adopted sterner measures. Many memorialists, among them Yi Man-son, were apprehended and punished with banishment. On June 11 the government circulated a small pamphlet entitled *Ch'ŏksa yunŭm* (Royal message concerning the rejection of heterodoxy) in an attempt to emphasize its role as the guardian of Confucian orthodoxy. It appealed to the confused populace to be morally armed against subversive influences from abroad. The conflict between the government and the Confucian dissidents reached its climax when Hong Chae-hak was beheaded outside the city walls of Seoul on September 13 after a dramatic trial. The king reportedly was especially angry with Yi Yu-wŏn who, by leaking the text of his secret correspondence with Li Hung-chang to the public, was mainly responsible for the uproar. Yi, although very old, was mercilessly sent into banishment. Kim Hong-jip did not deny his role in bringing the controversial document to Korea. He repeatedly submitted his resignation from government service in a gesture of self-accusation, but it was not accepted.[49]

The Confucianists' protest movement, regarded by the government as a serious challenge but hardly a real threat, had an unexpected aftermath. Taking advantage of the general excitement and unrest, a group of disgruntled men, inspired and possibly even controlled by the deposed Taewŏn'gun, tried in the fall of 1881 to realize their political program: the deposition of the king, the removal of the queen and the Min clan, and the ouster of all those high ministers who welcomed foreigners into the country. The final aim was the reestablishment of the Taewŏn'gun. Rarely before in the Yi dynasty had such a direct attack on the king and the royal house been attempted. The group was headed by the older illegitimate son of the Taewŏn'gun, Yi Chae-sŏn, aided by An Ki-yŏng and Kwŏn Chŏng-ho, both former royal secretaries, and a small number of dissidents. The plotters, however, dissented among themselves and were unable to advance the necessary preparations. Before they could strike, they were betrayed to the government authorities. They were put on trial, and Yi Chae-sŏn had to commit suicide on December 25. His abortive attempt to turn the course of history would have been just another episode of the protest movement had it not drawn support from the Taewŏn'gun, who still commanded a considerable amount of political power. This plot added a new dimension to the struggle between those who strove to open the country to the outside world and those who wanted to preserve Korea's isolation. The stage was set for the 1882 incident, an upheaval which contributed greatly to the increase of foreign interference in the peninsula.[50]

ㅆㅆㅆㅆㅆㅆㅆㅆㅆㅆㅆㅆㅆㅆㅆㅆㅆㅆㅆㅆㅆㅆㅆㅆㅆㅆ

The force of the dissenters' attack on Korea's early self-strengthening stood in small proportion to the program's actual success. There can be no doubt about the sincerity of King Kojong's commitment to self-strengthening. He and his ministers came to see the dimensions of the task and made serious efforts to formulate an adequate policy, but they failed to develop the necessary means to implement it. Korea's traditional economic system did not provide the surpluses to sustain even a small-scale self-strengthening program. The king did not devise economic measures, for example taxing trade or lifting the ban on mining, that would have furnished the needed funds. As a result, the ideological commitment was not supported by economic commitment. When the government did use government rice to support the new elite army unit, it provoked serious discontent and precipitated the violent end of Korea's first phase of self-strengthening. Despite its limitations, however, the new program epitomized the government's determination to lead the country out of its centuries-old isolation into the modern world. Unique in the Korean case was the fact that self-strengthening preceded the conclusion of treaties with Western powers. Also unique was the fact that the impetus for self-strengthening came just as much from the fear of her neighbors as from the fear of the West.

KOREA'S OPENING TO THE WEST

Before 1880, the seclusion policy was accepted as the fundamental law of the country. The treaty with Japan in 1876 did not significantly change this outlook. In the fall of 1880, however, the debates on Huang Tsun-hsien's treatise broke through the narrow confines of Korean-Japanese relations and confronted Korea with the realities of her international position. The Koreans finally realized that their country's situation was precarious. To ward off the surrounding dangers, they considered self-strengthening their first task. They also recognized that the conclusion of treaties with Western powers was a strategy for security, but they had little chance to participate; Korea's first treaties with the West were devised outside Korea.

Korea's seclusion remained a challenge to the West. Rumors about the Taewŏn'gun's retirement and the new regime's friendly disposition toward foreigners reached the outside world early in 1874. The German minister in Tokyo, Max von Brandt, suggested to his government in Berlin that the establishment of treaty relations with Korea would be in the best interests of the European powers. The Foreign Office in Berlin, however, did not act upon this recommendation.[1] The British representatives in the Far East received word about a "revolution in Corea" with skepticism. The British minister in Tokyo, Sir Harry S. Parkes, only suggested that surveys be conducted along the Korean coast. The friendly treatment that the shipwrecked crewmen of the British merchant ship *Barbara Taylor* received from authorities on Cheju Island in the fall of 1878 seemed to confirm the

Koreans' changed attitude toward foreigners. But when Parkes sent Ernest Satow to Cheju and Pusan to deliver a message thanking the authorities for the kindness shown to the shipwrecked British, the letter was not accepted by the Korean officials,[2] although Satow's reception was courteous.

Western reaction to the conclusion of the Kanghwa Treaty was favorable,[3] but the Japanese were fearful of the West's competition in the peninsula. Therefore, in their talks with Western representatives, they tended to downgrade the value of the Korean market. Toward the end of the 1870s, Japan became increasingly apprehensive of Russian designs and hesitantly began soliciting Western contacts with Korea. Japan also hoped that a Western involvement in Korea would facilitate the practical implementation of her own treaty with Korea. This caused a dilemma as far as Japan's commercial interests in the peninsula were concerned, but political advantage seemed at this point to outweigh the possibility of commercial loss.[4]

The Western nations, especially England and Germany, did not answer Japan's call for cooperation in Korea with much enthusiasm. Their fear of being rebuffed by the Korean government still lingered. Also, the practical value of Japan's overture was small. Although the Japanese government wanted Western allies, it did not want the task of introducing the Western nations to Korea. It repeatedly asserted that "such assistance would neutralize, and probably annul, the advantages she had with much difficulty obtained in Korea."[5]

The American Initiative: Commodore Shufeldt's Mission in 1880

The history of American interest in Korea dates back to 1845 when a resolution recommending a commercial arrangement with Korea was introduced into the House of Representatives. Nothing came of the resolution. More than twenty years later, after the *General Sherman* affair, Washington received reports from its representative in China strongly recommending the negotiation of a Korean treaty similar to those the United States already had with China and Japan. Although this proposal was welcomed in Washington, it could not be easily translated into action because it was based only on rumors about Korea's readiness to accept the American advances.

Early in 1871, the new American minister in Peking, Frederick F. Low, asked the Tsungli Yamen to convey a message to Korea announcing that America intended to send a naval expedition there to open diplomatic negotiations. The Chinese reluctantly sent the American letter to Seoul where it was rejected by the Korean government. Before the rejection arrived back in Peking, the American expedition left Shanghai and headed toward military defeat in Korea. In April 1878, a new resolution demanding an American-Korean accord through Japanese intercession was introduced into the Senate by Senator A.A. Sargent of California. This was the last resolution concerned with the Korea question before Commodore Robert Wilson Shufeldt of the US Navy set out aboard the flagship *Ticonderoga* in December 1878.[6]

The purpose of Commodore Shufeldt's voyage was to stimulate and expand American trade in Africa and Asia. Korea's inclusion in the itinerary seems to have been due to the commodore's ambition of "becoming the pioneer of a more enlightened policy in the East." The United States government was interested in the success of the mission, but it inadvisedly instructed Shufeldt to ask for the good offices of the Japanese rather than that of the Chinese in making contact with the Korean government. Shufeldt was further directed to visit a Korean port and deliver a letter addressed to the king of Korea. In a conciliatory tone, this letter assured the king that the events of 1871 were long since forgotten, and it emphasized America's wish to enter into friendly relations with Korea by concluding a commercial treaty and arranging for the care of shipwrecked seamen. Negotiations with the Koreans, Shufeldt's instructions concluded, would be conducted in a peaceful way.[7]

The American minister in Tokyo, John A. Bingham, approached the Japanese Foreign Ministry in March 1880 and requested that the Japanese government pave the commodore's way with official or personal letters to the Japanese officials in Korea and also to the Korean government. Foreign Minister Inoue Kaoru received this appeal coldly and tried to rid himself of the delicate task by arguing that the Korean-Japanese treaty was not yet fully functioning. Furthermore, Inoue maintained, the Korean government was not familiar with foreign relations and still appeared disinclined to open the country to foreigners. When Shufeldt reached Nagasaki on April 15, Bingham had only been able to secure for him a letter of introduction from Inoue to the Japanese consul at Pusan.[8]

Shufeldt's first appearance in Korea was brief and unfortunate. After landing at Pusan on May 4, he entrusted the initial talks with the Korean officials to the Japanese consul, Kondō Masuki. Kondō immediately went to see the prefect of Tongnae, Sim Tong-sin, and begged him to transmit to Seoul the American letter addressed to the king of Korea. Sim declined the Japanese demand, termed the American project "unreasonable," and urged the speedy departure of the foreign ship.[9]

When Shufeldt returned to Japan, he and Bingham entreated Inoue to enclose the American letter in a Japanese letter addressed to the Korean authorities in Seoul. This new request put Inoue in a dilemma. Not only did he fear that repeated Japanese action on behalf of the Americans would do irreparable harm to Japanese-Korean relations, he also was concerned about affronting the Americans. After securing the approval of Sanjō Sanetomi, Inoue at last announced to Bingham that he would cooperate on the condition that Shufeldt would await the answer in Nagasaki. A time limit of sixty days was fixed.[10]

Inoue's letter to the president of the Department of Rites, Yun Chasŭng, briefly outlined the American intentions and admonished the Koreans to change their seclusion policy and welcome foreigners into the country. Shufeldt's letter did not seem to stir up a great controversy in Seoul because one look at the envelope convinced the Koreans that the document was unacceptable. They did not even open it. The summer of 1880—it was prior to the debate on Huang Tsun-hsien's treatise—was an extremely unfavorable time for a discussion on foreign relations. Yi Yuwŏn apparently shared the general fear of contamination by heterodox thought from the West, but he felt that a negative answer would not deter the foreigners from repeating their call in the future. Chief State Councillor Yi Ch'oe-ŭng did not waste his time with such reflections. He ordered Kim Hong-jip, who was to go to Japan, to hand the unopened American letter back to the Japanese authorities. The reason for this rejection, contained in Yun's answer to Inoue, was laconic: on the American envelope Korea was designated as "Koryŏ" instead of "Chosŏn," and the letter itself was addressed to the king of Korea instead of to the president of the Department of Rites. For these two reasons, Yun asserted, the American communication was unacceptable. Thus the American overture was rebuffed by the Korean government, and the hope for success through Japanese assistance came to naught.[11]

Shufeldt was indignant at the blow to his ambitions and blamed the failure on his restriction to the use of peaceful means and on the lack of good faith on the part of the Japanese. The latter assertion Bingham did not support. He considered the Korean reply an insult directed against

Japan as well as the United States. Both Shufeldt and Bingham concurred that the Japanese government should again be asked to submit the American letter, and Bingham lost no time in suggesting such a course of action to Inoue. This time, however, the Japanese government refused the American appeal politely, but firmly.[12]

The reason for Korea's negative reaction lay in the unfortunate time which Shufeldt inadvertently chose for the realization of his plans in Korea. Moreover, Li Hung-chang was supporting the king's deep suspicion of Japanese intentions toward Korea and repeatedly warned that Korea should beware of Japan's plotting with Western nations for profit in Korea's open ports. Li's warnings were illustrated by Shufeldt's Japanese-American overture, an example which discredited Japan and presumably strengthened Korea's faith in Li's political perceptiveness. In any case, Japan's assumption that China's advice to Korea was still more potent than her own seemed to have been borne out.[13]

Even before his departure for Pusan, Shufeldt was informed that the Chinese government was encouraging the Koreans to conclude treaties with Western nations. His informant was the Chinese consul at Nagasaki, Yü Ching, who reportedly visited the commodore aboard the *Ticonderoga* on April 15. During this visit, which almost certainly was arranged without Li Hung-chang's prior knowledge, Yü apparently intimated to Shufeldt that the American should ask for China's good offices in his Korean venture. Shufeldt, however, was committed to Japanese assistance by his instructions, and he was unable at this time to take up Yü's suggestion.[14]

Li Hung-chang heard of Shufeldt's debacle in Japan through Yü Ching and presumably was quite delighted at Japan's failure to lead the American to success in Korea. He was quick to realize that he could make use of the commodore to China's advantage. In a letter dated July 23, he invited Shufeldt to China, a call which Shufeldt followed without much hesitation. On August 25, Shufeldt arrived in Tientsin, and on the next day he was received by the viceroy. Korea, Shufeldt told Li, did not have much to offer the United States from a commercial point of view. However, for the protection of American seamen and goods shipwrecked off Korea's coasts, the United States government intended to conclude a treaty of friendship with that country. Li Hung-chang gracefully accepted the commodore's solicitation of Chinese help. Assured that his mission would eventually be successful, Shufeldt returned to the United States on September 11.[15]

Secret Diplomacy: The Composition of the Korean-American Treaty

The peculiarity of the Korean-American Treaty is that it was composed not on Korean soil by Korean negotiators and an American representative, but in China in almost total secrecy by Li Hung-chang, his Chinese assistants, and Commodore Shufeldt. Li was not high-handed, nor was he oblivious to the Korean situation and to Korea's desires. Yet, after the fiasco of Shufeldt's mission using Japan as a reluctant go-between, he felt that it was China's duty to lead her tributary to the conclusion of its first treaty with a Western nation. The true aim, to be sure, lay in protecting China's eastern flank by strengthening the peninsula's security. It was difficult to enlist Korea's active participation in the treaty negotiations. The centers where China's policy vis-à-vis Korea was formulated in the early 1880s were Paotingfu and Tokyo, and the lines of communication to and from Seoul were cumbersome. Since the latter half of 1877, the Tokyo assignment was in the hands of the Chinese minister to Japan, Ho Ju-chang, and the counselor, Huang Tsun-hsien. Li Hung-chang had asked Ho to pay close attention to the relationship between Korea and Japan and to collect every bit of information possible on the subject.[16]

Stationed in a diplomatically strategic post, Ho Ju-chang took his mission very seriously. On the basis of his frequent contacts with Japanese, Korean, and Western diplomats, he developed his own views about how China should guide Korea's fate. Ho shared the anxiety of the Japanese government about Russia's designs on Korea. China, he feared, might not be able to protect Korea against a Russian onslaught. British Ambassador Parkes repeatedly told Ho that China should encourage Korea to conclude treaties with Western nations. Ho drew conclusions from this information and developed his own policy. Huang Tsun-hsien developed Ho's thoughts in the booklet *Chao-hsien ts'e-lüeh* (A policy for Korea). With this, Ho supplemented and clarified the arguments that he presented orally to the Korean envoy, Kim Hong-jip, in the summer of 1880.[17]

Ho Ju-chang evidently had high hopes for the impact his policy suggestions would have on the Korean government. He eagerly awaited a letter from Kim Hong-jip announcing their acceptance in Seoul. Then, around October 20, Ho was visited by the enigmatic Yi Tong-in who brought him transcripts of the discussions King Kojong had with Chief State Councillor Yi Ch'oe-ŭng and his high ministers about Huang Tsun-hsien's treatise.[18] Yi also gave Ho an allegedly secret personal message from the Korean king which asserted that the opinion at court had become favorably disposed toward concluding treaties with the West, and that Kim Hong-jip would be ordered to write a letter to Ho urging him to encourage the United States to send an envoy to Korea for the conclusion of a treaty. Based on this information, Ho developed his ideas further in a brief paper entitled *Chu-chih Chao-hsien wai-chiao i* (A proposal for the management of Korea's foreign relations). In the face of Russia's threat, he stated, Korea had to conclude a treaty with a third power. Because China would not tolerate the recognition of Korea as an independent country, it was imperative, Ho argued, that China follow one of two policy alternatives: the Chinese government should send an envoy to Korea to take care of the negotiations for the conclusion of a Korean-American treaty, or it should ask for an imperial edict ordering Korea to enter into treaty relationship with another country and directing that this order be included in the treaty preamble. When the Tsungli Yamen transmitted this document to Li Hung-chang for comment, the viceroy opposed such an interventionist policy. Korea, he feared, might not be receptive to a Chinese order, and the Western countries would hold China responsible for the fulfillment of such treaties. The dispatch of a Chinese envoy, Li argued further, might induce the Westerners to take the Western treaties with China as a blueprint for their treaties with Korea. This would not be of advantage to Korea.[19]

Before Ho received Li's negative answer in February 1881, he was told by a "secret agent," T'ak Chŏng-sik, that the king and his ministers wanted to conclude a treaty with the United States, but that they were afraid of the public uproar if such a decision became known. Therefore, T'ak entreated Ho, China should support the royal party with an imperial edict. A similar request was made in Kim Hong-jip's letter that arrived on December 30. T'ak also informed Ho that he was secretly instructed by the king to tell him that a second attempt by the Americans to conclude a treaty would not be rebuffed by Korea again. Ho thereupon contacted Bingham and confidently told him China would advise Korea to first conclude a treaty of commerce with the United States. He showed the American a draft treaty which was substantially the same as the United States-Japan treaties of 1857 and 1858. Ho also gave a copy of this draft to T'ak, who shortly afterward returned to Korea.[20]

Ho's concept of a Korea policy was rejected by the Chinese government. It also could not be implemented in Korea. When T'ak met Ho again in May 1881, the Korean asserted that the political climate in

Seoul had not changed much since his last visit. This was confirmed by a secret letter from Kim Hong-jip addressed to Ho, who passed the information on to Bingham with the apologetic remark that "at present my proposal on that matter cannot yet be carried out." With Shufeldt's second visit to Tientsin, Ho lost the opportunity to pursue his policy. The locus of the dialogue between China and the United States shifted away from Japan to northern China.[21]

After Shufeldt's first visit and retreat from Tientsin in the fall of 1880, Li Hung-chang started preparations for the conclusion of a Korean-American treaty. For this he used the Korean emissaries who went back and forth between Seoul and Peking as his secret couriers. Pyŏn Wŏn-gyu arrived in Tientsin in the middle of October, just after Shufeldt's departure. He was the first Korean to whom Li Hung-chang could convey his plan of action. Li told Pyŏn that Korea should take the initiative in concluding commercial treaties with Western countries. Li also expressed his concern about the possibility of Russia forcing its way into northeastern Korea. A treaty, Li claimed, was the only way to stop such a move. The young Chinese navy was not strong enough to assist Korea in case of a Russian attack.[22]

When Pyŏn Wŏn-gyu transmitted this message to the Korean government in January 1881, he found receptive listeners. During Pyŏn's absence from Korea, the king and his closest ministers had worked out a new strategy of concluding treaties with the West. A turn of mind was clearly reflected in the documents the assistant president (*chisa*) of the Board of Officials-without-Portfolio, Yi Yong-suk, brought to Tientsin in February 1881, and in what he told Li on the 18th. Yi gave Li a letter in which Chief State Councillor Yi Ch'oe-ŭng expressed his deep regrets at his harsh rejection of the American letter in the summer of 1880, and in which he announced Korea's readiness to conclude a treaty with the United States. From what Yi Ch'oe-ŭng wrote and Yi Yong-suk said, it is clear that Huang Tsun-hsien's treatise had acted as the catalyst that changed Seoul's rethinking of Korea's international position. Li brushed aside references to Ho Ju-chang's role as an adviser to Kim Hong-jip with the remark that China was absolutely unwilling to influence Korea's decision on the rejection or acceptance of another Western overture for treaty relations. He warned Yi once more that Korea was exposed to danger not only from the north but also from Japan. Then he instructed Ma Chien-chung and Chou Fu to compose a draft treaty as an instrument of reference for the Koreans.[23]

No documents exist to tell what happened after Yi Yong-suk delivered the Chinese papers to the king on May 4. It is certain, however, that the literati's protest movement greatly hampered swift action on the part of the Korean government and forced the king and his close collaborators to maneuver in almost total secrecy. The greatest problem they were facing, it would seem, was the difficulty of transmitting their own thinking to Tientsin. Lack of documentation leaves much of the reconstruction of this stage of the exchange to conjecture, but this much is clear: in September 1881, Cho Pyŏng-ho, accompanied by Yi Cho-yŏn, left for Japan to thank the Japanese government for Hanabusa's third trip to Seoul.[24] Cho met Ŏ Yun-jung at Kobe on October 23. Ŏ was in Japan as a member of the secret inspection tour. Five days later Ŏ left for Shanghai, where he arrived on November 3. Ŏ met Li Hung-chang once on December 1. They probably talked about the impending negotiations with Commodore Shufeldt, who was already present at Tientsin. Ŏ, who came without plenipotentiary powers, must have urged Li to postpone the negotiations with the American until the arrival of Kim Yun-sik.[25] Prior to Ŏ's unexpected and seemingly not too productive appearance in Tientsin, Li sent the Korean emissary, Yi Ŭng-jun, back to Seoul with a secret communication in which he pressed the Korean king to dispatch a plenipotentiary envoy to Tientsin. Yi met Kim Yun-sik, who was on his way to Tientsin with the Korean students and artisans, at the border station of Ŭiju and undoubtedly informed him about the American advances. Kim, however, had to continue on his trip and could not wait to be empowered as official Korean negotiator.[26]

Commodore Shufeldt was back in Tientsin in June 1881 under instructions to finish the American project by getting Li Hung-chang to fulfill his promises. He found Li unexpectedly reluctant to start negotiations. Li apparently tried to convince Shufeldt that the Korean court had still not settled on a common policy and that he should wait for a more opportune time. Shufeldt and the American minister to Peking, James B. Angell, surmised that the conclusion of the Treaty of St. Petersburg between China and Russia in February of the same year had lessened the viceroy's concern about Russia's designs against Korea. Whatever the value of the Americans' conjecture, it seems certain that one of the main reasons for Li Hung-chang's apparent recalcitrance was his unwillingness to start negotiations with Shufeldt without the presence of a high Korean official. It was not until mid-December that Li sent the commodore a note telling him that a Korean official had reached Tientsin and that Korea was willing to negotiate a treaty with the United States. Li undoubtedly referred to Ŏ Yun-jung. As soon as Kim Yun-sik arrived in Tientsin in mid-January, the Chinese-American negotiations got under way. Although Kim had no official authority to negotiate, he was the highest-ranking Korean in Tientsin. Li Hung-chang considered him an adequate representative of the Korean government.[27]

Kim Yun-sik and Pyŏn Wŏn-gyu arrived at Paoting on January 16, 1882, and met with Li Hung-chang several times during the following days. Kim told of the precarious situation in which the Korean king and his ministers found themselves. A secret letter which Kim handed to Li endorsed the conclusion of a treaty with America and entreated the Chinese to back the king's position with an imperial edict. Li Hung-chang found this appeal unacceptable and declined to act upon it. He was annoyed at Korea's indecision and pointed out to Kim that he had repeatedly turned a deaf ear on Russian and English plans to conclude treaties with Korea, yet he was determined to guide the American-Korean treaty to success. He was equally impatient with the fact that his call for a plenipotentiary had not been answered. Kim immediately sent Pyŏn Wŏn-gyu back to Seoul to repeat the Chinese order for the urgent dispatch of a plenipotentiary envoy to Tientsin. In the meantime Kim Yun-sik, who lacked the authority of an official spokesman, nevertheless assumed the role of unofficial consultant. He was the only Korean to witness the genesis of the American-Korean treaty.[28]

Although not all of Li Hung-chang's preconditions for negotiations with Shufeldt were fulfilled yet, Li received the more than tacit approval of the Korean king and a set of treaty propositions that members of the T'ongnigimu Amun had composed for Li's reference. Ordered by an imperial edict of January 23, Li began to work on a document which he envisaged as the basis for all future treaties between Korea and Western nations. The preparations were undertaken in an atmosphere of near secrecy. Li Hung-chang seems to have shared Korea's apprehension that certain bystanders, notably Russia and Japan, might dislike the idea that Korea was concluding a treaty with America with Chinese help. Shufeldt had reasons of his own for avoiding the attention of the foreign representatives in China and therefore declined to meet Li Hung-chang at Paoting for the treaty discussions. The Chinese draft treaty was drawn up by the Tientsin customs taotai, Chou Fu, and Ma Chien-chung, an expert on international law. They also conducted the preliminary negotiations with Shufeldt, who used a draft treaty he had composed on the model of the Japanese-Korean treaty. Shufeldt was at times assisted by the American chargé d'affaires at Peking, Chester Holcombe.[29]

The central problem of the negotiations between Li Hung-chang and Shufeldt turned out to be Korea's political status. Li insisted that the first article of the treaty should clearly declare Korea's dependence on China. Here was an opportunity to remedy some of the damage done by the Japanese-Korean treaty of 1876. The draft proposals Kim Yun-sik had handed to Li did not allude to the problem, but Kim preferred the formulation that "for China, Korea is a dependent country; for all others, Korea is independent."[30]

Not surprisingly, Li Hung-chang's ideas differed considerably from Shufeldt's. America, the commodore maintained, could conclude a treaty with Korea without recognizing the latter's dependent status since Korea, as repeatedly stated by China, acted as a sovereign in matters of foreign relations. If Korea needed China's approval for the treaty, this was of no concern to the United States. Yet the treaty between the two countries would be concluded on the basis of complete equality between the two partners. Li Hung-chang at one time hoped to find a supporter for his viewpoint in the American chargé d'affaires. Holcombe had apparently suggested earlier that the Tsungli Yamen insert into the treaty a paragraph depicting Korea's dependent status. However, when he joined the increasingly heated debate between Li and Shufeldt on April 12, he reversed his previous stand, arguing that the matter was wholly the commodore's responsibility. The negotiations became deadlocked, and Li Hung-chang, not wanting to pursue the issue, suggested that Shufeldt should ask for telegraphic instructions from Washington.[31]

While the issue of Korea's political status was dropped from the discussions for the time being, the Chinese and the two Americans worked out the remaining treaty text. After many bargaining sessions throughout the second half of April, the different drafts were amalgamated into one document. The final product seems to have satisfied Li Hung-chang, for "compared to the original Chinese and American versions and the Japanese-Korean treaty, the passages which assure benefit and guard against harm seem to be more tightly and completely worded." Shufeldt received no further instructions from his government and was unwilling to yield to Li's formulation of the first treaty article containing a confirmation of Korea's dependent status. They finally agreed on the compromise that the Korean king would, after signing the treaty, send a communication to the president of the United States declaring Korea's dependency on China. Li affixed his seal, and Shufeldt signed the finished treaty, which significantly bore the date according to the Chinese calendar. Li considered the established text as binding for both contracting parties, although he conceded that minor changes still could be negotiated between Shufeldt and the Koreans.[32] Shufeldt greeted the end of the negotiations with a sigh of relief. He was tired of the tedious discussions and complained that he rarely had a chance to meet the Korean representatives. He was convinced that Li was trying to make the treaty for China's benefit.[33]

The treaty text was finished, yet no Korean plenipotentiaries were in sight. In mid-April, Li Hung-chang had received a letter from Chief State Councillor Yi Ch'oe-ŭng that announced the appointment and dispatch of Ŏ Yun-jung and Yi Cho-yŏn to Tientsin in answer to Li's request.[34] Shufeldt refused to postpone his May 7 departure for Korea in order to wait for them. Li and Kim Yun-sik then decided to entrust Yi Ŭng-jun, who was again in Peking as a member of the Korean winter solstice mission, with hurrying the treaty to Seoul. Presumably afraid that the treaty text alone might not be guarantee enough for a smooth understanding with the Koreans, Shufeldt proposed that the Chinese government place some experts at his disposal to assist him in Korea. The idea seemed to fall in line with Li Hung-chang's concern that if Shufeldt went to Korea alone, he might soon find himself in conflict with the Koreans. Moreover, Kim Yun-sik had expressed similar apprehension. Nobody in Korea, he asserted, was familiar with the conduct of foreign affairs, and nobody was fluent in foreign languages. Following this general agreement, Li Hung-chang chose Ma Chien-chung and Admiral Ting Ju-ch'ang to accompany the commodore to Korea. This double appointment was to demonstrate China's magnanimity toward Korea.[35]

The Signing of the Korean-American Treaty in Korea

Commodore Shufeldt left Chefoo aboard the *Swatara* on May 7, 1882. Ma Chien-chung and Ting Ju-ch'ang sailed one day earlier with the three Chinese ships, *Wei-yüan, Yang-wei,* and *Chen-hai.* When Ma and Ting reached the mouth of the Han River on the 8th, they found Hanabusa's ship anchored there. The Japanese envoy, who had just returned from Japan, evidently was anxious to observe the events from close by. On the same day, Ma led preliminary talks about the treaty with some lower Korean officials, among them Yi Ŭng-jun, who had come from Seoul to greet him.

The Koreans prepared for the reception of the American party by establishing a reception house at Inch'ŏn and, on May 11, appointing Sin Hŏn, then a member of the T'ongnigimu Amun, as chief receptionist (*chŏpkyŏn taesin*), Kim Hong-jip as deputy (*pugwan*), and Sŏ Sang-u as attendant (*chongsagwan*). Shufeldt did not reach Inch'ŏn until the next day, May 12.[36]

Before the Korean negotiators appeared, Ma Chien-chung made a last attempt to gain Shufeldt's consent for ordering the Korean king to issue a declaration of Korea's dependency on China prior to the conclusion of the treaty. Ma's initiative, however, failed through Shufeldt's determined opposition. Sin Hŏn and Kim Hong-jip arrived at Inch'ŏn on May 14. Their only objection to the treaty concerned the original article 9, which was to grant the Korean king the right to prohibit temporarily the exportation of Korean grain. Sin and Kim pleaded for a general prohibition. The dispute over this point lasted for a few days, until Kim Hong-jip proposed adding a general prohibition limited to the port of Inch'ŏn. Shufeldt, who was in a hurry to finish his mission, finally agreed to the Korean addition. On May 22, Shufeldt and his party proceeded to the reception tent where Sin Hŏn, Kim Hong-jip, Ma Chien-chung, and Admiral Ting Ju-ch'ang waited. In a short ceremony, Shufeldt, Sin Hŏn, and Kim Hong-jip signed and sealed the *Treaty of Friendship and Commerce* in fourteen articles. "The event was signalised by a salute of twenty-one guns from the ship [the *Swatara*], and everything passed off in a very friendly and harmonious manner." Shufeldt left Korea on the following day and returned to America after an extended stay in Japan.[37]

The American-Korean treaty of May 22, 1882, generally called the Shufeldt Convention, was the first treaty Korea concluded with a Western power. Article 1 guaranteed perpetual peace and friendship between America and Korea and provided for the good offices of either government in case of oppression by another power. Article 2 stipulated the exchange of diplomatic and consular representatives. Protection for navigation was secured in article 3. According to article 4, extraterritorial jurisdiction was to be maintained until Korean statutes and judicial procedure would be so far modified and reformed as to be in conformity with those of the United States. Article 5 fixed the import tariffs on articles of daily use at 10 percent ad valorem, on that of luxury goods at 30 percent, and the export tariff on native products at 5 percent ad valorem. Concessions for the Americans in Korea were to be established in the open ports on the basis of article 6. The importation of opium was prohibited by article 7. Article 8 gave the king of Korea the right to decree a temporary prohibition on the export of foodstuffs whenever they might become scarce within Korea; the export of rice and grains of every description was prohibited from the open port of Inch'ŏn. Article 9 restricted the importation of all kinds of arms into Korea. Article 10 permitted the employment of natives for lawful work in either country. The exchange of students was established in article 11. Further negotiations for detailed commercial provisions and regulations were to be conducted within five years according to article 12. Article 13 prescribed English and Chinese as the two official languages in the communications between the two countries. Article 14 contained the most-favored-nation clause. Attached to the treaty was a *Despatch from the King of Korea to the President of the United States of America* in which the Korean king acknowledged that Korea was a tributary of China, but independent in regard to both internal administration and foreign affairs. After the establishment of relations between the two nations on terms of equality, the document asserted, "the King of Korea, as an independent monarch, distinctly undertakes to carry out the Articles contained in the Treaty, irrespective of any matters affecting the tributary relations subsisting between Korea and China, with which the United States of America has no concern." While the treaty was ratified by the American government, this declaration by the Korean king caused embarassment in Washington and was never officially published in any record. The Chinese government was well pleased with the result of Li Hung-chang's efforts, and in Korea the absence of any provision concerning the propagation of the Christian religion was noted with particular satisfaction.[38]

The British and German Treaties with Korea: The First Phase

British policy toward Korea in the second half of the 1870s was guarded. British representatives stationed in the Far East were observers rather than initiators. Gradually perceiving that Korea's commercial potential for British trade was minimal, Great Britain did not attempt to open the Korean market to British traders. Increasingly, British thoughts were occupied with political calculation. In the late 1870s, the British minister in Peking, Sir Thomas Wade, rarely missed an opportunity to describe to the Chinese government Korea's precarious situation between Russia and Japan. In Wade's eyes Korea's predicament was primarily a challenge to Korea and China, and only secondarily did it involve Britain. In October

1880 he told Li Hung-chang that England really did not intend to enter into relations with Korea. His country, however, would watch Russia's moves closely. This essentially unambitious line was also followed by the British minister at Tokyo, Harry S. Parkes. In 1878 he did not respond to the Japanese solicitation of Western participation in Korea. Moreover, when the Italian minister in Tokyo, Count Barbolani, suggested in the summer of 1880 that the maritime powers of Great Britain, France, Germany, the United States, and Italy should make a combined naval demonstration to induce the Koreans to conclude treaties and open the country to foreign trade, the British answer was cool. Britain, the Italian was told, considered such a demonstration unnecessary and would conclude treaties only after the successful opening of the country by others.[39]

British policy, in essence followed by the Germans, was stimulated in the early 1880s by various factors: Shufeldt's attempts to conclude a treaty with Korea; reports about the Korean government's changing mood toward entering into treaty relationship with the West; and Japan's continued efforts to induce England and Germany to break the ground for Western countries in Korea. Parkes' analysis linked Korea's reported readiness to negotiate treaties to her awareness of the Russian threat to Korean territory. He recommended to London that Britain should avail herself of this favorable disposition without loss of time. Should Russia's pressure lessen, he reasoned, Korea might retreat to her old concept of seclusion. The German minister at Tokyo, Eisendecher, did not favor separate German action and sought to coordinate German policy with the British. He was particularly concerned about the concentration of a large Russian fleet at Nagasaki and thought that in case Shufeldt should reach his goal without the use of force, Germany should follow suit.[40]

The British government was willing to take exploratory steps on the basis of intelligence received from Korea. It ordered Wade to probe the possibility of receiving China's good offices. In Berlin the Prussian government found no motive for direct action. To both, Shufeldt's frustration in Korea was disillusioning. In the British view, the conclusion of the Chinese-Russian treaty in February 1881, and the subsequent departure of the Russian fleet greatly diminished the political advantage of opening communication with Korea. At this stage the Korea policy of the European powers was formulated on an ad hoc basis and thus closely followed the vicissitudes of political expediency.[41]

When Shufeldt's negotiations with Li Hung-chang in the early spring of 1882 finally made positive gains, the Europeans looked on with a certain amount of anxiety. Parkes worried that the Americans, whose commercial interests in Korea were negligible, would only concentrate on making the first treaty with Korea. High tariffs granted to the Koreans, he feared, might seriously harm the prospects of future British trade in Korea. Vice-admiral George O. Willes of the China Station was ordered to cruise the Korean waters and observe Shufeldt's actions in Korea. Eisendecher was not concerned about the prospects for German trade, but considered it a matter of political prestige for Germany to play a role in Korea.[42]

Presumably on Wade's recommendation, Britain at last decided to seek the conclusion of a British-Korean treaty. Willes had authorization to negotiate, "if necessary," with Korean authorities to secure for Britian the advantages of the most-favored-nation treatment. It remained Wade's task to make the behind-the-scenes arrangements. He advocated using the American treaty with Korea as the basis for a British agreement. To be sure, Wade found the American-Korean treaty less liberal than the treaties between China and foreign states. He was convinced, however, that he could not obtain more favorable terms than the Americans had without resorting to arms. Furthermore, he reasoned, there was enough provision for later modification built into the treaty. Wade reportedly urged a meeting upon Li Hung-chang, who had just retired from active office because of his mother's death, to discuss sending Willes to Korea. Upon Wade's assurance that the British would use the wording of the American treaty without changing a single character, Li's initial reluctance toward the project seems to have disappeared. He gave Wade a copy of the American treaty and a letter of introduction to Ma Chien-chung.[43]

On May 25, 1882, Vice-admiral Willes sailed to Korea aboard the dispatch-boat *Vigilant*, and Wade's secretary, C.T. Maude, sailed on the gunboat *Sheldrake*. They anchored off Inch'ŏn on the 27th. The English ships surprised Ma Chien-chung and Ting Ju-ch'ang when they returned to Inch'ŏn from a royal audience in Seoul on the evening of the same day. Maude immediately contacted the Chinese who had to postpone their departure for China. At his first meeting with Ma, Willes reportedly wanted to add a few points to the American-Korean treaty in order to refine some of the provisions, but Ma opposed even the slightest change. In the end, Ma and the two Korean negotiators, Cho Yŏng-ha and Kim Hong-jip, who had been hurriedly dispatched from Seoul, agreed to three supplementary articles contained in a separate protocol: (1) the three ports of Wŏnsan, Pusan, and Inch'ŏn, which were open to Japanese trade, were, although not mentioned in the treaty, opened to British trade; (2)

British warships were permitted to enter any Korean harbor to buy provisions, tank fresh water, and do repair work; (3) the British navy was allowed to conduct surveys along the Korean coast to make navigation safer.

After Willes and Maude waited a few days in vain for a British interpreter to arrive at Inch'ŏn, Willes said that he would rely on Ma's assurance that the Chinese text corresponded in all points to the English. The British-Korean treaty was signed and sealed by Willes, Cho, and Kim in a tent near the beach on the afternoon of June 6, 1882. The treaty, the text of which was identical with the American-Korean document, was supplemented by a *Protocol* and a *Communication from the King of Korea to the Queen of England* which contained a declaration of Korea's dependency on China.[44]

Britain was the first to follow America's example. Germany became the second. Shortly after Willes' mission to Korea had received Li Hung-chang's consent, the German minister in Peking, Max von Brandt, met Chang Shu-sheng, the acting governor-general of Chihli, and expressed his intention to conclude a German-Korean treaty. He was not easily convinced that Chang would not allow a single change in the text that had been established for the Americans and British. After a few days of bickering, Brandt sailed to Korea accompanied by Ma Chien-chung and Ting Ju-ch'ang, both of whom had just returned from Inch'ŏn. Upon the exchange of credentials on June 27 with Cho Yŏng-ha and Kim Hong-jip, who again acted as the Korean plenipotentiaries, the German-Korean Treaty was signed and sealed on June 30, 1882. The treaty text, which was drawn up in Chinese and French in the form of the American-Korean treaty, was supplemented by a *Communication from the King of Korea to the King of Prussia* declaring Korea's dependency on China and by two notes exchanged between Brandt and the Korean plenipotentiaries which stipulated that German merchants were allowed to trade in the open ports even prior to the exchange of the treaty ratifications.[45]

Successive Petitioners for Treaty Favors: Russia and France

Korea's treaty commitments to Western nations through China's assistance was intensely observed. The Japanese were eager to catch a glimpse of the treaty text, but every time Hanabusa or Kondō Masuki approached Ma or the Korean negotiators, they were rebuffed with the answer that the treaties would be made public only after their ratification. It must have been a humiliating moment for the Japanese when Shufeldt praised'in Hanabusa's presence Li Hung-chang's efforts and Ma Chien-chung's help in his Korean mission.[46]

Even prior to Shufeldt's first mission in the summer of 1880, Russia had made a resolute, but premature attempt to conclude a treaty with Korea. In early March 1880, a band of mounted Russians crossed the frozen Tumen River and questioned the startled prefect of Kyŏnghŭng about the contents of the Korean-Japanese treaty and disclosed Russia's desire to enter into treaty relations with Korea. Upon the prefect's firm assurance that the agreement with Japan did not go beyond a reaffirmation of an old friendship and that Korea "did not have a law of foreign relations," the intruders retreated. Exactly two years later, contact was again sought across the Tumen River. This time, in March 1882, a Korean was sent by the local Russian authorities to the prefect of Kyŏnghŭng to deliver a letter which did not propose a treaty, but which intended to resolve a few local issues. This letter was received with surprise because it was written in *han'gŭl*. Although the government in Seoul ordered the local officials to answer with "nice words," it wanted to have it made unmistakably clear that further contact was not desired. Shortly afterward, however, the Korean government was again confronted with a Russian request for treaty relations. The Russian minister at Peking, Eugène de Butzow, approached Chang Shu-sheng early in June with the proposal that a treaty be negotiated which would grant overland trade and settle the border between the two countries. Chang instructed Ma, who was in Korea in the second half of June, to approach Kim Hong-jip about the Russian request. At the end of the month the Russian plan was rejected by Chief State Councillor Yi Ch'oe-ŭng, whose views were supported by Ma Chien-chung. Yi stated that the border area between Russia and Korea at the mouth of the Tumen River was too insignificant to render trade there feasible. It was therefore convenient, Yi insisted, "to wait for another day to conclude a treaty."[47]

The Koreans had expected that once they granted treaty favors to one nation, they would be forced to accommodate other nations as well. This expectation proved to be true. In the first days of June the French minister in Peking, M. Bourée, sent word to Chang Shu-sheng that France intended to conclude a treaty with Korea on the basis of the Korean-American treaty. The French, however, were not willing to sacrifice their special interests by accepting the same mold in which Korea's treaties with the

West had been cast. While the last preparations for the British-Korean treaty were made at Inch'ŏn, the French consul at Tientsin was sent to that port with a letter from Chang to Ma. During his brief encounter with Ma, he declared that France would ask for the insertion of a treaty article permitting Catholic missionaries to enter Korea. He retreated to Tientsin as soon as it became clear that his proposition met with Korean as well as Chinese opposition. One more attempt to win Chinese support failed. Chang refused to grant France more than had been granted to the other nations.[48]

The treaties Korea concluded with Western nations tied her at last to the legal structure of the "unequal treaties" which the West had begun imposing upon the Far East in 1842. The anomaly of the Korean case was that this process was started by Japan and finished with the help of China, both of whom suffered under the inequities of the same system. Japan had driven the first wedge into the eastern front of the Chinese world order; China presided over the distribution of treaty favors to Western powers. Although she was unsuccessful in incorporating her claim of suzerainty over Korea into the Western treaties, China left no doubt that she would not relinquish what she considered her special rights in the peninsula. Li Hung-chang did make efforts to let the Koreans participate in their country's opening to the West, but it was he who laid down the guidelines. The West did not oblige China with a written acknowledgment of her role in the negotiations. The Korean king's perfunctory declaration of his country's tributary status did not impress anyone.

To the Western powers, the conclusion of treaties with Korea was neither a political nor an economic necessity. It was a diplomatic nicety. The Westerners thought it convenient to have China's backing and were willing to accept Li Hung-chang's treaty concept. But the treaties to which the diplomats had acquiesced at Li's urging did not satisfy the traders. The British traders, especially, opposed the high tariffs which the treaties had imposed on prospective trade with Korea and forced the eventual revision of the British-Korean treaty. The political commitment of the Western powers in the peninsula remained small. But despite this indifference, the treaties of 1882 irreversibly marked the end of Korea's seclusion and opened the kingdom to outside pressures and influences of unforseeable dimension.

KOREA BETWEEN CHINA AND JAPAN

In 1882 the last obstacles to Korea's opening to the West were removed. China deemed it desirable and even necessary to give the Western powers the key to the hermit kingdom. Korea at last became tied in a peaceful way to the international community. A degree of stability in East Asia was established. This promised to heighten Korea's standing between her powerful neighbors and to begin her gradual development. China on the one side, and Japan on the other, considered Korea's treaties with the Western powers as guarantees against the other's securing special privileges in the peninsula. The eruption of violence in Seoul in the summer of 1882, however, jeopardized this well-designed scheme, and the treaties with the West lost much of their intended effect. No power seemed to be willing or strong enough to counterbalance Sino-Japanese interests in Korea. The Chinese could not allow the return to power of reactionary forces under the Taewŏn'gun and his supporters, and equally could not give Japan a free hand in the peninsula. China's reaction to the 1882 incident therefore determined the degree of her future involvement in Korea. China's maneuvers put Japan on the defensive. Japan had only two basic policy alternatives: war against China over Korea or acceptance of second place in the peninsula. She chose the latter.

The 1882 Incident

Internal and external events in the first two years of the 1880s shook traditional Korea. The government's modernization program, the increased
Japanese presence, and Western encroachment were not comprehended
by the Korean populace. They could not grasp the inevitability of these
developments and therefore saw them as a threat to their existence. The
government's adaptability and rather courageous response to the challenges
of the modern world were not shared and supported by the people. On
the contrary, the people interpreted the government's actions as a betrayal
of the old order and, more directly, attributed the plight of their daily
lives to the government's unorthodox policies. The literati movement of
1881 had been the prelude to the dissent, orchestrated by groups of Confucian scholars. The 1882 incident was the main movement, and it attracted
wide popular support. It was antigovernment and antiforeign.

Unrest had been smoldering among garrison soldiers for quite some
time because they had not been properly paid. There also was growing
tension between the old army units and the modern, which was receiving
preferential treatment. In the middle of July, soldiers of the Muwi Regiment clashed with granary officials in a bloody riot. When Min Kyŏm-ho,
who was in charge of the Tribute Bureau (Sŏnhyech'ŏng) and thus supervised the distribution of rice, chose to ignore the appeals of the excited
soldiers, they vented their anger by smashing Min's huge mansion. Min
barely escaped with his life. What had started as a minor incident widened
into a major upheaval after the Taewŏn'gun took over. He imposed upon
the unruly soldiers a firm program of action that included a strike against
the royal palace, the extermination of the Min family and its adherents,
and, most significantly, an attack against the Japanese legation. The
soldiers of the Muwi Regiment soon attracted groups from other units.
They were also joined by large numbers of common people.[1]

On July 23, soldiers and "hundreds of people" fiercely assaulted the
Japanese legation, which was located in the Ch'ŏngsugwan, a short distance
outside of Seoul. Hanabusa and his staff were completely unprepared for
the sudden outbreak of violence, although some reports and rumors had
reached the legation. After the mob set fire to their building and no government soldiers came to their rescue, the Japanese had to give up their
determined defense. At night, Hanabusa and a small group of legation personnel broke through the line of besiegers in a desperate attempt to reach
safety. When they got to the city wall the gates were closed, and Hanabusa

decided to flee to Inch'ŏn. Shortly after their arrival there in the afternoon of the following day, news of the events in Seoul caught up with the fugitives, and they were again molested by angry soldiers. Six Japanese were killed and five injured. The survivors retreated to Chemulp'o and then to Wŏlmi Island by boat. The British surveying ship *Flying Fish* rescued the small Japanese party and took it to Nagasaki. On the day of Hanabusa's flight from Seoul, the Japanese casualty list was lengthened when the Korean rioters killed the Japanese army instructor Horimoto Reizō, a Japanese language student, and a policeman.[2]

Simultaneously with the onslaught against the Japanese, the rampaging mob turned its anger against high government officials. Yi Ch'oe-ŭng, then the president of the Office of Royal Kinsmen, Min Kyŏm-ho, and the governor of Kyŏnggi province, Kim Po-hyŏn, were killed in the general unrest. The climax of the disturbances was reached when the royal palace itself came under fire, and the king was forced to take a last and desperate action: the reinstatement of the Taewŏn'gun. On July 25 the king formally announced that all government affairs, small and large, would henceforth be decided by the Taewŏn'gun. With this short decree, Korea's fate once again was put into the hands of the man who little more than a decade before had kept the country isolated from the outside world. On the day he received his new mandate, the Taewŏn'gun abolished the office which had been hailed as the symbol of Korea's changed attitude toward foreigners, the T'ongnigimu Amun, and reestablished the old Military Council (Samgunbu). In the military field, he switched back to the old system. Moreover, he undertook a far-reaching reassignment of personnel in the highest echelons of the government. An amnesty was decreed for Paek Nak-kwan and his partners who had played a role in the 1881 movement. One of the Taewŏn'gun's most ardent concerns, the extinction of the Min, was solved by the report that Queen Min had fallen into the hands of the rebels and had been killed. In reality, she had escaped unharmed from the beleaguered palace.[3]

Despite the Taewŏn'gun's efforts to use his regained authority to reverse the course of events, Korea's new position within the international structure of the Far East had been irreversibly fixed by the conclusion of treaties. Neither China nor Japan were willing to allow Korean retrogression or to surrender what they considered their duties and rights in the peninsula. On the contrary, the rebels of 1882 and the Taewŏn'gun unwittingly created the conditions that enabled Korea's neighbors to expand their influence in the peninsula.

Chinese Reaction: The Dispatch of Troops

News about the events in the Korean capital stunned the Chinese and Japanese governments. It reached Tokyo through Hanabusa on July 30, 1882, and Peking through telegraphic messages from Li Shu-ch'ang, the Chinese minister in Japan, two **days** later. The Chinese assessment of the situation profited from the opinions of Kim Yun-sik, who was still at Tientsin, and Ŏ Yun-jung, who had arrived there in the meantime. They seem to have agreed with Ma Chien-chung's interpretation that the combination of internal tensions and external grievances, the latter being stirred by the former, had led to the outbreak of violence. Fundamentally, Kim and Ŏ felt, it was a struggle for power between the king and his father, the Taewŏn'gun. The explosion of the soldiers' frustration had merely acted as the igniting spark. Kim Yun-sik feared that An Ki-yŏng, one of Yi Chae-sŏn's accomplices of 1881, might have been behind the attack against the Japanese legation. Ŏ did not try to conceal the fact that antiforeignism still was widespread in Korea. Kim and Ŏ concurred that the person responsible for what had happened was the Taewŏn'gun. The Chinese government readily accepted their judgment. King Kojong was favored by Peking because he had shown himself amenable to Chinese counsel.[4]

Whatever the local significance of the Korean disturbance, the issue acquired a new and more crucial aspect when it was raised to the level of Chinese-Japanese rivalry in the peninsula. It was clear to the Chinese government that Japan would take advantage of the opportunity to interfere in Korean affairs. Central to the Chinese considerations, therefore, was the search for a rationale for immediate action on the part of the Chinese themselves. The concept that Korea was her dependent country still seemed a realiable foundation. China, the argument ran, had the duty to "be kind to the weak," and furthermore she was bound to protect Japan, with which she had treaty relations, within the territory of her tributary. During a brief skirmish with the Japanese government on this subject, however, the Japanese once again rejected the Chinese formula and adamantly contended that their difficulties in Korea, an independent country, were of no concern to China. Japan made it clear that she felt free to act according to her own will. The traditional notion of a paternalistic China protecting a subordinate Korea by the prestige of her predominant position in the Far East faded into diplomatic obsolescence. The year 1882 signaled a fundamental change in China's Korea policy: China had no means left to assert her authority in the peninsula except through direct military intervention.[5]

The news that Japan was about to dispatch troops to Korea, transmitted to Peking by Li Shu-ch'ang on August 1 and 3, stirred the Chinese government into action. In his telegraphic reports, Li himself urgently requested an immediate dispatch of Chinese troops to Korea. Acting governor-general of Chihli, Chang Shu-sheng, apparently intended to wait for the Korean king to appeal for help. Both Kim Yun-sik and Ŏ Yun-jung urged swift military action. Kim and Ŏ were strongly backed by Hsüeh Fu-ch'eng, who argued that the Chinese government should assume the initiative by taking military measures to anticipate Japanese operations in Korea and to avoid a second Ryūkyū. Chang finally accepted these recommendations and, after receiving permission through an imperial edict on August 7, sent Admiral Ting Ju-ch'ang and Ma Chien-chung to Korea with three Chinese ships. Accompanied by Ŏ Yun-jung, they arrived at Inch'ŏn on August 10. On that day, the first Japanese ship was in view off Inch'ŏn. After two days, Ting Ju-ch'ang sailed back to Tientsin to report in person about the situation in Korea and to transmit Ma's call for quick reinforcement by land forces. In the meantime, General Wu Ch'ang-ch'ing was ordered to ready the six regiments under his command in Shantung. With an advance force of two thousand men, Wu arrived at Masanp'o (Namyang) on August 20. Ting Ju-ch'ang and Kim Yun-sik who, with Ŏ Yun-jung, received from Chang Shu-sheng the temporary appointment of "guide to the Chinese troops," escorted the force.[6]

After landing on Korean soil, Wu Ch'ang-ch'ing and Ting Ju-ch'ang led their troops toward the capital. The atmosphere there was tense. The negotiations between the Taewŏn'gun and Hanabusa Yoshitada, who had come to Seoul shortly before, were stalled. The first objective of the Chinese operations was clear: the removal of the Taewŏn'gun from power. The chance to act came on August 26, 1882, when the Taewŏn'gun repaid Ma's visit of the previous day. Ma reprimanded him seriously for having taken governmental power in such an arbitrary fashion. Ma disclosed to the Taewŏn'gun the plans for taking him to Tientsin, a scheme which enjoyed the support of the Chinese government. The Taewŏn'gun was forced into a sedan chair and abducted by the Chinese under cover of night. They went first to Namyang and then sailed to China.[7]

The abduction of the Taewŏn'gun solved only half the problem. Although government control was returned to the king, the rebels were under the command of the Taewŏn'gun's eldest son, Yi Chae-myŏn, and they still presented a formidable threat to peace and security. The king apparently sent Cho Yŏng-ha to the Chinese headquarters to extend his thanks and to transmit a secret request to initiate a pacification program. While Yi Chae-myŏn was being detained, Chinese troops moved against the rebels' strongholds, the villages of It'aewŏn and Wangsimni. The commander of this campaign was Yüan Shih-k'ai. When advance news reached the rebels, a number of them escaped the Chinese attack, and only about 170 persons were captured. Most of these were released after an investigation. The operation ended with the banishment of a few men who had held high military appointments during the Taewŏn'gun's brief return to power and the decapitation of some men of lower positions. The successful termination of the campaign earned Wu Ch'ang-ch'ing and Yüan Shih-k'ai high honors from the Korean king. Ma Chien-chung and Ting Ju-ch'ang returned to Tientsin on September 7. They were escorted by the king's personal emissaries, Cho Yŏng-ha, Kim Hong-jip, and Yi Cho-yŏn, who transmitted royal thanks for Chinese help to the Chinese government. Wu Ch'ang-ch'ing and his troops were ordered to stay temporarily in Korea. Ting Ju-ch'ang rejoined them later.[8]

From a military point of view, China's intervention was a success. The Chinese troops acted swiftly and with determination. They carried the Taewŏn'gun into exile in China and restored King Kojong to power. Despite their positive evaluation of their performance, however, the Chinese knew that what they had achieved was not the reestablishment of the status quo ante. The presence of Chinese as well as of Japanese troops in Korea escalated the Sino-Japanese rivalry from verbal confrontation to military confrontation. Nobody suggested moving against the Japanese in the peninsula by force. But Japanese domination had to be prevented by well-considered political and economic countermeasures.

Japan Presents Additional Demands: The Treaty of Chemulp'o

Chinese military intervention was only one result of the 1882 uprising. The other was Japan's presentation of some additional demands to the Korean government. As soon as Hanabusa reported the news of the uprising to Tokyo, Foreign Minister Inoue Kaoru called an urgent government session on July 31. Some strong resolutions were immediately adopted:

Japan demanded an apology and an indemnity from Korea; Hanabusa would be sent back to Seoul as plenipotentiary envoy, protected by a strong guard of soldiers and sailors; Inoue would be sent to Shimonoseki to instruct Hanabusa personally; warships would be dispatched to Pusan and Wŏnsan to protect the Japanese residents in those ports. On August 5, Miyamoto Koichi, the old Korea hand, was sent to Shimonoseki to inform Hanabusa about the future course of action at Seoul. They were joined two days later by the foreign minister himself. Most important, Hanabusa was not to use his complement of troops and warships for any offensive acts; their dispatch was a purely protective measure. On the whole, however, Hanabusa was given a wide range of alternatives from which he could choose, depending on the situation in Korea.[9]

Hanabusa's return to Seoul was prepared by Kondō Masuki, who arrived aboard a warship at Inch'ŏn on August 10. He announced the impending mission to the local authorities. Hanabusa himself reached Korea three days later, escorted by a number of ships carrying a large contingent of troops. He was received by Cho Yŏng-ha, who had been appointed chief receptionist, and his deputy, Kim Hong-jip. When he entered Seoul with a military guard on August 16, Ma Chien-chung was already in control of the situation in the Korean capital. At this time the Taewŏn'gun was still controlling government affairs. His announcement that the course of Korea's foreign policy would not be changed was intended, presumably, to smooth the way for a peaceful accord with Japan. Hanabusa's firmness of action, however, seemed to go beyond Korean anticipation. He refused to delay his entrance into the capital in view of the still unsettled atmosphere there, and he brushed aside Korean apprehension about his heavy military guard. Moreover, the Japanese demands which Hanabusa presented to the king during a royal audience on August 20 were stiff: (1) punishment of the culprits within 15 days; (2) adequate funerals for the victims; (3) payment of 50,000 yen to the families of the dead and to the wounded; (4) indemnity for the damages inflicted upon the Japanese and compensation for the maintenance of the Japanese troops; (5) extension of the travel limit at Inch'ŏn, Pusan, and Wŏnsan to one hundred *i*, opening of Yanghwajin as a new marketplace, and permission of commercial traffic to such places as Hamhŭng and Taegu; (6) inland travel for the Japanese minister, the consuls, and their suites and dependents; (7) stationing of one Japanese battalion for the protection of the Japanese legation for five years. One day later, the eighth demand, which requested the dispatch of a Korean envoy to Japan to apologize for the happenings, was added to the list. Hanabusa demanded an answer within three days. Shortly later, he received news that Chief State Councillor Hong Sun-mok was leaving town to take part in the mourning services for Queen Min and that the negotiations would be postponed until his return. Hana-busa felt slighted and accused the Korean government of lack of good faith. Leaving Kondō in charge, he angrily left Seoul in the morning of August 23 in a demonstration of protest.[10]

Hanabusa's retreat from Seoul left the field to the Chinese. Ma Chien-chung had been fully informed about the Japanese intentions and demands when he met Hanabusa's assistant, Takezoe Shinichirō, upon the arrival of the Japanese delegation on August 16. Takezoe had assured Ma that Japan did not harbor any designs of territorial aggrandizement in Korea or inter-ference in the country's internal affairs. "Our earnest hope is a quick settle-ment and nothing else." Ma, who apparently had tried to get the Japanese to tone down some of their ʻdemands, became fully involved in the Japanese-Korean negotiations when the Taewŏn'gun called him to Seoul for arbitration. Ma reached the capital on the evening of the day of Hanabusa's sudden departure.[11]

The new duty seems to have fit Ma Chien-chung's plans. He hurried to Inch'ŏn the next day to see Hanabusa and hold him back with the assurance that the Korean government did not want a rupture with Japan. It was also an opportunity to impart to the Japanese his scheme of restoring the king's independence of action. Clearly, Ma was tactically the master of the situation, and it was not long before the Chinese also dominated the scene militarily. The removal of the Taewŏn'gun from Seoul cleared the way for the resumption of the negotiations. A royal edict on August 27 appointed Yi Yu-wŏn as plenipotentiary envoy, Kim Hong-jip as his deputy, Sŏ Sang-u as attendant, and Kim Pyŏng-si as receptionist. Even prior to Ma's mediation, Hanabusa realized the difficult position he had maneuvered himself into through his rashness and agreed to meet the Korean negotiators at Chemulp'o on that same day.[12]

Negotiations were opened aboard the Japanese warship *Hiei* on Au-gust 28. The sessions apparently took place in an atmosphere of intense bargaining. Yi Yu-wŏn and Kim Hong-jip had obtained in advance Ma Chien-chung's opinions on the various Japanese demands and took them as their guidelines. During the negotiations Ma kept himself entirely in the background. Hanabusa, who received additional instructions through Inoue Kowashi on August 28, added some points to his original demands. The most controversial were the amount of indemnity and compensation due according to the fourth demand, and the stationing of troops requested in point six. On August 30, the two negotiating parties were ready to reach an accord through compromise. The treaty text was immediately drafted, and on the evening of the same day the *Treaty of Chemulp'o* and the *Additional Convention* were signed. The six articles of the treaty read as follows: (1) The Koreans were to capture and punish the culprits within twenty days. Japan would send an observer, and, if this deadline could not be kept, the Japanese would make their own arrangements. (2) Proper funerals were to be provided for the Japanese killed during the disturbances. (3) 50,000 yen would be paid to the families of the dead and to the wounded. (4) 500,000 yen would be paid in five yearly installments for damages suffered by the Japanese nation and for the maintenance of the Japanese soldiers guarding the legation. (5) Korea was to build and maintain quarters for the Japanese soldiers who could, under certain circumstances, be withdrawn after one year. (6) An envoy was to be sent to Japan to apologize for the incident. The *Additional Convention* stipulated in article 1 that at each of the ports of Wŏnsan, Pusan, and Inch'ŏn the treaty limits would be extended to fifty *i* (Korean measurement) and after two years to one hundred *i*; after one year the port of Yanghwajin would be opened to trade. Article 2 permitted free inland travel to the Japanese minister, the consuls, and their suites and families with passports issued by the Department of Rites.[13]

After the conclusion of the treaty, Hanabusa stayed on to supervise the implementation of the stipulations. He reentered Seoul on September 7, and he and Kondō were received by the king on September 16. On the same day, a royal edict ordered that the texts of all treaties which Korea had concluded with Japan and Western nations be made known. It also ordered the removal of the stone tablets which the Taewŏn'gun had erected to exhort the people's antiforeign sentiments. Both measures seem to have been suggested to the king by Hanabusa. His immediate mission fulfilled, Hanabusa left Kondō in charge of the legation and sailed on the *Meijimaru* back to Japan on September 20, 1882. He was accompanied by a Korean mission of apology consisting of Pak Yŏng-hyo, who had been appointed envoy (*susinsa*) and minister plenipotentiary, his deputy Kim Man-sik, and Sŏ Kwang-bŏm, the attendant (*chongsagwan*).[14]

With Hanabusa's departure, the 1882 incident was settled. The demands which he had exacted from the Koreans were less than the Chinese feared. In the Chinese view, the *Treaty of Chemulp'o* was a stopgap which for the moment prevented a headlong collision with Japan.[15] The Japanese were not prepared to go to war against China. For them, the *Treaty of Chemulp'o* was a face-saving device. They had even gained some additional privileges. They knew, however, that China's troops on Korean soil seriously challenged their position in the peninsula. But the time had not come to counter this challenge by force.

China's Military Presence in Korea

After the 1882 incident, three thousand Chinese soldiers were stationed in and around Seoul. The Chinese troops were faced by about six hundred Japanese soldiers whose presence was sanctioned by treaty. The stationing of Chinese troops in Korea was a temporary measure. To reassert China's prerogatives, new and more permanent strategies had to be developed. In reaction to the happenings in Seoul, two rather radical action papers were presented. One was authored by Chang Chien, who had sailed to Korea as a member of Wu Ch'ang-ch'ing's suite. Apprehensive about Japan's future moves, Chang put down the conclusions he had drawn from his firsthand inspection of the scene in a small treatise titled *Chao-hsien shan-hou liu-ts'e* (A six-point program for the solution of the Korea problem). He presented this treatise to Wu Ch'ang-ch'ing in September 1882. Chang boldly proposed Korea's incorporation into China, as had been done in Han times when Korea had been divided into four Chinese-controlled provinces. As an alternative policy, Chang suggested the installation of a high commissioner (*chien-kuo*) to supervise the reorganization of the government, and the stationing of a strong military force for the protection of the seaports. Alternatively, the Koreans should be ordered to undertake a governmental reorganization, establish a new-style army, and keep in close contact with China's Three Eastern Provinces.[16]

A somewhat more moderate program under the similar title of *Chao-hsien shan-hou liu-shih* (Six points for the solution of the Korea problem) was presented in a memorial of October 27, 1882, by Chang P'ei-lun. Like Chang Chien, Chang P'ei-lun was preoccupied with the possibility that Japan would eventually swallow up Korea. The source of Korea's troubles, he thought, was her foreign relations. Since foreign relations determined the fate of a country, he suggested that the Koreans be provided with guidelines for their diplomacy. He urged that China should send a high official to Korea as trade commissioner (*t'ung-shang ta-chen*) who would be put in charge of the country's foreign relations. Furthermore, China should impress upon Korea the fact that Japanese instructors and arms had not been the best solution for her army and provide her with Chinese instructors and arms. Chang went on to demand that China counteract the effects of the treaty Korea had been forced into by Japan. How could a poor country like Korea raise the necessary military funds? Chang urged that Li Hung-chang be ordered to support Korea not with a loan, but with military assistance. Chang, however, considered the stationing of Wu Ch'ang-ch'ing's troops a temporary measure. The Koreans, he argued, would sooner or later resent the presence of foreign troops on Korean soil. China should therefore shift her energy and hurriedly construct a number of ships, train naval personnel, and station this maritime force at Inch'ŏn for Korea's protection. Moreover, Chang included the adjacent Chinese provinces in his strategy for Korea's protection. He felt that, in particular, Fengtien's defense system should be strengthened since this province would fulfill an important role in a possible campaign in Korea. In addition, Korea's eastern coast should be defended. Chang considered Russia an even greater threat than Japan. He was convinced Russia would sooner or later attempt to bring the ice-free harbor of Port Lazareff (Yŏnghŭng) into its possession.[17]

It is uncertain whether Chang Chien's recommendations ever reached Li Hung-chang. It is rather unlikely. There is no reference to them in Li's works. Li was ordered by edict to study Chang P'ei-lun's program and to formulate an opinion. Evidently Li did not share Chang's views on all points. He especially opposed the idea of sending a high commissioner to Korea. His reasons were similar to those he had put forward late in 1880 when Ho Ju-chang had first recommended such a course. Li felt that this would involve China too deeply in the actual management of Korean affairs. All responsibility for the country's foreign relations would then lie with China. Li admitted that Korea's situation had grown increasingly complicated because of the treaties she had concluded with Western powers. Li knew that difficulties would arise from the fact that Japan recognized Korea as an independent country, whereas the Western nations had been all but forced to include in their treaties a declaration of Korea's dependency. A Chinese commissioner conducting Korea's foreign affairs, Li argued, might have to handle all the treaties—the Japanese as well as the Western—in the same way, which "would not be an easy thing." Li cautiously endorsed Chang's recommendation that China should furnish instructors and arms for Korea's military development and that

China's maritime strength should be reinforced.[18]

It is clear that Li Hung-chang, even at this point, hesitated to use the unrest in the peninsula to expand China's role in Korean affairs as conspicuously as his subordinates demanded. He had other methods in mind to reassert his country's suzerain rights. In October 1882, he ordered the Tientsin Arsenal to send a large shipment of arms to Korea for rearming and training Korean units. He did this in answer to a direct Korean request and because he could justify it as an emergency measure. In November he asked for imperial permission to withdraw three of Wu Ch'ang-ch'ing's regiments from Korea in the following spring, leaving the remaining soldiers until the complete withdrawal of the Japanese troops. This demand was partly motivated by Li's concern about the worsening situation in Annam where a headlong collision between China and France seemed imminent. It may also have reflected Li's desire to lower China's military profile in the peninsula as soon as possible, even at the risk of being accused of failing to develop a long-range military plan for China's eastern front. His proposal for a troop reduction revealed that Li was not aware of how decisive a role the Chinese military had come to play in Korean politics. Li's request was overruled by objections raised by Wu Ch'ang-ch'ing, who was back in Tientsin at the end of March 1883, and the personal plea the Korean king sent through Pyŏn Wŏn-gyu. Consequently, the Chinese troops were ordered to remain in Korea "for the time being." The atmosphere in Seoul remained uncertain. The Chinese resented the continued, even if reduced, presence of Japanese troops. The Chinese military became increasingly involved in the quagmire of Korean politics. This involvement led to serious disputes between Wu and his subordinate, Yüan Shih-k'ai. In May 1884, three regiments were drawn back to Fengtien, this time with Wu Ch'ang-ch'ing's approval. The rest, some 1,500 men, were placed under the command of General Wu Chao-yu, who was assisted by Yüan in a civilian capacity.[19]

China Secures Special Trade Privileges

When Ŏ Yun-jung and Yi Cho-yŏn, who had been sent to negotiate with Shufeldt, reached Tientsin in the middle of May 1882, they delivered a royal letter in which the king pleaded for the abolition of the old rule prohibiting the use of the seaway between the two countries (*haegŭm*). It would be timely, the letter continued, to allow Chinese and Korean merchants to trade in the opened ports so that they could share the profits reaped now by the foreigners alone.[20] This initiative immediately raised the problem of how such trade relations would affect the Koreans' tributary status. An imperial edict of June 14 ordered that Sino-Korean trade was henceforth to be handled by the Tsungli Yamen while the regular tributary matters continued to be managed by the Board of Rites. It also ordered Li Hung-chang to study the feasibility of trade regulations. The issue was pushed into the background by the events of July and August 1882, but in October, when Li Hung-chang was back at his post, he brought it up again for discussion with the Korean emissaries, Cho Yŏng-ha, Kim Hong-jip, and Ŏ Yun-jung. He was searching for a means, other than military, of asserting China's prerogatives in Korea. He also concurred with the Koreans' opinion that the Chinese-Korean trade had to be freed from inflexible traditions, and also shared their view that foreigners should not be allowed exclusive trade rights. After very brief negotiations, at which Chou Fu and Ma Chien-chung assisted, the *Regulations for Maritime and Overland Trade Between Chinese and Korean Subjects* was signed and sealed on October 4, 1882.[21]

An analysis of the eight articles in this document shows that its political implications were at least as important as its commercial stipulations. This was the first written understanding between China and one of her vassals. The word "regulations" in the title, it was explained to the Koreans, meant something that was granted by the imperial court and therefore did not need to be ratified by the two countries. China admittedly did not intend to make a treaty in the modern sense and reserved for herself the advantage of incorporating safeguards for all her interests without opposition. Korea was a subject country and therefore a second-rate partner. There is evidence that the scope of the Chinese formulations far surpassed the original ideas presented by the Koreans. The preamble of the Regulations made the apprehensive Koreans look ungrateful. At the same time it invalidated in advance any claim that other powers might put forward under the most-favored-nation clause. It read: "But the new regulations for the maritime and overland trade now decided upon are understood to apply to the relations between China and Korea only, the former country granting to the latter certain advantages as a tributary kingdom, and other nations are not to participate therein."[22]

A few examples will illustrate that Li Hung-chang, the chief architect of this document, had no difficulty in making the "certain advantages" work in China's rather than in Korea's favor. Article 1 gave the super-

intendent of the Northern Ports the right to appoint commissioners of trade
to reside at the opened ports of Korea for the special purpose of exercising
jurisdiction over Chinese merchants resident there. These commissioners
were to deal with Korean officials "on the footing of perfect equality." On
the other hand, it was the Korean king who was to delegate a high official
to reside at Tientsin and send other officers to the open ports of China to
take care of commercial matters. All of these Koreans were to be treated
"on the footing of equality" with the local Chinese authorities, that is the
taotai, the prefect, or the magistrate of the place in question. This article
in fact put the superintendent of the Northern Ports, Li Hung-chang, on
an equal footing with the Korean king. Moreover, the Korean chief commissioner was not to reside in Peking but at Tientsin, holding approximately
the status of a Western consul. Article 2 granted extraterritorial jurisdiction to the Chinese officials stationed in Korea, but "all such civil and
criminal cases which may arise with Korean merchants at any of the open
ports in China will be tried according to law by the Chinese local authorities, irrespective of the nationality of either the plaintiff or the defendant."
The Korean official had only the right to be informed of the case and to
appeal to "the high authorities" for a revision of the verdict. According to
Article 4, the merchants of both countries were allowed to trade in the open
ports, to rent land or houses, and erect buildings. Korean merchants,
moreover, were permitted to trade at Peking, and Chinese merchants to
establish themselves at Yanghwajin and Seoul, but neither the Koreans
nor the Chinese were allowed to send merchandise into the interior of the
other country. Native products could only be brought from the interior
upon the issuance of a special certificate and the payment of all local taxes
and the *likin* tax, putting the Korean merchants at a disadvantage even
in comparison to their Western counterparts. Travel in the interior was
allowed under passport. Article 5 permitted Chinese and Koreans to trade
at Ch'aengmun and Ŭiju on the Yalu River and at Hun-ch'un and Hoeryŏng on the Tumen River, the duties to be 5 percent ad valorem on all
goods except red ginseng. The Korean government also was required to
subsidize a Chinese steamship that was to make trips between Korea and
China at a fixed date once every month. In sum, these Regulations were
made to fit the "fundamental structure" (*t'i-chih*) of relations between China and Korea. But soon, the other powers who had concluded treaties
with Korea began to challenge this agreement which granted the Chinese
privileges in Korea that they themselves did not enjoy. Li Hung-chang's
attempt to retain some of China's traditional authority in the modern

age proved to be a difficult task.[23]

With the conclusion of the Regulations, the Korean market was opened to Chinese traders. Many came to Seoul and Inch'ŏn to try their luck on the peninsula. Li Hung-chang soon became concerned about the growing Western competition that the Chinese traders were facing in Korea's treaty ports. He urged that a civilian commissioner be sent to Seoul. This official would also supervise commercial affairs at Inch'ŏn. Li's recommendation was supported by the Tsungli Yamen, and an edict of August 22, 1883, handed down the imperial approval. Li's nominee was Expectant Taotai Ch'en Shu-t'ang, who had been consul at San Francisco and was fluent in English and familiar with trade matters. Ch'en was to reside at Seoul and carry the title of high commissioner of trade (*tsung-pan Chao-hsien ko-k'ou shang-wu*). He was instructed to see to it that on every official occasion he would be seated in a place suited to the rank of the representative of the suzerain state. According to Chinese diplomatic regulation, his tenure was three years.[24]

Ch'en Shu-t'ang arrived at Seoul on October 16 and took office on the 20th. Four days later, he announced his arrival in a proclamation reportedly posted on one of the gates of the city. In this document Ch'en put special emphasis on Korea's dependent status. Since the Koreans had always been obedient subjects, the proclamation read, and the prohibitions on trade between the two countries had been abolished, "the Court of China has now granted special permission to Korea to engage in foreign trade, that she may reap the advantages thereof, and hold the profits to be gained by this commerce in her own hands." The haughty tone of this introduction was painful to the Koreans, and it laid the foundation for markedly cool relations between the Chinese commissioner and the representatives of the other foreign nations at Seoul.[25]

Difficulties arose from the fact that China deemed it improper to establish "diplomatic relations" with Korea, her vassal. This was clearly reflected in the ambiguous status of the Chinese high commissioner of trade. Although he was put in charge of the maritime trade between China and Korea, he gradually expanded his title and strove to give his position an importance it originally was not supposed to possess. This development presumably was due to two factors. The Koreans, Ch'en thought, felt a particular distaste for people dealing with trade, and slighted the Chinese by confronting him with low officials. Moreover, the foreign representatives, who considered Ch'en's position as equivalent to that of a consul general, accorded him only a second-rank status. Ch'en wanted to be treated on an equal footing with the ministers plenipotentiary. His desire for more power was fulfilled in the fall of 1884 when he received a new seal from Li Hung-chang. The inscription read: "Chief Commissioner of Diplomatic and Commercial Affairs for the Several Korean Ports" (*tsung-pan Chao-hsien ko-k'ou chiao-she t'ung-shang shih-wu*). The foreign envoys, who from the beginning took Korea's dependent status much less seriously than the Chinese wished, disliked Ch'en's transformation. In particular, the British minister in Peking, Sir Harry S. Parkes, was anxious to get a precise definition of Ch'en's position from the Tsungli Yamen. The commissioner of trade, the Yamen replied, was not directly appointed by the throne, and therefore Ch'en's status was not commensurate with the Chinese representatives appointed to reside in foreign countries. When Parkes asked for a written statement to this effect, the Yamen changed its stand slightly—presumably after consulting with Li Hung-chang—and answered that although the appointment was sanctioned by the throne, the commissioner's rank was equal to that of a consul general.[26]

Li Hung-chang was intent on tightening China's authority by imposing upon the Koreans the Trade Regulations rather than by strengthening the Chinese military presence in the peninsula. The Trade Regulations, however, contained all the contradictions that arose from China's insistence on upholding her suzerain status despite greatly changed circumstances. The document resembled a trade treaty, but it sharply emphasized the two countries' political inequalities. Ch'en, the man in charge of supervising the implementation of this document, was a minor official who presumed that because of the prestige of the country he represented he would be accorded a special position. But even in the age of "unequal treaties," the Trade Regulations proved to be too unequal to go unchallenged by the other treaty powers in Korea. China's exercise in "tributary diplomacy," therefore, was largely ineffective.

Japan and Korea after 1882: A Policy of Caution

For Japan, the 1882 incident was settled quickly by an agreement that even contained some moderate advantages. This document, however, could not hide the fact that Japan's position in Korea was severely shaken. China's physical presence in the peninsula well illustrated the fact that Korea's independence, which Japan had tried so hard to establish, was a fiction.

Foreign Minister Inoue Kaoru deplored that a great deal of what he and Hanabusa Yoshitada had accomplished over the years seemed to have been swept away almost overnight. Inoue was realistic enough not to get carried away by suggestions sent in from Europe by Itō Hirobumi that Japan should actively support Korea's independence and make the Korean king rescind earlier declarations of his country's dependency on China. In view of the Korean government's weakness, Inoue regarded such a policy too risky. Under no circumstances did he want to provoke a confrontation with China as the price for Korea's independence. Inoue's policy was limited to encouraging Korea to conclude further treaties with other nations. By so doing, he hoped Korea would eventually be recognized as an independent country.[27] On the other hand, Inoue expected that Japan would get what she wanted: the relaxation of China's grip on Korea. Japan did not want to take unilateral action. Instead, she sought to enlist Western cooperation. In the fall and winter of 1882, Inoue had his subordinates in Tokyo and Peking sound out the Western representatives about his plan for a joint international conference of England, France, Germany, Russia, the United States, and Japan. Inoue wanted the conferees to guarantee the independence or neutrality of Korea. The reaction to this initiative was lukewarm. Those who were approached were glad to defer an answer by following the tactics of the American minister in Peking, John Russell Young, who referred Japan to his government in Washington.[28]

While Inoue was taking stock of the West's willingness to lend a hand in a joint venture, the Korean mission of apology arrived in Tokyo on October 13, 1882. This gave Inoue a chance to put into practice his policy of cautious support for Korean independence. He received the Koreans, and, after Pak Yŏng-hyo submitted Korea's letter of apology, he smoothed the way for a quick transaction of official business. On October 26, Inoue graciously accepted Pak's request for a ten-year extension on the period within which Korea had to pay the indemnity of 500,000 yen. The details were settled the next day. The two parties exchanged the ratifications of the *Additional Convention* on October 31. Undoubtedly because of the foreign minister's active intercession, Pak was able to receive a loan of 170,000 yen from the Yokohama Specie Bank without proper credentials. The Japanese government guaranteed the loan on December 18. The next day, Pak sent Inoue 50,000 yen of this money in payment of the compensation Korea owed Japan according to article 3 of the *Treaty of Chemulp'o*. While Pak was in Japan, Inoue appointed a new Japanese minister to Seoul. His appointee was Takezoe Shinichirō, who was well versed in Chinese literature, and who had been Japanese consul at Tientsin. It is possible that Inoue replaced Hanabusa, who personified Japan's uncompromising open-Korea policy, because he was determined to pursue a low-profile policy in Korea in the wake of the 1882 incident. Takezoe was to implement this new policy that aimed simultaneously at relaxing Japanese-Korean relations and at avoiding a provocation of the Chinese.[29]

Pak Yŏng-hyo's presence in Japan also provided Inoue Kaoru with the opportunity to tackle the solution of the most intractable question still pending between Seoul and Tokyo: the problem of the customs tariff. Serious negotiations at Seoul in the summer of 1882 between Hanabusa and the Korean plenipotentiaries, Kim Po-hyŏn and Kim Hong-jip, had been interrupted by the disturbances before an agreement could be reached.[30] Inoue was unwilling to accept as high a tariff as that stipulated in the Korean-American treaty. He insisted on treatment equal to that accorded to the Chinese in the Trade Regulations. Although Inoue blamed the Korean government for the long delay of tariff negotiations, he was aware of the adverse effect the failure to come to an agreement would have on foreign opinion. Since Pak did not have the plenipotentiary powers to enter into tariff discussions, Inoue admonished him that the Korean government should take immediate steps to meet Japanese negotiators for "fair discussions." Although the Japanese government originally insisted on conducting the negotiations at Tokyo for fear of undue Chinese interference, the parleys were held at Seoul. The *Regulations under which Japanese Trade is to be Conducted in Korea* was finally signed by Takezoe Shinichirō and the head of the Korean Foreign Office, Min Yŏng-mok, at Seoul on July 25, 1883.[31]

Japan's attempt to establish Korea as a neutral buffer between herself and China and Russia failed. Because of the many political and economic problems that clouded the outlook on Korea, the Japanese government decided to resort to caution. It would seem that self-preservation was the major motive for doing so. The Japanese were neither willing nor prepared to entangle themselves militarily in the peninsula. China's strengthened presence in Korea was a serious challenge to Japan's Korea policy, but, because of the uncertainty about Russia's designs in the area, the Japanese leaders could not risk an open conflict with China. For the moment, they had to content themselves with a lowered profile in the peninsula. They concentrated on courting the Koreans by settling the remaining issues of the 1882 incident as smoothly as possible.

мммммммммммммммммммммммм

The 1882 incident started as a military mutiny by some dissatisfied soldiers and ended as a major international crisis. For the first time since the Hideyoshi invasions at the end of the sixteenth century, Chinese and Japanese troops faced each other again in the peninsula. China and Japan dispatched troops to emphasize their respective claims, but neither side wanted war. Although it was a bloodless confrontation, both sides knew that the potential for a major conflict was present and tried not to ignite the spark. Li Hung-chang attempted to bolster China's suzerain status by a commercial agreement that reflected his ambivalent attitude toward Korea: he was sympathetic to Korea's modernization efforts, which included the conclusion of treaties with Western powers, but he clung with authoritarian tenacity to China's special claims over the peninsula. The Japanese dismissed those claims as unrealistic, but recognized that the force with which they were defended was real. Short of war, the Japanese had no other alternative but to withdraw. It was a precautionary, tactical withdrawal. The Korean issue was far from solved.

CONSOLIDATION OF POSITIONS: KOREA AFTER THE OPENING

The events of the summer of 1882 had far-reaching international repercussions. They also affected Korea's internal affairs. The upheaval, which had such strong antigovernment overtones, was costly to the king's prestige and to the standing of the Min. It also badly disrupted Korea's fledgling self-strengthening program. In the fall of 1882, after peace and order were restored, a general search for revitalization began. The majority of the officialdom had not supported the Taewŏn'gun's attempt to isolate Korea from the modern world. Their question in the fall of 1882, then, was not whether to continue the modernization program, but in what direction and at what speed. Ideas and suggestions proliferated; they illustrate the vitality of Korea's modernization efforts. Out of the shattering experience of 1882 came a new and stronger commitment to strengthening the country with modern knowledge and modern technology. The Min took over the leadership, and the second phase of Korea's self-strengthening unmistakably carried the imprint of their political and economic ambitions. Under their aegis the first foreign advisers entered Korean service. The Min also presided over the conclusion of further treaties with Western powers and welcomed the first Western representatives who arrived at their posts after the treaties were signed. The period immediately following the 1882 incident was one in which the course of Korea's development into a modernized country would be determined.

"New Beginning"

An edict of August 31 announced the end of the 1882 upheaval, "the likes of which had never happened in a thousand years." King Kojong announced to "soldiers and citizens" the successful conclusion of the campaign against the insurgents and granted a general amnesty to calm the anxious and disturbed populace.[1] The events of the summer of 1882, however, were not easily relegated to the past by a stroke of the royal brush. On the contrary, the king himself took them as the starting point for a catharsis of unprecedented proportions. On September 2, the king again addressed the people. He accused himself of commiting a series of grave mistakes since ascending the throne and pleaded with the people to give him another chance to correct his past errors and find a new basis for future action. Promising to abrogate all government measures that had been harmful to the people in the past, the king then tried to enlist his subordinates' cooperation in a "new beginning" (*kaengsi*).[2]

With this call, the king appealed to the many people who felt that the events of 1882 were the result of a general moral, social, and economic decay. They had been longing for a fundamental revitalization, and their response to the royal solicitation of suggestions and opinions was overwhelming. By the end of the year, more than one hundred memorials had poured into Seoul. Eager memorialists suggested a wide spectrum of remedies, from Confucian-rooted postulates such as the rectification of names and the clarification of the people's social status to more practical demands such as the lessening of the poor people's tax burden, the eradication of nepotism and the use of the "right men" in government, and general economic frugality. The formula of "internal strengthening and expulsion of the foreigners" (*naesu oeyang*), the slogan that had been effective in mustering the people's resistance to foreign intrusion, still emerged here and there. But the presentation of more pracical measures, such as accelerating military preparedness and selecting competent officials, was much more prevelant.[3]

This emphasis on practicality was a remarkable trend away from Confucian orthodoxy toward a more realistic assessment of the problems Korea faced at that time. Some memorialists revealed that they had been absorbing Western knowledge and ideas that had penetrated the country.[4] A lecturer at the State Confucian Academy, Pak Ki-jong, proclaimed that while "Western teaching" (i.e., Christianity) should be rejected, Western technology could be useful for raising the people's living standard. The concept of "enriching the well-being of the people by taking advantage of the useful" (*iyong husaeng*)[5] became the new rallying call. It was echoed in many memorials. A Confucianist from Hongsan, Cho Sŏng-gyo, saw the usefulness of Western technology for the promotion of agriculture, weaving, and armament, and he thought that it should be taught for the benefit of the people. The rise of Korea's technological level, another Confucianist insisted, would break the peninsula's isolation and make her an equal partner of her neighbors. The government's most urgent task, therefore, would be the selection of capable and talented students to learn the secrets of modern technology and eventually build such useful things as steamships, cannons, and telegraph lines. This argument was also supported by Confucianist Chi Sŏg-yŏng who blamed the people's total ignorance of the outside world for the prevailing unrest. He offered a surprising plan: collect foreign books on international law and other specialized topics, collect Korean books on contemporary affairs authored by such people as Kim Ok-kyun and Pak Yŏng-hyo,[6] and install them in a specially built institute. The most far-reaching program for change was conceived by a Seoul Confucianist, Ko Yŏng-mun. He presented his ideas in seven points: (1) For the purpose of introducing Western technology, envoys should be sent abroad to familiarize themselves with modern trends and to invite foreign instructors. (2) A deliberative body consisting of specially selected men should be established. (3) Mining should be encouraged and the circulation of money stimulated. (4) A new police system should be introduced. (5) A chamber of commerce and a national bank should be founded. (6) A navy should be built. (7) The tax system should be restructured.[7]

This amazing proliferation of "enlightened" thought proved to be more than a by–product of the 1882 incident. A new way of thinking had been forming for quite some time. King Kojong's self-abasement helped it come to the fore. This thinking pivoted on the concept of revitalizing the nation by adopting modern skills and ideas. Some postulated that the country's moral basis should be preserved intact and that all that was needed was a change in technology. This was the stand the Min adopted: modernization was conceived and implemented in material terms, and modern technology could be grafted onto the body of traditional wisdom. During the years following the 1882 incident, the younger officials who came to form the enlightenment party (*kaehwadang*) saw modernization not only in terms of technological innovation but as a fundamental reform of society as a whole. These two approaches to modernization eventually led to conflict.

Second Phase of Self-Strengthening: The Consolidation of Min Hegemony

The 1882 incident had sharply interrupted Korea's self-strengthening program and had disrupted the ranks of those who had been the movement's principal sponsors. The Min and their collaborators had to bear the brunt of the popular wrath. With the deaths of Min Kyŏm-ho, one of the clan's most prominent members, and of Yi Ch'oe-ŭng and Kim Po-hyŏn, the generation which had laid the foundation of the Min's rise in government nearly disappeared. The only survivor of that generation was Min T'ae-ho. Min prestige and power henceforth depended upon his position and that of his son, Min Yŏng-ik. Min T'ae-ho continued to further consolidate his power within the government during the second phase of self-strengthening.

After the restoration of royal rule on August 30, first priority was accorded to institutional reorganization. The T'ongnigimu Amun, which had been abolished by the Taewŏn'gun, was not restored. A royal edict of September 7 declared that because governmental affairs were numerous, a new deliberative body had to be created. The result of this order was the establishment of the Kimuch'ŏ, Office for the Control of State Affairs, within the precincts of the royal palace. This office had a deliberative function, and its members convened every day. Depending on the nature of the matter under discussion, they then had to meet with the chief state councillor to prepare a recommendation for decision. The appointees of this office were all trusted men: the minister of the Department of War, Cho Yŏng-ha, the minister of the Department of Revenue, Kim Pyŏng-si, and Kim Hong-jip, Kim Yun-sik, Hong Yŏng-sik, Ŏ Yun-jung, and Sin Ki-sŏn.[8]

The Kimuch'ŏ soon proved to be too small to handle the increasingly complex matters of state. The need for a more comprehensive government body that would deal with international and commerical affairs became obvious. One memorialist demanded the reestablishment of the T'ongni-gimu Amun because, he argued, all Western countries had such an office to observe the political behavior of other countries and to regulate important trade matters. Responding to the exigencies of the time, King Kojong ordered by an edict of December 26, 1882, the establishment of a new office, called T'ongni Amun, for the management of foreign affairs. On January 12, 1883, it was renamed T'ongni kyosŏp-t'ongsangsamu Amun, Office for the Management of Diplomatic and Commercial Matters—in short, the Foreign Office.

The Foreign Office was subdivided into four departments:(1) Department of Diplomatic Affairs (Changgyosa);(2) Department of Revenue and Port Administration (Chŏnggaksa);(3) Department for the Promotion and Exploitation of National Resources (Pugyosa); (4) Department of Communications (Ujŏngsa). Its officials were classed into four levels of appointments: one president (*p'alli samu;* after January 12 *tokp'an samu*), four vice-presidents (*hyŏpp'an samu*), four councillors (*ch'amŭi samu*), and a number of secretaries (*chusa*). The first president was Cho Yŏng-ha who was replaced on February 19, 1883, by Min Yŏng-mok (who was last governor of Kyŏngsang). Kim Hong-jip, Min Yŏng-ik, and Hong Yŏng-sik (since February 19, 1883) occupied second level positions. Serving as councillors were Kim Ok-kyun, Yi Cho-yŏn, Pyŏn Wŏn-gyu, Cho Pyŏng-p'il, and Kim Man-sik. The office was assisted from the very beginning by two foreign advisers: Paul Georg von Moellendorff, who first held the position of councillor and in January 1883 was promoted to vice-president, and Ma Chien-ch'ang. Including a number of secretaries, the Foreign Office was staffed by twenty-five persons at the end of 1883 (twenty in August 1884). In the spring of 1884, Kim Pyŏng-si moved from the Home Office to the Foreign Office and became its third president on April 8. With him went Yun T'ae-jun and Kim Yun-sik, who were appointed vice-presidents. On January 22, 1885, Kim Yun-sik became president after this post had been held for short periods by Kim Hong-jip and Cho Pyŏng-ho.[9]

One day after the establishment of the Foreign Office, on December 27, 1882, the king declared that internal matters should also be considered. He ordered the Council of State to arrange for the creation of a separate office that would deal exclusively with internal affairs. The official deliberations on the subject reveal that the model for this clear distinction between internal and external affairs was no longer provided by China, but by Western countries. The king as well as the chief state councillor, Hong Sun-mok, and the left state councillor, Kim Pyŏng-guk, considered the creation of these two offices a clear demonstration of the government's will to restore stability and peace to the badly shaken country.[10]

Originally called T'ongninaemu Amun, Office for the Management of Internal Affairs, on January 12 the new office was renamed T'ongni kun'guksamu Amun, Office for the Management of Military and National Affairs, commonly known as the Home Office. It was housed within the palace precincts, and the old Kimuch'ŏ and the Military Council (Samgunbu) were incorporated into the new office at the end of January.

The manifold tasks which the Home Office had to perform were assigned to seven specialized departments.[11] The hierarchy of its official posts was equivalent to that of its counterpart, although at its very top there were two, later three, overseers (*ch'ongni samu*). Hong Sun-mok and Kim Pyŏng-guk were (presumably ex officio) the first occupants of these positions, joined on April 23, 1883, by the right state councillor, Kim Pyŏng-dŏk. The real power of the Home Office lay in the hands of its four, later five, presidents (*p'alli samu*; after January 12, 1883, *tokp'an samu*) each of whom was in charge of one or two of the departments. Serving as presidents were Min T'ae-ho, Yun Cha-dŏk, Kim Yu-yŏn, Kim Pyŏng-si, Cho Yŏng-ha (transferred from the Foreign Office on February 20, 1883), and Chŏng Pŏm-jo (appointed on February 24, 1883). The second level positions of vice-president (*hyŏpp'an samu*) were held by such officials as Kim Yun-sik (who later moved to the Foreign Office), Pak Chŏng-yang, Cho Chun-yŏng, Min Chong-muk (all three had been members of the gentlemen's inspection tour to Japan in 1881), Han Kyu-jik, and Min Yŏng-ik. The councillors (*ch'amŭi samu*) were recruited from among equally well-known men: Hong Yŏng-sik (a short time later in the Foreign Office), Ŏ Yun-jung (later vice-president), Sin Ki-sŏn, Yun T'ae-jun (later vice-president), Yi Chung-ch'il, and Min Ŭng-sik. A Chinese adviser, Wang Hsi-ch'ang, acted in this office in the capacity of councillor. The complete staff of the Home Office, including a number of secretaries (*chusa*), consisted in December 1883 of thirty-three persons (twenty-nine in August 1884).[12]

An analysis of the personnel structure of the two new offices makes it clear that despite the temporary setback in 1882, the Min and their partisans were again on the advance. During 1881 and 1882, it is difficult to determine the exact extent of their influence, but there can be no doubt that from the end of 1882 they were in control of the nerve centers of the government. Although the Foreign Office and the Home Office were remarkable innovations in tune with the exigencies of the time, they provided the Min with platforms from which they could conveniently manipulate government power to their own advantage. Moreover, the Min could concentrate their faithful collaborators effectively at strategic points of power. The man who emerged as the new symbol of Min ambition and authority was Min T'ae-ho. He successfully assumed the leadership and turned the Home Office into his personal power base. It is not surprising that there was a definite shift of power from the Council of State to the Home Office. The weakening of the Council of State is shown by the fact that the post of chief state councillor was left vacant from July 1883, when Hong Sun-mok retired, until June 1884, when Kim Pyŏng-guk succeeded to the post which had become the highest in name only. Despite the fact that most government business was transferred to one or the other of the new offices, no attempt was made to discard the traditional government organization. All officials in the Foreign Office and the Home Office concurrently held traditional posts. Significantly, tenure in the new offices was not subject to the frequent personnel changes which paralyzed the functioning of the traditional government apparatus. It is evident that the new offices, which were grafted onto the old government body, were the instruments through which the Min chose to consolidate their domination. Moreover, the Min made use of people who had special expertise and had seen the outside world. Some of the younger officials of the Foreign Office and the Home Office had gone to Japan as members of the gentlemen's inspection tour. The principal exponents of what later became known as the enlightenment party (*kaehwadang*), Hong Yŏng-sik, Kim Ok-kyun, and Pak Yŏng-hyo (who was appointed commissioner of Seoul on February 6, 1883, upon his return from Japan) initially held posts in the new government structure the Min were building. They hoped they would be able to realize their reform ideas with the backing of Min power.[13]

The Min did not stop at just putting their men in key positions in the new government offices. They underpinned their influence with a number of projects that further assured their control over Korea's modernization program. Foremost was their effort to find a solution for the government's chronic financial plight. The new offices, in particular, drained the government's economic strength. The most effective way to alleviate the dearth in its coffers, the government decided, was to fall back on a method that had proved useful many times before: the minting of money. On January 22, 1883, Min T'ae-ho was put in charge of minting operations (*chujŏn tangsang*), and on March 1 he was instructed to supervise the establishment of some temporary mints for producing copper coins. Barely four weeks later, on March 26, the chief state councillor, Hong Sun-mok, recommended the minting of higher denomination coins and named them *tangojŏn*, "equivalent to five copper coins." The minting was done at three different places[14] under Min T'ae-ho's general supervision. The *tangojŏn* was soon beset by an age-old problem: the copper content of the new coin fluctuated because of the erratic supply of raw materials. The circulation of money that had a face value greater than its intrinsic value was profitable for the government, but it encouraged counterfeiting. The worsening monetary situation and the urgent need for more cash led to the decision on August 7, 1883, to centralize minting operations in Seoul and to found a permanent mint. Called Chŏnhwan'guk, the new mint was closely tied to the Home Office through Min T'ae-ho, who took general control and staffed it with his followers. The establishment of the Chŏnhwan'guk signified an innovation insofar as it was Korea's first permanent mint, but modern minting techniques were not employed until later.[15] The mint continued to issue large amounts of *tangojŏn* which helped finance the Min's other ventures.[16]

Another important new installation was the Kigiguk, Machine Hall, which was established on June 15, 1883, to house the machinery purchased by Cho Yŏng-ha and Kim Yun-sik at Tientsin in the late fall of 1882 and the steam engine bought by von Moellendorff at Shanghai in the early spring of 1883. The new workshop was designed for repairing and manufacturing military equipment. At the same time, it was planned as a training center for Koreans. It was staffed by a number of students who had received training at Tientsin and by four especially hired Chinese artisans. The overall direction of the Machine Hall was given to Kim Yun-sik, Yun T'ae-jun, Pak Chŏng-yang, and Yi Cho-yŏn. Pyŏn Wŏn-gyu and Han Kyu-jik joined the staff in February and April, 1884, respectively. In November of the same year Min Yŏng-ik became one of the principal officials of the Machine Hall.[17]

The keystone of Min power was undoubtedly the new Chinese-trained army units. The events of the summer of 1882 left the Korean army disorganized and leaderless. In the late fall a request was sent to General Wu Ch'ang-ch'ing to provide instructors. Upon Wu's recommendation, his secretary, Yüan Shih-k'ai, who had won medals and fame for his successful campaign against the rebels of 1882, became the new chief instructor of the Korean army on November 3. For the new units (*sin'gŏn ch'in'gun*), Yüan personally selected one thousand able-bodied soldiers and divided them into the left and right barracks. Chinese officers were put in charge as instructors, and Yi Cho-yŏn and Yun T'ae-jun were appointed as commanders (*kamdok*) of the left and right barracks, respectively. The new units were clad in uniforms that apparently combined Chinese as well as Western elements and were equipped with arms sent from the Tientsin Arsenal through Li Hung-chang.[18]

In November 1883, the new army was augmented by a new training unit, the front barracks (*chŏnyŏng*), under the command of Han Kyu-jik.[19] After the withdrawal of half of the Chinese forces in May 1884, rear barracks (*huyŏng*) were added. By mid-September, Korea's modern army consisted of 2,000 men who were organized into four units and commanded by four staunch Min supporters assisted by Chinese personnel. Han Kyu-jik commanded the front barracks, Yi Cho-yŏn the left barracks, Min Yŏng-ik the right barracks, and Yun T'ae-jun the rear barracks. A month later, an edict decreed that the four commanders (renamed *yŏngsa*) were to hold concurrent military appointments in the Home Office.[20]

The Min made full use of the Chinese military potential in Korea. Using essentially the same tactics they had used earlier, they tied the military organization closely to the Home Office through concurrent appointments.[21] Moreover, they undertook extraordinary efforts to provide enough funds to support the new force. In December 1883, a special planning office (Chuhyangguk) was established to coordinate military provisions. Large sums of the recently minted *tangojŏn* were spent on the new units, and in the spring of 1884 the ban on mining was partially lifted to permit the exploitation of mines as an additional source of military support.[22]

The relationship between the Min and the Chinese army was, however, more than a one-sided reliance of the Min on the military. Wu Ch'ang-ch'ing, whose troops were divided into five camps stationed inside and and just outside Seoul and at Suwŏn, had a firm grip on the capital[23] and made his voice heard in a wide range of matters outside the military sphere. Wu had urged the establishment of the Foreign Office, while emphasizing the necessity of counterbalancing foreign relations by giving special consideration to internal affairs. He seems to have been also instrumental in the decision to mint the *tangojŏn*. Wu was a frequent guest in the royal palace, and the king honored him by visiting the drill grounds.[24] The Chinese military became very influential in Korea's political life. It effectively used the Min's dependence on Chinese support to pursue its own goal of keeping Korea under firm control.

The second phase of Korea's self-strengthening differed from the first phase in several crucial respects. In the second, the Min assumed the leadership and shaped the program according to their own designs. It was a much broader and a much more successful program. Ideologically, this second phase was based on a wide consensus within the officialdom that the country's chronic ills could only be cured by introducing Western technology. Economically, the Min made great efforts to support the program with measures that were independent of the traditional sources of state revenue. Furthermore, by establishing specialized institutions such as the Machine Hall and the Mint, the Min could employ trained workers. As a result, self-strengthening under the Min was more advanced and better organized.

The second phase of self-strengthening also had political implications. During the first phase, the king had been the initiator and leader. After 1882 he seems to have lost at least part of this role to the Min. It is possible that King Kojong was aware of and feared the Min's advance through the T'ongnigimu Amun and therefore tried, in the fall of 1882, to get the country's affairs under tighter control by establishing the Kimuch'ŏ within the palace precincts. The king, however, eventually had to give in to the demands for the erection of a foreign office and a home office. Through the growth of the Min's power, the king's position and authority were undoubtedly weakened. The Min, in turn, were gradually less dependent on the king's backing because they interlocked their interests with the Chinese military. Royal authority was once more threatened by the advance of a royal in-law clan.

Foreign Advisers in Korean Service: Paul Georg von Moellendorff

Korea's relations with the outside world expanded, and the need for people trained in the conduct of foreign affairs became obvious. Ma Chien-chung played the role of intermediary in the spring and summer of 1882 when Korea concluded its first treaties with Western powers under Chinese tutelage. Ma's assignment was only temporary, however, and Kim Yun-sik, who was still at Tientsin in June 1882, raised the problem in his conversation with a Chinese official: "We urgently need someone who is thoroughly familiar with international relations, Western languages, and commercial affairs." At first he indignantly rejected the suggestion that Korea should hire a Westerner, but he gradually resigned himself to the idea.[25]

The Korean request for an adviser on foreign affairs was officially transmitted to Li Hung-chang by Cho Yŏng-ha in mid-September. It was repeated in a royal letter that Cho was again ordered to take to Tientsin two months later. In this letter the king expressed his anxiety that in view of the rapidly approaching dates for the ratifications of the treaties "the diplomatic and commercial matters are still in confusion." Li Hung-chang strongly recommended Paul Georg von Moellendorff, "a good-natured and sincere man," to fill the position of adviser. He praised the German's expertise in diplomatic affairs and fluency in foreign languages. Li, however, felt that he should give von Moellendorff the assistance of Chinese officials who would go to Korea with him. Li Hung-chang intended to secure for China a permanent voice in Korean affairs by placing his own men in key positions within the Korean government. He ordered Ma Chien-chung's older brother, Ma Chien-ch'ang, and Wang Hsi-ch'ang to go to Korea. Ma Chien-ch'ang was appointed vice-president of the Foreign Office and adviser to the Council of State (*Ŭijŏngbu ch'amŭi*) on February 2, 1883. These civil appointments were rendered ineffective, however, by China's ambiguous attitude concerning Korea's political status. Even Li Hung-chang had second thoughts about the appointment of a Chinese official (Ma was an expectant taotai) to a concurrent Korean post. For this reason, Ma presented his resignation on May 10 and presumably left Korea shortly afterward.[26]

Paul Georg von Moellendorff was the first European to occupy a high position in the Korean government. His appointment came at a very crucial juncture in Korea's history; it was also the climax of his career. Von Moellendorff was born on February 17, 1847, into a noble family living in Zedenik, a small town in the Prussian province of Brandenburg. In 1865 he began the study of jurisprudence, philology, and Oriental languages at the University of Halle a.d.S. Four years later, in 1869, he was called to Berlin because Robert Hart was recruiting young Germans for the Chinese Maritime Customs. Von Moellendorff followed this call rather reluctantly since he was preparing himself for a diplomatic career. However, he left for Shanghai on September 1 of the same year and entered the Imperial Maritime Customs Service there on October 27. His career in China was somewhat erratic. He held several minor posts in the Customs Service, became frustrated because the prospect of advancement was dim, and finally decided to quit Hart's services on June 30, 1874. By that time he had become proficient in the Chinese language, which he reportedly was studying intensively. In the fall of 1874 he received an appointment as interpreter in the German consular service and was sent to Canton. One year later he was called back to Peking. Then he was sent to Shanghai and after a prolonged stay was appointed vice-consul with Germany's consular

affairs at Tientsin in September 1879. It was during his tenure at Tientsin
that he came into contact with Li Hung-chang. Disappointed that he had
not advanced to the post of consul, he left German service in the spring of
1882. He apparently had been approached several times by the Chinese to
accept a Chinese appointment. In the summer of 1882 he became a member of Li Hung-chang's staff and was primarily occupied with secretarial
work involving foreign languages. He reportedly enjoyed the viceroy's full
confidence and was on friendly terms with people like Chou Fu and Ma
Chien-chung. Li Hung-chang chose von Moellendorff because of the qualifications the German had acquired through his work in the customs and
consular services. A brief remark to Kim Yun-sik reveals that the viceroy
had still another motive in mind. The Japanese, he said, stand in great
awe of the Germans and dread von Moellendorff; von Moellendorff would
be able to contain them.[27]

Von Moellendorff's contract was signed for the Korean government
by Cho Yŏng-ha at Tientsin on November 18, 1882. It contained six stipulations: (1) Von Moellendorff was to assist the diplomatic negotiations
between Korea and foreign countries in an advisory function with absolute
sincerity according to the practices observed by other countries. (2) He was
to draw upon his experiences during his service in the Chinese Maritime
Customs to establish a Korean maritime customs office. (3) Von Moellendorff was to use Korean assistants in the maritime customs administration. In exceptional cases, he could hire foreigners for limited terms with the
approval of the Korean government. During these periods, the foreigners
were to teach the Koreans so that they could take over later. Matters such
as salaries were to be determined by the Korean government for foreigners
and Koreans alike; von Moellendorff was not to act at his own discretion.
If the general expenditures could not be covered by the customs revenue,
they were to be supplemented from other sources. (4) The Korean government was to receive von Moellendorff with the utmost courtesy. His salary
was to be fixed at 300 taels a month. Incidentals such as rent and travel
allowance were to be covered separately as long as there was no fixed
estimate of expenditures. (5) In case von Moellendorff did not observe the
above rules, the Korean government could dismiss him at any time. Either
side could terminate this contract upon three months' notice. (6) This
contract was to be signed by Cho Yŏng-ha and von Moellendorff, and one
copy was to be sent to Li Hung-chang and another to the Korean king for
ratification.[28]

Von Moellendorff's nomination was not received everywhere with enthusiasm. The German minister in Peking, Max von Brandt, who was von Moellendorff's former boss, did not approve of his going over to Korean service. Sir Robert Hart reportedly felt unhappy that he was not allowed to send his own people to Korea to establish the customs service. Although the British representative at Peking, T.G. Grosvenor, credited von Mollendorff with the best intentions, he nevertheless commented critically: "I cannot but think that his somewhat spasmodic changes of career since he has been in China, and his relations to His Excellency Li, do not offer the guarantee requisite for so delicate an operation as the establishment of a Foreign Customs Service in a new country." Von Moellendorff's enthusiasm for his new job did not seem to be dimmed by these critical voices. A few days prior to the conclusion of his contract, he exulted in his diary that he was going to receive "one of the finest and most influential positions in the Far East, better paid than any ambassador and more powerful than any East Asian minister of state." He also did not hesitate to announce his ideas about the innovations he would introduce into Korea, which ranged from the reorganization of the Korean army to the opening of mines for coal and ores.[29]

After having been lavishly entertained by Li Hung-chang, the Koreans and von Moellendorff left Tientsin on December 4. It was a colorful group, reflecting the great changes Korea was experiencing. Besides Cho Yŏng-ha's official party there were Kim Yun-sik, von Moellendorff and Ma Chien-ch'ang, Ch'en Shu-t'ang (who was to study Korea's commercial possibilities) and the head of the China Merchants' Steam Navigation Company, T'ang T'ing-shu (Tong King-sing), the English engineer G.A. Butler (who had been working in the K'ai-p'ing mines), and two Chinese students who had recently returned from the United States, T'ang Shao-i and Wu Chung-hsien. On December 8, the Chinese ship approached the Korean coast, but because of a rough sea the passengers could not disembark until December 12. Carried in a sedan chair, von Moellendorff caused a sensation among the many curious villagers who lined the road to the capital. When he entered Seoul he was on horseback, and an immense throng of people awaited him to see the first European officially welcomed to Korea.[30]

Cho Yŏng-ha reported von Moellendorff's arrival in Korea directly to the king on December 14 and submitted the contract he had concluded with the German.[31] The king was pleased and received von Moellendorff in audience on December 26. On the same day, von Moellendorff was given the position of councillor in the newly established Foreign Office. In mid-

January he was promoted to vice-president of the Department of Revenue and Port Administration (Chŏnggaksa). The king presented to von Moellendorff Min Kyŏm-ho's mansion in Paktong which had stood empty since the violent death of its former owner. The German soon immersed himself in Korean life. With his beard trimmed in the Korean style and wearing the official costume of a nobleman of the second rank, he was scarcely recognizable as a foreigner. He became known as *Mok ch'amp'an*, "Moellendorff Vice-president."[32]

As his contract stipulated, von Moellendorff's principle duties were connected with the Foreign Office. As an adviser, he collaborated closely with Cho Yŏng-ha and subsequently with Min Yŏng-mok and was present at all diplomatic and commercial negotiations. In the summer of 1883 he apparently was instrumental in concluding the tariff negotiations with Japan. He knew the Japanese minister, Takezoe Shinichirō, from his days at Tientsin. In the fall of the same year, von Moellendorff actively took part in the renegotiations of the British and German treaties and the Trade Regulations and was present when the ratifications were exchanged in the spring of 1884. He apparently was not an easy negotiating partner. Reportedly, he was a "headstrong and opinionated man" and, intent on doing things his own way, conducted business with an iron hand. He was critical toward the other foreign diplomats and traders. He did not lack an imaginative approach to his tasks, but apparently he often failed to follow a consistent policy. Exclaimed an exasperated client: "There is no system at the Foreign Office and everything is done by fits and starts." Nevertheless, von Moellendorff savored his work. He enjoyed King Kojong's confidence and was intimate with Min Yŏng-mok and Min Yŏng-ik.[33] His two brief appointments to concurrent posts in the traditional hierarchy as vice-minister of the Department of Works (April 24 to June 13, 1884) and as vice-minister of the Department of War (December 15, 1884, to February 6, 1885) seem to have been special signs of royal favor.[34]

Besides his duties in the Foreign Office, von Moellendorff held a host of other responsibilities. His role as the head of the Maritime Customs Service will be discussed in the next chapter. On March 14, 1884, he was called upon to serve as the chief of the new mint, Chŏnhwan'guk. He tried to realize far-flung modernization plans by bringing two German minting experts and a technician to Korea and importing modern minting machinery through the German firm of Heinrich Constantin Edward Meyer & Co. He ambitiously designed fourteen new coins, none of which was minted during his tenure. He supported the Min's decision to mint large amounts of *tangojŏn*[35] and invited a German geologist to explore the mineral resources of the country.[36] He was also active in the Machine Hall (Kigiguk) for which he bought a steam engine in Shanghai,[37] and he is credited with installing the first steam-operated electric generator in Korea.[38]

Driven by his determination to accelerate Korea's entry into the modern age, von Moellendorff also ventured into the field of education. He helped establish the government language school (Tongmunhak) which was attached to the Foreign Office in September 1883 and placed under the supervision of Kim Yun-sik's elder cousin, Kim Man-sik. The school's first teachers of English were the two Chinese, T'ang Shao-i and Wu Chung-hsien, who had come to Korea with von Moellendorff. Shortly later, von Moellendorff employed a British telegrapher and sailor, Thomas E. Hallifax, as an instructor in English.[39] It was also on von Moellendorff's initiative that a German, A.H. Maertens, was called to Korea in the fall of 1884 to promote modern methods of sericulture. Half a year later, while in Japan, von Moellendorff persuaded another countryman, Helm, to buy equipment with which to introduce modern agricultural techniques into Korea.[40] Von Moellendorff's partiality to Germans brought him much foreign criticism.[41]

Von Moellendorff ventured into activities that went beyond the vaguely worded assignments of his contract. Through his position in the Foreign Office he also influenced Korean diplomacy. Exposed to international intrigue and pressure, von Moellendorff developed his own ideas about Korea's diplomatic future. He doubted that China would be strong enough to keep Japan in check and therefore only Russia, he thought, would be an effective counterbalance. America was too weak militarily to play such a role, and England was siding with Japan against Russia. It was for this reason that von Moellendorff strongly favored the conclusion of the treaty with Russia in the summer of 1884. This treaty, he was convinced, would secure for Korea a certain degree of independence from Japan as well as from China. His venture into power politics, however, cost him dearly. He was severely attacked by the Chinese representative, Ch'en Shu-t'ang, and, undoubtedly because of Chinese pressure, temporarily suspended from his post in the Foreign Office on July 8. Summoned to Tientsin by an angry Li Hung-chang, he left Korea with Karl Waeber, the Russian representative who had signed the Korean-Russian Treaty, on July 13. According to a newspaper report, von Moellendorff went to China "in order to avoid the heat in Seoul," where he found the atmosphere in the viceroy's yamen even hotter. He managed, however, to placate Li's anger and was back in Korea on August 23.[42]

Von Moellendorff was not reappointed to the Foreign Office upon his return, but he continued to serve in his other duties. More than ever before, he stood in the Chinese-Japanese cross fire, although he apparently still enjoyed royal favor. After the crisis of December 1884, he was suddenly called back to the Foreign Office and propelled into the role of mediator between Korea, Japan, and China. In his effort to establish Russia as a third power in the peninsula, von Moellendorff used his new assignment to conduct unauthorized negotiations for hiring Russian army instructors. When this secret diplomacy came to light in the summer of 1885, he was swept out of office by a general storm of disgust which was shared by the Chinese, the Japanese, the British, and the Americans alike. Von Moellendorff was dismissed from the Foreign Office on July 27. On September 4 he had to quit the Maritime Customs and on October 17 the Mint. An American contemporary summed up von Moellendorff's role in Korea with the angry and somewhat overstated words: "The conduct of this man would seem to be without a parallel in history!"[43]

There is no doubt that von Moellendorff left his imprint on Korea. His role as an imaginative innovator, however, was overshadowed by his manipulations in power politics. His approach to Korea's modernization was enthusiastic, but too diverse to be effective. He was guided by visions rather than by a cool assessment of reality. He also acted too independently. Although he enjoyed the Min's backing, he was not popular with the general officialdom. His attitude toward the enlightenment party was hostile.

The Arrival of the First Americans in Korea

For the Western countries that had concluded treaties with Korea, the relationship between China and Korea remained a perplexing problem. No formula could be found to bridge the contradiction between recognizing Korea as a quasi-dependent country and treating her at the same time as an equal. This was a diplomatic anomaly without precedent. The Trade Regulations between China and Korea, which the Westerners believed were forced upon Korea by Li Hung-chang, provided no clarification. On the contrary, they deepened Western uncertainty toward Korea. While this document was considered a tactical move against Japan,

China's demand for special diplomatic and commercial privileges left the Westerners aghast and raised a number of puzzling questions. What, for example, would be the status of the president of the United States vis-à-vis the Korean king if the latter were put on the same footing with the governor-general of Chihli? What would be the official relationship between the diplomatic and consular representatives of Western nations in Korea and the Chinese commercial agents appointed by the superintendent of trade for Northern Ports? These problems seemed to defy solution and made the Western powers apprehensive about formulating new Korea policies. The possibility of colliding with other interests was unusually high. Also, the commercial prospects of the peninsula were uncertain and not worth the risk of a diplomatic embroilment with either China or Japan.[44]

Not everyone welcomed the American-Korean treaty. The Japanese were alarmed at the high tariffs the Americans had granted Korea. Their concern was shared by the British and the Germans. When Lucius H. Foote was appointed the first envoy extraordinary and minister plenipotentiary of the United States to Korea, however, the news was interpreted in Tokyo as a sure sign that the United States recognized Korea's independence from China. Li Hung-chang was relieved when he was informed of Foote's arrival in Seoul. He viewed the American action as a manifestation of American sincerity and friendship. It seemed to disprove rumors, presumably fabricated by the British, about the US Senate's refusal to ratify the treaty.[45]

Lucius H. Foote arrived at Chemulp'o aboard the USS *Monocacy* on the evening of May 13, 1883, after a brief stopover in Japan. He was received by the local Korean officials. On the 17th he and his suite, consisting of his secretary, Charles S. Scudder, some interpreters (among them Yun Ch'i-ho), Captain Cotton, and eight officers of the *Monocacy*, left the port and reached the capital after a ten-hour trip. "Thousands were congregated upon the hillsides to watch our approach," Foote wrote. He and the captain were lodged in von Moellendorff's house. On May 19, he exchanged the ratifications with the president of the Foreign Office, Min Yŏng-mok, and was received in audience by the king on the following day.[46]

Foote was given great freedom in his new assignment since the general situation at Seoul had first to be explored. Only a few broad principles were laid down. Foote had to make it clear that "as far as we [the Americans] are concerned, Corea is an independent sovereign power with all the attendant rights, privileges, duties and responsibilities." The United

States, therefore, would not interfere in Korea's relationship with China unless it was detrimental to American interests. Although American trade with Korea was as yet nonexistent, Foote was advised to pay special attention to those points in the Chinese-Korean trade regulations that were discriminatory against non-Chinese traders, but he was to take no active steps in the matter because the provisions of the most-favored-nation clause would eventually secure the same benefits.[47]

Foote's relationship to the Korean government, and especially to the king, were cordial and confidential. His advice on diplomatic and administrative matters was eagerly solicited. In this function, he inevitably came into conflict with von Moellendorff, who was jealous of the royal confidence Foote enjoyed and suspicious of American designs. Foote's position was extremely delicate and exacting. He witnessed the growing struggle between China and Japan on both the Korean and international scenes. Because he had no firm American policy backing, he found himself powerless to exert any significant influence, and he could not effectively support Korea in her endeavors to seek an alternate source of help outside the orbit of her neighbors. From October 1883 onward, the king frequently asked Foote for an American adviser on foreign affairs and for instructors for the Korean army. To the king's disappointment and Foote's embarrassment, action on this request was repeatedly delayed and Shufeldt, who had originally promised to take the post of adviser, declined to do so after all.[48]

Foote received some reinforcement in June 1884 in the person of George C. Foulk, Ensign, USN, who was appointed naval attaché to Seoul at the request of Min Yŏng-ik. Foulk accompanied the first Korean mission in the United States back to Korea. Linguistically very talented, he learned Korean during this trip and thus became an invaluable aide to Foote. But Foote was soon to face the hardest blow to his career when the Diplomatic and Consular Act of July 7, 1884, reduced his post to the rank of minister resident and consul general. Unwilling to bear the implications of this loss of rank in his relationship to the Korean government, Foote tendered his resignation. It was granted on February 4, 1885. He left Foulk in charge of the legation, the business of which the American government was unwilling to transfer to Peking as suggested by the Chinese. Foulk inherited Foote's position of confidential adviser to the king, but he was powerless in view of the increasingly complex tangle of events. He was also unable to secure the appointment of American military instructors. On February 18, 1886, Foulk asked to be relieved from his post after having carried on his work under the most difficult circumstances.[49]

Foulk's aim had been to strengthen Korea's independence through Western assistance. Neither he nor Foote was successful in contributing much toward the fulfillment of this goal. Both were close to the king, but they seem not to have had more than a working relationship with the Min. Not backed by any real interest on the part of their own government and largely ignored by the Min, they were unable to realize an American alternative in the peninsula. In the first phase of its relations with the distant kingdom, the United States exerted no significant influence. It contributed little toward strengthening Korea's independence.

Korea's Treaties with England and Germany: The Second Phase

The British-Korean treaty that Vice-admiral George O. Willes concluded in May 1882 was heavily criticized as soon as it was publicized. Its most fervent opponent was the British minister in Tokyo, Harry S. Parkes. He considered the document anachronistic, he pictured Willes' helplessness in Ma Chien-chung's hands, and he regretted "that Li Hung-chang should have been allowed such a good opportunity for promoting his particular policy." His alarm at the possible ill effects this treaty might have on both China and Japan was shared by T. G. Grosvenor in Peking. British mercantile communities in China and Japan raised loud protests. They feared that Willes' treaty set a bad precedent both diplomatically and commercially and would cripple British trade with Korea from the outset.[50] British apprehensions were deepened by the violent outbreak in July 1882, and news about the conclusion of the Trade Regulations between China and Korea, which reached Tokyo in mid-December, further stiffened Parkes' resistance to accepting terms less favorable than those between China and Korea. He had several opportunities to impart his views directly to Pak Yŏng-hyo and Kim Ok-kyun, who were on an official mission to Japan in the fall of 1882. The Koreans were eager to represent Korea as an independent country and took great pains to point out to Parkes that the Trade Regulations were forced upon Korea by China. They repeatedly expressed their hope that Great Britain would ratify the treaty soon. Although Parkes was not unsympathetic to Korea's precarious position, as described by her envoys, he recommended to London a policy of caution and circumspection.[51]

Perhaps persuaded by the Koreans' repeated, even if unofficial, assurance that changes in the treaty might be arranged between the two governments, Parkes decided to send William George Aston, the British consul at Nagasaki and a long-time Far Eastern expert, on an unofficial mission to Seoul in March 1883. He was to explore "the state of affairs in Corea" and to probe the Korean government's attitude toward the ratification of the British-Korean treaty. Aston, who was accompanied by Kim Ok-kyun, visited the Foreign Office on March 30 and found the Koreans reluctant to make concessions in respect to the high tariffs, although their professed desire to enter into treaty relationship with the British was unabated.[52] In the meantime, Parkes received word from London, dated April 22, that the British government had decided, in agreement with the German government, to seek a postponement of the ratifications of their respective treaties with Korea for six months on the grounds that further consideration was required in respect to certain provisions. Aston returned to Tokyo, but Parkes sent him back to Seoul on May 15 to sign declarations for the British and German governments that postponed the ratification of both treaties until December 31, 1883.[53]

Parkes lost no time in drafting, with Aston's assistance, a completely revised version of the British-Korean treaty. Transferred to Peking at the end of August, Parkes was instructed to reopen negotiations at Seoul in October without giving notice to the Chinese government. On his way to Shanghai to board the ship to Korea, he briefly met Li Hung-chang at Tientsin. The viceroy was angry at British audacity in bypassing him and sent a communication to the Korean government warning that only changes in the commercial arrangements would be tolerated by Peking. After sending Aston ahead for preparatory negotiations, Parkes arrived at Chemulp'o on October 26 and met the German plenipotentiary, Eduard Zappe, who had come over from Yokohama. Together they prepared the final treaty draft which they handed to the Foreign Office on November 3. The negotiations, conducted on the Korean side by Kim Hong-jip, Yi Cho-yŏn, and von Moellendorff, proceeded smoothly, and agreement was easily reached on the treaty. Opinions on the trade regulations and the tariff, however, differed considerably. The Koreans clung to the trade regulations which they had concluded with Japan shortly before. Agreement was finally reached on November 24. Two days later, on November 26, the British-Korean treaty was signed by Parkes and the president of the Foreign Office, Min Yŏng-mok. The German-Korean treaty was signed by Zappe and Min. On the following day, Parkes and Zappe were received by the king.[54]

Parkes' treaty was an expansion of Willes' treaty both in general scope and in detail. The gist of the lengthy articles is as follows: Article 1 declared perpetual peace and friendship between England and Korea. Article 2 provided for the exchange of diplomatic representatives and the appointment of consular officials in the opened ports. Extraterritorial jurisdication was guaranteed according to article 3. Besides Inch'ŏn, Pusan, and Wŏnsan, two other places, Hanyang (Seoul) and Yanghwajin, were opened to British subjects in article 4. Article 5 secured for the British the fullest liberty of trade at each of the opened ports without the interference of Korean officials. Article 6 provided against smuggling and article 7 for the protection of shipwrecked British ships. Article 8 permitted ships of war to visit all ports of the other power. Article 9 allowed employment of Koreans by British subjects and vice verṣa. Article 10 contained the most-favored-nation clause. Article 11 specified the revision of the Treaty and the Tariff by mutual consent in ten years. English and Chinese were chosen as the two official languages in all official communications according to article 12, and article 13 provided for the exchange of the ratifications as soon as possible or at least within one year. Appended to the treaty were *Regulations under which British Trade is to be Conducted in Corea*, a *Protocol*,[55] and an *Import Tariff* which provided for ad valorem rates of 5, 7.5, 10, and 20 percent. Significantly, the text of the treaty did not allude to China's claim of suzerain rights over Korea. The text and provisions of the Korean-German treaty were identical to the Korean-British treaty.[56]

The second British-Korean treaty was well received. British traders in the Far East especially appreciated its tariff, which was lower and more flexible than those in either the American or Japanese treaties. Even Li Hung-chang approved of the treaty, for he found nothing in it "which concerned China in the least degree." Li's initial approval, however, turned into opposition in the spring of the following year. He had been severely criticized in Peking for having failed to send a Chinese official along with Parkes, a procedure which Li had considered impolitic at the time. The scapegoat in Seoul was Min Yŏng-mok, the chief negotiator on the Korean side, who had to resign as president of the Foreign Office because of Chinese pressure. Before Chinese objections to the ratification of the treaty reached Seoul, however, Parkes secured through his secretary, W.C. Hillier, an official declaration from the Korean government that the treaty had been ratified by the king. The exchange ceremony took place at Seoul on April 28, 1884. On May 1, Parkes and his suite were received splendidly by the king, and Parkes presented his credentials and a letter from Queen Victoria.[57] The ratifications of the German treaty were exchanged half a year later, on November 18, between Captain Zembsch and the president of the Foreign Office, Kim Hong-jip. On the same day, Zembsch was received in audience by the king.[58]

Great Britain appointed its minister in Peking concurrently to the post of minister to Korea. Britain's local representatives in Korea were a consul general residing at Seoul and a vice-consul stationed at Inch'ŏn. The consul general was responsible to the minister at Peking. This arrangement had also been recommended by Li Hung-chang. The first consul general was William G. Aston, who held a position which enabled him to communicate with the president of the Korean Foreign Office on all questions, personally or in writing. Germany was represented by a consul who was directly responsible to Berlin. Captain Zembsch was the first to hold this office. Since April, German interests had been represented by Vice-consul Hermann Budler. In November, Budler was sent to Inch'ŏn to take charge of consular affairs.[59]

The British and the German treaties served as models for most of the later treaties Korea concluded with Western nations. First to follow was Italy. On June 26, 1884, Italy's minister to China, Ferdinand de Luca, signed the Italian-Korean treaty at Seoul. Less than a month later, Karl I. Waeber, the Russian consul at Tientsin, arrived in the Korean capital to sign the Russian-Korean treaty on July 7, 1884. The last treaty Korea entered into in the 1880s was that with France on June 4, 1886.[60]

After Korea had concluded her first Western treaty, the other Western powers engaged her in treaty relationships in an almost routine manner. The conclusion of treaties with the distant kingdom was not a matter of necessity, but it had become a political expediency. The only people who were really interested in obtaining an open door to Korea were the men on the scene. Among them, only the British were concerned with trade. They insisted on a revision of some of the stipulations in the American treaty that had been used as a general blueprint. The West's treaties with Korea contained all the privileges that had become the hallmark of the unequal treaties. But as long as there was no real commitment, whether political or economic, the West's role in the peninsula remained small. Western presence, therefore, was too insignificant to become a counterbalance for the growing Chinese and Japanese interests in Korea.

In the fall of 1882, an unusual sense of common cause seemed to prevail among the officials. The threat of regression into international isolation and cultural stagnation jolted the officialdom into an unprecedented commitment to national revitalization. The king seems to have obtained the solid support for self-strengthening that he had previously lacked. But his leadership role was challenged by the Min, who advanced into the top decision-making offices, the Foreign Office and the Home Office, faster and more decisively after the 1882 incident. The Min used the self-strengthening program for their own purposes. They widened the economic foundation of the program, but gradually narrowed its political and ideological focus. Self-strengthening became a vehicle for political domination, losing its original aim of national improvement. In their bid for power the Min enjoyed the backing of the Chinese and therefore showed little interest in an active foreign policy. They did not use the treaties with the West as a means for gaining national independence. The Min's one-sided reliance on Chinese support and their single-minded drive to make self-strengthening work for their own aggrandizement eventually caused a serious rift within the self-strengthening movement itself. Political factors once again threatened to hamper the progress of Korea's modernization.

TRADE ON THE KOREAN COAST

Korea's foreign trade had been entirely in Japanese hands from 1876 until the early 1880s. Then, the conclusion of treaties with the Western powers and the signing of the Trade Regulations with China brought an end to Japanese domination in the opened ports. Keen competition developed between Japanese and Chinese traders. Although the Japanese government adopted a more cautious Korea policy after 1882, Japanese traders seem to have been little affected by their government's diplomatic retreat. They were, by then, well established and less dependent on government support. The few Western traders who ventured into the Korean treaty ports internationalized the growing foreign settlements, but they were hardly dangerous competitors. The Koreans responded to the expansion of foreign trade with some important new measures. The most significant was the establishment of the Maritime Customs Service. Moreover, there were signs that the government's traditionally negative attitude toward commercial activities had begun to change. For the first time, Korean merchants could pursue business without the handicaps imposed on them by centuries of official prejudices and restrictions.

The Establishment of the Korean Maritime Customs Service

One of the most important innovations introduced into the opened ports as a result of Korea's opening to the outside world was the Maritime Customs Service. Unfamiliar with the function of such an institution and hesitant to fix customs duties without Chinese advice, the Koreans had, prior to 1882, taken no active steps toward establishing a customs service.[1] Immediately after the conclusion of the American-Korean treaty on May 22, 1882, Ma Chien-chung reminded the Korean negotiators that they should give serious thought to establishing maritime customs. The subject was brought up again when Cho Yŏng-ha discussed the future of Chinese-Korean commercial relations with Li Hung-chang in September of the same year. After the setback of that summer, the Korean government put high priority on building a controlled foreign trade. Two major obstacles had to be overcome: the lack of sufficient funds and the absence of trained personnel. The Koreans solicited Chinese help for solving these problems. Consequently, a loan was contracted on October 1, 1882, and P. G. von Moellendorff was hired on November 18.[2]

The possibility of borrowing a large sum of money from China was explored as early as May 1882. Ma Chien-chung warned the Koreans of the possible political implications of such a loan and advised them to spurn any Japanese offers and to turn instead to China for help. In late September, Cho Yŏng-ha presented the Korean government's wish to borrow the sum of 500,000 taels and started negotiations on this matter with Ma Chien-chung and T'ang T'ing-shu, who represented the China Merchants' Steam Navigation Company and the K'aip'ing Mines. This project evidently enjoyed Li Hung-chang's support. A contract that assigned 300,000 taels of the loan to the China Merchants' Steam Navigation Company and 200,000 taels to the K'aip'ing Mines was signed at Tientsin on October 1, 1882, by Cho Yŏng-ha and Kim Hong-jip for the Korean government and by T'ang T'ing-shu for the Chinese. This contract stipulated that the money had to be used exclusively for the promotion of trade. The interest was fixed at 8 percent per annum, and the capital repayment was to begin after five years and completed within twelve years. The security for this loan was a specified amount of the Korean customs. In case this was not sufficient to pay the annual interest, the Korean government was obliged to supplement it with the duties on red ginseng, or the K'aip'ing Mines could arrange with the Korean government for the exploration and eventual exploitation of Korean mineral deposits under a special contract. Similar cooperation with the China Merchants' Steam Navigation Company was also possible. The contract was to become valid after ratification by the Korean king.

After von Moellendorff was appointed head of the Korean Maritime Customs Service, he, Min Yŏng-ik, and Yi Cho-yŏn were dispatched to Shanghai in January 1883 to transmit the royal ratification and discuss the details of the payment of the loan. These negotiations with T'ang T'ing-shu and Ma Chien-chung unexpectedly turned out to be inconclusive. T'ang insisted on being minutely informed about the way the money would be used, and he was unwilling to make the loan without receiving the Chinese government's guaranty. In the end, the dealings became so complex and unsatisfactory that the Korean delegation decided to go to Tientsin to ask for Li Hung-chang's mediation. On February 18, Min Yŏng-ik and von Moellendorff met the viceroy and apparently were able to win his sympathy. Li finally ended the dispute by ordering the China Merchants' Steam Navigation Company to lend the Korean government the sum of 200,000 taels. No further amounts appear to have been lent later.[3]

The organization and the administration of the customs service under von Moellendorff are difficult to reconstruct because of the lack of documentation. The records pertaining to all three ports apparently were destroyed when the customhouse at Inch'ŏn burned on July 15, 1885.[4] According to his contract, von Moellendorff was authorized to hire foreigners as assistants. After securing at least part of the Chinese loan, he chose his staff from among the foreigners in Shanghai. Most of the newly hired employees arrived in Korea in the summer of 1883. The collection of duties started provisionally at Inch'ŏn on June 16, 1883, on the basis of the tariff laid down in the American-Korean treaty. The actual planning and organization of the maritime customs, however, began only after the conclusion of the trade regulations with Japan. In this document, November 3 was stipulated as the date from which the duties would be levied. Von Moellendorff personally supervised the establishment of the maritime customs at Pusan, still the most important treaty port for trade with Japan. Accompanied by a small retinue, von Moellendorff stayed in Pusan during the first half of October. There he conferred with the prefect of Tongnae, Kim Sŏn-gŭn. The collection of duties started on November 3, 1883, as planned.

Von Moellendorff's representative at Pusan was the commissioner of customs, the German W.N. Lovatt, who worked with the deputy of the Korean treaty port superintendent (*kamni*). At Wŏnsan, the collection of duties seems to have started a few days earlier under the supervision of the Englishman F.W. Wright. Another Englishman, A.B. Stripling, was commissioner of customs at Inch'ŏn. The three commissioners were each assisted by a staff consisting of a tidewaiter, clerks, and local attendants. From the beginning, the customs service was so overstaffed that the small customs revenue was insufficient to pay all the salaries. Concerned about high costs, the Korean government apparently studied the possibility of hiring Japanese instead of European personnel. This idea was flatly rejected by von Moellendorff.[5]

The early phase of the customs service was complicated by the fact that the Chinese were bound by no fixed tariff on maritime trade and thus demanded that they be taxed according to the trade agreement most favorable to foreign traders. The Chinese high commissioner of trade, Ch'en Shu-t'ang, claimed that the Korean government had overcharged the Chinese merchants at Inch'ŏn prior to November 3, and he pressed for recompensation. Subsequently, the Chinese traders were charged duties according to the revised British treaty. In the summer of 1884, the Chinese traders at Pusan insisted that they be accorded the same treatment. The Foreign Office then instructed the commissioner of customs at Pusan to adopt the customs procedure in force at Inch'ŏn.[6] The Japanese filed similar complaints and invoked the most-favored-nation clause. In August 1884, the treaty port superintendents were ordered to accord to the Japanese traders in the three opened ports the privilege of paying the lower duties stipulated in the British treaty.[7] A certain uniformity of customs duties collection was therefore attained only in the fall of 1884. A major problem was the mode of payment. At Wŏnsan, for example, the commissioner of customs wanted to levy duties in foreign currency (presumably in Japanese yen or Mexican dollars), but the Japanese consul disputed this decision and insisted that the levies be made in Korean money.[8]

Von Moellendorff was dismissed as the head of customs on September 4, 1885. He was succeeded by an American, Henry F. Merrill.[9] At the time of von Moellendorff's appointment in the fall of 1882, Sir Robert Hart resented the fact that he was not asked to nominate one of his own men to organize the Korean customs service. He also urged the Tsungli Yamen to incorporate the Korean customs into the Chinese. When the Chinese government rejected this suggestion as too bold a policy, Hart proposed that the Korean customs should be a separate establishment, but placed under his supervision. Li Hung-chang did not pay much attention to Hart's ideas and appointed von Moellendorff. Although Hart had not gotten his way then, he was asked by Li Hung-chang to name von Moellendorff's successor in 1885. His choice was Henry F. Merrill of the Chinese Maritime Customs Service, a man bound to him by unfailing loyalty. When Merrill was called to Tientsin for an interview with Li Hung-chang, however, the viceroy made it clear that it was he, Li, who sent Merrill to Korea. He instructed the American to adhere strictly to the rules and regulations observed in the Chinese Maritime Customs and to devote himself exclusively to the administration of the customs. The head of the Chinese customs service could recall him from Korea at any time through the viceroy. Clearly, the instructions Merrill received bore no resemblance to von Moellendorff's loosely worded, open-ended contract.

Merrill took office as chief of the Korean customs (*haegwan ch'ongsemusa*) on October 23, 1885. He was disgusted at the disorganization and disorder he found at his new post. He made it his first task to reduce the staff and to introduce some uniformity of system in all the three ports. He eventually dismissed the original commissioners of customs and replaced them with his own men who had been trained in the Chinese service. As a means of increasing the customs revenue, Merrill suggested that the cultivation of red ginseng be intensified and the ban on its exportation lifted. He also devised stern measures to suppress smuggling. Under Merrill's leadership, the customs income increased rapidly and became one of the most dependable sources of funds for Korea's modernization program. Although Merrill was at all times in close touch with Hart, whom he consulted on all major decisions, he preserved for himself some independence of action and tried to prevent undue Chinese interference in Korean affairs.[10]

The Maritime Customs was the first modern institution in Korea that was built up and staffed entirely by foreigners. The model was the Chinese Maritime Customs Service, and China was instrumental in providing Korea with personnel and funds. In its early phase under von Moellendorff, however, the customs serice suffered from the contemptuous attitude the Chinese officials and traders in Korea took toward things Korean. Moreover, absorbed in too many projects, von Moellendorff seems to have paid too little attention to organizational and administrative details. The customs service therefore did not make its significant financial contribution to Korea's modernization until Merrill's tenure.

The Development of the Port and the Foreign Settlements at Inch'ŏn

In the early 1880s, three treaty ports—Pusan, Wŏnsan, and Inch'ŏn—were opened to foreign trade and residence. Naturally, the port lying closest to the capital, Chemulp'o, was destined to become the most important gate to Korea. Chemulp'o was situated in the embouchure of the Han River directly opposite Wŏlmido (Roze Island). A few miles to the southeast lay the old prefectural town of Inch'ŏn, the administration of which was transferred to the port of Chemulp'o when it was officially opened to foreign trade on January 1, 1883. Chemulp'o then became known as the modern Inch'ŏn. Chemulp'o was by no means an ideal port. Having a daily tide of thirty-three feet, half of the day the waterfront was muddy flats where the landing and shipping of cargo was extremely difficult. Wŏlmido divided the port into an inner and outer harbor, the outer affording good anchorage and accommodation for the largest ships. Communication with the landing place, however, was possible only with a favorable tide. Chemulp'o was known to foreigners as the place where Korea's first treaties with the West were signed. At the time of its opening it was a hamlet of fifteen houses. The nearby old Inch'ŏn was a town of 185 houses with an estimated population of 750. It reportedly had a decayed and desolate appearance. Only the houses of the prefect and his immediate subordinate and the local Confucian shrine were tiled.[11]

The establishment of the foreign settlement at Inch'ŏn differed from that of Pusan and Wŏnsan. The Japanese settlement at Pusan grew out of the former Japan House which had been in existence since the early fifteenth century. The settlement at Wŏnsan was intentionally patterned on the Pusan model and was planned as a purely Japanese settlement at a time when the only foreign traders in Korea were Japanese. The conventions for both settlements were rather loosely worded. They arranged for leasing the grounds to the Japanese government for an annual rent of fifty yen,[12] and no time limit for terminating these leases was set. Although the maintenance and operation of the settlements were the responsibility of the Japanese government, the Korean government apparently did not give up police control over the areas. In neither document was the question of sovereignty touched upon.

At Inch'ŏn, the Korean government planned to establish one settlement for all foreign traders. The agreement on the opening of Inch'ŏn to the Japanese antedated Korea's finalization of treaties with Westerners, and, without waiting for the official opening of the port, the Japanese took quick action to secure for themselves an advantageous position in the port. In April 1882, Kondō Masuki, who had been instrumental in the building up of the Japanese settlement at Pusan, was appointed consul of the yet unopened port to supervise the preparatory work. Some temporary houses were constructed on a flat piece of land close to the waterfront, and in that summer Hanabusa repeatedly urged the Foreign Office to discuss the construction of the quay and the laying out of the settlement. In mid-July, a group of legation officials staked out the area of the Japanese settlement. These preparations were interrupted by the 1882 incident, and the official opening of the port was then postponed to January 1, 1883. The Japanese gained some advantages by the *Additional Convention* of August 30 which extended the travel limits in all three ports from ten to fifty *i* in all directions.

Once Inch'ŏn was opened to foreign trade, the Japanese traders were the first to arrive, and by the summer of 1883 they had built a number of wooden houses. The Korean government hesitated to conclude a separate settlement agreement with the Japanese because it intended to build one general foreign settlement at Inch'ŏn. However, the rapid influx of Japanese traders and perhaps also the approaching date for levying customs duties seems to have made separate action inevitable. During the early fall, von Moellendorff urged the conclusion of an agreement that would restrain the Japanese from any further construction. On September 30, 1883, Min Yŏng-mok and Takezoe Shinichirō signed the *Agreement Concerning the Japanese Settlement at Inch'ŏn*. According to article 1 of this agreement a portion of the projected general foreign settlement was especially assigned to Japanese subjects as a place of residence "in acknowledgment of their priority of arrival." This area was to be leased to individual Japanese by the Korean government in lots which were to be put up to public auction. Ground rent had to be paid to the Korean superintendent of trade by the individual title holders according to the class of land thus leased. One-third of the rent was to go to the Korean government, and the remaining two-thirds were to constitute a municipal fund jointly administered by the Japanese consul and the Korean treaty port superintendent. The fund was to be used for the maintenance of roads, watercourses, bridges, street lamps, police, and other municipal requirements. The construction of these facilities, which was the duty of the Korean government, was finished a year later after some delay.[13]

After 1883, the fiercest competitors of the Japanese were the Chinese, who had acquired the right "to proceed to the open ports . . . for trade" and were "allowed to rent land or houses and erect buildings" according to article 4 of the *Regulations for Maritime and Overland Trade*. Because the Chinese had received the privilege of settling in Seoul, Inch'ŏn was specially important to them as a port of entry for their supplies. By the end of 1883, some sixty-three Chinese traders had opened their shops in Inch'ŏn, but preparatory work for a Chinese settlement started only in January 1884. Its site had been chosen by von Moellendorff and Ch'en Shu-t'ang during an inspection tour in early December of the previous year. Ch'en's personal representative in the port was the newly appointed commissioner of trade, Li Nai-yung. After some preliminary negotiations, an *Agreement for the Establishment of a Chinese Settlement* was concluded on April 2, 1884. In its general outline this document resembled that signed with Japan. The Chinese settlement was situated northwest of the Japanese settlement in a slightly elevated area, hitherto uninhabited. Ch'en demanded quick action from the Korean government, which was responsible for laying out the settlement, and requested a special site for the construction of a kiln to produce bricks, China's universal building material.[14]

Although the Americans were the first Westerners to obtain the right to resort to Korea's opened ports "to reside [there] within the limits of concessions, and to lease buildings or land or to construct residences or warehouses therein," the British were the most eager to secure a suitable piece of ground to establish a foreign settlement. When Aston was in Korea in the spring of 1883, he personally selected and marked off a site for the British consulate, even though Great Britain did not have at that time a valid treaty with Korea. Parkes visited Chemulp'o in November and found the proposed settlement undeveloped. The treaty he had just signed actually laid the broadest legal foundation for all foreign settlements in Korea in its stipulation that the British subjects would have the right to rent or purchase land or houses in the opened ports. While the American treaty "expressly agreed that land so acquired in the open ports of Chosen still remains an integral part of the Kingdom, and that all rights of jurisdiction over persons and property within such areas remain vested in the Authorities of Chosen" (if not relinquished by extraterritoriality), the British treaty did not mention Korea's sovereignty and in fact put it in abeyance through a tightly formulated extraterritorial system. Moreover, the authority of the British representative was strengthened in matters such as the selection and determination of the limits, the laying out of the sites of the foreign settlements, and the sale of land.[15]

Planning the establishment of a foreign settlement continued during the spring and summer of 1884. The Korean government originally suggested Wŏlmido as the site of the "European" settlement. This was rejected by the Western representatives. On May 1, Foote, who was looking for a piece of ground for the American consulate, and Parkes seem to have reached an informal agreement on a site on the mainland for a foreign settlement. Parkes advocated the formation of one general settlement for all foreigners since this would facilitate its administration according to treaty stipulations. Parkes was not permanently residing at Seoul, so most of the preparatory work and the drafting of the agreement was entrusted to Aston. At the end of July, a provisional Municipal Council, in which the Chinese and the Japanese were not represented, was organized to coordinate the preparations. Parkes himself put the finishing touches to the *Agreement Respecting a General Foreign Settlement at Inch'ŏn (Land Regulations)* that was signed by Korea, America, England, Japan, China, and subsequently also by Germany. Originally undated, this document later bore the date of October 3, 1884.[16]

The General Foreign Settlement covered an area of 647,107 square meters (approx. 160 acres). Its greatest portion was situated on the hillside and surrounded the Japanese and Chinese settlements, reaching the waterfront only at its northern and southern ends. The opinion that the Japanese and Chinese had picked the best sites for themselves was widespread. The settlement was divided into four classes of lots— A, B, C, and D—according to their position. Only subjects of treaty powers that had signed the agreement were allowed to purchase or hold land there. The Korean government, but no Korean, was permitted to hold lots with the same responsibilities as the others. The seawall and the jetty were to be constructed and kept in repair, and the streets and roads of the settlement laid out and constructed at the expense of the Korean government. Expenses such as street lighting and cleaning, police protection, and other municipal activities were to be paid by the settlement out of its own funds. A Municipal Council was to be formed. It was to consist of a Korean official of suitable rank, the consuls of the treaty powers whose subjects or citizens held land in the settlement, and three registered landholders to be elected by the other landholders. The council was empowered to make bylaws regulating the public life of the settlement, but had no judiciary powers. Whereas other nationals were excluded from the Japanese and Chinese settlements, both the Chinese and the Japanese were allowed to live in the General Foreign Settlement.[17]

On the fringe of the foreign settlements a "Korea town" developed. The influx of Korean merchants was rather rapid, especially in the spring and summer of 1884. By 1885, there were some 120 houses and a population of 700. The highest Korean representative on the scene was the treaty port superintendent (*kamni Inch'ŏn t'ongsang samu*) who was first appointed on September 19, 1883. The first incumbent was Cho Pyŏng-jik who, as a member of the gentlemen's sightseeing group (*sinsa yuramdan*) in 1881, had studied the port facilities of Yokohama. Assisted by a small staff, he started his work on October 22. His duties and powers were manifold. He was responsible for smooth relations between the Korean population and the foreign settlers, and he was in charge of dealing with the foreign representatives, supervising all matters connected with foreign trade, and tending to administrative affairs in the foreign settlements. He was also the head of the local police force, but he was relieved from this duty by the appointment of a police officer in May 1884. The officer was given the support of ten patrolmen (*sunp'o*) in September. The office of the *kamni* (*kamnisŏ*), a simple Korean-style structure, stood near the waterfront. Cho's successor in April 1884 was Hong Sun-hak. A little more than a year later, Hong was concurrently appointed prefect of Inch'ŏn following the example of Pusan and Wŏnsan.[18]

Despite the obvious disadvantages of Chemulp'o as a port, the foreign settlements grew rather fast because of the increasing volume of trade. The Japanese were most active in developing their settlement. By the beginning of 1884, it comprised almost one hundred established shops, and the Japanese consul applied for an extension of the settlement boundaries. The Japanese consulate, built in European style, rose conspicuously above the multitude of smaller structures. Near the beach fairly extensive warehouses were erected, and in August of the same year plans for a hospital were drawn up. In the spring of 1884, Chinese merchants, especially from Shantung and Fengt'ien, flocked into the Chinese settlement in increasing numbers. Many of them did not settle permanently, but sailed back and forth between the opened ports. The Chinese population grew from 63 persons at the end of 1883 to some 235 one year later. This figure decreased slightly in the two subsequent years. In contrast, the development of the Western foreign settlement was much slower. This was generally ascribed to the difficulties the Korean government encountered in fulfilling its new obligations. Moreover, the Westerners seem to have clung too rigidly to the model of foreign settlements in China and Japan. In 1885, the General

Foreign Settlement comprised only 146 houses. At the beginning of 1886, the settlement was not yet fully laid out, and a qualified Municipal Council was not yet elected.[19]

Chemulp'o was connected with Seoul by a road on which ponies and bullocks transported passengers and goods. It was widened in the spring of 1883 in expectation of an increase in traffic. With a good horse, the distance could be covered in four hours. The other route to the capital was the Han River, which was navigable up to Map'o, but because of the uncertainty of the tide most travelers seem to have preferred the road.

In the early 1880s Seoul was a town of some 200,000 inhabitants. Together with Yanghwajin, an important fortified place on the Han River, Seoul was opened to foreign trade by the Trade Regulations with China and again by the revised British and German treaties. In search of lucrative business, Chinese merchants sailed up the Han River to the capital. From late 1883 to the end of 1884 the Chinese merchant community at Seoul swelled from 59 to 352 persons. The Chinese ships had to clear their cargo and pay duties at Inch'ŏn before they were allowed to sail upstream. This procedure, which had to be repeated on the return trip, made a waiting period of several days necessary. A controversy arose over the question of whether a customs station should be erected at Yanghwajin. Before this problem was solved, the foreign representatives, who had visited Yanghwajin with Yun T'ae-jun and von Moellendorff in June 1884, decided against establishing a general foreign settlement there and in October chose instead a site at Yongsan, three miles from Seoul on the Han River. Work was never started on it because the foreigners preferred to stay in Seoul. Late in 1886, Yüan Shih-k'ai attempted to move the Chinese merchants to Yongsan. This was interpreted as an attempt to exclude all foreigners, especially the Japanese, from the capital. The Western powers protested and ignored the treaty stipulations that would have forced them to relinquish their rights to reside in Seoul as soon as the Chinese did. They wanted to stay in the capital because most of their nationals pursued missionary work there. No provisions for a general foreign settlement were ever made for Seoul, and the foreigners bought land in all parts of the town.[20]

Pusan and Wŏnsan after 1883

The opening of Inch'ŏn had a marked impact on the development of the two other opened ports, Pusan and Wŏnsan. Pusan, the oldest foreign settlement on Korean soil, was a busy port by the time of Inch'ŏn's opening. At the beginning of 1883, the population of the Japanese settlement at Pusan was somewhat less than 2,000. The settlement spread over eleven moderately wide and paved streets and included the office of the consul general, a civil judicial court, a town hall, a commercial assembly house, a police station, a hospital, and some larger commercial establishments, notably those of Mitsubishi and Daiichi Ginkō. The place presented to one visitor a "clean, well-kept appearance." The consul was assisted by an elective Municipal Council, the composition and work of which was guided by the Municipal Regulations promulagted in 1881. In April 1884 the Japanese government, through Chargé Shimamura Hisashi, proposed turning the Japanese settlement into a general foreign settlement. Foreign reaction to this suggestion was guarded because both Foote and Parkes feared Japanese interference and considered the conditions the Japanese attached to this arrangement unacceptable. Parkes also found the Japanese settlement too crowded and its best lots already taken up by the Japanese themselves. He wanted to further investigate a site that Aston had selected in the spring of 1883 and, if it were found suitable, make it into a foreign settlement. This project, however, apparently did not leave the discussion stage, and subsequently the Westerners purchased land wherever it was available. This procedure later made common action impossible.

For the Chinese, Pusan was of lesser significance than Inch'ŏn, and they found it difficult to penetrate this Japanese commercial stronghold. In the fall of 1883, two Chinese merchants rented a shop in Pusan from a Japanese to set up business; they were immediately ordered by the Japanese consul to close it. Upon Ch'en Shu-t'ang's protest, von Moellendorff was sent to the port to look into the matter and to select a site for a Chinese settlement. He was accompanied by Ch'en and the newly appointed treaty port superintendent, Yi Hŏn-yŏng. It was not until August 1884, however, that the Chinese commissioner of trade for Pusan, Ch'en Wei-hun, and the treaty port superintendent staked out the settlement at Ch'oryang between the Japanese settlement and the Korean town. Shortly afterward, they concluded a settlement agreement on the basis of that already in force at Inch'ŏn. The Chinese foothold in the southern port remained small because only a few merchants settled there. The majority chose to sail to the port more or less regularly from Inch'ŏn.[21]

Although considered by the Koreans as one of the great commercial centers of the country, Wŏnsan never gained much importance for trade other than that with the Japanese. A considerable portion of its trade, which had been important especially for Seoul and P'yŏngyang, was diverted to Inch'ŏn after 1883. In December of that year, the Council of State received royal approval cf its suggestion (based on a report by Ŏ Yun-jung) to transfer the seat of the prefecture from Tŏgwŏn to Wŏnsan. This move was to facilitate the prefect's work as concurrent treaty port superintendent (*kamni*). A contemporary visitor wrote enthusiastically about the area. "Surely if any town has a right to call itself spick and span, that town is Gensan [Wŏnsan]. Japanese houses of a substantial class, wide streets, a stream flowing through the town, the sea in front of it, and in comparison with Corean towns, made the place to me look clean beyond compare." The Japanese settlement, which comprised a consulate general, a hospital, and toward the end of 1883 some 180 mercantile houses, grew at a slower rate than those at Inch'ŏn and Pusan. The Japanese community was administered by the consul general with the assistance of an elective Municipal Council. No general foreign settlement was ever laid out, and when the Chinese commissioner of trade for Wŏnsan, Liu Chia-ts'ung, arrived in the port in the fall of 1884, he found the best sites already occupied by the Japanese. A small Chinese settlement developed to the north of the Japanese settlement, and by the end of 1884 about sixty-three Chinese merchants were registered. The majority of them stayed in the port only for short periods of time.[22]

Foreign residence was limited to the treaty ports, but the foreigners were allowed to freely move and trade within an area beyond the settlement boundaries that was fixed by treaty. Originally these travel or treaty limits (*hanhaeng ijŏng*) were measured by ten Korean *i* from the landing-place (according to the Additional Articles of August 24, 1876). They were extended to fifty *i* at all three ports on the basis of the Additional Convention of August 30, 1882. Takezoe Shinichirō and Min Yŏng-mok determined the exact course of the treaty limits for each opened port in the *Agreement with Japan Regarding the Treaty Port Limits* on July 25, 1883. A further agreement, signed on November 29, 1884, stipulated a second extension to one hundred *i* as provided for in the Additional Convention. This extension would have opened Seoul to the Japanese, had the capital not been already opened to foreigners by the revised British and German treaties. These treaties also gave to the nationals concerned the right to rent or purchase land or houses within a distance of ten *i* beyond the limits of the foreign settlements. Such arrangements, however, were subject to local

Korean regulations and taxes. The travel limits were marked off by poles bearing an inscription saying that foreigners were not allowed to pass beyond that point. Inland travel beyond the treaty limits was permitted only with a passport. Passports were issued by the respective foreign consul and countersigned or sealed by the Korean treaty port superintendent. The British and the Germans were the first who, in addition to the right to purchase native goods in the interior, obtained authority "to transport and sell goods of all kinds" in any part of the country. This privilege caused the Chinese, in the spring of 1884, to press for a revision of article 4 of the *Regulations for Maritime and Overland Trade* that had allowed only for buying Korean goods. The foreigners in Korea, thus, were able to expand their activities gradually to all parts of the country. Treaty limits lost much of their original purpose of containing the foreigners within the narrow confines of the treaty ports.[23]

Shipping and the Telegraph

The growth of the ports and the foreign settlements depended largely on regular shipping connections. A Mitsubishi steamer apparently sailed to Inch'ŏn on government orders twice a year beginning in 1881. Presumably after the 1882 incident, a warship ran twice a month between Shimonoseki and Inch'ŏn. A regular service was established only in the fall of 1883. From October of that year, the Mitsubishi Steam Navigation Company began including Inch'ŏn in its monthly run from Kobe to Pusan via Nagasaki. A Mitsubishi steamer also visited Wŏnsan monthly.[24]

The Chinese imposed shipping obligations on Korea in article 7 of the *Regulations for Maritime and Overland Trade*. Representing the China Merchants' Steam Navigation Company, Ch'en Shu-t'ang started negotiations with von Moellendorff in the late fall of 1883 and concluded a contract on November 5. This agreement, which could be renewed after one year, opened a monthly steamer line between Shanghai and Inch'ŏn. The Korean government was responsible for compensating losses incurred within one year from the date of the ship's first run. The funds were to come from the Inch'ŏn customs income. From the outset, the establishment of the line was motivated by politics rather than by commercial interests. It was a Chinese attempt to impress her suzerain rights on Korea.

The Chinese ship *Fuyu* arrived at Inch'ŏn on December 17 for the first time and took Ch'en Shu-t'ang and von Moellendorff aboard to sail on to Pusan. It apparently became clear to Ch'en that the line would not be profitable. He proposed to von Moellendorff that the contract be amended in such a way that the steamer would run without fixed schedule either from Shanghai via Chefoo to Inch'ŏn, Pusan, Nagasaki, and Shanghai, or from Shanghai via Nagasaki to Wŏnsan, Inch'ŏn, Chefoo, and back to Shanghai. An additional agreement to this effect was signed on January 11, 1884. Despite this rerouting, the line suffered such losses on its first three trips that its operations were suspended in April. The Korean government was sued for compensation, and there is no evidence that the service was ever reopened afterward.[25] The *Fuyu*'s competitors were not only the ships that were chartered by particular mercantile enterprises, but also the *Nanzing*, the Jardine, Matheson steamer, which started service between Shanghai and Korea at the same time.

Foreign ships were bound by treaty to call only at the opened ports. The Koreans strengthened the coastal patrols, but numerous incidents involving foreign, mostly Chinese, boats that engaged in smuggling along the coast and in the unopened ports were reported.[26]

The ports also came to be connected with the outside world by telegraphic lines. After preparatory talks in January and February 1883, Takezoe Shinichirō and Min Yŏng-mok signed on March 3 an agreement that provided for the building of an underwater telegraphic cable between the northwestern coast of Kyūshū (Nagasaki) via Tsushima and Pusan. Work started in the middle of October with the assistance of a cable steamer from the Danish Great Northern Telegraph Company. After the cable reached land in March of the following year, a telegraph station was opened at the southwest end of the Japanese settlement on March 22.[27] More than two years later, on July 15, 1885, the Korean government concluded with the Chinese a contract for establishing an overland telegraphic line between Korea and China. The line was to run from Inch'ŏn via Seoul and P'yŏngyang to Ŭiju on the Sino-Korean border. It was financed by a Chinese loan of 100,000 taels. Technicians and equipment were shipped from Tientsin in the first days of September, and the part of the line between Inch'ŏn and the capital was apparently finished at the end of the month when the Telegraph Bureau (Chŏnboguk) was opened at Seoul. A branch office at P'yŏngyang was set up at the beginning of October, and on November 22 the line reached Ŭiju.[28] As soon as the Japanese heard about Korea's new telegraphic venture using Chinese help, they filed a complaint claiming that the Koreans had broken their contract with Japan. The contract

gave Japan the exclusive rights to construct telegraphic lines in the peninsula for twenty-five years. The Korean government argued that China was
building an overland and not an underwater telegraphic line. In the end,
Korea was forced to sign on December 21, 1885, an additional agreement
with Japan promising to hook up the Chinese line with Pusan within six
months.[29]

Trade and Traders

Inch'ŏn was not a commercial center at the time of its opening. When
Aston arrived there in the spring of 1883, he found "the only representative of trade being a Korean who sat in front of his cabin with a scanty stock
of straw shoes, eggs, and dried persimmons displayed on a mat before
him."[30] The Japanese started trading actively at Inch'ŏn during the second
half of 1883. Besides Mitsubishi Steam Navigation Company, the most
important Japanese enterprise to branch out to Inch'ŏn was the Daiichi
Ginkō, which established an agency there in November 1883. In addition
to its normal financial transactions, this bank started its most important
venture in Korea: it became the banker to the Korean Maritime Customs.
Trade had become more complicated for the Japanese because of their new
obligation to pay customs duties to the Korean government, but the Korean
currency was hardly a viable financial instrument for this new function.
For this reason, the Daiichi Ginkō petitioned the Foreign Ministry in June
1883 for permission to conclude an agreement with the Korean government that would entrust the Japanese side of the customs transactions to
the Daiichi Ginkō. This would enable the Japanese merchants to pay their
dues henceforth with drafts drawn on that bank. On February 24, 1884, an
agreement was finally concluded between von Moellendorff and the Pusan
branch manager, Ōhashi Hanshichirō, to the effect that all financial responsibilities to the Korean customs in the three ports of Inch'ŏn, Pusan,
and Wŏnsan would be handled by the Daiichi Ginkō under the supervision of the commissioners of customs. As security, the bank advanced to
the Korean government a loan of 24,000 Mexican dollars.[31]

The majority of the Japanese merchants who opened shops at Inch'ŏn
seem to have come from Pusan. Their main motive in moving north apparently was the profitable trade in Japanese copper and tin that the
Korean government imported in large quantities to mint *tangojŏn* in late

1883 and 1884.[32]

While the Japanese were concentrating their activities in the ports, many Chinese moved into Seoul. The greatest influx of Chinese merchants was in the years 1884 and 1885. In 1884 the names of seventeen Chinese firms were registered; in 1885 this number increased to twenty-two. Their main trading items were foodstuffs, foreign cloth, and kerosene. Some Chinese got into business by supplying the Chinese community with locally produced bricks and vegetables. In the summer of 1884 the Chinese merchants in Seoul bought a Korean house which they turned into a kind of central meeting and coordinating place (Chung-hua hui-kuan).[33] Both the Chinese and the Japanese merchants frequently applied for passports to go inland to purchase native Korean goods. They were usually accompanied by an interpreter and some guards supplied by the Korean government. Despite these precautionary measures, there were numerous incidents involving foreign traders who were robbed of their purchases or were accused of extorting goods from Koreans.[34] In October 1885 the Japanese could at last fulfill their longtime wish of participating in the Taegu fair. According to the most-favored-nation clause, the Korean government finally acknowledged the Japanese merchants' right (which derived from article 4 of the revised British treaty) to transport and sell their wares at the famous inland market.[35]

Though the Western governments always had been skeptical about Korea's commercial potential, the country's unexplored mineral deposits nevertheless stimulated the Western traders. Moreover, well-publicized evidence that the Korean government had changed its attitude toward foreign traders further encouraged them. In the summer of 1883 the first representative of a Western firm, B.A. Clarke of the British firm Jardine, Matheson & Company (Ihwa yanghaeng), arrived at Inch'ŏn. Some British contracts with the Korean government had been discussed with von Moellendorff when he was in Shanghai during the spring of that year. Clarke's reports from Inch'ŏn enthusiastically described the capabilities of the country as "very great." Jardine, Matheson's primary interest was mining. Prospecting for mineral deposits began immediately after a contract was signed on July 18 that allowed the firm an initial period of nine months to locate a suitable site for a mine and a further nine months to start working it. Thirty percent of the profits was to go to the Korean government. A mine was opened in the summer of 1884 at a small village near Kimsŏng (Kangwŏn) and worked by fifty miners, some of them called in from China. The samples taken from this mine were disappointing, and new prospects were investigated in the provinces of Kangwŏn, Hwanghae, P'yŏngan, and Hamgyŏng. Local interference at a site some forty miles northeast of Seoul, where the British hoped to find gold, and the Korean government's demand for a loan in return for granting mining concessions (a deal Jardine, Matheson rejected) brought the mining venture to an end in the fall of 1884.[36]

Jardine's second interest in Korea was shipping. An agreement was concluded on November 15, 1883, which secured for the firm the regular steam communication between Shanghai and the Korean treaty ports. The *Nanzing*, which ran the route fortnightly, was in constant financial difficulty due to the lack of passengers and cargo. The steamer line never became profitable. Jardine also faced stiff competition from Mitsubishi. Negotiations for a contract that would have secured for Jardine the right to transport tax rice from Pusan to Inch'ŏn dragged on inconclusively into the summer of 1884. Discouraged by the poor results of its efforts in Korea, the headquarters in Shanghai, in October 1884, directed that the Inch'ŏn agency close on November 15. At that time the *Nanzing* stopped its service. Much of Jardine, Matheson's failure in Korea was attributed to the poor handling of foreign contracts by the Korean government. Von Moellen-dorff was a key figure in all Korean negotiations with Westerners. He and his Korean colleagues were courted by the Western diplomatic represent-atives who were acting as lobbyists for their respective nationals. Frequently the Koreans gave the same contract to two different parties at the same time, with the result that many damage claims were presented to the Korean government.[37]

About the time Jardine, Matheson & Company was ready to close its Korean branch, Carl Wolter, the representative of the German firm Heinrich Constantin Edward Meyer & Company (Sech'ang yanghaeng), arrived on one of the *Nanzing*'s last voyages from Shanghai. Wolter was primarily interested in persuading the Korean government to hire German instructors for the Korean army in the hope of receiving large orders for German arms. This plan failed not only because of Korea's refusal, but also because of the German government's unwillingness to mingle political and commercial affairs. Yet, there was plenty of other business for Wolter. The Korean government ordered modern minting machinery through Meyer. It arrived at Inch'ŏn in October 1885. Inch'ŏn had to rely entirely on Japanese steamer service after the *Nanzing* stopped running between Shanghai and Korea, so the Korean government commissioned Meyer & Company to rent a steamship at Shanghai which was to connect that port with Pusan and Inch'ŏn via Nagasaki and a port in Chŏlla. This ship, the *Hsi-hua*, which was first rented for the six-month period between March and September 1885, apparently was profitable because it had the privilege of transporting fixed quotas of government rice. Although the Koreans refused to grant mining concessions to Meyer, they hoped to receive a loan from the German firm to repay their debts to Japan. Negotiations began in December 1885, and a final contract was signed on January 2, 1886. According to this document, Meyer & Company loaned the Korean government the amount of 20,000 English pounds which was to be repaid quarterly, with an interest of ten percent, within two years. In case the Koreans were unable to raise the quarterly installments, they were obliged to pay them from the income of the maritime customs. On the same day, Meyer also secured the right to transport fixed amounts of tax rice from Mokp'o to Inch'ŏn by commercial steamer. Both transactions between the Korean government and Meyer were disapproved of by the Chinese who feared undue competition and consequent loss of business.[38]

Perhaps the first American trader to go to Korea from Japan was George B. Mott. He died shortly after his arrival in the summer of 1883.[39] When Kim Ok-kyun became development commissioner and visited Japan for the third time, he concluded a contract "to work for the Korean Government account, the timber of the Island of Ullunto [Ullŭngdo]" with a representative of the American Trading Company of Yokohama, Walter D. Townsend, in April 1884. In early May, Townsend arrived in Korea with Kim Ok-kyun and eventually executed considerable commission business for the Korean government. He imported several kinds of stock animals from America for the Korean government farm, tableware and furniture for the palace, and arms and ammunition. By May 1885 he had transacted $175,000 worth of business. Townsend also dealt in rice. His contract to cut Ullŭngdo timber involved him in a drawn-out controversy with the Foreign Office. The Foreign Office had concluded a similar contract with the Englishman J.F. Mitchell in December 1884, allowing him to go to the island in May 1885. Mitchell was to sell his timber only in Shanghai. The matter was further complicated by the illegal cutting of Ullŭngdo timber by some Japanese. This had started as early as 1881.[40] In July 1884, the American John Middleton and the Englishman Henry Gribble, representing the American firm of Middleton and Company, formed a steamship company and received permission from the Korean government to run a ship along the peninsula's coast and on its rivers and even to sail to some unopened ports. Another American, W.A. Newell, acquired in November 1885 the right to fish for pearl oysters along the Korean coast. All of these Western merchants concentrated their business at Inch'ŏn, and none of them ever became permanently established in Pusan or Wŏnsan.[41]

Korea's Changing Attitude Toward Foreign Trade

Intensified contact with the outside world did not fail to have an impact on the Korean government's attitude toward domestic and foreign trade. A significant indication of this change was the official repudiation of the venerated concept that members of the yangban class should not engage in trade (although some of them had done so for centuries). On February 5, 1883, King Kojong proclaimed that since foreign trade was beginning, yangban as well as commoners were henceforth allowed to "increase and circulate their wealth," that is, to engage in trade.[42] Trade was officially recognized as an effective means of enriching the country. The best way to encourage trade, it was agrued, was to outlaw the old institutions that had hitherto impeded its growth. On July 26, 1883, one day after the trade regulations with Japan were signed, the Korean government abolished the rights of the monopolists (*togo*) and abrogated taxes and levies on trade.[43] The abolition of the monopolists, however, was not welcomed by everyone. In the summer of 1882, the Japanese at Pusan had protested that the Korean traders who monopolized the dealings in cow hides were seriously threatening trade by levying special taxes. One year later, foreign traders deplored the monopolists' disappearance because they had played the important role of middleman.[44]

Despite the official abrogation of taxes on trade, the old concept of granting government protection to trade in return for taxing it continued to prevail. Taxation was an efficient means of official supervision and, of course, a sure source of government income. This was true for the traditional as well as for the more modern sectors of Korea's foreign trade. The innkeepers (*kaekchu* and *yŏgak*) continued to play an important role as trading partners of the foreign merchants in the opened ports. Under government supervision they formed trade deliberation bodies (*sangŭiso*). The first such organization came into being at Wŏnsan in 1883. A similar one was established at Inch'ŏn in 1885, and somewhat later a *sangŭiso* was also set up at Pusan. These organizations—their exact structure is unknown—

apparently were closely controlled by the treaty port superintendents and seem to have kept a check on the goods exported from the ports. In the summer of 1884, for example, the Japanese chargé d'affaires, Shimamura Hisahi, complained to the Foreign Office that the treaty port superintendent at Pusan had given orders to register all goods with an innkeeper before their sale. The Japanese protested this measure as undue interference with trade.[45]

From the ports, imported goods were carried inland by the peddlers (*pobusang*). Their organization, too, reflected the traditional demand for government protection. Through the abolition of the Military Council they had lost their protector, and in the fall of 1883 they again demanded effective support against the growing number of private traders who infringed upon what they considered their special privileges. This was one reason that the Office for the Benefit of Trade (Hyesang kongguk) was established under the aegis of the Home Office in September 1883.[46] The government continued to protect those from whom it expected the greatest profit. On the other hand, the licensed merchants (*kongin*), who hitherto had been the major suppliers for the government and the royal palace, suffered from the fact that the government started to deal directly with foreign firms. This deprived the licensed merchants of taking an active part in foreign trade and worsened their financial plight.[47]

Although the traditional features of Korean trade continued to dominate the commercial life in the treaty ports, there were important new developments. Concepts of Western trade organization and management found their way into enlightened thinking, and the establishment of modern commercial companies became one of the modernizers' demands for building a modern and strong nation. The first such company was founded at P'yŏngyang sometime in the middle of 1883. Called Taedong sanghoe, it apparently received some protection in the form of tax reductions from the Foreign Office. When members of this company wanted to go inland, they received passports which freed them from all local duties normally levied on trade. A similar commercial establishment named Ŭisin sanghoesa was opened in Seoul in 1884. Toward the end of that year it established branches at Kimch'ŏn (Kyŏngsang) and also at Pusan. It evidently enjoyed a measure of government protection because strict orders were sent to Pusan not to interfere with its activities in that port. In the fall of 1884, another company called Sunsinch'ang sanghoesa opened its doors at Inch'ŏn and in return for some financial contributions seems to have received government favors. Although the structure and organization of these companies are unknown, it would seem that they had some guild-like characteristics and perhaps specialized in certain kinds of goods. Despite government support, they apparently had run into serious financial difficulties by 1885.[48]

After 1882, Korea not only opened her ports to foreign traders, she also permitted her nationals to go abroad for trade. The legal foundation for this was laid down in the *Regulations for Maritime and Overland Trade* which allowed Koreans to trade in China under passport. The first sign that the Korean government intended to use this reciprocal right was the official permission given in November 1882 to any Korean to buy steamships or sailboats, thus lifting the centuries-old ban on overseas trade.[49] It was apparently not until April 1885 that a Korean bought a steamer from a Japanese. By 1887 at least two steamships were owned by Koreans. These Korean ships were treated like foreign ships and had to register with the treaty port superintendents and the Maritime Customs. They sailed mainly between Korean ports. A few Koreans ventured across the Yellow Sea to trade at Tientsin and Shanghai from the spring of 1884, but they had to rely on foreign transportation. There is also evidence that some Korean traders went to Japan.[50] The opening of maritime trade to Koreans made it necessary to dispatch a Korean representative to China, as stipulated by the Sino-Korean trade agreement. With Chinese help, a site at Tientsin was chosen and a building erected in November 1883 to house the Korean agent. In February 1884, Nam Chŏng-ch'ŏl was sent to China as the first permanent Korean trade representative.[51]

Despite these important developments, the majority of the trade partners of the Japanese and the Chinese remained the small, financially weak Korean merchants who brought some products to the ports at irregular intervals. On the other hand, Western traders continued to rely on Korean purchasing agents. Jardine, Matheson & Company, for example, tried their luck with a comprador, but without much success. Numerous accounts testify to the difficult relationship between foreign and native traders. Chinese merchants, in particular, frequently complained of being assaulted and robbed by Koreans. Friction seems to have intensified toward the end of 1884. In many cases, money advanced to Koreans for making purchases in the interior was stolen or embezzled. The Koreans' growing insolvency, moreover, seriously hampered foreign trade. Attempting to reduce the number of complaints, in the summer of 1884 the Foreign Office issued the order that whenever a foreign trader advanced money to a Korean a guarantor had to be sought. A year later, the Foreign Office demanded that each contract concluded between a Korean and a foreign merchant be countersigned by that office.[52]

Money continued to be one of the most persistent obstacles in the way of the smooth development of trade. Although the government made repeated efforts to widen the circulation of money by permitting money to be substituted for tribute rice and some other taxes, money still did not seem to have assumed an important role as a medium of exchange in the Korean economy. The most popular coin, the *sangp'yŏng t'ongbo*, varied considerably in size and value. In the spring of 1883 the conversion rate was 400 copper cash to one Mexican dollar; the rate in the summer of the same year seems to have dropped to 500 to 520 copper cash to one Mexican dollar. This depreciation was mainly due to an increased demand for the foreign coin, and the Korean government countered this development by fixing the rate at 525 cash to one Mexican dollar. The minting of the *tangojŏn* in the early summer of the same year did little to relieve the worsening monetary situation because the new coin did not meet expectations. Officially, the *tangojŏn* contained six parts of copper to four of lead, but the clumsily made coins varied greatly in size, and some contained three times as much metal as others. The minting of the *tangojŏn* made increased imports of Japanese copper necessary. Depreciation began, however, almost as soon as the coins came out. In the fall of 1884, for example, the rate stood at 200 *tangojŏn* to one Mexican dollar. Its circulation never extended far beyond the capital area, although the Korean government issued frequent exhortations to use the new coin. The overproduction of *tangojŏn* caused a steep rise in consumer prices. Since the Korean coins could not be the only means of payment, a large part of the trade was transacted by barter, and many bills of exchange were issued by the Daiichi Ginkō. Furthermore, the Chinese sycee (silver ingot) was used to some extent, and the Mexican dollar circulated freely in the open ports.[53]

After 1882, the general outlook on trade changed. Foreign trade, in particular, was no longer uncompromisingly regarded as a threat to the domestic economy. The government loosened its traditional control over trade and abolished the monopolistic rights it had granted to some select groups of traders. This policy liberalized trade as an economic activity and, as an occupation, made it socially acceptable to yangban who had hitherto been barred from it. The growth of new commerical companies was stimulated, but this encouragement of trade lacked a solid foundation: the change of attitude toward trade was not accompanied by a more fundamental assessment of Korea's economic needs. Korea's economy remained a basically non-commercial economy. Despite the government's repeated efforts to reduce official protection of traders, the traders inevitably turned to the government for protection. Moreover, the monetary system, upon which trade depends, remained undeveloped. Because the traditional, pre-modern economic system could not assure the new Korean companies a sustained growth, their impact on Korea's economic life at that time was probably small. Although the Korean government changed its stand on trade, it was still little interested in an overall program of modernizing the Korean economy.

The Development of Trade, 1883–1885

In 1883 nearly all import trade was still in Japanese hands. In contrast, the figures for 1884 and 1885 clearly reflect the challenge of the Chinese traders who began to compete for a share in the Korean market. The total value of trade with Japan took a steep plunge during this period. This was mainly due to the decreased imports of copper and foreign textiles from Japan. Chinese merchants were able to ship British textiles directly from Shanghai at a cheaper rate. By doing so, they cut into Japan's brisk business of reexporting foreign textiles. Foreign, mainly British, textiles accounted for approximately half of the value of Korea's imports. Metals (mainly copper and lead) followed next.

Compared to the value of the imports, that of the exports was small: 19 percent of the total foreign trade in 1885, and 21 percent in 1886. Cow hides were a principal export item, followed by rice and beans and some gold dust. After 1884, when commercial activities were briefly interrupted by the disturbances in December of that year, Korea's foreign trade showed continuous growth and more than tripled by the end of the decade.[54]

To the detriment of trade at Pusan and Wŏnsan, Inch'ŏn became the principal center of Korea's foreign trade. At Pusan, trade decreased considerably between 1883 and 1884—imports by one-half and exports by more than two-thirds.[55] The decline of trade at Pusan reflected the fact that the foreign traders were concentrating their activities at Inch'ŏn, close to the capital. Korea's foreign trade remained principally in Japanese and Chinese hands. The Western share was never very substantial.

The treaties that Korea concluded with the Western powers in 1882 ended Korea's seclusion in theory. The influx of foreign traders and the establishment of foreign settlements in the opened ports ended Korea's seclusion in fact. The treaties with the West expanded the diplomatic and commercial contacts with Korea, but the Japanese and the Chinese were, through the most-favored-nation clause, the principal beneficiaries. Because of Seoul's importance as the administrative and cultural center of the country, nearby Inch'ŏn grew into Korea's most important foreign trade center within a short time. Inch'ŏn was the only port during the early treaty days that acquired an international image. Pusan continued to be a Japanese stronghold, but it lost its former position as Korea's point of contact with the outside world. Wŏnsan never had more than provincial significance. At Inch'ŏn, the Western presence was small; the Japanese and the Chinese traders dominated the life of the port and competed for the largest share in Korea's foreign trade.

Korea responded to the demands of international trade by establishing the Maritime Customs Service. More difficult, however, was the rethinking of the traditional concept of trade. The government made efforts to free trade from its institutional and social shackles, but it did little to support the traders in their dealings with foreign merchants. The government did not consider trade as a part of the country's total economy and thus did not develop new resources and products that could have benefited Korea's foreign trade. The second phase of Korea's post-1876 foreign trade was characterized by some institutional innovations, but the economic basis, upon which foreign trade could have grown, improved only slightly.

THE END OF A DECADE

The 1882 incident gave impetus to the self-strengthening movement and stimulated a great variety of ideas on modernization. Even before 1882, a group of young officials had become fascinated by Japan's experiment with Western ideas and institutions. Initially they worked within the framework of the Min-controlled self-strengthening movement, but they eventually became disillusioned with the narrow scope of the Min's modernization program. The ensuing rift between the Min and the enlightenment group led to the deeper involvement of China and Japan in Korea's domestic affairs. Once more, Korea's development was interrupted by a bloody conflict. This conflict was not sparked by the question of whether Korea's modernization should be continued or not, but rather by controversy over the direction and the goal of modernization.

Japan as the Source of Liberal Inspiration

In the early 1880s, debate began to center on change and reform. King Kojong opened the subject to court discussion. Privately, the problem of modernization was scrutinized by younger officials who had become absorbed in finding ways and means to eliminate the stifling influence of Confucian orthodoxy. They saw the need to revitalize Korea by integrating Western ideas and values into Korean society.

199

It is possible that the enigmatic Yi Tong-in was the first Korean to secretly slip out of the country, absorb knowledge about the West as it had become popularized in Meiji Japan, and carry it back to the few Koreans with receptive minds. These young Koreans were not completely unprepared for Yi's ideas; they gathered frequently in Pak Kyu-su's house where they pursued *sirhak* studies and heard accounts from various people who had observed Western things in China.[1] To this group belonged Pak Yŏng-hyo (1861–1939), Kim Ok-kyun (1851–1894), Hong Yŏng-sik (1856–1884), Sŏ Kwang-bŏm (1859–1897), Sŏ Chae-p'il (1864–1951), and Ŏ Yun-jung.[2] When they listened to Yi Tong-in, whose first contacts with this group seem to have been through Kim Ok-kyun, they must have realized that Japan's interpretation of the West was less distorted and, in any case, more diverse than China's. Determined to leave the ruts of orthodox Confucian thinking, they were ready to venture into new intellectual territory. The dispatch of the gentlemen's inspection tour (*sinsa yuramdan*) in 1881 gave some of them an opportunity to see Japan with their own eyes. Hong Yŏng-sik and Ŏ Yun-jung were members of this mission, and Kim Ok-kyun and Sŏ Kwang-bŏm went to Japan for the first time in February 1882.[3] When Hong Yŏng-sik and Ŏ Yun-jung arrived in Japan, they were singled out by the Japanese as members of the enlightenment group, and Kim Ok-kyun was honorably referred to in the Japanese press as "a leader of Korea's enlightenment party."

These young, reform-minded Koreans were all drawn to Fukuzawa Yukichi, the great popularizer of Western thought in Meiji Japan.[4] Ŏ Yun-jung had visited him in the summer of 1881, and Kim Ok-kyun carried a letter of introduction to him from Ŏ. Fukuzawa was glad to have the opportunity to receive Koreans because he wanted to transmit to them his own ideas on Korea. He argued that Korea had been recognized by the treaty of 1876 as an independent country, and thus it was Japan's duty to support Korea's struggle for independence and enlightenment. Fukuzawa instilled in his Korean disciples concepts of national independence and sovereignty. He became Kim Ok-kyun's most important source of inspiration and remained his mentor throughout the following years.

In the fall of 1882, Kim Ok-kyun went to Japan for the second time as an unofficial member of Pak Yŏng-hyo's mission of apology. He spent much of his time with Fukuzawa, and this was the formative period of his thought. Although Pak Yŏng-hyo was occupied with official business and apparently was not introduced to Fukuzawa, he probably took a great interest in Kim's explorations, and he enrolled two members of his mission in Fukuzawa's school. When Pak returned to Korea, the many Japanese faces in his entourage bore testimony to the fact that Fukuzawa intended more than only verbal support of Korea's enlightenment. Fukuzawa encouraged Inoue Kakugorō, one of his favorite students, to go to Korea. Inoue later described his mandate with the words: "The purpose of my going to Korea was in a word to make Korea move toward civilization."[5] Besides Inoue, six technicians accompanied the Korean envoy as well as two Koreans who had graduated from Rikugun Toyama Gakkō. Takezoe Shinichirō joined the party to take up his duties as the new Japanese ambassador at Seoul.[6]

The Korean reformers do not seem to have been prolific writers, and therefore very little is known about their ideas before 1884. A memorial authored by Kim Ok-kyun in the fall of 1882 and carried back to Seoul by Pak Yŏng-hyo shows that Kim was not merely a vague idealist, but that he had definite priorities. Entitled "A Short Essay on the Construction of Roads," the memorial postulated three fundamental starting points for Korea's modernization: sanitation, agriculture, and roads. Subdividing his recommendations into seventeen points, he treated his subject in minute detail.[7]

Other postulates were contained in the well-formulated "Memorial on Enlightenment" which Pak Yŏng-hyo wrote in 1888 (when he was living in exile in Japan). The gist of them had undoubtedly been included in the party's pre-1884 program to modernize Korea's outdated socioeconomic system. Pak's memorial was a final, rather than a preliminary product of an intellectual crystallization process. To the discussion of each of his eight points, except the first one, Pak added a list of concrete requirements. In the following summary a few of the requirements are included in parentheses: (1) international situation; (2) law (equal law for all); (3) economy (prohibition of the sale of offices, reform of the land tax, promotion of industry, encouragement of commerce); (4) hygiene (construction of hospitals, prohibition of early marriages, installation of water pipes and places to bathe); (5) defense (establishment of military schools, new methods of recruiting soldiers); (6) education (establishment of schools, employment of foreign teachers who would teach such subjects as law, finance, politics, medicine, and languages, founding of a newspaper); (7) government (selection of able ministers and proper officials, administrative reorganization, relations with foreign countries, preservation of national sovereignty); (8) civil liberties (prohibition against taking concubines, remarriage of young widows, intermarriage between different social classes, and equal treatment for everyone).[8]

The enlightenment party (*kaehwadang*) did not aim at restoration but at a fundamental reform of Korea's political, social, and economic structure. Uppermost in the reformers' minds was their postulate of national self-strengthening and independence. They wanted to enroll the common people in this effort by giving them a modern education, and they hoped to free Korean society from the inequities of the past. It was an idealistic program that had little resemblance to the Min's more pragmatic approach to modernization. Inevitably, the reformers found themselves at cross purposes with the Min establishment.

Power versus Modernization

Returning from Japan full of ideas on reform and modernization, Pak Yŏng-hyo used his appointment as commissioner of Seoul to embark on modernizing the city's sanitation, improving roads, and introducing a police system. He also eagerly presented to King Kojong the idea of founding a newspaper. The king approved the project on February 28, 1883. Two weeks later, on March 13, a newspaper office was set up, and Pak delegated the main responsibilities to Yu Kil-chun. Yu had studied at Fukuzawa Yukichi's school in Tokyo and held the post of secretary at the Foreign Office. He was assisted by Inoue Kakugorō and some Japanese newspaper experts who had come to Korea with Pak Yŏng-hyo. Yu named the new office Pangmun'guk, the Office of Extensive Culture, and drafted its regulations. He intended to print the newspaper in a mixture of *han'gŭl* and Chinese characters to ensure it wide readership. Yu Kil-chun wrote the announcement of publication and eloquently set forth the ideas of enlightenment. Shortly afterward, Pak Yŏng-hyo was abruptly dismissed as commissioner of Seoul. Consequently, Yu retired from the Foreign Office, and the Japanese technicians who had come to assist him went home disillusioned. The newspaper venture, however, was continued under the aegis of the Min. The regulations of the Foreign Office stipulated the opening of a newspaper office as part of the government language school (Tongmunhak). The head of the school, Kim Man-sik, was put in charge of the Pangmun'guk in August 1883. Work started on September 20, assisted by Inoue Kakugorō whose services were retained. The first issue of the *Hansŏng sunbo* came forth on October 31, 1883. Printed in pure

Chinese, this newspaper appeared every ten days during a period of fourteen months until its publication was interrupted by the disturbances in December 1884.[9]

Pak Yŏng-hyo, who "entered into reform in Seoul with such over-energy that loud complaints came from the common people," apparently antagonized the all-powerful head of the Home Office, Min T'ae-ho.[10] His dismissal, therefore, was undoubtedly a first sign of a rift between the Min and the young reformers. Pak was appointed prefect of Kwangju (Kyŏnggi) on April 23, 1883.[11]

Upon his return from Japan in mid-March, Kim Ok-kyun assumed his post in the Foreign Office.[12] Uppermost in his mind were his reform plans. His ideas inevitably brought him into conflict with his superiors. His relationship with von Moellendorff was especially strained. They disagreed about fiscal policy. Von Moellendorff supported the Min's efforts to mint large amounts of *tangojŏn*; Kim Ok-kyun wanted to raise a loan. He needed money to support the Korean students, among them Sŏ Chae-p'il, whom he sent to Japan in the first half of 1883. Some of the students were to receive military training at the Rikugun Toyama Gakkō, some were to study at Keiō, and others were to undergo job training.[13] Another use of the money was to be the financing of a modern military unit Pak Yŏng-hyo intended to form with the help of the two military school graduates who had returned from Japan with him.[14] Von Moellendorff accused Kim of wasteful expenditures and of "being a dangerous schemer who had unfortunately got the ear of the king."[15]

On April 23, Kim received the royal appointment of "development commissioner for the southern and eastern islands and whaling commissioner." In June he set out to Japan for the third time to borrow three million yen. Official Japan, however, was not inclined to support the reformers. At Seoul, Japanese minister, Takezoe Shinichirō, avoided the reformers because he was pessimistic about their future. In Tokyo, Inoue Kaoru received Kim coldly because he did not recognize him as an official representative of the Korean government. Kim was unable to raise the loan from the Japanese government, and his attempt to do so through James R. Morse of the American Trading Company also failed. Kim's hopes were dashed, and in frustration and bitterness he plotted action that would get results more quickly and effectively. He returned to Seoul in the first days of May 1884.[16]

At least one Min showed more than a fleeting interest in the ideas of the reformers. This was Min Yŏng-ik. In the fall of 1882 he joined Pak

Yŏng-hyo's mission as an unofficial mission member. In Japan, he openly criticized China and conducted himself in such a way that a foreign observer took him for "the leader of the liberal party of Corea."[17] In the summer of 1883, the question of sending an embassy to the United States was under consideration. Min Yŏng-ik was chosen as the plenipotentiary envoy. He was accompanied by two members of the enlightenment party, Hong Yŏng-sik and Sŏ Kwang-bŏm. The mission took leave from the king on July 14. Hong Yŏng-sik returned to Korea via Japan in the winter of 1883. Min Yŏng-ik and Sŏ Kwang-bŏm, accompanied by Foulk, took the route via Europe and came back to Korea on the last day of May 1884.[18] Min Yŏng-ik confessed to Minister Foote: "I was born in the dark, I went out into the light, and now I have returned into the dark again: I cannot yet see my way clearly but I hope to soon."[19] These remarks reveal Min Yŏng-ik's ambivalent attitude toward the reformers. He was fascinated with their ideas, but not committed to their program of action.

Min Yŏng-ik's mission did stimulate some innovations. On April 22, 1884, Hong Yŏng-sik was instructed to establish a postal service (Ujŏng ch'ongguk).[20] Another mission member, Ch'oe Kyŏng-sŏk, built a model farm a short distance from Seoul.[21] Min Yŏng-ik himself was very active as a vice-president of the Foreign Office. Gradually he gravitated back to the ideological fold of his clan. After an apparent dispute with Sŏ Kwang-bŏm, he abruptly resigned from the Foreign Office on August 20 and became the commander of the right barracks of the new army units.[22] Min's entering military office led to a test of strength with Sŏ Chae-'pil and the thirteen other military graduates who had returned to Korea in July. Sŏ Chae-p'il was appointed commanding officer of the newly established Military Training Bureau (Choryŏn'guk) on August 20, and some of his companions entered service under Han Kyu-jik. Min Yŏng-ik presumably resented this competition, forced them all out of office, and replaced them with Chinese instructors. Min's estrangement from the reformers was evident by September 1884.[23]

The Min reached the zenith of their power in the summer of 1884. They had been concentrating on only a few select aspects of modernization. For them, strengthening themselves was first; strengthening the country was second. Initially, the Min staffed the lower ranks of the new offices with members of the enlightenment party and tolerated Min Yŏng-ik's close association with some of them. But the Min included only a few of the reformers' ideas in their program. The Min disagreed with the enlightenment party over domestic issues; they also held different views about Korea's international position. Pak Yŏng-hyo and Kim Ok-kyun set great hopes on the conclusion of treaties with Western powers because they believed that a link with the West would safeguard Korea's independence and check China's increasing pressure.[24] The Min, on the other hand, depended on Chinese backing and never considered using the treaties with the Western powers to assert a degree of independence. The Min's concept of modernization was narrow and self-serving; their concept of foreign relations was traditional. A rupture between the Min and the enlightenment party was therefore only a matter of time.

Min power gradually encroached upon King Kojong's sphere of action. Through their determined takeover of Korea's self-strengthening movement, the Min deprived the king of the chance to direct the "new beginning" for which he had solicited suggestions in the fall of 1882. It is certain that the king sympathized with the enlightenment party. He frequently received Pak Yŏng-hyo and Kim Ok-kyun and reportedly supported Kim's quest for a foreign loan. But the king's sympathy could never be more than a morale boost. Although King Kojong was losing his say in the daily operation of government, his prerogatives as the head of state were untouched, and he was free to entertain contact with foreign representatives. In the fall of 1883, he approached Foote with the request for American army instructors. This request, which he repeated several times, failed because of American indifference—not because of Min obstruction.[25] The Min did not intend to force King Kojong from the throne. On the contrary, they needed him to legitimize their own actions.[26]

The Coup d'état of 1884

The situation in the early fall of 1884 was complicated. The gap between the Min and the reformers had widened to an abyss. In particular, the smoldering enmity between Kim Ok-kyun and Min Yŏng-ik flared into open hostility. The fuel was provided by the coincidence that Kim Ok-kyun came back from Japan disillusioned and without money, and Min Yŏng-ik, upon his return from abroad, climbed to prominence and power. Kim Ok-kyun, supported by Pak Yŏng-hyo, Hong Yŏng-sik, Sŏ Kwang-bŏm, Sŏ Chae-p'il, and a few others, became convinced that the enlightenment party could not reach its goal within the power structure to which most of them belonged.[27] This insight led to the resolution that a seizure of power had to precede the pursuit of modernization. This decision was taken in the first days of October. It was an urgent decision: the reformers felt personally threatened by the Min and hoped that the Sino-French conflict over Annam might divert Chinese attention from Korea and give them an opportunity for unimpeded action in Seoul.[28]

By the end of October ominous clouds were hanging over the capital. Foulk, who was close to Sŏ Kwang-bŏm, became a witness of the deteriorating situation, and Minister Foote seems to have had foreknowledge of the reformers' violent plans. Consul General Aston noticed an "uneasy feeling at present among political circles," and he reported to Parkes that the enlightenment party regarded the presence of the Chinese garrison in Seoul as one of the chief obstacles to reform. Yet Aston thought the reformers' hope that Chinese difficulties with France might allow them to expel Chinese troops from Korea was quite unrealistic. Yüan Shih-k'ai, however, made this possibility the alarming theme of a secret communication to Li Hung-chang, but the viceroy was unwilling to send reinforcements.[29]

Takezoe Shinichirō returned to Seoul on the last day of October after a ten-month absence. During a royal audience on November 2, Takezoe's first official act was to announce that the Japanese government had decided to cancel Korea's outstanding 400,000 yen balance of the 1882 indemnity. This gesture was interpreted as an expression of Japan's desire to counteract Chinese influence. The official Japanese attitude toward the reformers also seems to have undergone a marked change.[30] The Japanese minister showed himself sympathetic and even offered encouragement when he met Kim Ok-kyun, but he used abusive language toward Kim Yun-sik and Kim Hong-jip for their allegiance to China.[31]

Although Kim Ok-kyun, Pak Yŏng-hyo, and their companions had originally plotted action that did not include Japanese help, by November 4 they hoped that the Japanese would assist in the seizure of power and forestall any Chinese intervention. From this day on, concrete preparations were made at evening gatherings, drinking parties, and secret meetings at which Takezoe, Shimamura Hisashi, and Inoue Kakugorō were the principal Japanese participants. Takezoe was uncertain about how far he should involve himself, although the involvement itself was not in question. He asked Tokyo for instructions on November 12. The Koreans did not seem to trust the Japanese fully, but because they needed them they had no alternative but to make them familiar with the details of the plot.[32]

During the first days of December, each person's role was decided and the targets for assassination selected. The scene of the coup was to be the inauguration party for the new Post Office in An'guk-tong on the evening of December 4. On the morning of that day, Takezoe received instructions—the Koreans had long been fearing a change in Japanese policy—that he should not interfere in Korean affairs by actively supporting one party against another. Therefore he shunned public appearance and delegated Shimamura to take his place at the banquet table. Among the other foreign guests were Foote, Aston, Ch'en Shu-t'ang, and von Moellendorff. Three of the designated victims, Min Yŏng-ik, Yi Cho-yŏn, and Han Kyu-jik, were also invited. The banquet dragged on in a dull atmosphere. About ten o'clock the cry of "Fire" broke the cold winter night. In the subsequent confusion, Min Yŏng-ik, who was the first to leave the hall, was stabbed. Kim Ok-kyun, Pak Yŏng-hyo, and Sŏ Kwang-bŏm hurried to Ch'angdŏk Palace, reported the coup to the king and queen, and persuaded them to take refuge in nearby Kyŏngu Palace. Immediately afterward, Pak Yŏng-hyo went to the Japanese legation carrying a note allegedly written by the king calling for Takezoe's help. The Japanese minister, alerted by two previous oral summons from the king, led two hundred legation guards into Kyŏngu Palace to protect the royal family. During the same night, Yi Cho-yŏn, Yun T'ae-jun, Han Kyu-jik, Min T'ae-ho, Cho Yŏng-ha, and Min Yŏng-mok were assassinated.[33]

On December 5, the day following this bloody night, Kim Ok-kyun and Pak Yŏng-hyo proclaimed a newly constituted government. The reform government was headed by Yi Chae-wŏn, a nephew of the Taewŏn-gun, as left state councillor. Right state councillor was Hong Yŏng-sik. The military and police functions were concentrated in the hands of Pak Yŏng-hyo and Sŏ Kwang-bŏm. Sŏ Chae-p'il was also given a military assignment. Direct communication with the king was assigned to Pak Yŏng-hyo's brother, Pak Yŏng-gyo, as first royal secretary. Kim Ok-kyun was vice-minister of the Department of Revenue, and Sin Ki-sŏn was appointed minister of the Department of Personnel and deputy director of the Office of Special Counselors. A striking feature of the new government, which included twenty-three people, was the great number of officials who were related to the Taewŏn'gun (six) and to the in-law clans (three: P'ungyang Cho and Namyang Hong). Two men who had been closely associated with the pro-Chinese Min, Kim Yun-sik and Kim Hong-jip, were appointed minister of rites and commissioner of Seoul, respectively. One Min, who had hitherto held no official function, was present in the new government.[34] This rather strange composition may indicate that the enlightenment party was limited to a very small circle of people. It may also suggest that the reformers intended to muster authority by relying heavily upon the royal clan.

By eliminating the Min and their associates, the reformers had seized power, the first of their two basic objectives. They then established the reform government, their second objective. The swiftness with which they executed both these steps shows that they were better prepared for the aftermath of the coup than the scant allusions to a firm program prior to December 4 would suggest. On the first day "in office," on December 5, the reformers drafted a fourteen-point proclamation that contained the ingredients of a far-reaching political and socio-economic policy. This document called for a total revision of the Sino-Korean relationship and demanded the immediate return of the Taewŏn'gun. Society was to be restructured in such a way as to ensure equal rights for everyone. The document called for economic measures such as reforming the land tax system, easing the people's financial burden, and curtailing government expenditures. The streamlining of government organization, the elimination of corruption and unqualified officials, and the appointment of honest and capable men were demanded. The abolition of certain institutions and the reorganization of the military and police system were also considered.[35]

On the morning of the 5th, the foreign representatives, Foote, Aston, and Zembsch, called on the king who "had little to say, and seemed to be in a state of excitement." In the late afternoon the king and his entourage returned to Ch'angdŏk Palace.[36] The reformers, busily preparing the program of their new government, apparently took little notice of what was going on beyond the palace walls.

Foreign Intervention

Both the Chinese and the Japanese maintained some of the troop contingents that they had moved into the peninsula in the wake of the 1882 incident. The reformers organized their new government under Japanese military protection. This was a challenge the Chinese could not leave unanswered. It is not certain how far the intentions of the reformers had become known before the Chinese countermove began. Ch'en Shu-t'ang reported the events of December 4 to Yüan Shih-k'ai who readied himself for quick action. Ch'en wanted to follow the suggestion of the foreign representatives that China "do nothing to disturb the peace or excite the populace, and avoid a conflict between Japanese and Chinese troops." Yüan, unwilling to follow such a timid course, solicited a call for help from the former right state councillor, Sim Sun-t'aek. During the afternoon of the 6th, leading a force of 1,500 men, he and Wu Chao-yu moved against Ch'angdŏk Palace where the king and the reformers were under the protection of the Japanese. A brief battle between the Japanese guards and the Chinese soldiers ensued. The reformers realized that they were facing an overwhelming adversary. They appealed to Takezoe to remove the king to Inch'ŏn. The Japanese minister declined this request and retreated to the Japanese legation. The desperate reformers, Kim Ok-kyun, Pak Yŏng-hyo, Sŏ Kwang-bŏm, Sŏ Chae-p'il, and a few others, followed him. Hong Yŏng-sik and Pak Yŏng-gyo, who stayed with the king, were killed.[37]

General excitement and the uncertainty about the whereabouts of the king drove the Korean populace into the streets. They went on a rampage, looting Japanese houses and stores and killing a number of Japanese. Westerners were unmolested. Aware that he could not withstand the onslaught of the outraged Koreans, Takezoe decided to evacuate the legation and, reminiscent of Hanabusa Yoshitada's flight to Inch'ŏn after the 1882 incident, fled to that port. Behind him, the legation went up in flames. Takezoe was accompanied by a number of Japanese merchants and artisans and by the defeated reformers who had put their fate in Japanese hands. While Takezoe stayed at Inch'ŏn, they and Inoue Kakugorō boarded the *Chitose maru* on the 11th and sailed into exile in Japan.[38]

With the Chinese in control of Seoul, the king was moved to Yüan Shih-k'ai's quarters. He stayed there until December 10. On December 7, the proclamation of the reform government was rescinded, and the former high ministers, including von Moellendorff, were called back to court. The most significant institutional change was the incorporation of the Home Office into the Council of State. The ill-fated Post Office was abolished. On the following day, Sim Sun-t'aek was appointed chief state councillor, Kim Hong-jip left state councillor, and Kim Pyŏng-si right state councillor. Min Yŏng-ik, too, was recalled to serve in his former appointments.[39] As soon as the Korean government was functioning again, the new president of the Foreign Office, Cho Pyŏng-ho, was sent to Inch'ŏn on the 8th to confer with Takezoe. The latter refused to return to the capital. The king appealed to the Western representatives to mediate, but Foote and Aston hesitated to take on the assignment without consulting with their superiors. The Koreans put the responsibility for the dramatic happenings on Takezoe and demanded the extradition of the Korean rebels. The Korean government decided to carry the matter directly to the Japanese government and appointed the vice-president of the Department of Rites, Sŏ Sang-u, as envoy plenipotentiary and von Moellendorff as deputy envoy on December 12.[40]

When the Japanese government learned about the coup on December 11 through the Chinese minister, Li Shu-ch'ang, and two days later by Takezoe's direct report, it was quick to emphasize that it wanted to resolve the conflict peacefully and directly with Korea. The most complicated and painful aspect of the matter was the uncertainty about the degree of Takezoe's involvement. On December 16, it was decided to send a plenipotentiary envoy to Korea. Inoue Kowashi was dispatched to Inch'ŏn to order Takezoe to return to Seoul without delay and to prepare for negotiations with the Koreans. Three days later, Foreign Minister Inoue Kaoru himself assumed the assignment of plenipotentiary. He was instructed to concentrate on finding out who was responsible for the destruction of the Japanese legation and property, and for the loss of Japanese life. He was to demand punishment, reparations, and an apology. This dispassionate, rather modest approach to a formidable challenge reflected Japan's earlier commitment to a cautious policy that would avoid an open conflict with China. Inoue departed on December 22, but left Shimonoseki only after receiving a military escort. He entered Seoul on January 3, 1885.[41]

News of the coup reached Peking earlier than Tokyo. On December 11, Li Hung-chang was ordered by edict to find a solution in consultation with Wu Ta-ch'eng. The edict made no secret of the fact that China, deeply involved in troubles of her own, could not afford a military confrontation with Japan. Urgent instructions were therefore sent to the Chinese officials on the scene to risk no open conflict with the Japanese. Escorted by Admiral Ting Ju-ch'ang and a force of five hundred soldiers, Wu Ta-ch'eng was sent to Korea to investigate the situation and restore peace and order. The report that Wu was dispatched with military force prompted the Japanese government to give Inoue a similar escort. Wu was not equipped with plenipotentiary powers to negotiate with the Japanese envoy as requested by the Japanese government. The Tsungli Yamen argued that Wu had the power to settle the internal disturbances of a vassal country and therefore could not possibly meet with the representative of a third country. Wu entered Seoul on December 29. Inoue declined to deal with Wu.[42]

Inoue started negotiations with the Korean plenipotentiary, Kim Hong-jip, on January 7. Kim was assisted by von Moellendorff. Preliminary talks between Cho Pyŏng-ho, von Moellendorff, and Takezoe had become deadlocked. The question of guilt threatened to stall the negotiations from the beginning. Only a quiet agreement between Kim Hong-jip and Inoue opened the way for a settlement on January 8. Kim withdrew his demand for expressly censuring Takezoe for collaboration with the rebels; Inoue promised to recall Takezoe. On the next day, January 9, 1885, the *Treaty of Seoul* was signed. It stipulated that: (1) Korea had to send a letter of apology to Japan; (2) Korea had to pay 110,000 yen as indemnity to the relatives of those who had lost their lives, to the injured, and to those whose property was damaged during the disturbances; (3) Korea had to apprehend and punish those who killed the military attaché of the Japanese legation, Captain Isobashi Shinzō; (4) The Japanese legation was to be moved to new grounds, and the Korean government was to provide the site and buildings and pay 20,000 yen to cover construction costs; (5) The housing of the legation guards had to be adjacent to the legation and maintained according to article 5 of the *Treaty of Chemulp'o*. Inoue refused the Korean request for the extradition of Kim Ok-kyun and his collaborators on the ground that they were political exiles. The foreign minister and Takezoe retired from Seoul on January 11 and left Kondō Masuki in charge of the legation under the protection of one battalion.[43] On January 28, Isobashi's murderers were executed,[44] and on February 5, Sŏ Sang-u and von Moellendorff were sent on a mission of apology to Japan.[45]

The coup d'état of 1884 was a failure. The reform government lasted only two days. Its impact on the domestic scene was slight; its international repercussions were disastrous. The basic cause of the events of 1884 was a clash between the Min and the enlightenment party over the principles and priorities of Korea's modernization program. The reformers failed to seize power for at least two reasons: they were outside the decision-making level of government politics and could not reach the apex of power by traditional means, and they were unable to raise enough money to finance their modernization projects. The reformers had contact with the king, who was sympathetic with their cause, but as a part of the traditional political establishment dominated by the Min, he could not help them.

As Kim Ok-kyun himself pointed out while in exile in Japan, it is not fruitful to see this struggle as a simple dichotomy of "pro-Chinese" and "pro-Japanese."[46] Foreign involvement in Korea's modernization, however, was considerable. The Chinese as well as the Japanese supported Korea's self-strengthening with ideas and economic aid. This support was primarily political although both sides also became militarily involved. When the pro-Chinese Min were menaced by the Japanese-backed reformers, China did not hesitate to defend her position within the peninsula. The involvement of China and Japan elevated the coup of 1884 beyond Korean domestic politics to the level of international politics. It was therefore inevitable that the final settlement of the coup had to be reached outside Korea.

The International Settlement of the 1884 Incident: The Convention of Tientsin

In Japan, outrage over the behavior of the Chinese troops toward Japanese nationals in Seoul created a new crisis atmosphere. Demands for immediate punitive action against China and the annexation of some Korean territory threatened to force the Japanese government to act precipitously. Foreign Minister Inoue Kaoru, however, was firm in continuing the moderate course that had brought him Western approval of his actions in Seoul.[47] He wanted to wait until public opinion calmed down and then start quiet negotiations with China on three principal points: (1) complete withdrawal of both the Chinese and the Japanese troops from Korea; (2) recognition of Korea's independence; (3) neutralization of the peninsula to be recognized officially by all concerned powers. Inoue had his doubts about Russia's cooperation, but he was apparently anxious to revive his neutralization scheme, although it had found no Western support two years earlier. The foreign minister's overriding concern was to avoid an open clash with China.[48]

Inoue hastened to let Peking know that his refusal to deal with Wu Ta-ch'eng in Korea did not mean a breaking off of negotiations on the Korean issue. In its search for a negotiation strategy, Tokyo had to consider Sir Harry Parkes' warning that China would refuse to withdraw her forces from Korea. Moreover, it took pains to counteract the hawkish opinions expressed by the Japanese envoy to Peking, Admiral Enomoto Takeaki. On February 24, Itō Hirobumi was appointed special ambassador to Peking. He was to secure two policy goals: first, the withdrawal of Chinese and Japanese forces from Korea and their replacement by a small,

Western-trained Korean force; second, the reprimand of the Chinese officers who had ordered their troops to attack the royal palace. Itō was not to raise the issue of China's suzerainty over Korea.[49]

Peking learned about Japanese intentions to send a delegation to China through a telegram from the Chinese minister in Tokyo, Hsü Ch'eng-tsu, and a direct report from the Japanese consul at Tientsin. Li Hung-chang realized that China would have no choice but to comply with Japan's proposal for a bilateral troop withdrawal. On March 11, he was appointed plenipotentiary negotiator by imperial edict. He seems to have received no other instructions than the emphatic order to reject any Japanese demands for the punishment of Chinese officers in Korea.[50]

The six negotiation sessions, which took place from April 3 to April 15, 1885, between Itō Hirobumi and Enomoto Takeaki and Li Hung-chang, assisted by Wu Ta-ch'eng and Hsü Ch'ang, centered on the settlement of the 1884 incident and the prevention of similar events in the future. The discussions had hardly gotten underway when they almost foundered on the unresolvable question of guilt. Itō insisted on a clear admission of the culpability of the responsible Chinese officers. Li countered by pinning the full blame for the bloody encounter between the Chinese and the Japanese at Seoul on Takezoe Shinichirō. Each questioned the other's claim to have rightfully obtained a Korean call for military intervention. Li also rejected Itō's demand for Chinese compensation to Japanese victims. Although a deadlock over these issues seemed unavoidable, neither side really wanted an irreparable breakdown of the negotiations. Both Li and Itō asked for urgent instructions from their governments. In the fourth meeting, on April 10, the discussions were narrowed down to the single topic of bilateral, simultaneous withdrawal of troops. The Chinese in principal approved this move, but they still faced the problem of how to defend their claim that China, as suzerain, had to be free to preserve peace in the peninsula. Itō objected to a proposed treaty clause that would give China the right, upon the Korean king's request, to send troops to Korea without Japanese interference. He also refused to accept any formula that would acknowledge China's suzerainty over the peninsula. Li Hung-chang had become aware that he could not include in the treaty of 1885 that which he had failed to include in the treaty of 1871. In the sixth session, a compromise text was drafted that settled the military aspects. The issues of guilt and compensation remained unsolved. After some deliberations, Itō agreed at last with Li's suggestion that these two problems should be taken care of in the form of an official communication. After some two weeks of tough negotiations, the *Convention of Tientsin* (also known as the Li-Itō Convention) was signed on April 18, 1885. It contained three stipulations: (1) Article one called for the bilateral withdrawal of troops within four months after the signing of the treaty. To avoid confusion, the Chinese troops were to be shipped from Masan (Ch'ungch'ŏng) and the Japanese troops from Inch'ŏn. (2) Article two contained the agreement to encourage the Korean king to hire foreign instructors for training a local peace-keeping force. China and Japan should refrain from sending their own instructors for this purpose. (3) The last article stipulated that if in the future either side wanted to send troops into Korea because of a renewed outbreak of disturbances, it had to give previous notice in writing to the other side. After the settlement of the incident, the troops would be withdrawn without delay and would not be stationed for any length of time.[51]

As soon as the treaty was ratified by China and Japan on May 21, preparations for the mutual withdrawal of troops got under way. The soldiers left on July 21. Japan notified Korea that the withdrawal of her security forces, which had been in Korea on the basis of article five of the *Treaty of Chemulp'o*, did not mean an invalidation of that treaty.[52] For Japan, the withdrawal of her troops from the peninsula was in tune with her low-risk foreign policy. For China, this same move came dangerously close to an admission that she was no longer able to act in Korea at will. On July 25, the Korean government notified all foreign representatives in Seoul that the protection of the foreign missions would lay henceforth in the hands of the Korean Foreign Office.[53]

Precarious Peace

Peace returned to the peninsula after China and Japan settled accounts at Tientsin in a way that gave Korea greater independence and freedom from interference from either country. Yet there was no time to feel relieved. Over the heads of both the Chinese and the Japanese, big power politics unexpectedly thrust a small island off Korea's southern coast into the limelight of international concern. The British were worried that the Russians would take the Sino-Japanese rift as an opportunity to move into Korea. To prevent this, four English war vessels took up "temporary" positions at the strategically important Port Hamilton on Kŏmun Island on April 15, 1885.[54] The Korean government received the first reports on the British action through Western sources. Although the Korean Foreign Office felt "apprehension and some indignation against England," there was nothing it could do against this occupation of its territory. Upon learning the news, Li Hung-chang proposed to Itō Hirobumi a secret Sino-Japanese security agreement. The Japanese rejected this, but there is no doubt that the relationship between the two statesmen became closer in their common fear of Russian designs against the peninsula from which they were about to withdraw their military forces.[55]

When the secretary of the Russian legation in Tokyo, Alexis de Speyer, secretly departed from the Japanese capital and took up residence as "agent provisoire" in Seoul in the middle of June, the Japanese interpreted the move as an ominous sign. The reason for Japan's heightened concern was secret intelligence that Russia was about to claim, under the most-favored-nation clause, that as a neighbor she was entitled under the privilege of article three of the *Convention of Tientsin* to send troops into Korea under certain circumstances. Japan's apprehension was shared by the British, who were well aware that de Speyer had a special friend in Seoul, Paul Georg von Moellendorff. Moreover, the Russian seems to have made no secret of the fact that he had "instructions to take steps for the annexation of ten times as much Corean territory as had been occupied by Great Britain unless the latter withdraws from Port Hamilton."[56] Before the Korean government could secure the mediation of the foreign representatives to effect the release of Port Hamilton—a special call for good offices went out to the United States—de Speyer defused the explosive situation by revealing that his mission to Korea had come to naught. In an effort "to preclude any erroneous opinions" he stated in early July that his purpose in Korea had been to sign a contract for the employment of Russian military training officers for the Korean army, a contract he had negotiated with von Moellendorff in Japan earlier that year. However, as the Russian found out, von Moellendorff had acted wholly without authority, and the Korean government knew nothing about such a deal.[57] De Speyer dramatized his "strong feelings of deep embarassment" with the veiled threat that Russia might force Korea to accept Russian officers. But von Moellendorff's expulsion from the Foreign Office on July 27, and the arrival of the Russian chargé d'affaires, Karl I. Waeber, who exchanged the ratifications of the Korean-Russian treaty, cleared the air in the Korean capital to some extent.[58]

In the summer of 1885, Japan's posture at Seoul was "apparently little more than that of a passive bystander." At that time, China had begun to restore her shattered image of suzerain. Several acts undertaken by Li Hung-chang point in this direction. He was anxious to eliminate the possibility of having Russian military personnel in Korea. He strongly pressed for the hiring of American instructors. His most daring act, however, was to release and return the Taewŏn'gun, despite opposition by Min Yŏng-ik, who had become the Min's principal spokesman. The Taewŏn'gun was not the only passenger on the Chinese gunboat that brought him back to Inch'ŏn on October 3. He was escorted by Yüan Shih-k'ai, who was to become the symbol of Chinese presence in the peninsula for the next decade. Yüan succeeded Ch'en Shu-t'ang and took charge of diplomatic and commercial affairs on November 16. His calling card bore the pompous English title "Director-General Resident in Korea of Diplomatic and Commercial Relations."[59] It looked as if China had regained the upper hand in the peninsula after all.

꙾꙾꙾꙾꙾꙾꙾꙾꙾꙾꙾꙾꙾꙾꙾꙾꙾꙾꙾꙾꙾꙾꙾꙾꙾꙾꙾꙾꙾꙾꙾

The international agreement reached between China and Japan at Tientsin in mid-April 1885 ended a stormy decade of Sino-Japanese conflict in Korea. The *Convention of Tientsin* was concluded without consulting the Koreans. It was a bilateral agreement between China and Japan that settled the military aspects of the two countries' involvement in the peninsula. Neither China nor Japan wanted war at this time, and the *Convention of Tientsin* was a face-saving device for both. The events of 1884 left the Korean political scene badly disrupted. The Min had lost their main leaders, and the reformers were in exile in Japan. The king had become a mere figurehead. The Chinese moved into this power vacuum in full force. They felt so much in command of the situation that they even risked the return of the Taewŏn'gun. The reformers had demanded his return because they had considered his detainment in China an undue interference in Korea's domestic affairs. Ironically, the Taewŏn'gun could be returned to Korea because of increased Chinese interference. The Japanese retreated and made no preparations for an immediate comeback. The decade that had started with Japan's opening of Korea ended with China's deepened political involvement in Korea.

The 1884 incident ended Korea's own attempt at modernization. To be sure, China and Japan were both concerned with Korea's modernization process to varying degrees, but the leadership lay in Korean hands. The fight for this leadership changed the focus of Korea's modernization effort. Self-strengthening, initially conceived as a means of defending the country against stronger neighbors, narrowed into a factional struggle. Korea's first decade of modernization not only failed to preserve the country against her stronger neighbors, but left her open to intensified foreign interference.

CONCLUSIONS

The two major forces that shaped Korea's first decade after her opening were the pressure of Far Eastern power politics and the challenge of modernization. Both these forces were set in motion by the Kanghwa Treaty of 1876.

Japan opened Korea to trade and diplomacy and exposed the obsolescence of the Sino-Korean tributary system. The Japanese government skillfully used the threat of war to gain privileges in Korea, but in actuality it did not regard war against Korea as a feasible policy alternative. By 1876, Japan had established a solid record of military victories in her other, relatively low-risk adventures at the periphery of the Chinese empire, but it is difficult to detect a strong expansionist drive against Korea in the thinking of such men as Iwakura Tomomi, Ōkubo Toshimichi, and (after 1873) Kido Kōin. Inoue Kaoru, who was a major leader of Japan's foreign policy for more than half of the period under consideration, also harbored no expansionist ambitions at that time. Outside the government, the clamor for active intervention in the peninsula never stopped, but it was an emotional call for expansion to which the Japanese government could not respond. Japan's priorities during these ten years did not and could not include the annexation of Korea. Japan was not prepared to risk defending militarily what she had won from Korea diplomatically.

China was unable to give the Sino-Korean relationship adequate and acceptable expression under the greatly changed circumstances of the late nineteenth century. China, however, would not disclaim suzerainty over Korea. If Korea's position could no longer be preserved within the traditional framework of the tributary relationship, China had to search for other means of controlling Korea. China was also concerned about protecting herself against a military attack on her eastern flank. Korea had become a security problem. In a display of strangely naive trust in the written word, China advised Korea to conclude treaties. Rather than binding Korea to China, these treaties, on the contrary, opened Korea to more outside pressure. China's own Trade Regulations were an ill-conceived and, in the long run, an ineffective instrument for defending her special interests in the peninsula. Although Li Hung-chang believed in the strength of diplomacy, in the end he had to rely on military force to defend Korea against Japan. It would seem that China, especially in 1882, overestimated Japanese intentions and capabilities and therefore moved into the peninsula with too great a military commitment. Within the decade, China changed her non-committal attitude toward Korea into a policy of active interference. The tributary system gave way to power politics.

The West played a small role in the dissolution of Korea's tributary status and in the intensified struggle between China and Japan. For varying reasons, China and Japan assigned to the Western powers the role of mediator. With no particular interests in Korea and bemused by the peculiarities of Far Eastern power politics, the Western powers were unwilling to risk important diplomatic stakes in the peninsula. The modest commercial prospects, moreover, provided no motivation for action. The United States could have aided Korean independence, but any initiative for action by its representatives in Korea was frustrated by Washington's indifference and indecision. Russia was a potential danger in the eyes of both the Chinese and the Japanese. The prospect of a Russian involvement in Korea prompted defensive action by Japan, China, and some Western powers. Instead of benefiting from a relaxation of tension through Western mediation, Korea faced the threat of becoming the arena of yet another struggle for supremacy in the region.

In the case of Korea, the immediate stimulus for modernization was Far Eastern power politics rather than Western aggression. Modernization, in turn, created factional schisms that involved China and Japan even more in Korea's domestic affairs. This eventually led to a widened rift between the two Far Eastern powers. In China's and Japan's view, the modernization of Korea was an imperative dictated by the international situation. Korea's relatively undeveloped state was a security risk for both of them. Therefore, Korea's modernization efforts were actively supported by China as well as by Japan. In this context, modernization was thought of primarily in terms of military and economic strengthening. Only secondarily did Japan come to support the reformers' drive for more fundamental changes in Korean society. The Japanese felt that Korea could not modernize without prior social reform. They wanted an independent Korea because her independence would free her from China's hold and make it easier for the Japanese to influence Korean affairs.

For Korea, modernization was a defensive measure made necessary by her opening to the outside world. In its initial phase, modernization revealed King Kojong's new perspectives on Far Eastern affairs. The king felt a personal commitment to explore ways of giving his country a stronger standing among her neighbors. Kojong's father, the Taewŏn'gun, had been successful in correcting some of the inadequacies of the traditional government system. He had acted in response to internal demands, but from a position of strength toward the outside world. His son's task was both more complex and more urgent. Kojong was under strong external pressures. His country's precarious international situation forced him to take measures that had nothing in common with his father's traditional concerns.

King Kojong's most outstanding achievement was the establishment of the T'ongnigimu Amun. The arrogance of seclusion had disappeared, and the king approached foreign policy with more sophistication and pragmatism than his father had. Despite this, Kojong's initiative failed. There were many reasons for his failure; most seem to have been of a personal nature. First of all, the Taewŏn'gun retained some of his power over the ultra-conservative sectors of the country's political life despite his retirement. Although some of the Taewŏn'gun's internal policies had been unpopular, his defense of the Confucian state against foreign adversaries had won him lasting fame. He therefore still commanded support in the realm of foreign policy and overshadowed his innovative son. King Kojong's credibility as a leader in the face of foreign threats was thus severely jeopardized. He could not easily win the irresolute bureaucracy over to his point of view.

In addition, King Kojong had to face the challenge of a recurrent nineteenth century phenomenon: the emergence of a strong in-law clan. Some of the Yŏhŭng Min used the T'ongnigimu Amun as a vehicle to power. Its establishment had changed the traditional pattern of political control, and it developed into a separate administration. In addition to advancing through the ordinary channels, the Min had to use this new office to gain dominance. This testifies to the fact that the old bureaucracy still commanded some of its traditional strength. Moreover, the Min's relationship to the royal house through marriage was not enough in itself to guarantee them a preeminent role in the traditional government structure. The Min did not work in alliance with the king and did not accept his leadership to achieve a "restoration." The Min seem to have been effective as a group, and there was no outstanding leader among them. In their lack of perception, they perverted Korea's modernization effort into their own self-aggrandizement. It was easy for the Chinese to take advantage of this lack of direction and impose their will on Korea.

As much as external forces inhibited Korea's response to modernization, retarding factors must be sought as well in the traditional system itself. The root of Korean conservatism was the preservation of the Confucian state. The Confucian state represented in every aspect of its political, economic, and social life a self-sufficient system that derived its inner momentum from its determination to recreate a glorified past in the present. Ideally, the past was the touchstone for all action. The Confucian state's remarkable resilience was in its ability to add to or subtract from the body politic those elements that had become necessary or obsolete. This process took place within the strict bounds of the traditional system and was not innovative. Innovation, according to one analysis,* does not result from the addition or subtraction of parts; it takes place only when there is a recombination of the parts. Innovation is thus a process of substitution that is first of all psychologically motivated. This may explain at least in part the nature of Confucian conservatism: the psychological disposition for substitution, that is, for fundamental change, was absent. Although this problem can not be dealt with adequately here and awaits more intensive research, it may be suggested that within Confucian thought it was the concept of "rectifying the names"—the concept of stratifying the sociopolitical life—that inhibited fundamental change most seriously. This concept emphasized the unchangeable hierarchical structure of the world and was thus inimical to innovation. In Confucian view, innovation was the enemy of the system itself. The major concern of the Confucian state was the preservation of its basic values through minor adjustments over time.

In the late nineteenth century, innovation was synonymous with

---

* See H.G. Barnett, *Innovation: The Basis of Cultural Change* (New York: McGraw-Hill, 1953).

modernization on Western terms. "Modernization" is generally understood as action that consists of several transformative processes: commercialization, industrialization, secularization, a diffusion of education, and
expansion of popular involvement in the political process. According to this
definition, the Min's program in the 1880s did not contain the criteria for
innovation because it did not go beyond adding new parts to the traditional
body. Government policy was not revised to encompass a new direction
for the country's development. At best, the adoption of new methods, if
not ideas, was convenient for the rationalization of some traditional government functions. This was the basic weakness of the Korean type of "modernization." It was a process of grafting, but even this was limited. New
agencies were pasted onto the traditional government structure, but the
revenue base did not change significantly and could not produce the means
to sustain new government programs.

In contrast, the program of the reformers contained genuine innovation; it envisaged a definite break with the Confucian past. But the
conditions under which the reformers wanted to implement their program
were not propitious. The Confucian system did not have the proper ante-
cedents that would have provided the reformers with a foundation for
launching their program. Moreover, the reformers did not create a
"popular" front for their ideas. They tried to work within the traditional
government, but they did not make it to the echelons of power, nor did
they solicit support from among their equals. They unrealistically aimed
at reforms, the need for which could not be grasped by those who would
have been their principal beneficiaries—the general populace. They failed
to replace the real power holders, the Min. The reformers did not want to
begin with popular support: this would have been the method of rebels.
They wanted to work down from the top: this was the method of the
Confucian gentlemen.

There was scant difference between the reformers and the Min as
far as the implementation of their plans was concerned. Their difference
lay in their programs and their pattern of action. The Min operated
within the traditional framework; they aimed at preserving the Confucian
state and did not hesitate to do this under China's protective umbrella.
The reformers operated at the periphery of the traditional system. They
aimed at the eventual overturn of the Confucian order and did not hesitate
to try this with Japanese help. Neither party was successful, and both were
responsible for creating the conditions that hastened the downfall of the
Confucian state and its replacement with a new order—an order that was

forced upon the Koreans from abroad. Because the Koreans could not resolve the conflict between the preservation of the traditional Confucian social and political order and the requirements of the modern age, the Japanese imposed a solution of their own: they gradually incorporated the peninsula into their own world order.

Recent Korean historiography has been intent on finding the preconditions for change in developments before 1876. Behind this endeavor may lie the desire to avoid giving all the credit for motivating and starting Korea's modernization to the impact of outsiders. Certain prerequisites for modernization are being identified in pre-1876 Korea. From the eighteenth century, for example, the emergence of private merchants and artisans who sold their products directly to the consumers is taken as the beginning of commercialization. With the growth of cities a certain amount of commercialization would seem to have been inevitable in order to supply the city dwellers with daily necessities. This process, however, showed the adaptability of the traditional society; the changes were strictly within the traditional system. That they did not signify the beginnings of modern commerce becomes clear when these trends are followed into the nineteenth century and especially to the post-1876 period. During the nineteenth century, the trend toward economic development was not sustained. Economic diversification was not supported by any changes in government policy. After 1876, the foreign goods which began to enter the country were distributed through traditional channels. The Kaesŏng and Suwŏn merchants, who had risen in the eighteenth century and had come to play an important role in Korea's unofficial foreign trade, were, after 1876, conspicuous by their absence. This does not mean that they were no longer operating; rather, it would indicate that they, too, lacked the basic requirements—capital and business acumen—to enter into trade relationships with foreign merchants. Foreign trade was thus not easily integrated into the old system, and it did not stimulate a diversified production of goods.

It was not only the indigenous economy that did not contain the prerequisites for development according to modern requirements. After 1876 the Min's self-strengthening program also failed to initiate economic modernization. For example, the country's natural resources remained largely unexplored. Foreign mining ventures failed because of bureaucratic stubbornness. The government's attitude toward taxing trade remained ambivalent. The establishment of the Maritime Customs Service did represent an innovation, but during its initial phase its returns were too small to finance new programs. Modern technology could be introduced only in some specialized sectors—in the Mint, for example. Von Moellendorff's endeavors suffered from lack of coordination, but more fundamentally they were bound to fail because they could not rely on proper financial and technological bases. In sum, the initiatives of foreign advisers and contact with foreign merchants were not sufficient to alter the traditional matrix of economic thinking and experience. The motivation for fundamental economic change was absent.

Korea's general unpreparedness for foreign trade (e.g., lack of cheap export goods and mercantile know-how) accelerated the penetration of Japanese capitalism into the ports. Initially, the Japanese were not bound by treaty to pay tariffs. They thus deprived Korea of a means of protecting her inefficient domestic handicraft industries. Moreover, Korea's defective monetary system led to the influx of foreign money. No efforts were made to counteract this by devising a new monetary system. It would thus seem that the inflexibility of the Korean economy, even more than the impact of foreign trade, was responsible for the relatively slow development of commercial activities inside and outside the treaty ports. In conclusion, then, the indigenous system of political and economic organization rather than the foreign challenge retarded the rapid and effective adaptation to the modern age. "Modernization" in the first decade did not go beyond a moderate self-strengthening movement, in itself too narrow and limited to save the country from the incursions of East Asian power politics.

Korea responded to the coming of the Japanese in the same way the Chinese and Japanese had responded to the coming of the Westerners. All three countries faced the foreign challenge with basically the same initial reaction: consternation and resistance to the foreign influence that threatened the traditional order. The opening of a Far Eastern country was a three-stage process of concluding treaties, violent reactions, and in the end more treaties. A country's adjustment to the opening determined its survival in the modern world.

Korea's response in the initial phase was neither slower nor weaker than that of China, and not much different from that of pre-Meiji Japan. Yet, Korea's subsequent pattern of adjustment resembled that of China and had little in common with Meiji Japan. The criteria which are commonly given to explain China's slow response to the West, however, do not fit Korea's case in all respects. Unlike either China or Japan, Korea suffered from the collapse of the tributary system. She became a pawn in the struggle between China and Japan over the restructuring of the Far East.

Korea thus had to deal with China's efforts to salvage her out-dated prerogatives in the peninsula and with Japan's drive for national security and economic expansion. Korea was not strong enough to hold her own against her two rivaling neighbors. Moreover, the international rivalry over Korea intensified the schism that had developed in Korea as soon as the debate over the country's opening to the outside world had started. Internal and external affairs came to be linked in such a way that Korea gradually lost the power to decide her own course of action. This, however, was the result rather than the cause of Korea's difficulties in finding a modus vivendi in the modern world. Like China, Korea was ideologically a less diverse country than Japan. In Korean hands Neo-Confucianism had become an inflexible creed that helped cement the socio-political status quo. It had earlier been impervious to reformist trends, and in the late nineteenth century it was, under the impact of Western thought, unable to add a new dimension without destroying its fundaments.

Unlike either China or Japan, Korea was a small, highly centralized country. Centralization meant that the decision-making process lay in the hands of the few who surrounded the king. The debate about the acceptance or rejection of the Japanese treaty, for example, never became a national debate. It remained confined to the capital and the highest government officials. Even the local officials who were to implement the new policies were badly informed and therefore balked at the orders of their superiors. The self-strengthening program, too, was centrally guided, and it was almost impossible for lower ranking officials to take part in its planning and execution. While in Meiji Japan the ruling class was widened to include elements that hitherto had taken part in the political process only at the lowest level, in Korea the inflexible traditional government structure ensured the upper echelons' domination in governmental affairs and prevented the common man from joining a process that made popular participation one of its basic requirements. The general populace thus was not compelled to act in unison with the government but instead was misled into xenophobic adventures. This xenophobia, directed against the Westernized Japanese, was not proto-nationalistic. It was stirred by uneasiness and frustration over developments that could not be understood (and thus was at times even directed against the government) rather than by the commitment to defend the country against foreign enemies.

Another internal impediment to a prompt adjustment was the inadaptability of Korea's economic system. Agriculture was the economic mainstay of the Confucian state and remained relatively untouched for purposes of self-strengthening. This was quite the opposite of Japan where agriculture and small-scale industry provided the foundation for industrial growth. Whereas in Japan real drive and momentum of economic development lay outside the government, in Korea economic policy was state controlled.

Is Korea's response, then, a replica of China's case? In certain respects, yes. Both China and Korea shared the Confucian heritage. In both countries it had the same retarding effect. But from an economic point of view, China, being a vast country with great resources, was more adaptable because it could respond on a regional basis. The establishment of modern arsenals, for example, was largely due to regional initiative and financing. Korea, in contrast, had neither local forces nor local resources that could have been easily developed. The smallness of the country had helped to preserve the pre-treaty seclusion. After 1876 it impeded a diversified, regional response. This was not only the result of geographical circumstances, it was also due to political organization. Because of the vastness of the country, China's centralization allowed for diversification. Korea's centralization worked for a more unified, but more rigid response.

It seems useless, however, to push the comparisons too far, especially if this is done in a different time frame. If, for example, Ch'ing diplomacy of the 1860s is compared to Korea's rigid and unresponsive seclusion policy, it is not hard to conclude that the ministers of the Tsungli Yamen steered a foreign policy course that was remarkably adaptable to international realities, one that stood in stark contrast to the Koreans' inflexible policy.* This contrast, however, would not be as evident if China's pre-1842 policy were compared to Korea's pre-1876 policy. Put in a wider time perspective, it is clear that the real turning-point in China's policy toward Korea did not appear until the late 1870s. Until then the Chinese government had not intended to relax the tributary ties and also had not encouraged Korea to conduct negotiations with the West as an independent nation. On the contrary, China's subsequent shift to active participation in Korean affairs must be seen as the direct result of China's frustration over her failure to preserve the tributary system in the modern world. Chinese policy after 1882, and even more distinctly after 1884, was designed to keep a close check on Korea's internal and external affairs. Western observers have generally felt that this interference retarded Korea's development. In the

---

* See Mary C. Wright, "The Adaptability of Ch'ing Diplomacy, the Case of Korea," *Journal of Asian Studies* 17.3: 363–381 (May 1958).

late 1880s China openly expressed regret that she had ever chosen to help the Western powers set foot in Korea.

ⱮⱮⱮⱮⱮⱮⱮⱮⱮⱮⱮⱮⱮⱮⱮⱮⱮⱮⱮⱮⱮⱮⱮⱮⱮⱮ

The decade 1875 to 1885 was a transitional period. The old order was eroded, but nobody spoke about dynastic decline. Korea's opening did not bring about the collapse of the country's traditional order, nor did the developments during this decade turn Korea into a modern state. Given her political and economic self-sufficiency and her intellectual seclusion, Korea had neither China's thrust to halt momentarily the West's impact with a restoration of the Confucian state, nor Japan's drive to rival the West with a forced program of modernization. Even if Korea had had the inner resources and unified leadership to develop more vigorously her modest beginnings of modernization, she would have had to cope with the external factors. The tributary heritage weighed heavily on the peninsula. Coupled with internal weakness, it was the dissolution of this system and Japan's search for an alternative more suitable to her purposes that stunted Korea's growth into a healthy and independent nation and laid her open to become the victim of Far Eastern imperialism.

APPENDIXES
NOTES AND BIBLIOGRAPHY
INDEX

APPENDIX 1

Major Protagonists of Min Power

Clan seat: Yŏhŭng (present-day Yŏju, Kyŏnggi)

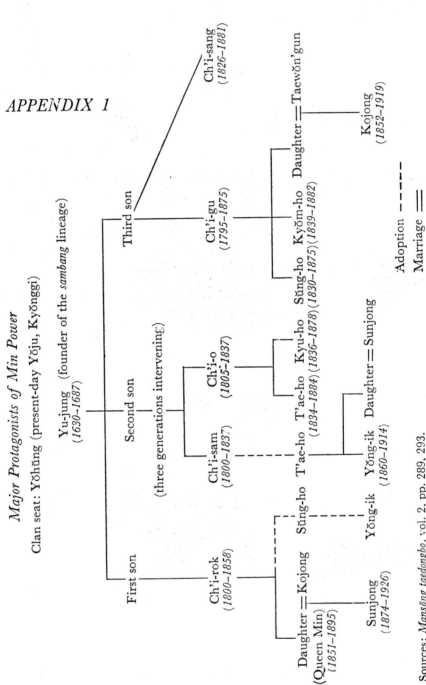

Sources: *Mansŏng taedongbo*, vol. 2, pp. 289, 293.
Yi Sŏn-gŭn, *Han'guksa, ch'oegŭnse-p'yŏn*, p. 352.

APPENDIX 2

Leading Members of the Enlightenment Party

Pak Yŏng-hyo (1861–1939): envoy and minister plenipotentiary to Japan (1882); commissioner of Seoul (1883); prefect of Kwangju (Kyŏnggi) (1883).

Kim Ok-kyun (1851–1894): trips to Japan (1882, 1882/83, 1883/84); Foreign Office (1883–1884).

Hong Yŏng-sik (1856–1884): member of the gentlemen's sightseeing group (*sinsa yuramdan*) (1881); Department of Military Matters (1882); Home Office and Foreign Office (1883); trip to US with Min Yŏng-ik (1883); Post Office (1884).

Sŏ Kwang-bŏm (1859–1897): trip with Kim Ok-kyun to Japan (1882); trip with Kim Ok-kyun and Pak Yŏng-hyo to Japan (1882/83); trip with Min Yŏng-ik to US and Europe (1883/84).

Sŏ Chae-p'il (1864–1951): Graduate of Rikugun Toyama Gakkō (1884); commanding officer in Military Training Bureau (1884).

Yu Kil-chun (1856–1914): Studied at Keiō (1881/82); Foreign Office (1883); in charge of Pangmun'guk (1883); with Min Yŏng-ik to US (1883).

Abbreviations used in the Notes

CJHSL	*Ch'ing-chi Chung-Jih-Han kuan-shi shih-liao*
CKHCJ	*Kuang-hsü-ch'ao Chung-Jih chiao-she shih-liao*
CSS	*Chōsen shi*
CWCSL	*Ch'ing-chi wai-chiao shih-liao*
FO17	Foreign Office, England (China)
FO46	Foreign Office, England (Japan)
FRUS	*Papers Relating to the Foreign Relations of the United States*
IS-KJ	*Ilsŏngnok* (Kojong period)
MHBG	*Chŭngbo munhŏnbigo*
NGB	*Dai Nippon gaikō bunsho*
PBTN	*Pibyŏnsa tŭngnok* ("b" after page nos. refers to lower half of the reproduced page)
TGIG	*T'ongni kyosŏp-t'ongsangsamu Amun ilgi*
Treaties	*Treaties, Regulations, etc. Between Corea and Other Powers, 1876–1889*

Dates are by year, month, and day of the king's reign. Kojong 13.6.12 means the twelfth day of the sixth month of the thirteenth reign year of King Kojong. Intercalary months are indicated by *. When a king's name does not precede a Korean date in this book, the reference is to King Kojong's reign. A KH preceding the year refers to the Kuang-hsü period.

NOTES

Chapter 1

1. The term "hermit nation" comes from William E. Griffis' work *Corea, the Hermit Nation* (New York, 1882).

2. Charles Gutzlaff, *Journal of Three Voyages along the Coast of China in 1831, 1832, and 1833* (London, 1834), p. 317.

3. Sinic Zone is a term coined by Prof. Fairbank. According to his definition, Korea, Vietnam, the Liu-ch'iu Islands, and, at times, Japan belonged to it. See John K. Fairbank, *The Chinese World Order* (Harvard, 1968), pp. 1–19.

4. Chŏn Hae-jong maintains that the label "tributary" (*chogong*) does not fit Sino-Korean relations prior to the fourth century. The term "tributary" was apparently first used in an institutional sense in the Chinese historical work *San kuo-chi*. Prof. Chŏn classifies tributary relations into two categories: formal and quasi. To the former belong the following aspects: economic (tribute and presents), ceremonial, military (mutual aid), and political (calendar, hostages). To the latter belong: political (border questions), economic (trade), and cultural (thought, religion, etc.). These categories are, of course, not rigid and in many cases the dividing lines are fluid. Chŏn Hae-jong, "Han-Chung chogong kwan'gye ko," *Tongyang sahak yŏn'gu* 1:14–18,21,23 (Oct. 1966).

5. In 1370 Koryŏ began to use Ming reign-titles; this practice was, however, interrupted several times afterward. In 1386 the frequency of sending tribute-bearing missions to the Ming was fixed at one mission every three years. Trade became a quasitributary feature. Chŏn Hae-jong, "Han-Chung chogong kwan'gye ko," *Tongyang sahak yŏn'gu* 1:34–35; Yi Sang-baek, *Han'guksa, kŭnse chŏn'gi-p'yŏn*, pp. 31–34.

6. Another responsiblity China had toward her tributary was help in case of internal rebellion.

7. For background information on the two Manchu invasions, see Yi Sang-baek, *Han'guksa, kŭnse hugi-p'yŏn*, pp. 87–107.

8. For the most detailed study on tributary missions exchanged between Korea and China, see Chŏn Hae-jong, "Ch'ŏngdae Han-Chung chogong kwan'gye chonggo," *Chindan hakpo* 29/30:239–284 (1967). For an English version of this article: "Sino-Korean Tributary Relations in the Ch'ing Period," in John K. Fairbank, ed., *The Chinese World Order*, pp. 90–111. Also see Kim Sŏng-ch'il, "Yŏnhaeng sogo," *The Yŏksa Hakpo* 12:1–79 (May 1960) and Fairbank and Teng, "On the Ch'ing Tributary System" in *Ch'ing Administration, Three Stndies*, pp. 107–246.

9. For details on the missions' composition, route, reception in Peking, etc., see Chŏn Hae-jong, "Ch'ŏngdae Han-Chung chogong kwan'gye chonggo," *Chindan hakpo* 29/30:244–253. A map of the tribute routes can be found in Yi Sang-baek, *Han'guksa, hugi-p'yŏn*, pp. 112–113.

10. In the remaining cases the Korean envoys brought the imperial commands back to Seoul. Chŏn Hae-jong, "Ch'ŏngdae Han-Chung chogong kwan'gye chonggo," *Chindan*

hakpo 29/30:253–254; Fairbank and Teng, "On the Ch'ing Tributary System," in *Ch'ing Administration, Three Studies,* pp. 193–197.

11. The most detailed treatment of Korean-Japanese relations up to the time of the Hideyoshi invasions is Lee Houn-jong's (Yi Hyŏn-jong) book entitled *Chosŏn chŏn'gi tae-Il kyosŏpsa yŏn'gu* (Seoul, 1964). Based on material drawn from the *Sillok,* the book has many useful tables. Nakamura Hidetaka in his monumental three-volume work *Nissen kankei shi no kenkyū* (Tokyo, 1965 and 1969) also studies various aspects of Korean-Japanese relations prior to the Hideyoshi invasions.

12. For the content of the Treaty of Kiyu (1609), see Ching Young Choe, "The Decade of the Taewŏn'gun," vol. 2, pp. 401–405. For an illuminating description of the seals and certificates (there were eight different kinds), see Yi Hyŏn-jong, *Chosŏn chŏn'gi tae-Il kyosŏpsa yŏn'gu,* pp. 34–59. For a brief discussion on the exchange of missions between Yi Korea and Tokugawa Japan, see George M. McCune, "The Exchange of Envoys between Korea and Japan during the Tokugawa Period," *Far Eastern Quarterly* 5.3:308–325 (May 1946).

13. Yi Hyŏn-jong, *Chosŏn chŏn'gi tae-Il kyosŏpsa yŏn'gu,* pp. 30–31; *Pusan yaksa* (Pusan, second ed., 1968), pp. 50–57; Yi Wan-yŏng, "Tongnaebu mit Waegwan ŭi haengjŏng sogo," *Hangdo Pusan* 2:11–75 (1963). For a picture of the Japan House, see Kim Ŭi-hwan, "Pusan kaehang ŭi yŏn'gu," *Hangdo Pusan* 3:25 (1963). Prof. Kim, an untiring historian of his native Kyŏngsang namdo, has published an excellent guidebook of historical Pusan, *Pusan ŭi kojŏk kwa yumul* (Pusan, 1969).

14. Han U-gŭn, *Han'guk kaehanggi ŭi sangŏp yŏn'gu,* p. 23.

15. *Sok taejŏn,* 5:12. The heavy tributes in gold and silver moreover induced the government to impose a ban on mining these metals in order to hide the country's mineral resources. Yi Kyo-sŏng, "Han'guk sanggongŏp sa," in *Han'guk munhwasa taegye,* II, 1096–1098.

16. Yi Nŭng-hwa, *Chosŏn kidokkyo kŭp oegyosa,* pp. 154–155.

17. For the encounters with the French and the Americans, see Ching Young Choe, *The Rule of the Taewŏn'gun, 1864–1873,* pp. 91–133.

18. A different view is stated in Mary C. Wright, "The Adaptability of Ch'ing Diplomacy, the Case of Korea," *The Journal of Asian Studies* 17.3:363–381 (May 1958). Mary Wright's point of view seems somewhat forced in the light of events in the late 1870s and the 1880s.

19. For the various Japanese missions to Korea prior to 1874, see Ching Young Choe, *The Rule of the Taewŏn'gun, 1864–1873,* pp. 139–165. For discussions on the *seikanron,* see Nobutaka Ike, *The Beginnings of Political Democracy in Japan,* pp. 47–59; Hilary Conroy, *The Japanese Seizure of Korea: 1868–1910,* pp. 34–50; Tabohashi Kiyoshi, *Kindai Nissen kankei no kenkyū,* I, 298–330.

20. For the draft version of the treaty, see *Ch'ou-pan I-wu shih-mo,* 82:33–37b. For its English version, see *Treaties, Conventions, etc. between China and Foreign States,* II, 1236.

21. Li Hung-chang, *Memorials,* 18:49b.

22. *Ch'ou-pan I-wu shih-mo,* 93:29b–30b. For the problems discussed in this section, consult the two older articles: Tsiang Ting-fu, "Sino-Japanese Diplomatic Relations, 1870–1894," *Chinese Social and Political Science Review* 17.1:first chapter (April 1933) and T.C. Lin, "Li Hung-chang: His Korea Policies, 1870–1885," 19.2:202–209 (July 1935).

23. See, for example, Kim Yun-sik, *Ŭmch'ŏngsa,* pp. 79, 96.

24. For the Taewŏn'gun's restoration of the royal house and the Council of State, see Ching Young Choe, *The Rule of the Taewŏn'gun, 1864–1873*, pp. 46–48, 64–69.

25. For the Taewŏn'gun's economic policies, see Ching Young Choe, *The Rule of the Taewŏn'gun, 1864–1873*, pp. 32–41.

26. For studies on the growth of commercialism, see Kang Man-gil, "Chosŏn hugi sangŏpchabon ŭi sŏngjang," *Han'guksa yŏn'gu* 1:79–107 (Sept. 1968) and "Kaesŏng sangin yŏn'gu—Chosŏn hugi sangŏpchabon ŭi sŏngjang," *Han'guksa yŏn'gu* 8:1–24 (Sept. 1972) and Yu Wŏn-dong, *Yijo hugi sanggongŏpsa yŏn'gu* (Seoul, 1968).

27. Chŏn Hae-jong, "Ch'ŏngdae Han-Chung chogong kwan'gye chonggo," *Chindan hakpo* 29/30:274–277 (1967).

28. Fairbank and Teng, "On the Ch'ing Tributary System," in *Ch'ing Administration, Three Studies*, p. 172. For a description of a typical market day, see *Kankoku shi*, pp. 109–110.

29. *Man'gi yoram, chaeyongp'yŏn*, pp. 725–729; Chŏn Hae-jong, "Ch'ŏngdae Han-Chung chogong kwan'gye chonggo," *Chindan hakpo* 29/30:277 (1967); Han U-gŭn, *Han'guk kaehanggi ŭi sangŏp yŏn'gu*, pp. 25–26.

30. For a detailed description of trade conditions prior to the Hideyoshi invasions, see Yi Hyŏn-jong, *Chosŏn chŏn'gi tae-Il kyosŏpsa yŏn'gu*, pp. 141–176, 208–218; Kang Man-gil, "Chosŏn hugi sangŏpchabon ŭi sŏngjang," *Han'guksa yŏn'gu* 1:93 (Sept. 1968); Kim Byung-Ha (Kim Pyŏng-ha), *Yijo chŏn'gi tae-Il muyŏk yŏn'gu* (Seoul, 1969).

Chapter 2

1. Throughout the subsequent discussion the members of the Yŏhŭng Min who came to power in the second half of the nineteenth century are collectively called "the Min," although they constituted only one particular segment (*p'a*) of the Yŏhŭng Min clan. See Appendix 1. The fullest account of the emergence of the Min clan can be found in Harold F. Cook, "Kim Ok-kyun and the Background of the 1884 Emeute" (unpublished Ph. D. thesis, Harvard 1968), chapter 2, pp. 24–45.

2. Prof. Yi Sŏn-gŭn in *Han'guksa, ch'oegŭnse-p'yŏn* (Seoul, 1961), pp. 342–349, summarizes the factors that led to the deep hatred Queen Min came to harbor against her father-in-law and presents five points which account for the rise of the Min faction: 1. the appointment of members of the Min clan to high office; 2. the recruitment of Queen Dowager Cho's nephews, Cho Yŏng-ha and Cho Sŏng-ha, for the Min cause by Min Sŭng-ho, Queen Min's brother by adoption; 3. the link-up with some members of the Andong Kim clan, for example with Kim Pyŏng-ik and Kim Pyŏng-guk, who resented the Taewŏn'gun's pressure against their clan; 4. the alliance with some of the Taewŏn'gun's own relatives, notably with his older brother, Yi Ch'oe-ŭng, and his oldest son, Yi Chae-myŏn; 5. Min Sŭng-ho's approach of some dissident Confuciantists, for example Ch'oe Ik-hyŏn. In conclusion, then, Prof. Yi tends to see the downfall of the Taewŏn'gun as a plot forged by the Min clan. A similar thesis is put forward by Tabohashi Kiyoshi in his *Kindai Nissen kankei no kenkyū* (Keijo, 1940), I, 331–332. Accounts of the events leading to the Taewŏn'gun's retirement can be found in Ching Young Choe, *The Rule of the Taewŏn-gun, 1864–1873* (Cambridge, 1972), pp. 166–176, and in James B. Palais, *Politics and Policy*

in Traditional Korea (Cambridge, 1975). Prof. Palais has treated the problems surrounding the Taewŏn'gun's downfall in the first two chapters of his "Korea on the Eve of the Kanghwa Treaty, 1873–1876" (unpublished Ph. D. thesis, Harvard 1968). Although from a different point of view, Palais treats in his thesis many problems under discussion in this and the following chapters.

3. *CSS*, pt. 6, vol. 4, pp. 309, 311, 344, 351–352, 364, 381. It should be noted that these appointments were rather long in comparison to the frequent shifts of personnel on the lower levels of the bureaucracy.

4. For a description of Yi Yu-wŏn's early career, see Ching Young Choe, *The Rule of the Taewŏn'gun, 1864–1873*, pp. 54–55; *Han'guk inmyŏng taesajŏn*, p. 695.

5. *CSS*, pt. 6, vol. 4, pp. 349, 350, 352, 353. For details, see Palais, "Korea on the Eve of the Kanghwa Treaty, 1873–1876," pp. 395–406.

6. Yi Sŏn-gŭn pictures Yi Ch'oe-ŭng as a man who harbored deep resentment against his younger brother and therefore was especially disposed to accept the courting of the Min clan. *Han'guksa, ch'oegŭnse-p'yŏn*, pp. 355–356; *Han'guk inmyŏng taesajŏn*, p. 745. Here again Yi Sŏn-gŭn relies on Hwang Hyŏn's *Maech'ŏn yarok*, p. 22.

7. *CSS*, pt. 6, vol. 4, p. 364. After his retirement as chief state councillor, Yi Yu-wŏn continued to serve in various capacities.

8. Ching Young Choe, "The Decade of the Taewŏn'gun," vol. 2, pp. 310–319; Yi Ki-baek, *Han'guksa sillon*, p. 296; Yi Sŏn-gŭn, *Han'guksa, ch'oegŭnse-p'yŏn*, pp. 354–355.

9. *Han'guk inmyŏng taesajŏn*, p. 103; Yi Sŏn-gŭn, *Han'guksa, ch'oegŭnse-p'yŏn*, p. 356. Prof. Yi describes Kim Pyŏng-guk, who was a member of the Andong Kim clan, as an archenemy of the Taewŏn'gun. Kim Pyŏng-guk became left state councillor on September 14, 1878.

10. Yi Sŏn-gŭn maintains that these four individuals were appointed to high office because they were easy puppets in the hands of the Min. It is evident that Yi Sŏn-gŭn based himself too one-sidedly on Hwang Hyŏn's *Maech'ŏn yarok*, a work which overstresses the power of the Min clan. Yi Sŏn-gŭn, *Han'guksa, ch'oegŭnse-p'yŏn*, p. 356.

11. For brief biographical sketches of Kim Pyŏng-hak, Hong Sun-mok and Kang No, see Ching Young Choe, *The Rule of the Taewŏn'gun, 1864–1873*, pp. 55–58. Hong and Kang were pardoned as early as February 11, 1874. Even Han Kye-wŏn who had been punished with banishment was released in mid-February and pardoned on March 25, 1874. *CSS*, pt. 6, vol. 4, pp. 312, 316, 317, 322. For a thorough discussion of the question of personnel, see James B. Palais, "Korea on the Eve of the Kanghwa Treaty, 1873–1876," pp. 105–107, 140–141.

12. In his detailed study of the emergence of the Min clan Harold Cook states that the basis of emergence of the Min was exactly the same as it had been for the Andong Kim, namely the marriage of a clanswoman to the king. However, their ascendence to power was delayed by several factors: the Taewŏn'gun started to rule; the Andong Kim were still strong; Queen Min did not immediately have a son. Cook, "Kim Ok-kyun," p. 34. The Taewŏn'gun was married to a sister of Min Sŭng-ho.

13. Min Sŭng-ho died, as the story goes, when a package exploded while he unwrapped it. The bomb was presumably sent to him by the Taewŏn'gun. *CSS*, pt. 6, vol. 4, pp. 348–349. Min Sŭng-ho was Queen Min's brother through adoption. Another mysterious explosion took place in Kyŏngbok Palace, reportedly in Queen Min's sleeping quarters. Yi Sŏn-gŭn, *Han'guksa, ch'oegŭnse-p'yŏn*, pp. 358–360.

14. *CSS*, pt. 6, vol. 4, pp. 473, 476. For a brief list of representative Min appointments between 1866 and 1873, see Yi Sŏn-gŭn, *Han'guksa, ch'oegŭnse-p'yŏn*, p. 347. It is also interesting to note that in the period between 1800 and 1866 only nineteen members of the Min clan passed the *munkwa* examination, whereas between 1866 and 1884 twenty-four Min passed it. Cook, "Kim Ok-kyun," p. 44.

15. Prof. Yi Sŏn-gŭn presents the view that in January 1874 Queen Min started to rule in the name of the king. Since she could not appear outside the palace, she let close kinsmen such as Min Sŭng-ho and Min Kyu-ho represent her. Yi Sŏn-gŭn, *Han'guksa, ch'oegŭnse-p'yŏn*, p. 353. Prof. Yi undoubtedly based this statement on Hwang Hyŏn's *Maech'ŏn yarok*. This assertion can not be supported by the court records.

16. For a detailed discussion of the abolition of Ch'ing cash and the reestablishment of the Mandongmyo, see Palais, "Korea on the Eve of the Kanghwa Treaty, 1873–1876," chapters 3 and 4.

17. In the *Ilsŏngnok* a great number of these missions are reported: *IS–KJ*, 1.3.28 (vol. 7), 1.5.23 (vol. 10), 2.2.6 (vol. 21), 3.8.23(vol. 44), 6.4.5 (vol. 84), 7.4.15 (vol. 96), 9. 4.4/30 (vol. 121). For a detailed discussion of the contents of the reports brought back from China, see Han U-gŭn, "Kaehang tangsi ŭi wigiŭisik kwa kaehwasasang," *Han'guksa yŏn'gu* 2:112–115 (Dec. 1968).

18. *IS-KJ*, 9.12.26 (vol. 130).

19. *IS-KJ*, 11.3.30 (149:38–48).

20. *CSS*, pt. 6, vol. 4, pp. 333–334; Yi Sŏn-gŭn, *Han'guksa, ch'oegŭnse-p'yŏn*, pp. 369–370. The Tsungli Yamen's assessment of the possibility of an attack on Korea by Japan was apparently based on the opinion of the Frenchman Prosper Giquel who was employed in Shen Pao-chen's navy yard.

21. *IS-KJ*, 11.6.25 (152:74–78b; 81b–82b); *Kao koryak*, vol. 4: "Pukchahu nonpyŏng sa-kye" (Discussion of military matters after receipt of the Chinese communication). There was great uncertainty about the role Christianity played in the West's fast advance in East Asia. Pak Kyu-su, for example, thought that Christianity was a major factor in the Meiji Restoration. *IS-KJ*, 11.6.25 (152:78b). Generally it was thought that Prince Kung had helped the Western powers from within. He was pictured as a traitor. For example, see *IS-KJ*, 9.4.30 (vol. 121).

22. *IS-KJ*, 11.6.29 (152:94–95), 12.1.22 (163:22b); *CSS*, pt. 6, vol. 4, pp. 335, 336, 342, 343, 360; *PBTN*, 256: 743a.

23. *IS-KJ*, 11.1.3 (146:16b–17), 11.1.9 (146:28–29b), 11.1.10 (146: 32). Pak Che-gwan was formerly prefect of Andong and had impeccable credentials.

24. For a discussion on the formation of foreign policy in early Meiji Japan, see Marlene J. Mayo, "The Korean Crisis and Early Meiji Foreign Policy," *Journal of Asian Studies* 31.4:793–819 (Aug. 1972).

25. *NGB*, vol. 7, Nos. 210–212, pp. 362–371.

26. *IS-KJ*, 11.6.29 (152:94–95); Pak Kyu-su, *Hwanjae-chip*, 11:1–3b (letter to the Taewŏn'gun, spring 1874).

27. *IS-KJ*, 11. 8. 9 (154:17a–b); *CSS*, pt. 6, vol. 4, p. 341; *NGB*, vol. 7, No. 218, pp. 404–414. From a discussion between King Kojong and Yi Yu-wŏn during an audience it becomes clear that the only term they found unacceptable in the Japanese documents was *chŏnja*, "Son of Heaven." Upon the king's terse question why China had hitherto tolerated Japanese use of this term, Yi had to concede that even China could not but put up

with it because of "geographic distance." *IS-KJ*, 11.9.20 (155:42b–43).

28. *NGB*, vol. 8, No. 18, p. 53. If Korea called herself independent and made the Korean king and the Japanese chief minister (*dajō-daijin*) or the Japanese foreign minister and the Korean minister of rites counterparts and proposed the restoration of the old friendship, Moriyama was instructed to answer immediately in a positive sense. If, however, Korea called herself independent and proposed to carry on the relationship on the level of ruler to ruler, or if she presented herself as a country dependent on China and insisted that all things be handled by China, Moriyama had to refer to Tokyo for a decision. Moriyama Shigeru was to carry two letters to Korea: one in which Sō was to inform the vice-minister of the Korean Department of Rites of the changes in Japan since the Meiji Restoration and another which was to introduce Moriyama to the vice-minister of the same department and to demand that an official be sent to Tongnae to negotiate a new agreement with Moriyama. *NGB*, vol. 8, No. 15, pp. 46–48.

29. *NGB*, vol. 8. No. 14, pp. 45–46.

30. *NGB*, vol. 8, No. 23, pp. 55–58; *CSS*, pt. 6, vol. 4, pp. 356.

31. *NGB*, vol. 8, No. 23, pp. 57–58; No. 25, pp. 61–68; No. 26, pp. 68–69; *CSS*, pt. 6, vol. 4, p. 357.

32. *IS-KJ*, 12.2.5 (164:7–9, 12a–b); *PBTN*, 256:728b–729; *CSS*, pt. 6, vol. 4, p. 356.

33. *IS-KJ*, 12.2.9 (164:27b–28); *PBTN*, 256:729.

34. *IS-KJ*, 12.3.4 (165: 11a–b); *PBTN*, 256:742b.

35. *NGB*, vol. 8, No. 32, pp. 75–79; *PBTN*, 256:763.

36. *NGB*, vol. 8, No. 28, pp. 70–71.

37. *NGB*, vol. 8, No. 29, pp. 71–72; No. 30, pp. 72–73; No. 34, p. 83; No. 35, pp. 90–91.

38. The audience of June 13 was attended by 35 high officials (Tabohashi counts 34, although he lists the names of 35). Among them were elder statesmen, state councillors, heads of ministries, and some military men. Although the Min clan was directly represented by Min Kyu-ho and Min Ch'i-sang, they did not express views of their own. *IS-KJ*, 12. 5. 10 (167:20–30, 36a–b); 12.5.25 (167:71a–b); *PBTN*, 256:763, 765; Pak Kyu-su, *Hwanjae-chip*, 11:3b–5(letter to the Taewŏn'gun), 10b–11 (letter to Yi Ch'oe-ŭng); Tabohashi Kiyoshi, *Kindai Nissen kankei no kenkyū*, I, 380–385. In the summer of 1874, Pak Kyu-su began to exchange letters with the Taewŏn'gun. Pak evidently was disgusted about how the relations with Japan were handled in the summer of 1875. In one letter he wrote: "Although you do not wish to have worldly affairs reach your ears, these matters [concerning Japan] are of paramount importance for the existence [of Korea]. ." As a last resort for a quick settlement of the dispute with Moriyama, Pak even considered a temporary return of the Taewŏn'gun to the capital "to give leadership in mapping out a strategy." *Hwanjae-chip*, 11:6a–b. Pak did not repeat such a demand in public, however. I believe that James Palais overinterprets this passage. See Chapter 13 in his book, *Politics and Policy in Traditional Korea*.

39. *NGB*, vol. 8, No. 39:100–101.

40. *IS-KJ*, 12.6.3 (168: without page numbers); 12.6.14 (168:38b–39b); 12.6.19 (168:49); 12.7.8 (169:11–12b); 12.7.9 (169: 14b–15); 12.8.6 (170:16); *PBTN*, 256: 777a–b, 786a–b; *NGB*, vol. 8, No. 42, pp. 109–112; No. 46, p. 116; No. 47, p. 118; Pak Kyu-su, *Hwanjae-chip*, 11:5–10b (letters to the Taewŏn'gun), 10b–15b (letters to Yi

Ch'oe-ŭng). In two letters to Yi Ch'oe-ŭng, Pak Kyu-su suggested that the Korean government should demand official apology from the Japanese government for Yabe Junshuku's slandering articles of 1867 as the condition for acceptance of the Japanese communications. *Hwanjae-chip*, 11:15b–17. For the background, see Ching Young Choe, *The Rule of the Taewŏn'gun, 1864–1873*, pp. 142–144.

41. *NGB*, vol. 8, No. 36, pp. 91–94.

42. For a detailed description of the incident, see Inoue Yoshika's report:*NGB*, vol. 8, No. 57, pp. 130–132.

43. *CKHCJ*, 1:10b; *T'ongmun kwanji* (repr., Keijo, 1944), 11:92 (the letter of the Korean king to the Chinese Board of Rites).

44. *IS-KJ*, 12.8.23 (170:43b–44), 12.8.24 (170:45b), 12.8.25 (170:49), 12.8.26 (170: 50a–b); *PBTN*, 256: 788b, 789, 790a–b, 796b, 798b–799. On September 25, an edict promoted Inch'ŏn to the status of a defense regiment (*pangŏyŏng*), and Yŏngjong, which was strategically most important "at the gate of the sea," was attached to the defense unit of Inch'ŏn.

45. *IS-KJ*, 12.8.29 (170:53, 56b–57); *PBTN*, 256:793a.

46. *NGB*, vol. 8, No. 48 and No. 49, p. 119; No. 53, pp. 122–124.

47. *NGB*, vol. 8, No. 60, pp. 137–138.

48. *FRUS*, 1876, No. 181: Bingham to Fish, October 6, 1875.

49. *NGB*, vol. 8, No. 56, pp. 127–129; No. 57, pp. 129–130.

50. *NGB*, vol. 8, No. 59, p. 137; *CKHCJ*, 1:1.

51. *Asien*, Nov. 25, 1875: Brandt to Bülow; *NGB*, vol. 8, No. 61, pp. 139–140; vol. 9, No. 38, p. 142.

52. *NGB*, vol. 9, No. 37, pp. 140–141; FO 17/719, Wade's 6, January 12, 1876. Wade considered England's difficulties with China over Yünnan as the principal reason his discussions with the Tsungli Yamen would fail at that particular moment.

53. *CKHCJ*, 1:1, 2a–b; *NGB*, vol. 9, No. 39, pp. 143–145; *CJHSL*, No. 206, pp. 264–265.

54. *NGB*, vol. 9, No. 39, pp. 142–162. The *NGB* gives the different versions of this conversation, including the transcript made by the secretaries of the Tsungli Yamen.

55. *CKHCJ*, 1:1b–2.

56. *CKHCJ*, 1:2–3; *NGB*, vol. 9, No. 38, pp. 141–142; No. 41, pp. 163–165.

57. *CKHCJ*, 1:3b–7; *CWCSL*, 4:35a–b; *CJHSL*, No. 208, pp. 267–268; No. 212, p. 270; No. 217, p. 273; No. 230, p. 293; No. 232, p. 293; No. 235, p. 295; *NGB*, vol. 9, No. 41, pp. 165–166; No. 42, pp. 166–167; No. 46, pp. 181–183; No. 47, pp. 184–185; Wang Yün-sheng, *Liu-shih-nien-lai Chung-kuo yü Jih-pen* (Tientsin, 1932–1933), vol. 1, pp. 86–90.

58. *NGB*, vol. 9, No. 44, p. 168.

59. Li Hung-chang, *Communications to the Tsungli Yamen*, 1:49.

60. Yi Yu-wŏn was appointed chief master of the investiture of the crown prince on February 12, 1875, and went to Peking in the capacity of envoy to request this investiture. Back from Peking, he was received in royal audience on January 12, 1876. *IS-KH*, 12.12. 16 (174:29–33b).

61. Li Hung-chang, *Communications to the Tsungli Yamen*, 4:31–32; *Kao koryak*, vol. 1 (without page numbers).

62. Li Hung-chang, *Communications to the Tsungli Yamen*, 4:30–31; *CJHSL*, No. 224, pp. 276–277.

63. Later the Chinese authorities apparently stated to foreign representatives in Peking that Mori had forced his visit on Li Hung-chang. FO17/720, Wade's 61 (conf.), February 16, 1876.

64. *CKHCJ*, 1:3b–4, 7–9b; Li Hung-chang, *Communications to the Tsungli Yamen*, 4:32b–33b; *NGB*, vol. 9, No. 44, pp. 168–169; No. 45, pp. 169–180; No. 46, pp. 180–183; No. 47, pp. 183–185. The Chinese and Japanese versions of the conversation between Li Hung-chang and Mori Arinori differ on some points not essential to our discussion.

65. Li Hung-chang, *Communications to the Tsungli Yamen*, 4:33a–b.

Chapter 3

1. *NGB*, vol. 8, No. 54, pp. 124–126; No. 58, pp. 133–137.

2. *NGB*, vol. 8, No. 64, 143–145.

3. *NGB*, vol. 8, No. 64, pp. 145–148.

4. *NGB*, vol. 8, No. 64, pp. 147–148.

5. *NGB*, vol. 8, No. 69, pp. 151–166; *Asien*, Eisendecher to Bülow, December 10, 1875; HC42/3933: Parkes to Derby, Yedo, December 31, 1875.

6. *NGB*, vol. 8, No. 62 and No. 63, pp. 140–143.

7. *NGB*, vol. 9, No. 3, pp. 23–24.

8. *NGB*, vol. 9, No. 6, p. 29.

9. *NGB*, vol. 9, No. 3, pp. 2–9. For more details of the expedition, see Kuroda's diary in the *NGB*.

10. *PBTN*, 257:837b, 842b; *Waesa ilgi*, 12.12.26/27/28/29. For the negotiations between Korea and Japan in the second half of the 1870s, the Korean side is richly documented. Besides the *Ilsŏngnok*, the most important collections of primary materials are the *Waesa ilgi* (Diary [of the negotiations] with the Japanese envoys) and the *Waesa mundap* (Questions and answers [in the negotiations] with the Japanese envoys), both kept in the Kyujanggak archives in Seoul. The *Waesa ilgi* (in 14 volumes) covers the period between KJ12.12.26 (January 22, 1876) and 17.12.29 (January 28, 1881). The *Waesa mundap* (in three volumes), starting with 13.1.4 (January 29, 1876) and ending with 16.7.17 (September 3, 1879), duplicates a great number of documents found in the *IS* and the *Waesa ilgi*. There are still other compendia containing materials for the late 1870s, for example the *Ilsa munja* (Documents concerning the Japanese envoys) or the *Ilbonin mundap chamnok* (Various documents pertaining to the negotiations with the Japanese). They reveal, however, little additional information. For a detailed description of these materials, see Chŏn Hae-jong, *Kŭnse taeoe kwan'gye munhŏnbiyo* (Seoul, 1966), pp. 131–133.

11. *Waesa ilgi*, 13.1.4; *Waesa mundap*, 13.1.4; *NGB*, vol. 9, No. 3, pp. 15–17; *IS-KJ*, 13.1.4 (175:19–22).

12. O Kyŏng-sŏk had long been interested in foreign policy. He regretted the long stalemate of the relations between Japan and Korea. Having been in China several times, he apparently realized the necessity of Korea's opening to the outside world. He reportedly expressed this opinion as early as 1871 at the time of the American expedition and was therefore called *kaehangga* ("advocate for the opening of the ports"). See *Han'guk inmyŏng taesajŏn*, p. 471.

13. *IS-KJ*, 13.1.4 (175:22–24b); *Waesa ilgi*, 13. 1. 4; *Waesa mundap*, 13.1.4; *NGB*, vol. 9, No. 5, pp. 26–27.

14. *IS-KJ*, 13.1.6 (175:29), 13.1.6 (175:32); *Waesa ilgi*, 13.1.5/7; *Waesa mundap*, 13.1.7; *NGB*, vol. 9, No. 3, pp. 18–19; No. 6, pp. 27–39 for the lengthy transcript of the conversation between the Japanese and Koreans.

15. *IS-KJ*, 12.11.15 (173:28b–29). As a result of Yi Ch'oe-ŭng's memorial, the prefect of Tongnae, Hong U-ch'ang, sent the language officer to the Japan House to inform the Japanese about the decision of the Korean government. On December 22 Hong apparently met secretly with Hirotsu Hironobu, who had arrived in Pusan to announce Kuroda's impending mission. Hong presented Hirotsu with the proposal that the Koreans would accept the revised letters from the Japanese Foreign Ministry on the condition that Kuroda's mission to Kanghwa would be stopped. The Japanese did not give this proposal serious consideration. *NGB*, vol. 9, No. 7, pp. 39–40; Tabohashi Kiyoshi, *Kindai Nissen kankei no kenkyū*, I, 407–409.

16. *IS-KJ*, 12.10.13 (172:29–30b). I believe that the text in *Ilbonin mundap chamnok* (without page numbers) is the article in the *Wankuo kungpao*. However, the rest of the material in this collection dates from 1879 and later.

17. *IS-KJ*, 12.12.16 (174:29–33b).

18. *IS-KJ*, 13.1.13 (175:47b); *Waesa ilgi*, 13.1.10; *CKHCJ*, 1:10–12; *T'ongmun kwanji*, 11:92. It took approximately three weeks for a communication sent by fast mail to get from Peking to Seoul. The transcripts of Mori Arinori's discussions with Li Hung-chang and a second letter with the copies of the correspondence between Mori and Prince Kung were sent by the Board of Rites on February 24 and arrived in Seoul on March 16.

19. *IS-KJ*, 13.1.2 (175:10b–12b). The prefect of Tongnae at that time was the newly appointed Hong U-ch'ang. Before leaving for Tongnae, Hong was received by the king who reminded him that royal orders did not exclude personal initiative! *IS-KJ*, 12. 8. 5/10 (170:11b–12, 22–23). The Council of State recommended that Hong and the governor of Kyŏngsang, Pak Che-in, be punished for extreme negligence. *IS-KJ*, 13.1.3 (175:16b–17); *Waesa ilgi*, 13.1.3.

20. *IS-KJ*, 13.1.5 (175: 25a–b); *PBTN*, 257:843a–b; *Waesa ilgi*, 13.1.5.

21. *IS-KJ*, 13.1.10 (175:39–41); *Waesa ilgi*, 13.1.10; *Waesa mundap*, 13.1.10; *NGB*, vol. 9, No. 2, p. 20; No. 9, pp. 44–49.

22. *IS-KJ*, 13.1.11/12/13/14 (175:42b–51b); *Waesa ilgi*, 13.1.11/12/13; *Waesa mundap*, 13.1.12/13; *PBTN*, 257:848b; *NGB*, vol. 9, No. 10 and No. 11, pp.49–57; No. 13, pp. 58–65.

23. *IS-KJ*, 13.1.15 (175:53b), 13.1.16 (175:55b–56), 13.1.17(175:58b–60); *Waesa ilgi*, 13.1.16/17; *Waesa mundap*, 13.1.17; *NGB*, vol. 9, No. 14, pp. 65–66.

24. *IS-KJ*, 13.1.20 (175:74b–78), 13.1.21 (176:1b–2); *Waesa ilgi*, 13.1.20/21; *Waesa mundap*, 13. 1. 20/21. The text of the thirteen articles of the draft treaty can be found in *IS-KJ*, 13.1.21 (176:2b–6); *NBG*, vol. 9, No. 14, p. 68; No. 17, pp. 87–92.

25. *IS-KJ*, 13.1.20 (175:68–69, 72b–73); *PBTN*, 257:850b.

26. *IS-KJ*, 13.1.24 (176: 26a–b); *Waesa ilgi*, 13.1.24.

27. *IS-KJ*, 13.1.25 (176:28b–29); *Waesa ilgi*, 13.1.25; *PBTN*, 257:850b.

28. *IS-KJ*, 13.1.29 (176:45b–46); *Waesa ilgi*, 13.1.29.

29. *NGB*, vol. 9, No. 14, pp. 67–69; Tabohashi Kiyoshi, *Kindai Nissen kankei no kenkyū*, I, 508–511.

30. *IS-KJ*, 13.1.20 (175:78a–b). For a discussion of the disenchantment of Confucian literati with King Kojong, see James B. Palais, *Politics and Policy in Traditional Korea*, chapter 12.

31. *IS-KJ*, 13.1.23 (176:20b–21b).

32. *IS-KJ*, 13.1.23 (176:21b–24); Tabohashi Kiyoshi, *Kindai Nissen kankei no kenkyū*, I, 511–512; Han U-gŭn "Kaehang tangsi ŭi wigiŭisik kwa kaehwasasang," *Han'guksa yŏn'gu* 2:116–118. In this connection it is important to note that the literati remained consistent in their antiforeign stand. This may also indicate that at the time when they demanded the Taewŏn'gun's retirement they were not a mere tool of the Min.

33. *IS-KJ*, 13.1.27 (176:35b–36b).

34. *IS-KJ*, 13.1.25 (176:29), 13.1.26 (176:31b–32), 13.1.27 (176:36b–37, 37–38b), 13.1.28 (176:43b–44b), 13.1.29 (176:48b–50), 13.1.30 (176:58).

35. *PBTN*, 257:849b; *IS-KJ*, 13.1.27 (176:35b–36b). Also see the memorial by the right state councillor, Kim Pyŏng-guk, *PBTN*, 257:850a.

36. *IS-KJ*, 13.1.28 (176:41b–43b).

37. *Waesa ilgi*, 13.1.21, 13.1.26; *NGB*, vol. 9, No. 20, pp. 97–99. For a convenient contrasting of the Korean and Japanese points of view, see Tabohashi Kiyoshi, *Kindai Nissen kankei no kenkyū*, I, 472–491.

38. *Waesa ilgi*, 13.1.26; *Ilsa munja*, 13.1.26; *NGB*, vol. 9, No. 32, pp. 131–134. It is interesting to note that the proposals Sin Hŏn presented to the Japanese contained demands that had been put forward by the opposition. Compare the remaining proposals of the Koreans to the final version of the Trade Regulations disucssed in the following chapter.

39. *NGB*, vol. 9, No. 14, p. 71; No. 21, pp. 99–105; Nos. 23 and 24, pp. 107–113; *CSS*, pt. 6, vol. 4, pp. 399–400.

40. *IS-KJ*, 13.1.30 (176:51–55); *Waesa ilgi*, 13.1.30; *PBTN*, 257:850b.

41. *NGB*, vol. 9, No. 14, p. 72.

42. *IS-KJ*, 13.2.5 (177:8b–14b); *Waesa ilgi*, 13. 2. 5; *Waesa mundap*, 13.2.5; *NGB*, vol. 9, No. 14, pp. 72–77; Nos. 28 and 29, pp. 120–121.

43. *NGB*, vol. 9, No. 14, pp. 77–78.

44. For the complete treaty text, see *Treaties*, pp. 1–6; *NGB*, vol. 9, No. 26, pp. 114–119; *PBTN*, 257:851b–854a.

45. *IS-KJ*, 13.2.5 (177:14b–15b); *PBTN*, 257:857b–859a.

46. As the immediate result of the treaty, the military alert in the districts along the coast of Kanghwa Island and Kyŏnggi was called off. *IS-KJ*, 13.2.5 (177:17b).

47. The Koreans also accepted extraterritorial jurisdiction because under the old system operative at Pusan criminal cases involving Japanese were either judged by the local Japanese officials or sent back to Tsushima. Tabohashi assumes that Kuroda himself added the article stipulating extraterritorial jurisdication. Tabohashi Kiyoshi, *Kindai Nissen kankei no kenkyū*, I, 489–490.

48. The texts of the treaty and the ratification were copied and distributed to all parts of the country. *PBTN*, 257:857a–b; *Waesa ilgi*, 13.2.9.

49. *Waesa ilgi*, 13.2.12/20; *PBTN*, 257:857a; *T'ongmun kwanji*, 11:92; *CKHCJ*, 1:10–11.

50. *CJHSL*, Nos. 234–244, pp. 300–303; No. 252, p. 308; No. 258, p. 312; No. 268, pp. 325–326.

51. *Asien*, Brandt to Bülow, Peking, March 16, 1876.

Chapter 4

1. *CKHCJ*, 1:12b; *NGB*, vol. 9, No. 30, pp. 122–123.

2. *IS-KJ*, 13.2.22 (177:56), 13.2.24 (177:59a–b); *PBTN*, 257:860a–b; *Iltong kiyu*, 1:1–2. Following traditional practice, the Korean government sent an official message to the Chinese Board of Rites to announce Kim Ki-su's dispatch to Japan. *IS-KJ*, 13.3.2 (178:4b); *PBTN*, 257:866b; *T'ongmun kwanji*, 11:92; *CKHCJ*, 1:12b.

3. *IS-KJ*, 13.3.12 (178:26b–27); *Waesa ilgi*, 13.3.10; *PBTN*, 257: 868a; *NGB*, vol. 9, No. 51, p. 188; No. 52, p. 189; Nos. 53–55, pp. 191–193.

4. *IS-KJ*, 13.4.4 (179:6b–8), 13.5*. 18 (181:25a–b); *Waesa ilgi*, 13.5.2, 13.5.3, 13. 5.4, 13.5.5, 13.5.8; *Iltong kiyu*, 1:2–3, 6, 11, 12; *NGB*, vol. 9, No. 52, p. 191; No. 56, pp. 193–195.

5. Kim Ki-su's mission to Japan is richly documented by the *Iltong kiyu* and the *Susinsa ilgi*, both of which are contained in *Susinsa kirok* (Seoul, 1958). *Waesa ilgi*, 13.5*. 18; *Iltong kiyu*, 1:21, 2:45–47, 4:83–85; *NGB*, vol. 9, Nos. 58 and 59, pp. 198–200; No. 60, p. 200. Kim presented to Terashima a letter from the minister of rites, Kim Sang-hyŏn, and to Miyamoto Koichi a similar message written by the vice-minister of rites, Yi In-myŏng.

6. *Iltong kiyu*, 2:26, 28–29, 3:66, 4:102–103.

7. *Iltong kiyu*, 4:109–110.

8. *Iltong kiyu*, 4:86–87. For a day-by-day account of Kim's activities in Japan, see *Susinsa ilgi*, 1:113–136; *NGB*, vol. 9, No. 64, pp. 205–209.

9. *IS-KJ*, 13.6.1 (182:1–7); *Waesa ilgi*, 13.6.1, 13.6.11; *Susinsa ilgi*, 1:129–136; *CKHCJ*, 1:14; *T'ongmun kwanji*, 11:93; *MHBG*, 176:18b. Also see Yi Kwang-rin's article "*Hai-kuo t'u-chih* ŭi Han'guk chŏllae wa kŭ yŏnghyang" (The transmission of the *Hai-kuo t'u-chih* to Korea and its influence), in *Han'guk kaehwasa yŏn'gu*, pp. 2–18. For an older article on Kim Ki-su's mission, see Sohn Pow-key, "The Opening of Korea—A Conflict of Traditions," *Transactions of the Korea Branch of the Royal Asiatic Society* 36:101–128 (April 1960).

10. *NGB*, vol. 9, No. 35, pp. 136–137.

11. *NGB*, vol. 9, No. 67, p. 216. In the meantime Japanese language studies were intensified by selecting and training linguistically gifted students. *IS-KJ*, 13.2.27 (177: 68); *PBTN*, 257:862b–863a.

12. *IS-KJ*, 13.5*.24 (181:41a–b), 13.6.2 (182:8a–b), 13.6.7 (182:17a–b), 13.6.8 (182:20), 13.6.11 (182:24a–b); *Waesa ilgi*, 13.6.2/3/7/8; *PBTN*, 257:892b, 896b–898a. Cho In-hŭi, who had been made a vice-minister of the Department of Punishment, was elevated a few days later to the rank of a *tangsang* so that he would be able to participate in the government deliberations. *IS-KJ*, 13.6.6 (182:14).

13. *IS-KJ*, 13.6.12 (182:26a–b); *Waesa ilgi* 13.6.10 13.6.12; *PBTN*, 257:898a, 899a; *NGB*, vol. 9, No. 74, pp. 221–224; No. 76, pp. 226–228.

14. The most complete transcripts of the negotiations between Miyamoto and the Koreans can be found in the *Waesa mundap* and the *Waesa ilgi*. *Waesa mundap*, 13. 6. 18, 13.6.20, 13.6.21, 13.6.22, 13.6.24, 13.6.27, 13.6.28, 13.6.29, 13.7.1, 13.7.3, 13.7.5. Also

see *Waesa ilgi* under the same dates. The Japanese draft treaty can be found in *Waesa ilgi*, 13. 6. 16. The Koreans used the same arguments in their opposition to giving the Japanese trade superintendent and the Japanese envoy the right to travel inland accompanied by their families. This proposition had been made in art. 2 of the draft treaty. *Waesa mundap* and *Waesa ilgi*, 13.7.5. Also *NGB*, vol. 9, Nos. 80–91, pp. 230–274; *IS-KJ*, 13.6.15 (182:33a–b).

15. *Waesa mundap* and *Waesa ilgi*, 13. 7. 6. Both give the texts of the *Supplementary Treaty* and the *Trade Regulations*. Also see *PBTN*, 257:904a–907b and *NGB*, vol. 9, No. 92, pp. 275–283. An English translation is found in *Treaties*, pp. 7–17. The foreign envoys in Tokyo were especially satisfied with article 10 of the supplementary articles which provided for kind treatment of shipwrecked people belonging to nations with which Japan had concluded treaties. *NGB*, vol. 9, No. 103, pp. 306–307 and No. 105, pp. 308–309.

16. The prohibition of the sale of opium had been demanded by Sin Hŏn.

17. For these documents, see *NGB*, vol. 9, No. 92, pp. 283–287. For an English translation, see *Treaties*, pp. 18–23. A few days later the Korean government distributed the texts of the *Supplementary Articles* and the *Trade Regulations* into all parts of the country. *Waesa ilgi*, 13. 7. 13.

18. *IS-KJ*, 13. 7. 16 (183:34a–b); *Waesa ilgi*, 13.7.16; *PBTN*, 257:911a; *NGB*, vol. 9, No. 95, pp. 288–289. A similar letter was sent by Cho In-hŭi to Miyamoto a few days later. *NGB*, vol. 9, No. 96, p. 289.

19. Miyamoto repeatedly argued that the Korean government conceived of diplomacy in the traditional terms of exchanging envoys on the occasion of royal funerals, weddings, etc. and therefore was unprepared to admit a Japanese envoy to the capital on a permanent basis. He also supported the idea of fixing the route from T'ongjin to Seoul. *NGB*, vol. 9, No. 100, pp. 298–300.

Tabohashi gives a somewhat different story of the exchange of notes. He provides a third memorandum which Miyamoto apparently sent to Cho In-hŭi on the day of the conclusion of the supplementary treaty. In this document Miyamoto assured his Korean colleague that envoys would only be sent for diplomatic matters (*kyobing*), and that commercial matters would be handled solely by the Japanese trade superintendent in the ports. Furthermore he promised that the route to the Korean capital would be fixed. Yet, since Miyamoto's authority was not great enough to ensure the enforcement of these promises, the president of the Department of Rites, Kim Sang-hyŏn, asked Terashima to add them to the supplementary treaty. The Japanese government, however, did not agree with this viewpoint, and Miyamoto, who was responsible for the confusion, had to send a reply to Kim in which he disclaimed the content of his memorandum and stressed the validity of article 2 of the treaty. See Tabohashi, *Kindai Nissen kankei no kenkyū*, I, 614–617.

20. *NGB*, vol. 10, No. 107, pp. 214–215.

21. *Waesa ilgi*, 13.7.17.

22. *NGB*, vol. 9, No. 15, pp. 79–80; vol. 10, Nos. 110 and 111, pp. 217–219.

23. Hanabusa was also instructed to continue talks about the two touchy subjects that had been dropped from earlier negotiations: the residence of the Japanese minister in the Korean capital and his travel route there. The Japanese government apparently was ready to make a slight concession. Since it was convinced that the Korean government did not understand the importance of the issues and was unaccustomed to receive foreigners, Hanabusa was allowed to choose between Kanghwa and Inch'ŏn (whichever

would be opened as a port) as a temporary residence. *NGB*, vol. 10, No. 117, pp. 222–226.

24. *IS-KJ*, 14.10.13 (198:21b–22); *Waesa mundap*, 14.9.2, 14.10.4, 14.10.20; *Waesa ilgi*, 14.9.2, 14.10.4, 14.10.12, 14.10.20; *MHBG*, 176:19; *NGB*, vol. 10, Nos. 118–119, pp. 226–227; No. 129, pp. 235–236; No. 130, pp. 236–237; No. 132, p. 289 and p. 294.

25. *IS-KJ*, 14.9.28 (197:43–44b); 14.10.12 (198:20a–b); 14.10.15 (198:24–27b); 14.10.18 (198:41b–42b); 14.10.19/20/21/22/23 (198:43b–47); 14.11.16 (199:26a–b), 14.11.17 (199:28); *Waesa mundap*, 14.10.22, 14.10.23, 14.10.27, 14.10.30, 14.11.3, 14.11.12, 14.11.15; *Waesa ilgi*, 14.10.22, 14.10.23, 14.10.27, 14.10.30, 14.11.3, 14.11.12, 14.11.15, 14.11.16; *PBTN*, 258:135a, 147b; Kim Ki-su, *Susinsa ilgi*, 1:137–144; *NGB*, vol. 10, No. 126, pp. 230–232; No. 130, p. 237; No. 132, pp. 239–308; *Treaties*, pp. 30–32. On the recommendation of the Council of State a report about Hanabusa's mission to Korea was sent to Peking. *IS-KJ*, 14.11.17 (199:27a–b); *CKHCJ*, 1:23a–b.

26. *NGB*, vol. 11, No. 142, pp. 287–289.

27. *IS-KJ*, 14.12.12 (200:21), 14.12.25 (200:57b–58), 15.4.21 (205:36b–37b), 15.4.23 (205:41), 15.5.1 (206:1b–2b), 15.5.5 (206:13–15), 15.5.20 (207:17b–20), 15.5.27 (207:56b–58b), 15.6.11 (208:17–19), 15.8.7 (210:11b–15b), 15.8.17 (210: 40–43), 15.8. 20 (210:48b–52b), 15.8.24 (210:63–65), 15.8.26 (210:72b–73b), 15.8.27 (210:84–86b), 15.9.10 (211:15–18); *Waesa mundap*, 15.4.15, 15.4.21, 15.5.20, 15.8.7, 15.8.13. Same dates in *Waesa ilgi*. *NGB*, vol. 11, No. 144, pp. 290–292; No. 145, pp. 292–293; No. 146, pp. 293–294.

28. *NGB*, vol. 12, No. 120, p. 212.

29. Hanabusa's advance up to Chemulp'o is very well documented on the Korean side. It would, however, be meaningless to enumerate here all the entries in the *Ilsŏngnok*, vols. 218 and 219. The *Waesa ilgi* also contains these documents.

30. *IS-KJ*, 16.2.28 (216:51b–52), 15.10.26 (212:79b–80); *Waesa ilgi*, 15.10.26; *PBTN*, 259:241b.

31. Day-by-day transcripts of the negotiations between Hong U-ch'ang and Hanabu-sa Yoshitada can be found in vol. 3 of *Waesa mundap* and vols. 11–13 of *Waesa ilgi*. *IS-KJ*, 16.4.30 (219:87b–88b); *NGB*, vol. 12, No. 124, pp. 218–222.

32. *IS-KJ*, 16.5.15 (220:33–34b), 16.5.23 (220:45a–b), 16.5.28 (220:54b–55); *Waesa mundap*, 16.5.19; *Waesa ilgi*, 16.5.19.

33. *Waesa mundap*, 16.5.22, 16.6.30, 16.7.6; *Waesa ilgi*, 16.5.22, 16.6.30, 16.7.6; *Chōsen jimu shimatsu satsuyō*, vol. 3.

34. *Waesa ilgi*, 16.7.11, 16.7.14; for the text of the Convention, see *NGB*, vol. 12, No. 124, pp. 221–222; *Treaties*, pp. 36–38. A report about it was also sent to China. *CKHCJ*, 1:37a–b.

35. *Waesa mundap*, 16.5.23, 16.6.2, 16.6.9, 16.6.14, 16.6.21, 16.7.9; *Waesa ilgi*, 16.5.23, 16.6.2, 16.6.7, 16.6.9, 16.6.14, 16.6.21, 16.7.12; *NGB*, vol. 12, No. 124, p. 221.

36. *IS-KJ*, 15.8.27 (210:76–78b), 16.7.1 (222:1b–2), 16.7.11 (222:21).

37. *IS-KJ*, 16.6.17 (221:37a–b).

38. *IS-KJ*, 16.7.16 (222:31–32), 16.7.17 (222:33a–b), 16.7.18 (222:36a–b), 16.7.22 (222:47–48), 16.8.3 (223:5b–6b), 16.8.4 (223:9a–b), 16.8.11 (223:21a–b), 16. 8. 14 (223: 28–29). Yi Sŏn-gŭn explains the government crisis by saying that some opportunistic high ministers flattered the Min and agreed to the opening of the country in order to secure their positions. They became confused by the increasing demands put forward by the Japanese and sought to shift the responsibility upon others. This interpretation is, of course,

in line with the general thesis of Min dominance after 1875. See *Han'guksa, ch'oegŭnse-p'yŏn*, p. 423.

39. The envoy was Kim Hong-jip who was sent to Japan in the summer of 1880 primarily to continue the discussions about the customs duties. *Susinsa ilgi*, 2:151; *NGB*, vol. 13, No. 161, p. 420. See the following chapters.

40. *IS-KJ*, 17.11.13 (239:24a–b), 17.11.22 (239:39b), 17.11.23 (239:41), 17.11. 24 (239:42b–43), 17.11.26 (239:46a–b); *Waesa ilgi*, 17.11.13, 17.11.22, 17.11.23, 17.11.24, 17.11.26; *NGB*, vol. 13, No. 161, pp. 420–421; No. 162, pp. 425–428; No. 165, pp. 429–430. When Yi Yong-suk visited Li Hung-chang in March 1881, he asked for Li's opinion about how the Japanese "state letter" (i.e., Hanabusa's credentials) was to be answered. The Koreans had objected to the presentation of such a document because the treaty provided only for an exchange of communications between the Japanese Foreign Office and the Korean Department of Rites. Li advised that Korea should send in return a "state letter" in which Korea should use her tributary title. *CJHSL*, No. 355, pp. 488–489.

41. In preparation for Hanabusa's arrival, Kim Hong-jip who had become vice-minister of the Department of Rites a few days before, was appointed negotiator (*kang-sugwan*) and concurrently chief receptionist (*panjŏpkwan*), while Yi Cho-yŏn was appointed to second him. *IS-KJ*, 17.11.14 (239:25b), 17.11.16 (239:29); *PBTN*, 261:446a–b; *Waesa ilgi*, 17. 12. 5. Hanabusa's intention to present his credentials apparently triggered a crisis in the Department of Rites. The unwillingness to bear the responsibility for it led to a chain of resignations by the various ministers. The situation was saved by concurrently appointing Kim Hong-jip negotiator. Tabohashi Kiyoshi, *Kindai Nissen kankei no kenkyū*, I, 727–728.

42. *Waesa ilgi*, 17.12.5, 17.12.9, 17.12.15, 17.12.25; *NGB*, vol. 14, No. 140, pp. 328–331; No. 141, pp. 331–340; *North China Herald*, April 8, 1881.

43. *Waesa ilgi*, 17.12.29; *NGB*, vol. 14, No. 141, pp. 340–342; No. 144, pp. 347–349; No. 146, pp. 352–354. At one point Kim Hong-jip advanced economic reasons for postponing the opening. He argued that the exportation of rice from Kyŏnggi, which itself had to rely for rice on the southern provinces would lead to popular unrest. Hanabusa took up residence at Seoul in May 1882, and was instructed to discuss the details of Inch'ŏn's opening. Tabohashi Kiyoshi, *Kindai Nissen kankei no kenkyū*, I, 733.

44. *NGB*, vol. 15, No. 111, p. 208; No. 113, pp. 209–212.

45. *NGB*, vol. 14, No. 143, p. 344, 347. The *North China Herald* reported rumors about a movement to expel the Japanese from the vicinity of Inch'ŏn. The paper went on to say, "it is pretty well known that the whole affair is got up by the government in order to delay the opening of the port." *North China Herald*, April 8, 1881. Such an assertion is, however, difficult to prove.

Chapter 5

1. *NGB*, vol. 9, No. 112, p. 322; *North China Herald*, May 11, 1878; FO46/217, Parkes' 50, April 2, 1877; *PBTN*, 258:77b.

2. For a detailed discussion of Kojong's financial policies, see James B. Palais

Politics and Policy in Traditional Korea, Chapter 10: "The Abolition of Ch'ing Cash."

3. *CSS*, pt. 6, vol. 4, pp. 330, 347.

4. Memorials treating economic issues can be found throughout the second half of the 1870s. For example, *IS-KJ*, 13.10.23 (186:46b–48b); 16.1.24 (215:66–69b); 17.11.11 (239:19b–21b); 17.12.17 (240:37–39).

5. It was only in 1883 that the wishes of the Korean government concerning the exportation of grains were respected to some extent. In the *Regulations under which Japanese Trade is to be Conducted in Corea* signed on July 25, 1883, Regulation 37 reads: "Whenever the Corean Government shall have reason to apprehend a scarcity of food within the limits of the Kingdom, or whenever a case of emergency shall arise, such as an inundation, drought, war, etc., that Government may, by Decree, temporarily prohibit the exportation of all breadstuffs..." *Treaties*, p. 101.

6. *IS-KJ*, 16.4.2 (219:7b); *Waesa ilgi*, 16.7.13. Many more references could be cited.

7. The appointment of the *p'anch'algwan* was entrusted to the Department of War. The new seal was cast by the Department of Rites. At the same time the *pyŏlch'a* was renamed *yŏkhak* (interpreter). *IS-KJ*, 13.10.22 (186: 45a–b), 14.1.4 (189:14); *PBTN*, 257:34a; *NGB*, vol. 9, No. 112, p. 321; No. 116, pp. 338–339; No. 118, p. 342.

8. See article 4 of the Korean-Japanese treaty.

9. For a description of the Japan House, see Chapter 1.

10. *Sinjŭng Tongguk yŏji sŭngnam*, 23:1–5b; *NGB*, vol. 9, No. 3, pp. 10–11; Isabella B. Bishop, *Korea and Her Neighbours*, pp. 23–26; Foulk, *Korean Coast*, pp. 8–9; for a description of the historical sites, see Kim Ŭi-hwan, *Pusan ŭi kojŏk kwa yumul*. The building of the Tongnae prefecture is preserved today and still serves administrative purposes.

11. The appointment of the trade superintendent was provided for by article 8 of the treaty. For Miyamoto's suggestions to Foreign Minister Terashima about the functions of the trade superintendent, see *NGB*, vol. 9, No. 102, p. 305; No. 109, pp. 315–316. The trade superintendent was also in charge of the post office that was opened in November 1876.

12. *NGB*, vol. 9, No. 107, p. 314; No. 112, p. 321.

13. *Waesa mundap*, 13.11.10, 14.1.9; *Waesa ilgi*, 13.11.10, 14.11.9; *Sinyak hu kanrikan yŏ Tongnae pusa yakchoch'o* (1876) for the seven-point proposal Kondō brought with him; *NGB*, vol. 9, No. 114, pp. 324–325, 333–334. The rules which were established for the "caretaker" period were modelled after the Trade Regulations. See *NGB*, vol. 9, No. 114, pp. 325–326.

14. *Ilsa munja*, 13.11.28. For the whole text of the document, see *Treaties*, pp. 25–26. Another important document which Kondō Masuki and Hong U-ch'ang agreed upon later, on July 3, 1877, was concerned with the treatment of Koreans shipwrecked off the Japanese coast. *NGB*, vol. 10, No. 105, pp. 210–211.

15. Ōkura Kihachirō (1837–1928) was one of the most active traders and industrialists of the Meiji period. In 1872, he took a trip abroad and later started branches in London, Korea, and Southeast Asia. See Johannes Hirschmeier, *The Origins of Entrepreneurship in Meiji Japan* (Harvard, 1964), pp. 233–236.

16. *Shibusawa Eiichi denki shiryō*, 16:8–9.

17. For the full text of the government notifications nos. 128 and 129, see *Treaties*, p. 24.

18. *NGB*, vol. 9, No. 138, pp. 316–317.

19. *NGB*, vol. 9, No. 3, p. 10; No. 112, p. 321. At the very end of 1874, a Korean source estimated the population of the Japan House at fifty to sixty persons. *IS-KJ*, 11. 12. 13 (160:61). When Ōkura Kihachirō came to Pusan, he counted some ninety Japanese. *Shibusawa Eiichi denki shiryō*, 16:9 and *Daiichi Ginkō shi*, p. 416. In November 1876, eighteen Japanese ships anchored at Pusan; eleven anchored there in the first half of December. *NGB*, vol. 9, No. 115, p. 337.

20. FO46/218, enclosure in Parkes' 71, May 8, 1877; *NGB*, vol. 9, No. 115, p. 337; *Shibusawa Eiichi denki shiryō*, 16:10.

21. It is not quite possible to calculate the exact area of the new Japanese settlement from the available data. The *Pusan yaksa* on p. 152 says that the area was approximately 110,000 *p'yŏng*, which would be the approximate equivalent of 90 acres. The shape of the area seems to have been rectangular, yet the measurements given do not add up to the area mentioned above.

22. *North China Herald*, July 27, 1877; *Pusan yaksa*, p. 163.

23. Ishihata Tadashi, *Chōsen kikō yoroku*, 1:13b. Ishihata Tadashi came to Pusan as a member of Kondō Masuki's staff. He wrote one of the very few eyewitness reports about Pusan in the late 1870s to which he added some nice illustrations. The work is preserved in the Pusan City Library.

24. Kim Tae-sang, "Kaehang chikhu Pusan ŭi sahoe-munhwa," *Hangdo Pusan* (Pusan, 1967), VI, 165–167.

25. Ishihata Tadashi, *Chōsen kikō yoroku*, 1:18b.

26. Kim Tae-sang, "Kaehang chikhu Pusan ŭi sahoe-munhwa," *Hangdo Pusan* (Pusan, 1967), VI, 197; *IS-KJ*, 14.8.4 (196:10). The harbor dues differed according to the size of the ship. See Trade Regulation VII.

27. Kim Ŭi-hwan, *Pusan ŭi kojŏk kwa yumul*, pp. 72–73.

28. *IS-KJ*, 14.1.21 (189:57a–b), 14.2.25 (190:48b); *PBTN*, 258:64b–65a, 77a–b; *NGB*, vol. 10, Nos. 133 and 135, pp. 309–312. The Koreans evidently held the opinion that article 2 of the Japanese draft of the Supplementary Articles, which would have allowed Japanese envoys to travel inland accompanied by their families, also would have included Japanese merchants. Since this article was dropped from the final treaty text at Korean insistence, the matter was settled as far as the Korean side was concerned. Also see Tabohashi Kiyoshi, *Kindai Nissen kankei no kenkyū*, I, 618.

29. *IS-KJ*, 14.1.25 (189:74a–b); *PBTN*, 258:68a.

30. *IS-KJ*, 14.4.24 (192:53b–54), 14.4.27 (192:63–64), 14.6.29 (194:65a–b); *PBTN*, 258:68a, 94b–95b, 100a.

31. *IS-KJ*, 17.11.11 (239:20); *Waesa mundap*, 16.5.22; *Treaties*, p. 10.

32. *Shibusawa Eiichi denki shiryō*, 16:5–10, 639–640; *Daiichi Ginkō shi*, pp. 414–416. The second point in the Ōkura-Shibusawa petition to the government in August 1877 concerned the re-opening of the steamship line between Nagasaki and Pusan, which had been interrupted when the government requisitioned the steamers for action against Satsuma. Mitsubishi Kaisha was allowed to resume the steamer service with the old schedule in September 1877. *Shibusawa Eiichi denki shiryō*, 16:639; *NGB*, vol. 10, Nos. 137–139, pp. 315–318; *North China Herald*, December 6, 1877.

33. *IS-KJ*, 16.3*.23 (218: 43b); *Waesa mundap*, 16.5.22; *Waesa ilgi*, 16.7.13; *NGB*, vol. 14, No. 147, p. 356; FO17/857, Wade's 5, February 18, 1881; FO46/246, Parkes'

105, May 15, 1879; *Shibusawa Eiichi denki shiryō*, 16:8,10; *North China Herald*, March 21 and 28, 1878; December 24, 1879. Ishihata Tadashi reported that a Korean needed approximately ten *mun* daily to feed himself. A cash string (*ilgwan*) contained 1,000 *mun* and was (in 1875?) the equivalent of two Japanese *yen*. This clearly shows the unwieldiness of the Korean currency. Ishihata Tadashi, *Chōsen kikō yoroku*, pp. 3, 9b; *Pusan yaksa*, p. 179.

34. *IS-KJ*, 14.2.25 (190:48b), 14.8.4 (196:6–7); Ishihata Tadashi, *Chōsen kikō yoroku*, 1:5b, 37b, 56–57b; *NGB*, vol. 9, No. 115, p. 337; *The Tokyo Times*, vol. 11, No. 3, July 21, 1877.

35. Shikata Hiroshi, "Chōsen ni okeru kindai shihonshugi no seiritsukatei," pp. 151–152, 189; Han U-gŭn, *Han'guk kaehanggi ŭi sangŏp yŏn'gu*, pp. 181–182 (his treatment, however, draws on documents of the late 1880s); *North China Herald*, December 24, 1879, March 7 and 21, 1882; *The Tokyo Times*, vol. 2, No. 3, pp. 40–41; FO46/218, Parkes' 71, May 8, 1877; FO17/857, encl. in Wade's 5, February 18, 1881; Ishihata Tadashi, *Chōsen kikō yoroku*, pp. 18b, 37b, 46a.

36. FO46/243, Parkes' 16, January 22, 1879 (inclosure).

37. Ishihata Tadashi, *Chōsen kikō yoroku*, pp. 21b, 45b–46; *North China Herald*, July 27, 1877; April 28, 1882. This aspect of the trade is, of course, very difficult to document.

38. *IS-KJ*, 15.7.19 (209:50), 15.8.10 (210:20b–21); *Waesa ilgi*, 15.8.10; *PBTN*, 259:219b.

39. *Waesa ilgi*, 15.9.10; *NGB*, vol. 11, No. 150, p. 305; *Shibusawa Eiichi denki shiryō*, 16:8.

40. *Waesa ilgi*, 15.9.24. An eyewitness report can be found in the *Nichinichi shimbun* of November 27, 1878; *North China Herald*, December 14, 1878.

41. *North China Herald*, November 14, 1878; December 14, 1878.

42. At the time of the conclusion of the supplementary treaty and the trade regulations, Moriyama had been instructed to concede a tariff of five percent, if necessary. This issue was never fully discussed between him and Cho In-hŭi. As a kind of afterthought, Moriyama made up for this in his subsequent correspondence with Cho in which he gave assurance that the Japanese government would tax neither the imports from Korea nor the exports there for a number of years. Evidently he expected the same from the Korean government. In response, Cho consented to such a provision. FO46/231, Parkes' 125 (conf.), December 2, 1878; *NGB*, vol. 9, No. 71, p. 219; No. 92, pp. 283–285; *Treaties*, pp. 18 and 23.

43. *IS-KJ*, 15.10.26 (212:79b–80); *Waesa ilgi*, 15.10.26, 15.11.15, 15.11.26, 15.12. 14; *Waesa ilgi*, 16.5.18, 16.6.30, 16.7.3, 16.7.11, 16.7.13; *NGB*, vol. 11, No. 150, pp. 304–314. The seven demands that the Japanese government formulated in place of an indemnity were presented by Hanabusa to the Korean government in the summer of 1879. Most of the demands in fact reemphasized stipulations which had been laid down in previous agreements. The Korean negotiator, Hong U-ch'ang, accepted all of them except demands 5 and 6. Demand 5 would have given the Japanese the right to explore Korea's interior for natural resources and demand 6 would have allowed Japanese merchants to visit the spring and autumn fairs at Taegu. Both of these demands were firmly rejected by the Korean government and subsequently dropped from the negotiations. On the other hand, the Japanese government acknowledged that the Koreans had the right to fix and collect customs duties, if this was done within the concept of "free trade." *NGB*,

vol. 12, No. 120, pp. 212–214; No. 124, pp. 218–219; *IS-KJ*, 16.3*.12 (218:19b); *Waesa ilgi*, 16.3*.12.

44. *IS-KJ*, 16.3*.4 (218:5a-b), 16.3*.5(218:7a-b); *Waesa ilgi*, 16.3*.4, 16.3*.5. The restrictions agreed upon between Yun Ch'i-hwa and Yamanoshiro provided for a temporary halt to Japanese visits to Tongnae; furthermore the Japanese were no longer allowed to enter official buildings, to visit the town on market days, or to wear arms. Yun was held responsible for the incident and was soon relieved from his post.

45. *NGB*, vol. 13, No. 153, p. 412; Nos. 154 and 155, pp. 413–414. For the special instructions to the consuls in Korea, see *NGB*, vol. 13, No. 156, pp. 414–416.

46. *IS-KJ*, 16.6.30 (221:65a-b), 16.7.8 (222:14–15), 16.7.10 (222:18b-19); *PBTN*, 260:309b-310a, 316a, 320a-b; the Tŏgwŏn language officer (*hundo*) was shortly afterward renamed *p'anch'algwan* on the Pusan model. *IS-KJ*, 17.2.16 (230:30b); *PBTN*, 261:384a.

47. *IS-KJ*, 16.8.27 (223:47b-48b), 16.9.1 (224:1b-2), 16.9.2 (224:3b-4), 16.9.9 (224:15b-16b), 16.9.12 (224:20b-21b); *Waesa ilgi*, 16.8.27, 16.9.2, 16.9.9; *Shibusawa Eiichi denki shiryō*, 16:11; *Tō-Chōsen*, p.53; *North China Herald*, November 14, 1879. Maeda Ken-kichi succeeded Yamanoshiro Sukenaga at Pusan in June 1879. *IS-KJ*, 16.5.3 (22:8a-b).

48. The Bay of Yŏnghŭng is the southern part of the larger bay called Tongchosŏn-man, the "Bay of Eastern Korea." The northern part is the Bay of Songjŏn (Port Lazareff), bounded on its east side by the long peninsula of Hodo which projects southward from the mainland. *Sinjŭng Tongguk yŏji sŭngnam*, 49:11–12; *Tō-Chōsen* (Eastern Korea), pp. 5–6, 28–30, 33; *Korean Repository*, Correspondence, No. 1 (1892); Buckingham and Foulk, *Observations upon the Korean Coast*, pp. 17–18; *Nichinichi shimbun*, October 28, 1879; *Tŏg-wŏnbu ŭpchi*. A Korean source estimated the population of Wŏnsan in 1879 at approximately one thousand households. *IS-KJ*, 16.2.28 (216:51b).

49. *IS-KJ*, 17.4.5 (232:9b); *Waesa ilgi*, 17.4.5; *NGB*, vol. 13, No. 148, p. 406.

50. *NGB*, vol. 13, Nos. 144–146, pp. 404–405; *Tō-Chōsen*, p. 53; *Echo du Japon*, June 12, 1880; *Waesa ilgi*, 17.4.17.

51. *IS-KJ*, 17.4.26 (232:55a-b), 17.6.17 (234:26b), 17.7.28 (235:43b), 17.8.10 (236:25–26), 18.1.15 (241:31a-b), 18.2.7 (242:10b); *Waesa ilgi*, 17.4.27, 17.5.25, 17.7.28; *North China Herald*, August 24, 1880; *Convention with Japan Regarding the Opening of the Port of Wŏnsan* in *Treaties*, pp. 36–38. The rent of the settlement was not agreed upon until August 4, 1881, when Maeda concluded with Kim Ki-su the *Agreement with Japan Regarding the Land Rent of the Settlement of Wŏnsan*. The rent was fixed at fifty yen per annum on the Pusan model. *Treaties*, pp. 39–40.

52. *NGB*, vol. 13, No. 140, pp. 400–401; *Tō-Chōsen*, p. 53.

53. *NGB*, vol. 13, No. 143, pp. 402–403; Nos. 150 and 152, pp. 408–411; No. 153, pp. 411–413.

54. *Shibusawa Eiichi denki shiryō*, 16:12.

55. *IS-KJ*, 17.6.3 (234:3–4); Foulk, *Corean Coast*, p. 18. Foulk visited Wŏnsan in 1883. An earlier visitor was Donald Spence, the British consul at Shanghai, who sailed to Wŏnsan aboard the *Vettor Pisani* as a member of the suite of the Duke of Genoa. He sent a very detailed report about his trip to the British government. FO17/857, Wade's 5, February 18, 1881; *Waesa ilgi*, 17.7.18. The *Tō-Chōsen* reports the population of Japanese settlers at Wŏnsan as follows: 1880, 235; 1881, 281; 1882, 260; 1883, 199.

56. *NGB*, vol. 14, No. 147, pp. 354–357; *Shibusawa Eiichi denki shiryō*, 16:12; *Daiichi Ginkō shi*, p. 416; *North China Herald*, August 24, 1880.

57. *NGB,* vol. 13, No. 139, p. 400; vol. 14, No. 147, pp. 354–357; *Tō-Chōsen,* p. 53.

58. Ch'oe Yu-gil, "Yijo kaehang chikhu ǔi Han-Il muyǒk ǔi tonghyang, "*Asea yǒn'gu* 47:175–221 (September 1972). Ch'oe Yu-gil bases his study on a large body of data published by the Customs Bureau of the Japanese Finance Ministry, *Dai Nippon gaikoku bōeki jūhachi konen taishōhyō,* which covers the period of 1868–1885 and has an appendix entitled *Chōsen kyūbōeki hachi konen taishōhyō,* which treats the period of 1877 to 1884 and was compiled on the basis of Japanese consular reports from Korea. The *Kankoku shi* (the Japanese translation of the Russian Finance Ministry report) gives statistical figures on pp. 110–116 which seem to be based on the above source. Hilary Conroy in *The Japanese Seizure of Korea, 1868–1910,* pp. 457–459, reproduces the material of the *Kankoku shi.* For comparative figures, see *North China Herald,* November 7, 1879; March 21 and July 28, 1882; FO46/243, Parkes' 16, January 22, 1879; FO 46/248, Kennedy's 189, October 27, 1879; and 46/257, Kennedy's 89, May 25, 1880. The figures given in FO46 supposedly are based on the reports of the Japanese customs. For a discussion of pre-1883 trade, also see Kitagawa Osamu, "Nisshin sensō made no Nissen bōeki," *Rekishi kagaku* 1:64–79 (1932).

59. For a convenient table showing Korea's imports and exports in total figures, see Ch'oe Yu-gil, "Yijo kaehang chikhu ǔi Han-Il muyǒk ǔi tonghyang," p. 180.

60. Ch'oe Yu-gil, "Yijo kaehang chikhu ǔi Han-Il muyǒk ǔi tonghyang," pp. 199–200.

61. For statistics on Wǒnsan for 1881, *NGB,* vol. 14, No. 147, p. 356.

62. *NGB,* vol. 13, No. 139, p. 400; FO46/218, Parkes' 71, May 8, 1877; *North China Herald,* March 28, 1878; November 14, 1879; for statistics, see July 28, 1882; Ch'oe Yu-gil, "Yijo kaehang chikhu ǔi Han-Il muyǒk ǔi tonghyang," pp. 181–188.

63. *Shibusawa Eiichi denki shiryō,* 16:8; FO17/857, Wade's 5, February 18, 1881; *North China Herald,* July 27, 1877; Ch'oe Yu-gil, "Yijo kaehang chikhu ǔi Han-Il muyǒk ǔi tonghyang," pp. 188–192.

64. The number of Japanese residents at Pusan in the second half of 1881 diminished by one thousand compared to the first half of that year. *North China Herald,* March 21, 1882; *Diplomatic Despatches, Japan,* Bingham to Frelinghuysen, April 18, 1883; Ch'oe Yi-gil, "Yijo kaehang chikhu ǔi Han-Il muyǒk ǔi tonghyang," pp. 191–192, 194–195.

65. Han U-gǔn, *Han'guk kaehanggi ǔi sangǒp yǒn'gu,* pp. 264–268.

66. Ishihata Tadashi reports that Japanese merchants bought Korean gold dust, hides, and seaweed for the equivalent of 100 yen and sold them in Osaka for three hundred yen. *Chōsen kikō yoroku,* p. 45b.

67. Ch'oe Yu-gil, "Yijo kaehang chikju ǔi Han-Il muyǒk ǔi tonghyang," pp. 185–186, 193.

68. Hilary Conroy reached similar conclusions. See *The Japanese Seizure of Korea: 1868–1910,* p. 484.

Chapter 6

1. *CWCSL,* 15:1b-3; *CSS,* pt. 6, vol. 4, p. 475. For instance, when French missionaries were jailed in Korea, the Yamen sent a note to Seoul urging the release of the missionaries

only after the French minister launched an indignant protest in the fall of 1879. *CSS,* pt. 6, vol. 4, pp. 510–511.

2. See T. C. Lin, "Li Hung-chang: His Korea Policies, 1870–1885," *Chinese Social and Political Science Review* 19.2:218–219 (July 1935).

3. FO17/809, Wade's 23 (conf.), Peking, July 3, 1879; *CKHCJ,* 1:31b-32b.

4. *CKHCJ,* 1:31b-32b; *CWCSL,* 16:11b-13; *CJHSL,* No. 309, pp. 363–364.

5. Li Hung-chang, however, rejected a proposal by a memorialist who suggested that China should build up a heavy defense system in the area of Chunggang and eastward to thwart a Russian attack. Li Hung-chang, *Memorials,* 39:37–38.

6. *CWCSL,* 16:14–17 (also in *NGB,* vol. 14, No. 154, pp. 370–371); 23:35–36; *CSS,* pt. 6, vol. 4, pp. 501–503; *Kao koryak,* vol. 1 (Letter from Li Hung-chang to Yi Yu-wŏn), fall of 1879.

7. Huang Tsun-hsien was counsellor of the Chinese legation in Japan.

8. The full text of Huang Tsun-hsien's treatise can be found in Kim Hong-jip, *Susinsa ilgi,* pp. 160–171. At the end of that document Huang outlined a full program for Korea's self-strengthening. *CJHSL,* No. 353, appendix 4 (Li Hung-chang to Yi Yu-wŏn), p. 472. Huang Tsun-hsien's booklet was brought back to Korea by Kim Hong-jip who had been sent to Japan in the early summer of 1880 to thank the Japanese government for Hanabusa's mission to Korea. *IS-KJ,* 17.2.9 (230:12a-b), 17.3.23 (231:30), 17.3.26 (231:33); *Waesa ilgi,* 17.2.9, 17.6.28, 17.7.7. For Kim's conversations with Ho Ju-chang and Huang Tsun-hsien, see Kim Hong-jip, *Susinsa ilgi,* pp. 171–189.

9. *CWCSL,* 23:35–36; *CKHCJ,* 2:32b.

10. *Chung-Jih chan-cheng,* 2:337–338; *CWCSL,* 16:12a-b, 13–14; *CJHSL,* No. 309, appendix 1 (Letter from Yi Yu-wŏn sent in 1878), pp. 364–365; Tabohashi Kiyoshi, *Kindai Nissen kankei no kenkyū,* I, 756–757. Tabohashi takes the view that Yi Yu-wŏn, being an ardent foe of the Taewŏn'gun, joined those who advocated opening the country because he knew that China's prestige was behind them.

11. Li Hung-chang, *Communications to the Tsungli Yamen* in *Chung-Jih chan-cheng,* 2:6–8; *CKHCJ,* 2:31; *CJHSL,* No. 309, pp. 363–364; No. 327, pp. 394–395, and appendixes 1 (Yi Yu-wŏn to Li Hung-chang, October 7, 1879) and 2 (Li Hung-chang to Yi Yu-wŏn), pp. 395–396; No. 329, p. 397, and appendix 1 (Yi Yu-wŏn to Li Hung-chang, December 24, 1879), pp. 398–400; *Ilbonin mundap chamnok:* Letter from Li Hung-chang and Yi Yu-wŏn's answer. Also see *Kao koryak,* vol. 1.

12. For the references to the Li-Yi correspondence, see footnote 16. Li Hung-chang, *Communications to the Tsungli Yamen* in *Chung-Jih chan-cheng,* 2:6–8; *CKHCJ,* 2:32b. The middleman who transmitted this correspondence was the prefect of Yung-p'ing (Chihli), Yü Chih-k'ai.

13. *IS-KJ,* 15.11.28 (213:53a-b); 16.3.25 (217:50b-53); *CWCSL,* 26:17a-b (Kim Yun-sik's secret report to Li Hung-chang); for the correspondence concerning the French missionary captured in Korea, see *CJHSL,* No. 280, pp. 339–340; Nos. 284 and 285, p. 342; No. 289, pp. 346–347; No. 297, p. 356; No. 300, p. 358; No. 317, pp. 384–385; Nos. 319 and 320, pp. 386–387; No. 325, pp. 391–392. The Chinese sent the French request for the missionary's release to Seoul. Yi Sŏn-gŭn, *Han'guksa, ch'oegŭnse-p'yŏn,* pp. 443–444.

14. *CJHSL,* No. 342, appendix 2, pp. 442–445.

15. *IS-KJ,* 17.8.28 (236:53); Kim Hong-jip, *Susinsa ilgi,* pp. 189–191; *NGB,* vol. 13, No. 136, pp. 394–396; *CJHSL,* No. 342, appendix 3, pp. 445–447; *CSS,* pt. 6, vol. 4, pp.

536–537, 539–540.

16. *CKHCJ*, 2:31–33; FO46/258, Kennedy's 179 (very conf.), Nov. 21, 1880; Kennedy's 180 (very conf.), November 22, 1880.

17. *IS-KJ*, 17.12.20 (240:45b), 17.12.21 (240:47a-b); *PBTN*, 261:452a,459b. For a detailed analysis of the records concerning the establishment of the new office, see Chŏn Hae-jong, "T'ongnigimu Amun sŏlch'i ŭi kyŏngwi e taehayŏ," *The Yŏksa Hakpo* 17/18: 687–702 (June 1962). As early as 1877, Hanabusa Yoshitada had urged the Korean government to create a high ministerial post which would exclusively manage the relations with foreign countries. *NBG*, vol. 10, No. 132, pp. 302–304. When the first news reporting the establishment of this new organ leaked to Japan, Japanese reaction was very enthusiastic. This development, it was felt, was pointing in the direction of extraordinary reforms in Korea, and Hanabusa even used the words *ishin*, "restoration," in evaluating it. *NGB*, vol. 14, No. 151, p. 361; No. 152, pp. 363–364.

18. The Military Council (Samgunbu), the functions of which had been taken over by the Pibyŏnsa, was restored under the Taewŏn'gun. See Ching Young Choe, *The Rule of the Taewŏn'gun, 1864–1873*, pp. 48–51.

19. For the twenty-two rules governing the organization of the new office, see *PBTN*, 261:460b-461a; 262:468a-b; *IS-KJ*, 18.1.7 (241:15b), 18.1.10 (241:19–20); *MHBG*, 216:520; *NGB*, vol. 14, No. 151, pp. 360–361. The twelve departments were to be managed jointly in the following combinations: the Department of Relations with China together with the Department of Neighborly Relations; the Department of Military Matters combined with the Department of Border Administration and the Department of Coastal Surveillance; the Department of Recruitment together with the Department of Language Study; the Department of Machinery jointly with the Department of Military Ordnance and the Department of Ships; and the Department of Foreign Trade together with the Department of Supply.

20. *IS-KJ*, 17.12.22 (240:50), 18.1.16 (241:33b); *PBTN*, 261:461b-462a. Min Ch'i-sang and Sim Sun-t'aek were not on the original list. Including them, there were actually twelve directors. At the beginning of each month the *Pibyŏnsa tŭngnok* gave the composition of the higher officialdom. Yi Ch'oe-ŭng remained chief state councillor, but not all of the newly appointed officials retained their former posts. For an extensive list of the members, see *NGB*, vol. 14, No. 152, pp. 364–365. The secretaries were assigned to the various departments on February 16. *IS-KJ*, 18.1.18 (241:38a-b).

21. *IS-KJ*, 18.1.17 (241: 36b), 18.1.18 (241: 38b-39b), 18.4.1 (244:1a-b); *CSS*, vol. 6, pt. 4, pp. 555, 556, 557; *MHBG*, 216:520. Kim Kyŏng-su, Pyŏn Wŏn-gyu, and Yi Ŭng-hŏn were appointed interpreters of Chinese and Hyŏn Sŏg-un interpreter of Japanese.

22. *IS-KJ*, 18.1.28 (241:53b-54b), 18.2.5 (242:6b-7), 18.11.4 (252:6b), 18.11.19 (252:35b), 18.11.21 (252:42a-b); *MHBG*, 216:520. Young-ick Lew says that the reorganization of the T'ongnigimu Amun in January 1882 was a result of reports submitted by the members of the secret mission to Japan (*sinsa yuramdan*). "Kabo Reform Movement: The First Modern Reform Movement under Japanese Control, 1894" (Unpublished Ph.D. thesis, Harvard, 1972), Chapter 6. Yi Chae-gŭng, who was a son of Chief State Councillor Yi Ch'oe-ŭng, died on February 21 and was replaced by Yi Chae-myŏn on February 26. Min Ch'i-sang was no longer listed on the personnel roster of January 10, 1882.

23. Ching Young Choe, *The Rule of the Taewŏn'gun, 1864–1873*, pp. 45–46.

24. The data to document the various Min careers are taken out of the *Chōsen shi*. They can easily be retraced there. Min Yŏng-ik made heir to Min Sŭng-ho: *CSS*, vol. 6, pt. 4, p. 351; posthumous appointment of Sŭng-ho, vol. 6, pt. 4, p. 489; Min T'ae-ho's daughter designated as bride of the heir apparent, vol. 6, pt. 4, p. 603. For a list of the Min, see Appendix 1.

25. Another piece of evidence that this was true is the fact that between 1800 and 1866 nineteen clan members passed the higher civil service examination (*munkwa*), whereas between 1866 and 1884 twenty-five passed. Harold F. Cook, "Kim Ok-kyun and the Background of the 1884 Emeute," p. 44.

26. The details documenting the careers of these men were taken out of the *Chōsen shi*, the *Ilsŏngnok*, the *Inmyŏng taesajŏn*, and Hwang Hyŏn's *Maech'ŏn yarok*.

27. *IS-KJ*, 18.11.21 (251:42a-b); *Inmyŏng taesajŏn*.

28. For Huang Tsun-hsien's sweeping proposals for Korea's self-strengthening, see Kim Hong-jip, *Susinsa ilgi*, 2:167, and Hanabusa's recommendations in *NGB*, vol. 14, No. 143, pp. 345–346.

29. *IS-KJ*, 17.4.30 (232:65–67), 17.5.25 (233:51a-b); *PBTN*, 261:402a; *Kao koryak*, vol. 1; *CJHSL*, No. 327, pp. 394–395 (with appendixes: exchange of letters between Yi Yu-wŏn and Li Hung-chang). Between the third and ninth month of 1880, Kim Pyŏng-guk was not the left state councillor, but a vice-president of the Board of Officials-without-Portfolio (Chungch'ubu).

30. *CKHCJ*, 2:5b-6; *CSS*, pt. 6, vol. 4, p. 532.

31. *CKHCJ*, 2:5b-6, 7b-8, 13a-b, 31, 32; Li Hung-chang, *Memorials*, 38:37–39, 44–45b; *PBTN*, 261:452a; *CJHSL*, No. 340, pp. 421–424; No. 341, pp. 430–436. In addition to the four general rules which Li Hung-chang worked out with Pyŏn Wŏn-gyu, Li instructed Pyŏn minutely about the criteria of age and skill according to which the artisans and students were to be selected for the various branches of industry. *CJHSL*, No. 340, pp. 421–428.

32. *IS-KJ*, 18.2.4 (242:4a-b), 18.2.26 (242:36a-b), 18.3.5 (243:8), 18.3.6 (243:11), 18.3.21 (243:37a-b), 18.3.26 (243:54), 18.3.27 (243:58), 18.4.6 (244:12a-b), 18.4.29 (244:59), 18.5.5 (245:5a-b), 18.6.13 (246:20b), 18.7.22 (247:32b), 18.7.*15 (248:25b); *CKHCJ*, 2:13a-b, 43a-b; *CJHSL*, No. 381, p. 536; No. 385, pp. 538–542; Kim Yun-sik, *Ŭmch'ŏngsa*, pp. 3, 9–10 (lists all the members of the mission), 12–14 (strict rules of behavior of the mission members), 35. On March 25, the assistant minister of the Department of Appointment, Cho Yong-ho, was appointed *yŏngsŏnsa*. He died on September 8. Another reason for the delay was the death of the widow of the Hsien-feng emperor (r. 1850–1861) and the dispatch of a Korean mission of condolence.

33. The group consisted of thirty-eight trainees, twelve officials, and nineteen attendants. Among the trainees there were twenty "students" and eighteen artisans. Kwŏn Sŏk-pong suggests that the former were yangban, whereas the latter presumably belonged to chungin class. Kwŏn Sŏk-pong "Yŏngsŏn sahaeng e taehan ilgoch'al, "*The Yŏksa Hakpo*, 17/18:277–312 (June 1962). To date, this article is the fullest account of the student mission to China.

34. Kim Yun-sik, *Ŭmch'ŏngsa*, pp. 60, 62, 67, 70–71, 75–76, 83–86, 100–102, 114, 119–120, 121–122, 124, 128–129, 136, 147, 151–152, 158, 179, 188, 197, 200, 201, 211; *IS-KJ*, 18.11.4 (252:5b-6b); *CWCSL*, 26:24b–25b, 30:11b-15; *CSS*, pt. 6, vol. 4, p. 659.

35. Yi Tong-in was a Buddhist monk who was disturbed about current events and

Korea's situation. He slipped out of the country and went to Japan in 1880. In a secret meeting he told Kim Hong-jip about his plans for Korea. Kim later told the king of Yi's plans. Yi transmitted to Hanabusa the alleged plans of the Korean government to hire Japanese military instructors, to raise a loan in Japan, and to get Japanese military equipment, an intimation which very presumably lacked any foundation. *NGB*, vol. 14, No. 122, pp. 290–294; No. 123, pp. 294–295. On February 28, Hanabusa presented a draft agreement of seven articles to the Korean government, but no firm commitments seem to have come out of this. In that agreement the Japanese generously offered their protection to Korea. Japan also would provide instructors and experts for the build-up of Korea's army and industry. Furthermore, Japan would welcome Korean students sent to Japan for specialized studies in military and industrial fields and would make available any number of weapons and ships the Korean government might care to acquire. *NGB*, vol. 14, No. 123, p. 300. For some more information about Yi Tong-in and his relationship to Kim Ok-kyun, see Harold F. Cook, *Korea's 1884 Incident* (Seoul 1972), pp. 33–35.

36. *NGB*, vol. 14, No. 127, pp. 305–306; Ŏ Yun-jung, *Chongjŏng yŏnp'yo*, p. 119. For an analysis of the composition of the inspection mission, see Chŏng Ok-cha, "Sinsa yuramdan ko," *The Yŏksa Hakpo* 27:114–119 (April 1965).

37. *NGB*, vol. 14, No. 127, pp. 305–306; No. 128, pp. 306–307; Ŏ Yun-jung, *Chongjŏng yŏnp'yo*, pp. 119–120, 123; *Ku Han'guk oegyo munsŏ, Ilan*, Nos. 72 and 73, pp. 56–57. Separate from the inspection mission, two groups of three Koreans each were organized to receive special training in Japan. The first went to Nagasaki to study customs regulations and the methods of customs management; the second went to Osaka to visit silver and copper mines and to buy equipment for tanning, minting, coal mining, and iron smelting. *NGB*, vol. 14, No. 125, p. 303; No. 129, pp. 307–308; Yi Sŏn-gŭn, *Han'guksa, ch'oegŭnsep'yŏn*, p. 438. Two assistants, Yun Ch'i-ho and Yu Kil-chun, who accompanied Ŏ Yun-jung on the inspection mission, were enrolled by Ŏ at Keiō in June 1881, Harold F. Cook, *Korea's 1884 Incident*, pp. 64, 66.

38. For a complete list of these reports, see Chŏng Ok-cha, "Sinsa yuramdan ko," pp. 140–142. They are preserved in the Kyujanggak Library.

39. *IS-KJ*, 18.8.30, 18.9.1. 18.9.2; for an analysis of the contents of the various reports submitted after the mission's return, see Chŏng Ok-cha, pp. 126–139. It is important to notice in passing that this mission also exerted considerable influence on Kim Ok-kyun's development because two of his friends, Hong Yŏng-sik and Ŏ Yun-jung, were mission members. The mission also met Fukuzawa Yukichi, who was to become one of Kim Okkyun's principal mentors. See Harold F. Cook, *Korea's 1884 Incident*, pp. 35–36. Ŏ Yunjung did not return to Korea with the inspection mission, but undertook a side trip to China. See the following chapter. Ŏ Yun-jung, together with Yi Chung-ch'il, Sin Ki-sŏn, and Pak Yŏng-hyo, was appointed secretary (*chusa*) in the T'ongnigimu Amun on March 20, 1882. *IS-KJ*, 19.2.2 (255:2b).

40. *CJHSL*, No. 340, pp. 428–429; No. 353, p. 468. Pyŏn was given a Western rifle to take back to Korea.

41. *IS-KJ*, 18.2.5 (242:6), | 18.2.10 (242:15a-b). There is uncertainty about this appointment. Yi Wŏn-hoe is also listed in various sources as a member of the inspection mission to Japan (*sinsa yuramdan*). Yi reportedly crossed over to Japan with this mission. Since Yi Tong-in never went to Japan with him and disappeared around that time, it is possible that Yi Wŏn-hoe was considered by most mission members as belonging to the

mission, although he evidently had a different task to perform.

42. Yi Kyŏng-ha (1811-1891) had a very successful military career under the Tae-wŏn'gun and was instrumental in repelling the French in 1866. He continued to be in high military office under King Kojong. *Han'guk inmyŏng taesajŏn*, p. 593.

43. *IS-KJ*, 18.6.20 (246:38); *PBTN*, 261: 461b; Li Hung-chang, *Memorials*, 38:37b-38; *NGB*, vol. 13, No. 159, pp. 418–419; vol. 14, No. 143, pp. 344–345; No. 153, pp. 365–369; *CSS*, pt. 6, vol. 4, pp. 567, 598, 600; Yi Sŏn-gŭn, *Han'guksa, ch'oegŭnse-p'yŏn*, pp. 439–440, 442–443. Hŏ Wŏn-sik, for example, complained about the different treatment accorded to old and new army units. *IS-KJ*, 17.12.17 (240:40). After his return from Japan, Hong Yŏng-sik wrote a three-volume manual on the Japanese army. See Harold F. Cook, "Kim Ok-kyun and the Background of the 1884 Emeute," p. 130.

44. *CWCSL*, 26:17b-18.

45. *IS-KJ*, 17.10.1 (238:2b-3b); *PBTN*, 261:430b.

46. *IS-KJ*, 17.12.17 (240:37–40b).

47. *IS-KJ*, 18.2.26 (242:40-42b); *NGB*, vol. 14, No. 155, pp. 372–375; Hwang Hyŏn, *Maech'ŏn yarok*, 1:50–51.

48. *IS-KJ*, 18.13.23 (243:41b-46b); the full text of Hong Chae-hak's memorial can be found in *NGB*, vol. 14, No. 156, pp. 376–381. A short biography of Hong is in *Kirosup'il*, pp. 8–14. Yi Sŏn-gŭn, *Han'guksa, ch'oegŭnse-p'yŏn*, pp. 447–457; Hyŏn Sang-yun, *Chosŏn yuhak sa*, pp. 443–459; Han U-gŭn, "Kaehang tangsi ŭi wigiŭisik kwa kaehwasasang," *Han'guksa yŏn'gu* 2:123–127.

49. *IS-KJ*, 17.10.2 (238:7b) (Yu Wŏn-sik's banishment), 17.10.3 (238:8–9), 18.3.2 (243:3b-4), 18.3.6 (243:12a-b), 18.3.18 (243:30b), 18.3.19 (243:34a-b) (Kim Hong-jip's case), 18.2.26 (242:42b) (king's response), 18.3.23 (243:46b), 18.3.25 (243:50b-51b), 18.3.26 (243: 56a-b) and almost daily entries in the fourth month (vol. 244) (Hwang Chae-hyŏn's trial and banishment), 18.4.1 (244:3a-b), 18.4.2 (244:5a-b), 18.4.3 (244:8) (Yi Man-son's trial and banishment), 18.5.9 (245:10a-b) (Han Hong-nyŏl's trial and banishment), 18. fifth month (vol. 245) is full of documents pertaining to Yi Man-son's trial, 18.7*.8 (248:10–11), 18.7*.14 (248:23b-24b), 18.7.*.15 (248:27a-b), 18.7*.25 (248:47b) (Yi Yu-wŏn's banishment), 18.7*.24 (248:44a-b), 18.7*.25 (248: 46b–47), 18. 8. 2 (249:3–4b) (Kim Hong-jip's case); 18.7*. 8 (248:11b), 18.7*.29 (248: 52b), and many more entries in vol. 248 concerning Hong Chae-hak's and Sin Sŏp's trials. The *Royal Message Concerning the Rejection of Heresy* can be found in *IS-KJ*, 18.5.15 (245: 19–21). A booklet which contains both the Chinese and the *han'gŭl* versions is preserved in the Kyujanggak Library. It is dated June 12, 1881. A memorialist who supported the royal call for moral unity was Kwak Ki-rak. For his memorial, see *IS-KJ*, 18.6.8 (246: 10b-13). *CWCSL*, 26: 17a-b; *NGB*, vol. 14, No. 157, pp. 382–383; Hwang Hyŏn, *Maech'ŏn yarok*, 1:50–52; Yi Sŏn-gŭn, *Han'guksa, ch'oegŭnse-p'yŏn*, pp. 448–457; Tabohashi Kiyoshi, *Kindai Nissen kankei no kenkyū*, I, 752–758.

50. *CSS*, pt. 6, vol. 4, pp. 586–594; Yi Sŏn-gŭn, *Han'guksa, ch'oegŭnse-p'yŏn*, pp. 457–461; Tabohashi Kiyoshi, *Kindai Nissen kankei no kenkyū*, I, 759–765.

Chapter 7

1. The reaction of the German consul at Newchwang was most enthusiastic. He urged his government to allow the German navy to play the Commodore Perry role in Korea. *Asien*, F. P. Knight to Auswärtiges Amt, March 19, 1874; von Brandt to Bismarck, March 30, 1874; Bülow to von Brandt, June 27, 1874; von Brandt to Bismarck, September 30, 1874. Max von Brandt had made a short trip aboard the warship *Hertha* to the port of Pusan. See Ching Young Choe, "The Decade of the Taewŏn'gun," II, 446–450.

2. FO17/672, Wade's 19, February 21, 1874; Wade's 25 (conf.), March 9, 1874; FO46/231, Parkes' 125 (conf.) and 127, December 2, 1878; Parkes' 136, December 12, 1878 (containing Satow's report on his trip to Cheju Island).

3. *FRUS*, 1876, No. 193, Bingham to Fish, March 9, 1876.

4. *FRUS*, 1876, No. 363, Bingham to Fish, March 21, 1876; FO46/231, Parkes' 141 December 18, 1878; Parkes' 147 (conf.), December 30, 1878; FO46/248, Kennedy's 190 (conf.), October 27, 1879; FO46/256, Kennedy's 52 (conf.), March 14, 1880; FO46/258, Kennedy's 185 (very conf.), November 26, 1880; *North China Herald*, December 2, 1880.

5. FO46/231, Parkes' 147 (conf.), December 30, 1878; FO46/248, Kennedy's 190 (conf.), October 27, 1879; FO46/256, Kennedy's 52 (conf.), March 14, 1880.

6. Charles O. Paullin, *Negotiations of American Naval Officers, 1778–1883*, p. 283. It should be remembered that the suggestion of 1868 and the action of 1870 were direct results of the *General Sherman* incident of July 1866. The American expedition of 1871 was launched before the answer from Seoul was received. For the whole background, see Ching Young Choe, *The Rule of the Taewŏn'gun*, pp. 109–133.

7. *NGB*, vol. 13, No. 172, pp. 438–442; Yi Po-hyŏng, "Shufeldt chedok kwa 1880 nyŏn ŭi Cho-Mi kyosŏp," *The Yŏksa Hakbo* 15: 65–66 (September 1961); Tyler Dennett, *Americans in Eastern Asia* (New York, 1922), p. 458; *North China Herald*, May 20, 1881. Commodore Shufeldt was no stranger to Korean waters. In January 1867 he had headed the mission that had gone to the Korean coast to investigate the fate of the *General Sherman*. See Ching Young Choe, *The Rule of the Taewŏn'gun*, pp. 117–118.

8. *NGB*, vol. 13, No. 169, pp. 435–436; No. 170, pp. 436–437; No. 171, p. 437; FO46/257, Kennedy's 75 (conf.), May 1, 1880.

9. *IS-KJ*, 17.4.10 (232:20b–21b); *Waesa ilgi*, 17.4.5, 17.4.6.

10. *NGB*, vol. 13, No. 173, pp. 442–443; No. 174, p. 443; FO46/257, Kennedy's 90 (conf.), May 25, 1880.

11. *NGB*, vol. 13, No. 175, pp. 443–446; No. 178, pp. 448–449; *Ku Han'guk oegyo munsŏ*, No. 64, pp. 48–49; No. 65, pp. 49–50; *Waesa ilgi*, 17.5.16; *CSS*, pt. 6, vol. 4, p. 532; *Kao Koryak*, vol. 1. Hanabusa seconded Inoue's letter with one of his own which was also addressed to the president of the Department of Rites.

12. *NGB*, vol. 13, No. 182, pp. 451–455, No. 183, pp. 455–456; *CJHSL*, No. 335, pp. 411–412. Yi Po-hyŏng, "Shufeldt chedok kwa 1880 nyŏn ŭi Cho-Mi kyosŏp," pp. 86–88.

13. *NGB*, vol. 14, No. 154, p. 370.

14. Yi Po-hyŏng, "Shufeldt chedok kwa 1880 nyŏn ŭi Cho-Mi kyosŏp," pp. 81–82.

15. Li Hung-chang, *Communications to the Tsungli Yamen*, 11: 43; Yi Po-hyŏng, "Shu-feldt chedok kwa 1880 nyŏn ŭi Cho-Mi kyosŏp, " pp. 82–84.

16. *CKHCJ*, 1:22a-b; *Chung Jih chan-cheng*, II, 337.

17. *CJHSL*, No. 332, pp. 403–404; No. 334, pp. 406–407; No. 335, pp. 411–412; No. 336, pp. 412–413. For a discussion of Huang Tsun-hsien's treatise, see Chapter 6.

18. It is not clear how Yi Tong-in, who reportedly had gone to Japan in September, received these transcripts from Korea. He could not have brought them himself because the court conference in question was held on October 11. It is possible that Yi's comrade, T'ak Chŏng-sik, brought them with him when he came to Japan in the last months of 1880. When Yi met Ho, he carried the documents in his travelling bag and was apparently most reluctant to have them copied. *CJHSL*, No. 342 and appendixes, pp. 437–446.

19. *CJHSL*, No. 342, pp. 437–442; No. 344, pp. 449–450; Li Hung-chang, *Communications to the Tsungli Yamen*, 11:42–43; *CKHCJ*, 2:31–32.

20. *CJHSL*, No. 345, pp. 451–452; *Diplomatic Despatches, Japan*, Bingham to Evarts, No. 1238, January 6, 1881. T'ak apparently left for Nagasaki on January 31, 1881, on his way home. T'ak died of the plague at Kobe in February 1884. The fact that Kim Ok-kyun was his chief mourner may be indicative of their close relationship. Harold F. Cook, *Korea's 1884 Incident*, p. 90.

21. *CJHSL*, No. 349, pp. 456–458; No. 360, pp. 500–501; No. 361, pp. 504–505. Ho Ju-chang also met Hong Yŏng-sik and Ŏ Yun-jung who confirmed what T'ak had told before. No. 364, p. 508; No. 365, p. 509. *Diplomatic Despatches, Japan*, Bingham to Blaine, No. 1318, June 20, and encl.: Ho to Bingham, June 16, 1881. Ho Ju-chang was replaced in the early winter of 1881 by Li Shu-ch'ang.

22. *CJHSL*, No. 341, pp. 432–436 (Li Hung-chang's conversation with Pyŏn Wŏn-gyu).

23. Yi Yong-suk arrived in Peking as a member of the regular winter solstice mission. The mission departed from Peking in the first days of March and was received in royal audience on May 5, 1881. *CJHSL*, No. 353, pp. 461–462 and appendixes, pp. 462–480 (Li Hung-chang's discussion with Yi Yong-suk, the Chinese draft treaty, and other documents); No. 354, pp. 480–482; No. 355, pp. 483–490; *CKHCJ*, 2:32–33. The specific questions which Yi Yong-suk put before Li Hung-chang were concerned with such practical problems as the management of the maritime customs, fixing the customs, tariffs, the invitation of Chinese merchants to trade in Korea's open ports, the stationing of Hanabusa in Seoul, and the use of Korean titles in foreign correspondence.

24. *IS-KJ*, 18.2.26 (242:36b-37). The envoy to Japan (*susinsa*) had henceforth to be appointed from among the members of the T'ongnigimu Amun: 18.7*.6 (248:7b), 18. 8.7 (249:10b), 18.11.29 (252:54). Originally, Kim Hong-jip was called upon to go to Japan, but he adamantly refused to go. *IS-KJ*, 18.4.9 (244:19a-b), 18.7*.6 (248:7a-b).

25. Ŏ Yun-jung, *Chongjŏng yŏnp'yo*, pp. 120–123; *CSS*, pt. 6, vol. 4, pp. 599–600. It is uncertain whether Ŏ had been instructed to go to China before his departure from Seoul. It is more likely that Cho Pyŏng-ho told him to do so. It is also not clear when the Koreans learned about Shufeldt's second trip to Tientsin. When the commodore passed through Japan in June, there was apparently no contact between Shufeldt and members of the secret inspection mission. Ŏ departed from Tientsin on December 1, returned to Nagasaki on the 21st, and returned to Korea with Cho Pyŏng-ho. He was received in royal audience on Feburary 2, 1882. *IS-KJ*, 18.12.14 (253:23). Ŏ was appointed to the

T'ongnigimu Amun on March 20, 1882. *IS-KJ*, 19.2.2 (255:2b); Ŏ Yun-jung, *Chong-jŏng yŏnp'yo*, p. 125. Ŏ seems to have been quite impressed by China's industrial progress, especially in the military field. He was aware of the potential danger Japan presented to Korea and was convinced that only trade relations with other countries could meet this challenge. On December 19, 1882, Ŏ Yun-jung had a lengthy conversation with the new Chinese minister to Tokyo, Li Shu-ch'ang, during which Ŏ repeatedly expressed his faith in international trade as a device which could restrain Japan's ambitions in Korea. *CJHSL*, No. 387, pp. 543–547.

26. *CWCSL*, 26:14; Kim Yun-sik, *Ŭmch'ŏngsa*, pp. 8, 27, 44; *CCS*, pt. 6, vol. 4, pp. 603–604.

27. *CWCSL*, 26:14; Tyler Dennett, *Americans in Eastern Asia*, p. 458; Paullin, *Diplomatic Negotiations of American Naval Officers, 1778–1883*, pp. 304–307; *Diplomatic Despatches, China*, Angell to Evarts, No. 187, July 16, 1881; Holcombe to Blaine, No. 30, December 19, 1881. Shufeldt actually was authorized to help Li Hung-chang organize the Chinese navy, and he therefore established himself in Tientsin. Yet his advisory role aroused the jealousy of the other foreigners in China who did not like to see an American exercise influence on Li Hung-chang. The intrigue against Shufeldt finally led to his complete retirement from naval matters.

28. *CWCSL*, 26:14–15, 18b; Kim Yun-sik, *Ŭmch'ŏngsa*, pp. 30, 44–47; *CSS*, pt. 6, vol. 4, p. 604. The fact that Cho Pyŏng-ho did not come to agreement concerning the tariffs with Japan was interpreted as a sure sign of Japan's sinister plans against Korea and made the speedy conclusion of a Korean-American treaty even more urgent. *CWCSL*, 26:15a-b.

29. *CKHCJ*, 2:45a; *CWCSL*, 26:19; Kim Yun-sik, *Ŭmch'ŏngsa*, pp. 52, 105; Li Hung-chang, *Communications to the Tsungli Yamen*, 13:7b, 33b; *CSS*, pt. 6, vol. 4, p. 608. Li Hung-chang suggested to Kim Yun-sik that the Korean plenipotentiary who would be sent to China should be dispatched under the pretext of investigating the Korean students at Tientsin to avoid drawing public attention. Kim Yun-sik, *Ŭmch'ŏngsa*, p. 46. For Shufeldt's draft of the American-Korean treaty, see *CWCSL*, 27:13b-18 and *Ŭmch'ŏngsa*, pp. 106–111. Li Hung-chang reportedly dismissed the Korean treaty propositions as "too sketchy in their wording." Among other things, they apparently suggested that the negotiations concerning the trade regulations and the dispatch of a resident minister should be postponed for five years. Li thought that Shufeldt was unlikely to agree to this point. In particular, Kim Yun-sik argued against allowing missionary work in Korea. *Ŭmch'ŏngsa*, pp. 52–53.

30. Li Hung-chang, *Communications to the Tsungli Yamen*, 13:8, 9; Kim Yun-sik, *Ŭmch'ŏngsa*, pp. 52–53; Chou Fu, *Collected Works*, 9:1a-b; *CSS*, pt. 6, vol. 4, p. 608.

31. *CJHSL*, No. 389, pp. 548–552; Li Hung-chang, *Communications to the Tsungli Yamen*, 13:8b, 23b–24b; *CSS*, pt. 6, vol. 4, p. 608.

32. *CJHSL*, No. 392, pp. 557–558; No. 393, pp. 559–560; Li Hung-chang, *Communications to the Tsungli Yamen*, 13:31b–33b; Kim Yun-sik, *Ŭmch'ŏngsa*, pp. 104, 106; Chou Fu, *Collected Works*, 9: 1b; *CSS*, pt. 6, vol. 4, p. 608. As for the reason Shufeldt did not receive an answer from Washington, Paullin suggests that Secretary of State Frelinghuysen did not want to see a Blaine administration appointee conclude a treaty with Korea. Paullin, *Diplomatic Negotiations*, pp. 324–325.

33. Henry G. Appenzeller, "The Opening of Korea: Admiral Shufeldt's Account of It," *The Korean Repository* 1:61 (Seoul, 1892).

34. *IS-KJ*, 19.2.2 (255:2b–3), 19.2.5 (255:9b), 19.2.17 (255:31); Ŏ Yun-jung, *Chongjŏng yŏnp'yo*, pp. 125–127, 130. According to Li Hung-chang's request, Ŏ Yun-jung and Yi Cho-yŏn were appointed "investigation officers" (*kosŏn'gwan*, later changed to *munŭigwan*) in order to disguise their real purpose. The king emphasized, however, that their primary task was to negotiate with the foreigner. Ŏ was also instructed to bring up for discussion the issue of the "prohibition of the seaway" (*haegŭm*). Ŏ and Yi departed on April 5 and arrived in Tientsin on May 15. Yi Ch'oe-ŭng's letter to Li Hung-chang can be found in *CJHSL*, No. 393, pp. 560–561.

35. Li Hung-chang, *Communications to the Tsungli Yamen*, 13:9a-b, 31b–32, 34; Kim Yun-sik, *Ŭmch'ŏngsa*, pp. 87, 93, 98–99, 103, 105, 113; *CSS*, pt. 6, vol. 4, pp. 608–609; Ma Chien-chung, *Tung-hsing san-lu*, 1:5. Li Hung-chang sent a letter through Yi Ŭng-jun to the Korean king in which he announced the impending mission of Ma Chien-chung and Ting Ju-ch'ang to Korea. *CJHSL*, No. 934, pp. 566–569; No. 397, pp. 575–577; No. 398, pp. 577–578. Paullin writes that Li Hung-chang agreed to waive article 1 of the treaty provided the commodore would make a request in writing for a messenger to accompany him to Korea as the representative of the Chinese government. No substantiation for this could be found in the Chinese documents. Paullin, *Diplomatic Negotiations*, p. 315.

36. *IS-KJ*, 19.3.15 (256:44), 19.3.20 (256:57b), 19.3.22 (256:60b), 19.3.24 (256:66); *CJHSL*, No. 419, p. 606; Ma Chien-chung, *Tung-hsing san-lu*, 1:7–11; *CKHCJ*, 3: 8b–9; *CCS*, pt. 6, vol. 4, pp. 609, 610; Paullin, *Diplomatic Negotiations*, pp. 319–320. Five officials of the CMSNC sailed to Korea with Ma to make an on-the-spot survey of the situation.

37. *CJHSL*, No. 419, pp. 606–609; *CKHCJ*, 3:9–10; Ma Chien-chung, *Tung-hsing san-lu*, 1:12–18; *CSS*, pt. 6, vol. 4, pp. 610–613; *North China Herald*, June 2, 1882; Paullin, *Diplomatic Negotiations*, pp. 321–322. Paullin used Shufeldt's *Korean Letter-Books*. For Ma Chien-chung's discussions with the Korean negotiators prior to the conclusion of the treaty, see "Conversations on the US-Korean Treaty in 1882 between the Korean Delegates and the Chinese Envoys," *The Yŏksa Hakpo* 22:121–132 (January 1964).

38. *CKHCJ*, 3:9b–10; see for the text of the treaty and the dispatch of the Korean king, *CKHCJ*, 3:10–13b and *Treaties*, pp. 41–52. *FRUS*, 1883, No. 85, Young to Frelinghuysen, December 26, 1882; Dennett, *Americans in Eastern Asia*, p. 464. The ratifications of the treaty were exchanged at Seoul on May 19, 1883.

39. FO17/672, Wade's 50 (conf.), March 31, 1874; FO17/719, Wade's 7, January 12, 1876; FO17/753, Fraser's 33 (conf.), February 10, 1877; FO17/809, Wade's 23 (conf.), July 3, 1879; FO46/257, Kennedy's 114 (conf.), July 1, 1880; 115, July 2, 1880. Li Hung-chang, *Communications to the Tsungli Yamen*, 11:43a-b.

40. The French minister in Tokyo came out in favor of assisting and encouraging Shufeldt's expedition to Korea because if it was successful Korea would be opened to all nations. FO46/257, Kennedy's 90, May 25, 1880; FO46/258, Kennedy's 179 (very conf.), November 21, 1880; 180 (very conf.), November 22, 1880; 185 (very conf.), November 26, 1880; 199 (very conf.), December 21, 1880; FO46/271, Parkes' memorandum, January 11, 1881; *Korea II*, Eisendecher to Auswärtiges Amt, June 23, 1880; Eisendecher to Auswärtiges Amt, July 22, 1880; Eisendecher to Auswärtiges Amt, December 4, 1880. It should be noted that the Korean, Yi Tong-in, who secretly went to Japan in 1880, was the informant to both Parkes and Eisendecher.

41. FO17/856, Granville's 7, January 20, 1881; FO46/272, Kennedy's 61 (very conf.), June 8, 1881; FO46/284, Kennedy's 5 (most conf.), January 10, 1882; *Korea I*, Auswärtiges Amt to Eisendecher, February 4, 1881; Eisendecher to Auswärtiges Amt, June 24, 1881.

42. FO46/283, Granville to Parkes, April 17, 1882; FO46/284, Parkes' 41 (conf.), March 25, 1882; FO46/285, Parkes' 57 (conf.), April 21, 1882; *Korea I*, Eisendecher to Bismarck, April 27, 1882.

43. FO17/897, Wade to Granville, May 27, 1882; FO17/912, Admirality to Under Secretary of State for Foreign Affairs (conf.), April 14, 1882; Kim Yun-sik, *Ŭmch'ŏngsa*, p. 124; *CSS*, pt. 6, vol. 4, p. 613.

44. *IS-KJ*, 19.4.12 (257:18a–b), 19.4.22 (257:35a-b); *CJHSL*, No. 434, p. 686; No. 455, pp. 718–726; *CKHCJ*, 3:19b, 24b; Kim Yun-sik, *Ŭmch'ŏngsa*, pp. 137, 159–161; Ma Chien-chung, *Tung-hsing san-lu*, 1:23–32; *CCS*, pt. 6, vol. 4, pp. 613, 614, 615, 616; FO17/897, Wade's 51 (conf.), July 6, 1882 (it contains Maude's report to Wade); FO17/915, George O. Willes' report to the Secretary to the Admirality, Nagasaki, June 9, 1882. For the text of the British-Korean treaty and the supplementary documents, see *CKHCJ*, 3:20–23b; *Treaties*, pp. 53–61.

45. *IS-KJ*, 19.5.7 (258:13), 19.5.10 (258:20b), 19.5.15 (258: 27b); *CJHSL*, No. 433, pp. 686; No. 435, p. 687; No 448, p. 705; No. 468, pp. 737–747; *CKHCJ*, 3:24b–30b; Kim Yun-sik, *Ŭmch'ŏngsa*, pp. 137, 148–149, 165–167; Ma Chien-chung, *Tung-hsing san-lu*, 2:41–45, 50–52; *CSS*, pt. 6, vol. 4, pp. 617, 618, 619; FO17/897, Wade's 63, July 28, 1882. Ma Chien-chung was decorated for his services by the Prussian emperor. *CJHSL*, No. 703, p. 1133; No. 717, p. 1148.

46. Ma Chien-chung, *Tung-hsing san-lu*, 1:19, 33; FO17/898, Grosvenor's 98, September 30, 1882.

47. *IS-KJ*, 19.2.7 (255:14a-b), 19.2.17 (255:31b–32); *CJHSL*, No. 412, p. 585; No. 447, pp. 701–704; Kim Yun-sik, *Ŭmch'ŏngsa*, pp. 148, 152, 162–163, 170; *CSS*, pt. 6, vol. 4. pp. 521, 619–621; Yi Sŏn-gŭn, *Han'guksa, ch'oegŭnse-p'yŏn*, pp. 763–766. The major problem which burdened the relationship between the two countries was the great number of Korean settlers who crossed over into Russian territory.

48. *CJHSL*, No. 402, p. 580; No. 405, p. 581; No. 409, p. 583; No. 410, p. 584; No. 414, p. 588; No. 415, p. 588; No. 452, p. 707; Ma Chien-chung, *Tung-hsing san-lu*, 1:30–31.

Chapter 8

1. *CSS*, pt. 6, vol. 4, pp. 622–623; Tabohashi Kiyoshi, *Kindai Nissen kankei no kenkyū*, I, 770–773. For a detailed description of the mutiny, see Ching Young Choe, "Yüan Shih-k'ai: His Role in Korea, 1882–1894" (Seminar paper, Harvard Regional Program, 1956–1957), pp. 1–7. It was also reported that on the modern training-field angry soldiers destroyed Western-style rifles. Ŏ Yun-jung, *Chongjŏng yŏnp'yo*, p. 135. For an analysis of economic factors leading to popular unrest, see Yi Sŏn-gŭn, *Han'guksa, ch'oegŭnse-p'yŏn*, pp. 466–470.

2. A vivid account is given by Kondō Masuki in *Keijō zokuto ikken temmatsu sho* (1882).

CSS, pt. 6, vol. 4, pp. 623–624, 626–627, 628; Tabohashi Kiyoshi, *Kindai Nissen kankei no kenkyū*, I, 776–780; Yi Sŏn-gŭn, *Han'guksa, ch'oegŭnse-p'yŏn*, pp. 473–479. For Hanabusa's reports to Inoue, see *NGB*, vol. 15, No. 116, pp. 215–216 and No. 118, pp. 216–221. A report by the commander of the *Flying Fish*, R.F. Hoskyn, can be found in FO46/287, Parkes' 98, August 9, 1882.

3. *IS-KJ*, 19.6.10 (259:16b); *CSS*, pt. 6, vol. 4, pp. 624–627; Tabohashi Kiyoshi, *Kindai Nissen kankei no kenkyū*, I, 780–783; Yi Sŏn-gŭn, *Han'guksa, ch'oegŭnse-p'yŏn*, pp. 479–487.

4. *CJHSL*, No. 463, p. 734; No. 464, p. 735; No. 470, pp. 748–751; No. 485, pp. 768–772; *CKHCJ*, 3:31; 4:4; Kim Yun-sik, *Ŭmch'ŏngsa*, pp. 177–179, 180–183; Ŏ Yun-jung, *Chongjŏng yŏnp'yo*, pp. 135–136; Ma Chien-chung in Tsiang T'ing-fu, *Chin-tai Chung-kuo wai-chiao-shih tzu-liao chi-yao*, II, 393–394; Ma Chien-chung, *Tung-hsing san-lu*, 3:64. It seems that rumors about an alleged refusal by the American Congress to ratify the Korean-American treaty circulated at the time of the disturbances. Yet, it is not celar what influence they had. *CKHCJ*, 3:34b; FO46/287, Parkes' 97, August 7, 1882.

5. *CKHCJ*, 3:31a-b, 33a-b, 34; Hsüeh Fu-ch'eng, *Yung-an wen-pien*, 2:33; *NGB*, vol. 15, No. 104, p. 164; No. 105, p. 164; No. 106, p. 165; No. 107, pp. 165–169.

6. *CJHSL*, No. 492, p. 776; No. 498, pp. 780–783; No. 503, pp. 786–787; No. 511, pp. 796–805; *CKHCJ*, 3:31a-b, 32, 34a-b, 36–37, 40a-b; Hsüeh Fu-ch'eng, *Yung-an wen-pien*, 2:33-35b; Ma Chien-chung, *Tung-hsing san-lu*, 3:55–56, 59–60, 68–69; Kim Yun-sik, *Ŭmch'ŏngsa*, pp. 179–183, 184–190, 192; Ŏ Yun-jung, *Chongjŏng yŏnp'yo*, pp. 136–137; *CSS*, pt. 6, vol. 4, pp. 633–635, 637; *Nan-t'ung Chang Chi-chih hsien-sheng ch'uan-chi*, pp. 32–43. As soon as the first reports about the incident reached Peking, an imperial edict ordered Li Hung-chang to hurry back north. He resumed charge of Korean affairs in the first days of September. *CKHCJ*, 3:33b–34; *CJHSL*, No. 545, p. 885.

7. *IS-KJ*, 19.7.11 (260:20), 19.7.12 (260:21); *CKHCJ*, 3:44–45, 46–47; Hsüeh Fu-ch'eng, *Yung-an wen-pien*, 2:35b; Ma Chien-chung, *Tung-hsing san-lu*, 3:73–74; *CSS*, pt. 6, vol. 4, pp. 639–640. For a description of the Taewŏn'gun's confinement at Paoting, see Yi Sŏn-gŭn, *Han'guksa, ch'oegŭnse-p'yŏn*, pp. 510–517.

8. *IS-KJ*, 19.7.16. (260:26); *Kojong sillok*, 19.8.9, 19.8.11, 19.8.16, 19.8.21; *CJHSL*, No. 520, pp. 824–825 (letter from Cho Yŏng-ha to Ting Ju-ch'ang and Ma Chien-chung); No. 544, pp. 883–884; *CKHCJ*, 3:44–45, 46b–47b; Ma Chien-chung, *Tung-hsing san-lu*, 3:74–89; *CSS*, pt. 6, vol. 4, pp. 640, 641, 642, 643; Tabohashi Kiyoshi, *Kindai Nissen kankei no kenkyū*, I, 851. According to the Chinese sources, the Chinese planned a campaign against the rebels before they were asked to do so by the Korean king. According to Tabohashi, it was Ŏ Yun-jung who transmitted to the Chinese the king's request to move against the rebels.

9. *IS-KJ*, 19.6.22 (259:43b), 19.6.30 (259:60b), 19.7.1 (260:1a-b), 19.7.3 (260:6b), 19.7.4 (260:9), 19.7.6 (260:13); *NGB*, vol. 15, No. 122, pp. 226–230; Tabohashi Kiyoshi, *Kindai Nissen kankei no kenkyū*, I, 788–795.

10. *NGB*, vol. 15, No. 110, pp. 204–207; *CSS*, pt. 6, vol. 4, pp. 632, 634, 635, 636–637, 638; Ma Chien-chung, *Tung-hsing san-lu*, 3:64–70, 71; Tabohashi Kiyoshi, *Kindai Nissen kankei no kenkyū*, I, 800–807. When Hanabusa sailed back to Korea, he was accompanied by Kim Ok-kyun and Sŏ Kwang-bŏm who had just finished their first visit to Japan. Kim and Sŏ had petitioned Foreign Minister Inoue Kaoru to dispatch under their command Japanese troops to punish the Taewŏn'gun. This proposal was not even taken

into consideration by the Japanese. Harold F. Cook, *Korea's 1884 Incident*, p. 48.

11. *NGB*, vol. 15, No. 110, p. 207; Ma Chien-chung, *Tung-hsing san-lu*, 3:64–69; *CSS*, pt. 6, vol. 4, pp. 638–639.

12. *IS-KJ*, 19.7.14. (260:23a-b); *NGB*, vol. 15, No. 110, pp. 195–199, 207; Ma Chien-chung, *Tung-hsing san-lu*, 3:71–74; *CSS*, pt. 6, vol. 4, pp. 640–641; Hsüeh Fu-cheng, *Yung-an wen-pien*, 2:35b.

13. *CJHSL*, No. 544, p. 883; *NGB*, vol. 15, No. 110, pp. 200–204, 207–208; No. 126, pp. 235–237; Ma Chien-chung, *Tung-hsing san-lu*, 3:74–87; *CSS*, pt. 6, vol. 4, pp. 641, 642. For the texts, see *Ku Han'guk oegyo munsŏ, Ilan*, No. 95, pp. 68–69; No. 96, pp. 69–70. For the English text of the *Additional Convention*, see *Treaties*, pp. 62–63. For a point-by-point discussion between Hanabusa and the Korean negotiators, see Tabohashi Kiyoshi, *Kindai Nissen kankei no kenkyū*, I, 814–817. In return for a reduction of the indemnity by 100,000 yen, Hanabusa demanded that the right to build telegraphic lines, to open mines, and to have access to the markets of Taegu and Hamhŭng be stipulated in the treaty.

14. When Pak Yŏng-hyo and his suite boarded the ship to Japan, the new Korean national flag, the *t'aegŭkki*, was raised for the first time. Pak Yŏng-hyo, *Sahwa kiryak*, pp. 197, 199. For a brief account about the origin of the Korean national flag, see Kwŏn Sŏk-pong, "Kukki chejŏng ŭi yurae e taehan kwan'gyŏn," *The Yŏksa Hakpo* 23:41–54 (April 1964).

15. *IS-KJ*, 19.7.25 (260:43a-b); *Kojong sillok*, 19.8.4, 19.8.5, 19.8.8; *CKHCJ*, 3:47a-b;4:17b–20b; *CSS*, pt. 6, vol. 4, pp. 646–647; Pak Yŏng-hyo, *Sahwa kiryak*, p. 195.

16. Tabohashi Kiyoshi, *Kindai Nissen kankei no kenkyū*, I, 861. It seems that the text of Chang Chien's treatise is not preserved in its entirety.

17. *CKHCJ*, 4:12–13; Chang P'ei-lun, *Chien-yü ch'üan-chi, tsou-i*, 2:63–66b. In an earlier memorial Chang was even more preoccupied with his notion that China should make a major effort to build up a strong navy. See Chang P'ei-lun, *Chien-yü ch'üan-chi, tsou-i*, 2:59–61; *CWCSL*, 29:22–24b. Two days later, on October 29, 1882, Chang P'ei-lun submitted another memorial in which he castigated Ma Chien-chung's inability to modify the terms of the *Treaty of Chemulp'o* and even accused him of being the intiator of the whole matter. On October 30, Li Hung-chang was ordered by edict to investigate these accusations. Chang P'ei-lun, *Chien-yü ch'üan-chi, tsou-i*, 2:67–68b; *CKHCJ*, 4:29b–30, 30b.

18. *CKHCJ*, 4:13, 31b–34b.

19. Li Hung-chang, *Memorials*, 45:6a-b; Chang P'ei-lun, *Chien-yü ch'üan-chi, tsou-i*, 3:42–43b; *CJHSL*, No. 589, p. 976; No. 614, pp. 1016–1017; No. 738, pp. 1168–1169; *CKHCJ*, 5:2b–3b, 5, 12b–14; *IS-KJ*, 20.2.6 (268:8b), 20.2.7 (268:10), 20.2.10 (268:16); *Kojong sillok*, 20.2.10, 20.3.20, 21.1.26, 21.2.1, 21.4.30; *CSS*, pt. 6, vol. 4, p. 716; Tabohashi Kiyoshi, *Kindai Nissen kankei no kenkyū*, I, 871–875.

20. Originally, Huang Tsun-hsien advocated in his *Chao-hsien ts'e-lüeh* the expansion of Chinese-Korean trade to the ports of Pusan, Inch'ŏn, and Wŏnsan. Kim Hong-jip, *Susinsa ilgi*, p. 167. The problem of stimulating Sino-Korean trade was afterward raised by Yi Yong-suk in February 1881. See note 23 of Chapter 7. *CKHCJ*, 3:16b–17b; *CWCSL*, 29:27–28b; Kim Yun-sik, *Ŭmch'ŏngsa*, p. 131; Ŏ Yun-jung, *Chongjŏng yŏnp'yo*, pp. 130–133. The whole issue of trade was discussed in detail between Chou Fu and Ŏ Yun-jung. *CJHSL*, No. 417, pp. 589–595 (transcript of Chou Fu's discussion with Ŏ Yun-jung on May 19, 1882), pp. 596–597 (letter of the Korean king), pp. 597–602 (Chou Fu's

discussion with Ŏ Yun-jung on June 3, 1882); No. 594, pp. 979–986. The main points raised during these discussions concerned the abolition of the trade towns along Korea's northern border, the dispatch of a Korean resident envoy to Peking in order to lessen the financial burden Korea accrued from sending special missions to China, the question of lifting the ban on communication by sea, and trade. For an analysis of these discussions, see Kim Chong-wŏn, "Cho-Chung sangmin suryungmuyŏk changjŏng e taehayŏ," *The Yŏksa Hakpo* 32:135–145 (December 1966). The request for a permanent Korean envoy at Peking was immediately rejected by an imperial edict. *CKHCJ*, 3:18b.

21. Ŏ Yun-jung, *Chongjŏng yŏnp'yo*, pp. 140–142; for the text of the *Regulations*, see *CKHCJ*, 5:9b–11b and *CJHSL*, No. 596, pp. 987–993 and for an English translation, *Treaties*, pp. 64–70.

22. Li Hung-chang, *Communications to the Tsungli Yamen*, 13:39–41b; *CKHCJ*, 4:20b–22; *Treaties*, p. 64. Cho Yŏng-ha brought with him a six-point program which contained the Korean ideas about a commercial agreement with China. *CJHSL*, No. 554, pp. 910–912.

23. From the beginning, Ŏ Yun-jung pleaded for separating trade from the traditional tribute relations and putting trade on a basis of equality. He especially objected to article 2. *CJHSL*, No. 417, pp. 589–595; No. 594, pp. 979–986. Also see Kim Chong-wŏn, "Cho-Chung sangmin suryungmuyŏk changjŏng e taehayŏ," pp. 150–156. Despite the conclusion of the *Regulations*, trade at Korea's northern border remained a problem. The Korean king apparently was greatly concerned about the opening of Ŭiju and Hoeryŏng to Sino-Korean trade. On November 22, 1882, he appointed Ŏ Yun-jung as intendant of Western and Northern border affairs (*sŏbuk kyŏngnyaksa*) to settle the details of the border traffic according to article 5 of the *Regulations* as soon as possible. In February 1883, Li Hung-chang sent Ch'en Pen-chih, the Eastern border taotai, to Fengt'ien to meet Ŏ and to discuss all problems. The result of this meeting was the establishment of the *Twenty-four Rules for the Traffic on the Frontier between Fengt'ien and Korea* sometime in late March or early April 1883. Ŏ also traveled widely in the Tumen region and, in the summer of the same year, concluded the *Sixteen Rules for the Trade between Kirin and Korea* with Chinese officials. *IS-KJ*, 19.10.7 (265:17b–18), 19.10.12 (265:35), 20.12.1 (279:1a-b); *Kojong sillok*, 20.12.3; *CJHSL*, No. 607, pp. 1009–1010; No. 609, pp. 1011–1013; No. 683, pp. 1110–1114; No. 684, pp. 1114–1115; No. 754, pp. 1186–1187; No. 755, pp. 1187–1188; No. 790, pp. 1250–1256 (Rules of Kirin); *CWCSL*, 30:31b–34; 34:12b–18b; 36:23b–24b; 38:4b–11; Ŏ Yun-jung, *Chongjŏng yŏnp'yo*, pp. 143–144, 146, 151–161; *Treaties*, pp. 71–81; Kim Chong-wŏn, "Cho-Chung sangmin suryungmuyŏk changjŏng e taehayŏ," pp. 162–165; Song Pyŏng-gi, "Killin-Chosŏn sangmin susimuyŏk changjŏng yŏkchu," *Sahak yŏn'gu* 21:193–207 (Sept. 1969).

24. *CKHCJ*, 4:22–23b; 5:9a-b, 11b–12b; *CWCSL*, 34:10–11; Li Hung-chang, *Memorials*, 46:59; *Treaties*, pp. 64–65; Kim Yun-sik, *Ŭmch'ŏngsa*, pp. 219–220; *CJHSL*, No. 741, pp. 1172–1175 (rules for handling commercial affairs in Korea); No. 748, pp. 1181–1182; No. 749, p. 1183. Ch'en Shu-t'ang was to be accompanied by two attendants, two secretaries, six messengers, one translator of English, and a Korean interpreter. In his correspondence with the Korean government, he was to use the protocol form of communication (*chao-hui*).

25. *TGIG*, 20.8.29, 20.9.19; *Hwasin*, KH9.8.5, KH9.9.19; *CJHSL*, No. 799, p. 1314; No. 800, pp. 1314–1316; *Diplomatic Despatches, Korea*, Foote's 38, October 30, 1883,

and Foote's 39, November 8, 1883 (inclosure 1); FO405/34, Parkes' 78, April 16, 1884 (inclosure); *Ku Han'guk oegyo munsŏ, Ilan,* Nos. 191–192, p. 103.

26. *CKHCJ,* 4:23b; FO17/952, Parkes' 36, November 27, 1884; *CJHSL,* No. 878, pp. 1471–1472; No. 883, p. 1477; No. 895, p. 1493; No. 896, p. 1494. Harry Parkes was transferred from Tokyo to Peking at the end of August 1883.

27. Tabohashi Kiyoshi, *Kindai Nissen kankei no kenkyū,* I, 905–907.

28. *Korea III,* Zedtwitz to Bismarck, October 25, 1882; von Brandt to Bismarck, January 7, 1883; Hilary Conroy, *The Japanese Seizure of Korea, 1868–1910,* pp. 116–119.

29. *NGB,* vol. 15, No. 162, pp. 294–195; No. 164, pp. 296–297; No. 165, pp. 297–298; *Ku Han'guk oegyo munsŏ, Ilan,* No. 98, pp. 70–71 (agreement concerning the payment of indemnity, October 27, 1882); No. 99, pp. 71–72 (exchange of ratifications, October 31, 1882). The *Treaty of Chemulp'o* did not need ratification. Pak Yŏng-hyo, *Sahwa kiryak,* pp. 202–203, 205–206, 215–220, 222–229, 234–235, 256; Tabohashi Kiyoshi, *Kindai Nissen kankei no kenkyū,* I, 907–908, 912. Tabohashi and Cook say that the 50,000 yen Pak gave Inoue were the first installment on the indemnity. This is in contrast to Pak's diary. Harold F. Cook, *Korea's 1884 Incident,* p. 65. The repayment of the loan was scheduled to start in 1885 in ten annual installments. The Japanese received the customs revenues of Pusan and the output of the gold mine of Tanch'ŏn as security. Yi Sŏn-gŭn, *Han'guksa, ch'oegŭnse-p'yŏn,* p. 550.

30. The Koreans, who had on several occasions turned to Li Hung-chang for advice on how to establish a tariff (they were warned not to take the Chinese treaties as a model), tried in vain from 1880 to enlist Japanese cooperation. *IS-KJ,* 19.4.19 (257:29); *CWCSL,* 26:15; Li Hung-chang, *Memorials,* 42:37–39; *CJHSL,* No. 341, p. 432 (discussion between Li Hung-chang and Pyŏn Wŏn-gyu); No. 355, pp. 485–486 (Yi Yong-suk and Li Hung-chang); No. 387, p. 545; *NGB,* vol. 16, No. 109, pp. 281–282.

31. *IS-KJ,* 20.6.11 (272:32); 20.6.23 (272:55a-b); *NGB,* vol. 16, No. 110, pp. 282–289; Pak Yŏng-hyo, *Sahwa kiryak,* pp. 200–201; FO46/288, Parkes' 140 (conf.), October 2, 1882; FO46/297, Parkes' 3 (conf.), January 2, 1883; Parkes' 26 (conf.), February 17, 1883; FO46/299, Parkes' 76(conf.), May 14, 1883; *Diplomatic Despatches, Korea,* Foote's 31, October 18, 1883. For the complete text of the agreement, see *NGB,* vol. 16, No. 110, pp. 283–289; *Kojong sillok* 20.6.22, and *Treaties,* pp. 82–119. The *Regulations* were ratified on September 27, 1883.These regulations in 42 articles laid down the procedure and restrictions governing the conduct of Japanese-Korean trade from that time. The last article contained a most-favored-nation clause. The tariffs were fixed at between 5 and 50 percent and became the model the Korean government wanted to adopt for later treaties. The regulations and the tariff became effective on November 3, 1883. On the same day, July 25, 1883, Min Yŏng-mok and Takezoe Shinichirō signed an *Agreement with Japan Regarding the Treaty Port Limits* and *Regulations for the Treatment of Japanese Fishermen Committing Offences on the Korean Coast, Treaties,* pp. 120–125.

Chapter 9

1. *IS-KJ,* 19.7.18 (260:29a-b).
2. *IS-KJ,* 19.7.20 (260:33–34); Yi Sŏn-gŭn, *Han'guksa, ch'oegŭnse-p'yŏn,* pp. 526–

527. Most of the mistakes were of an economic nature. On September 7, the news that Queen Min was still alive reached the capital. Under military guard, she was escorted back to the palace in solemn procession by civil and military officials. *IS-KJ*, 19.7.25 (260:42); *CKHCJ*, 4:15b-16; Yi Sŏn-gŭn, pp. 527–530.

3. *IS-KJ*, 19.7.2 (260:3b-6), 19.7.25 (260:44–45); 19.9.5 (263:16b–37), 19.9.6 (263:39b–42), 19.9.10 (263:55b–56), 19.9.14 (263:64–65, 66b–68), 19.11.19 (266: 44b).

4. For a background study of Korea's absorption of Western technology, see Kim Yŏng-ho, "Hanmal sŏyang kisul ŭi suyong," *Asea yŏn'gu* 31:295–312 (Sept. 1968). Yi Kwang-rin examines the foreign literature which influenced the formation of "enlightened thought" in *Han'guk kaehwasa yŏn'gu*, pp. 26–34.

5. For a discussion of this concept, see Kim Yŏng-ho, "Hanmal sŏyang kisul ŭi suyong," pp. 301–302.

6. For a brief discussion of the enlightenment movement of which Pak Yŏng-hyo and Kim Ok-kyun were the principal exponents, see Chapter 11.

7. *IS-KJ*, 19.9.5 (263:31b), 19.9.18 (264:4b–5), 19.9.20 (264:11–12), 19.9.22 (264:19a–b), 19.10.7 (265:15b–16b), 19.12.22 (267:60–61b); *Kojong sillok*, 19.8.23; Han U-gŭn, "Kaehang tangsi ŭi wigiŭisik kwa kaehwa sasang," *Han'guksa yŏn'gu* 2:130–134 (December 1968). For a topic-by-topic analysis of these memorials, see Yi Kwang-rin, *Han'guk kaehwasa yŏn'gu*, pp. 38–42.

8. *PBTN*, 263:615a-b; *IS-KJ*, 19.7.25 (260:45a-b); Ŏ Yun-jung, *Chongjŏng yŏnp'yo*, p. 139. Cho Yŏng-ha and Kim Hong-jip had been appointed the king's personal emissaries and had left Korea together with Ma Chien-chung and Admiral Ting Ju-ch'ang by the time they were appointed to the Kimuch'ŏ. Sin Ki-sŏn (1851–1909) had been appointed to the T'ongnigimu Amun with Ŏ Yun-jung, Pak Yŏng-hyo, and others on March 20, 1882. Sin was a close friend and later collaborator of Kim Ok-kyun. *IS-KJ*, 19.2.2 (255: 2b). Kim Pyŏng-si (1832–1898) was an Andong Kim who had entered high office under the Taewŏn'gun and continued to serve in various capacities under King Kojong. *Han'guk inmyŏng taesajŏn*, p. 104. Another new office, which was established on November 30, 1882, was called Kamsaengch'ŏng or Office for the Reduction of Government Expenditures. As indicated by its name, its purpose was to streamline and reduce government expenditures by abolishing certain privileges and offices, and by eliminating surplus officials. It was under Ŏ Yun-jung's direction that a large-scale program for action was designed for this office. However, opposition against it came from all government circles, and the office was abolished on June 5, 1883, before becoming fully operational. Ŏ was "demoted" to intendant of Western and Northern border affairs (*sŏbuk kyŏngnyaksa*) and sent to negotiate the various border agreements (see note 23 of chapter 8). *CSS*, pt. 6, vol. 4, pp. 662, 684; Ŏ Yun-jung, *Chongjŏng yŏnp'yo*, pp. 144, 147–151; Yi Sŏn-gŭn, *Han'guksa, ch'oegŭnse-p'yŏn*, pp. 554–556. For a full account about this office, see Yi Hyŏn-jong, "Kojong ttae Kamsaengch'ŏng sŏlch'i e taehayŏ" in *Kim Chae-wŏn paksa hoegap kinyŏm nonch'ong* (Seoul, 1969), pp. 311–330.

9. *IS-KJ*, 19.9.5 (263:25b), 19.11.17 (266:37), 19.11.29 (266:68a-b), 19.12.4 (267: 9), 19.12.5 (267:11b), 20.3.17 (270: 24), 20.4.9 (271:25; Yun Ch'i-ho appointed secretary), 21.3.13 (282:26), 21.10.20 (290:29b), 21.12.7 (292: 15b); *Kojong sillok*, 20.1.12 and 20.1.17; *PBTN*, 263:659b, 665a; *Hansŏng sunbo*, No. 7 (December 29, 1881), No. 31 (August 21, 1884); for the regulations of the new office, see Chŏn, pp. 15–16. For lists of

the Foreign Office personnel, see Chŏn Hae-jong, *Han'guk kŭnse taeoe kwan'gye munhŏn piyo,* pp. 208–214. Kim Yun-sik, *Ŭmch'ŏngsa,* p. 224; Ŏ Yun-jung, *Chongjŏng yŏnp'yo,* pp. 145–146. Cho Pyŏng-p'il (1835–1908) had passed the higher civil service examinations in 1871, but does not seem to have had much of an official career prior to his appointment to the Foreign Office. *Han'guk inmyŏng taesajŏn,* p. 878. The financing of the Foreign Office seems to have been a problem at all times, and various measures were introduced to raise sufficient funds. Early in 1885, for example, the salt producers of Kyŏngsang were charged a new tax of six *chŏn* per *sŏk* of salt. *P'alto sado samhanggu kwanmun,* vol. 2, 22.1.13, 22.2.16, 22.6.22; *T'ongni kyosŏp-t'ongsangsamu Amun sonap yŏmse chŏlmok* (1885).

10. *IS-KJ,* 19.11.18 (266:39); *Kojong sillok,* 19.11.18.

11. The departments of the Home Office were: 1. the Department of Supply (Iyong-sa); 2. the Department of Military Matters (Kunmusa); 3. the Department of Works (Kamgongsa); 4. the Department of Recruitment (Chŏnsŏnsa); 5. the Department of Agriculture and Sericulture (Nongsangsa); 6. the Department of Control (Changnaesa); 7. the Department of Agriculture and Commerce (Nongsangsa). Yi Hong-jik, *Kuksa taesajŏn,* I, 1606. The *Hansŏng sunbo* mentions only six departments, leaving out the Department of Agriculture and Sericulture.

12. *IS-KJ,* 19.11.19 (266:42a–b), 19.11.28 (266:68b), 19.12.4 (267:9), 19.12.5 (267: 10b–11b), 19.12.16 (267:46), 19.12.22 (267:60), 20.3.17 (270:23b), 20.8.14 (275:34b), 20.9.19 (276:29b), 20.9.30 (276:48b), 20.10.3 (277:3b), 21.4.1 (283:1b), 21.10.21 (290: 34); *Kojong sillok,* 20.1.12/13/17/19/22, 20.3.17; *Hansŏng sunbo,* No. 7 (December 29, 1883), No. 31 (August 21, 1884). The Home Office was incorporated into the Council of State on December 8, 1884. It was revived under the name Interior Office (Naemubu) on July 7, 1885. *CSS,* pt. 6, vol. 4, p. 772; Yi Hong-jik, *Kuksa taesajŏn,* I, 344. For a detailed description of this office, see *Tongnaebu kyerok,* vol. 9 (KH11.8.1). Kim Yu-yŏn (1819–1887) had held several high posts in the 1860s and was minister of the Department of Revenue at the time he was appointed to the Home Office. Han Kyu-jik (1846–1884) had been following a military career until he was appointed to serve in the Home Office as a military expert. See *Han'guk inmyŏng taesajŏn,* pp. 149, 987.

13. *IS-KJ,* 19.12.29 (267:79), 21. 5. 22 (284:31a–b); *CSS,* pt. 6, vol. 4, pp. 688, 718 (appointment of chief state councillors). The shift of power away from the Council of State is also documented by the fact that the material presented in the *Ilsŏngnok* gets increasingly scanty after 1884. From 1884, it contains only information on ceremonial matters, appointments to traditional posts, records of royal audiences, and occasional memorials on traditional subjects.

14. The three places were the Kŭmwi Regiment, Kanghwa Island (the prefect of which was Kim Yun-sik), and Ŭiju. *IS-KJ,* 20.2.21 (268:32), 20.4.11 (271:30), 20.6.3 (273:12).

15. It was not before von Moellendorff was put in charge of the Chŏnhwan'guk on March 14, 1884, that new minting machinery was purchased, and foreign experts were employed. See below.

16. *IS-KJ,* 20.2.18 (269:27), 20.2.21 (269:32), 20.2.24 (269:35), 20.7.5 (274:15), 20.7.13 (274:29a–b), 20.7.26 (274:62), 20.9.13 (276:23) 20.12.21 (279:32b); *Kojong sillok,* 20.1.22; *CSS,* pt. 6, vol. 4, p. 669; for the roster of the personnel of the Chŏnhwan-guk, see *Hansŏng sunbo,* No. 7 (December 29, 1883) and No. 31 (August 21, 1884). There were twelve individuals involved in its operations at the end of 1883 and fifteen in August

1884. For a comprehensive study on the Chŏnhwan'guk, see WŏnYu-han," Chŏnhwan-guk ko," *The Yŏksa Hakpo* 37:49–100 (June 1968). The same author has studied the history of the *tangojŏn* in "Tangojŏn ko," *The Yŏksa Hakpo* 35/36:313–339 (December 1967).

17. *IS-KJ*, 20.5.11 (272:23), 20.5.23 (272:47a-b), 20.5.24 (272:50), 20.5.25 (272:51), 21.3.28 (282:62b), 21.10.2 (290:3); *Kojong sillok*, 20.5.11, 21.1.23; *Hansŏng sunbo*, No. 1 (Oct. 31, 1883), No. 7 (December 29, 1883), No. 31 (August 21, 1884); Kim Yun-sik, *Ŭmch'ŏngsa*, pp. 168–171 (Kim's discussion with officials of the Tientsin Arsenal about the establishment of a machine shop), 174, 201–202 (Kim's discussion with Li Hung-chang), 211–213 (final discussions and purchase), 225. The old Kun'gisi or Ordnance Workshop which had been established at the very beginning of the dynasty was incorporated into the Kigiguk on October 15, 1884. *IS-KJ*, 21.8.27 (288:51b).

18. *IS-KJ*, 19.9.24 (264:28); *Kojong sillok*, 19.9.23; *CSS*, pt. 6, vol. 4, p. 658; Kim Yun-sik, *Ŭmch'ŏngsa*, pp. 194–195; Tabohashi Kiyoshi, *Kindai Nissan kankei no kenkyū*, I, 871. Yüan Shih-k'ai was also called upon to inspect the defense installations on Kang-hwa Island and to organize a new force of 500 men. Kim Yun-sik, *Ŭmch'ŏngsa*, pp. 221–223, 224; *CSS*, pt. 6, vol. 4, p. 664.

19. *IS-KJ*, 20.10.23 (277:33). Han Kyu-jik was concurrently commander of the traditional Ŏyŏng Regiment.

20. *IS-KJ*, 21.7.22 (287:43), 21.7.27 (287:55), 21.7.29 (287:59b), 21.8.26 (288:45a-b), 21.8.28 (288:54a-b).

21. The Min also made clever use of the paramilitary organization of peddlers (*po-busang*) who had for centuries been staunch supporters of the dynasty. At the recommendation of the left state councillor, Kim Pyŏng-guk, a special bureau called Hyesang kong-guk, Office for the Benefit of Trade, was established on September 19, 1883, to give the peddlers a new centralized organization (after they had become leaderless with the abolition of the Military Council). Min T'ae-ho presided over the new office, assisted by Han Kyu-jik, Min Yŏng-ik in absentia, Yun T'ae-jun, Min Ŭng-sik, and Yi Cho-yŏn. *IS-KJ*, 20.8.1 (275:4a-b), 20.8.30 (275:65a-b), 20.9.3 (276:8b); *Kojong sillok*, 20.8.19; *Han-sŏng sunbo*, No. 7 (December 29, 1883), No. 31 (August 21, 1884). The personnel roster remained the same. The Hyesang kongguk was transformed into one of the bureaus of the Interior Office (Naemubu) on September 18, 1885. *IS-KJ*, 22. 8. 10 (300:25).

22. *IS-KJ*, 20.5.4 (272:8a-b), 20.11.16 (278:35b), 21.1.6 (280:12), 21.3.6 (282:13b-14); *Kojong sillok*, 20.5.5, 20.7.1.

23. *CSS*, pt. 6, vol. 4, p. 648.

24. *Kojong sillok*, 19.11.7, 19.11.18, 19.12.6, 19.12.20; Chŏng Kyo, *Taehan kyenyŏnsa*, p. 18.

25. Kim Yun-sik, *Ŭmch'ŏngsa*, pp. 138, 141–142, 182; *CKHCJ*, 3:15.

26. *IS-KJ*, 19.12.25 (267:65); *Kojong sillok*, 20.4.4, 20.4.17; *CKHCJ*, 4: 34b-35b, 37; 5:4a-b; *CJHSL*, No. 623, pp. 1029–1030; No. 737, pp. 1166–1167; No. 829, p. 1342; Li Hung-chang, *Memorials*, 45:14b, 15; Kim Yun-sik, *Ŭmch'ŏngsa*, pp. 195, 197, 202, 206; *CSS*, pt. 6, vol. 4, pp. 656, 661, 662–663. Cho Yŏng-ha was sent to Tientsin the second time primarily to purchase modern arms. At the same time, Kim Yun-sik was sent to Tientsin to recall the remaining Korean trainees. For a study on the background of von Moellendorff's appointment, see Ko Pyŏng-ik, "Mok In-dŏk ŭi kobing kwa kŭ paegyŏng," *Chindan hakpo* 25–27 (combined issue):225–244 (December 1964). Von Moellen-dorff reportedly felt that the dispatch of Ma Chien-ch'ang to Korea served no other

purpose than to observe his movements and to report them to Li Hung-chang. FO46/ 300, Parkes' 91 (conf.), May 31, 1883.

27. Kim Yun-sik, *Ŭmch'ŏngsa*, p. 208. The only document that records von Moellendorff's career in China and his later activities in Korea is the short biography which was written by his wife, Rosalie von Moellendorff, *P. G. von Moellendorff, Ein Lebensbild* in Leipzig in 1930. This book is based on memories (Rosalie von Moellendorff accompanied her husband to China and, for a short period, to Korea), excerpts from letters, and von Moellendorff's personal diary. It seems to reflect very much the author's personal taste and unlimited admiration for her husband's accomplishments. It is a one-sided work, intended for her own family and therefore of questionable historical significance. Unfortunately, the original copy of the diary as well as the complete correspondence between the Korean king and von Moellendorff and "documents and diplomas" which were all in the widow's possession were dispersed during World War II and have not been recovered since. There is the possibility that they still exist somewhere in Eastern Germany.

28. *CJHSL*, No. 627, pp. 1045–1046; Kim Yun-sik, *Ŭmch'ŏngsa*, pp. 200, 202, 206–208; Chŏng Kyo, *Taehan kyenyŏnsa*, p. 17; Moellendorff, *Lebensbild*, p. 39; FO17/900, Grosvenor's 140 (very conf.), November 25, 1882; Wright, *Hart and the Chinese Customs*, p. 501.

29. Moellendorff, *Lebensbild*, pp. 33–34, 38, 39, 100–108; Kim Yun-sik, *Ŭmch'ŏngsa*, pp. 209–210; FO17/900, Grosvenor's 140 (very conf.), November 25, 1882; *Korea III*, Pelldram to Bismarck, Tientsin, November 30, 1882.

30. Kim Yun-sik, *Umch'ŏngsa*, pp. 218–220, 220–221; *CSS*, pt. 6, vol. 4, pp. 662–663; *CKHCJ*, 5: 4a-b; Moellendorff, *Lebensbild*, pp. 40–44.

31. *Kojong sillok*, 19.11.5.

32. *IS-KJ*, 19.11.16 (266:34b-35), 19.11.17 (266:37), 19.12.6 (267:16); Hwang Hyŏn, *Maech'ŏnyarok*, p. 66; Moellendorff, *Lebensbild*, pp. 44–49, 54–56; *North China Herald*, July 13, 1883.

33. Von Moellendorff's presence in the Foreign Office can be easily traced through the *Diary of the Foreign Office* (*T'ongni kyosŏp-t'ongsangsamu amun ilgi*). Moellendorff, *Lebensbild*, pp. 44, 49, 56–57, 59, 74; Chŏng Kyo, *Taehan kyenyŏnsa,* p. 18; Letters from Korea (Jardine Matheson Archives): Correspondence from Chemulp'o, 1884; *Diplomatic Despatches, Korea*, Foote's 34, October 23, 1883. According to von Moellendorff, Cho Yŏngha had to resign from the Foreign Office because of differences with Takezoe Shinichirō.

34. *IS-KJ*, 21.3.29 (282:64b), 21.5.20 (284:29), 21.10.28 (290:54), 21.12.22 (292: 42b); Moellendorff, *Lebensbild*, p. 67.

35. *IS-KJ*, 21.2.17 (281:27b); Wŏn Yu-han, "Chŏnhwan'guk ko," *The Yŏksa Hakpo* 37:56, 58, 74–76 (June 1968). The two minting experts were F. Kraus and C. Riedt; the technician was C. Diedricht. They arrived in Korea in early November 1885. Upon their arrival they faced certain difficulties because von Moellendorff was already dismissed from the Mint. See *Tŏgan*, vol. 3, for documents pertaining to their arrival.

36. Moellendorff, *Lebensbild*, p. 57.

37. See footnote 17.

38. Kim Yŏng-ho, "Hanmal sŏyang kisul ŭi suyong," *Asea yŏn'gu* 31:325 (September 1968).

39. Yi Kwang-rin, *Han'guk kaehwasa yŏn'gu*, pp. 94–95, 126–127; Moellendorff, *Lebensbild*, p. 58.

40. *Tōgan,* vol. 3, October 21, 1885; November 3, 1885; November 10, 1885. Because he was unable to buy land for his experiments, Helm returned to Japan in the early fall of 1885.

41. *North China Herald,* May 8, 1885.

42. *Kojong sillok,* 21.5*.22; *TGIG,* 21.5.16, 21.7.4, 21.7.8; *North China Herald,* June 13, 1884; Moellendorff, *Lebensbild,* pp. 60, 67–69. Undoubtedly on von Moellendorff's initiative, King Kojong had already, in October 1883, solicited the help of the American representative, Lucius Foote, for treaty negotiations with Russia (and France). Immediately after the conclusion of the treaty, Min Yŏng-ik conveyed to Foote the royal gratitude for assistance the king believed Foote had rendered. *Diplomatic Despatches, Korea,* Foote's 32, October 19, 1883; Foote's 92, July 7, 1884.

43. *IS-KJ,* 21.10.20 (290:30), 21.10.27 (290:52b), 22.6.16 (298:27), 22.7.26 (299: 49b), 22.9.10 (301:19); *TGIG,* 22.6.16, 22.7.26; *Tōgan,* vol. 3, October 23, 1885; *Diplomatic Despatches, Korea,* Foulk's 192 (conf.), July 5, 1885; Foulk's 211, August 4, 1885; Foulk's 214, August 16, 1885; Wright, *Hart and the Chinese Customs,* p. 501; Moellendorff, *Lebensbild,* pp. 70f. Also see the short appraisal of von Moellendorff's activities in Korea, in H. B. Morse, *The International Relations of the Chinese Empire,* III, 10–11. This is based on a memorandum written on Feburary 16, 1910, for the author by H. F. Merrill. There is a short description of von Moellendorff by Paul King who met him in 1887–1888 at Tientsin. See Paul King, *In the Chinese Customs Service,* pp. 88–89. For detailed discussions on von Moellendorff's dealings with the Russians, see Yi Sŏn-gŭn, *Han'guksa, ch'oegŭnse-p'yŏn,* pp. 791–800 and Tabohashi Kiyoshi, *Kindai Nissen kankei no kenkyū,* II, 1–18. After his dismissal from Korea, von Moellendorff returned to China and again entered Hart's customs service. His post as adviser to the Korean government was given to the American O.N. Denny. In 1897, von Moellendorff finally was appointed commissioner at Ningpo. Shortly before he was to return to Germany for a leave, he died mysteriously on April 20, 1901. Von Moellendorff was a gifted scholar. He knew a great many Chinese dialects and wrote several works on Far Eastern linguistics, among them a Manchu grammar, a Chinese Radical Dictionary, a Chinese-German-German-Chinese Dictionary, a Korean dictionary, an Encyclopedia of Chinese philology; he also translated a few Chinese literary works into German.

44. *FRUS,* 1883, No. 85, Young to Frelinghuysen, December 26, 1882 (inclosure 2, "Memorandum: Commercial regulations between China and Corea"); FO17/894, Granville to Wade, November 20, 1882; FO17/915, Memorandum respecting Corea, January 5, 1883; FO46/285, Parkes, 73, June 21, 1882; FO46/297, Parkes' 27, February 17, 1883; *Diplomatic Despatches, Korea.* Foote's 11 (conf.) June 30, 1883; Tyler Dennett, "Early American Policy in Korea, 1883–1887," *Political Science Quarterly* 38. 1: 84–85, 102–103 (March 1923); Robert T. Pollard, "American Relations with Korea, 1882–1895," *Chinese Social and Political Science Review* 16. 3: 430–431 (October 1932).

45. *CWCSL,* 33:10b–11b; FO46/299, Parkes' 69, April 28, 1883. The British repeatedly expressed their displeasure at Shufeldt's treaty and spread word to the Japanese and the Koreans that the United States would not ratify it. Harold F. Cook, *Korea's 1884 Incident,* pp. 69, 76.

46. *IS-KJ,* 20.4.13 (271:33b); Kim Yun-sik, *Ŭmch'ŏngsa,* p. 225; Chŏng Kyo, *Taehan kyenyŏnsa,* pp. 18–19; *FRUS,* 1883, No. 6, Foote to Frelinghuysen, May 24, 1883; No. 7, same to same, May 25, 1883; No. 10, same to same, June 29, 1883; *North China Herald,*

July 13, 1883; Moellendorff, *Lebensbild,* pp. 60–61; *Treaties,* p. 49. The US Senate approved the treaty on January 9, 1883.

47. *FRUS,* 1883, No. 85, Young to Frelinghuysen, December 26, 1882; *Diplomatic Instructions, Korea,* No. 1, Frelinghuysen to Foote, March 9, 1883; No. 3, Frelinghuysen to Foote, March 17, 1883; FO46/299, Parkes' 75 (conf.), May 14, 1883. Also see the introduction to McCune and Harrison, *Korean-American Relations,* I, 1–11.

48. *FRUS,* 1883, No. 34, Foote to Frelinghuysen, October 23, 1883. For documents pertaining to the appointment of an adviser on foreign affairs and of army instructors, see Section 2 "Securing American Advisers for the Korean Government" in McCune and Harrison, *Korean-American Relations,* I, 53–65 and "Introduction," pp. 1–19. The resolution to send military instructors to Korea passed the Senate on February 24, 1886, and they arrived in Seoul only in April 1888. For a detailed account on the American army instructors, see Yi Kwang-rin, *Han'guk kaehwasa yŏn'gu,* pp. 146–189.

49. Tyler Dennett, "Early American Policy in Korea, 1883–1887," *Political Science Review* 28. 1:86–99 (March 1923); Robert T. Pollard, "American Relations with Korea, 1882–1895," *Chinese Social and Political Science Review* 16.3:431–444 (October 1932); Payson Treat, "China and Korea, 1885–1894," *Political Science Quarterly* 49:506–543 (December 1934). Foulk's successor was William Parker, who proved to be unfit for this post. Foulk was ordered to go back to Seoul where he was in charge until W.W. Rockhill took office on December 9, 1886. Foulk stayed on as naval attaché. Rockhill was succeeded by Hugh O. Dinsmore as minister resident and consul general on April 1, 1887.

50. FO46/285, Parkes' 73, June 21, 1882; FO46/286, Parkes, private, July 13, 1882; FO17/898, Grosvenor's 98, September 30, 1882; FO17/900, Grosvenor's 148, December 5, 1882; FO17/913, Shanghai Chamber of Commerce to Granville, August 10, 1882; FO17/914, Hongkong Chamber of Commerce to Granville, July 28, 1882. The chambers of commerce in China and Japan were invited by Granville to comment on Willes' treaty. For their replies, see *North China Herald,* March 21, 1883; August 3, 1883; August 10, 1883; August 17, 1883. How much of Parkes' indignation at Willes' treaty was directed against Wade, who after all had been instrumental in preparing it, is difficult to determine. Li Hung-chang, for example, thought it considerable. Li, *Communications to the Tsungli Yamen,* 15:13b.

51. FO46/288, Parkes' 145 (conf.), October 16, 1882; Parkes' 153 (conf.) and 154 (conf.) October 24, 1882; FO46/290, Parkes' 172 (conf.), December 21, 1882; Parkes' 175, December 24, 1882; Parkes' 176 (conf.), December 29, 1882; Pak Yŏng-hyo, *Sahwa kiryak,* pp. 198, 213, 242–243.

52. *Oeamun ch'ogi, kii,* 20.2.18, 20.2.22; FO46/298, Parkes' 35, March 9, 1883 (with enclosures); FO46/299, Parkes' 64 (conf.), April 28, 1883 (inclosure 2: Aston's memorandum on his discussions at Seoul). Aston suggested that a preliminary treaty consisting of the first and last articles of the Willes' treaty should be concluded so that Korea would be opened to British subjects at the same time that it would be opened to those of other treaty powers. The issue was undecided when Aston left Seoul. Kim Ok-kyun had first suggested such a procedure to Parkes. See FO46/299, Parkes' 60 (conf.), April 21, 1883.

53. *IS-KJ,* 20.4.10 (271:27); *Oeamun ch'ogi, kii,* 20.4.8; FO46/296, Granville's 42, April 22, 1883; FO46/299, Parkes' 67 (conf.), April 28, 1883 (inclosure 2: Parkes to Min Yŏng-mok); Parkes' 78, May 14, 1883; Parkes' 81, May 21, 1883.

54. *TGIG,* 20.9.23, 20.9.27, 20.9.29, 20.10.4, 20.10.7, 20.10.19, 20.10.22, 20.10.27,

20.10.28, 20.10.29, 20.10.30, 20.11.1; *IS-KJ*, 20.10.27 (277:42); *CSS*, pt. 6, vol. 4, pp. 700–701; Li, *Communications to the Tsungli Yamen*, 15:19–20; FO17/920, Granville's 36, October 3, 1883; FO17/925, Parkes' 28, October 18, 1883; FO17/926, Parkes' 36, November 1, 1883; Parkes' 37 (conf.), November 3, 1883; Parkes' 38, November 7, 1883; Parkes' 39, December 1, 1883; Parkes' 42, December 6, 1883 (detailed report on the negotiations); for the draft Parkes drew up, see FO46/301, Parkes' 108 (conf.), June 22, 1883 (inclosure); *CKHCJ*, 5:17, 20–21. E. Zappe was German consul general at Yokohama.

55. The Protocol stipulated:1. that the extraterritorial jurisdiction would be relinquished as soon as Korea's laws and legal procedure would be modified and reformed; 2. that if the Chinese government gave up its claim of opening commercial establishments at Hanyang (Seoul), the British government would do likewise; 3. that all treaty provisions also applied to the British colonies.

56. For the whole treaty text, see *Treaties*, pp. 132–152.

57. In the summer of 1884, Foote addressed a note to the Foreign Office claiming all privileges of the British-Korean treaty under the most-favored-nation clause. *IS-KJ*, 21.4. 4 (283:8b), 21.4.7 (283:13); *TGIG*, 21.2.17, 21.4.4, 21.4.5; Li Hung-chang, *Communications to the Tsungli Yamun*, 15:13–17b (Li's conversation with Parkes); FO17/926, Parkes' 43, December 7, 1883 (inlcosure 1: Memorandum of Interview with the Grand Secretary Li); FO17/949, Parkes' 66 (conf.), March 31, 1884; FO405/34, Parkes' 78, April 16, 1884 (inclosure 1: Hillier to Parkes, April 14, 1884); FO17/950, Parkes' 1 (Corean series), April 28, 1884; Parkes' 6, May 2, 1884; FO17/951, Parkes' 19 (conf.), June 20, 1884; Parkes' 29, July 3, 1884; *North China Herald*, May 9, 1884.

58. *IS-KJ*, 21.10.1 (290:1a-b); *TGIG*, 21.8.27, 21.8.29, 21.10.1; *Tŏgwŏnan*, vol. 2, August 10, 1884.

59. FO17/927, Parkes' 54 (conf.), December 16, 1883; FO17/950, Parkes' 2, April 28, 1884; Parkes' 12 and 13, May 31, 1884; FO17/951, Parkes' 20, June 20, 1884. At the end of 1884, the Korean Foreign Office reportedly tried to claim that Aston's position was not sufficient to deal with international issues. This was apparently done at von Moellendorff's instigation. See FO17/953, Parkes' 37, December 12, 1884. Hermann Budler had been interpreter at the German consulate at Amoy and had assisted Consul General Zappe during the negotiations of the German-Korean treaty. *Tŏgan*, vol. 2, April 13, 1884; November 10, 1884. Nothing is known about Zembsch's background. He was a captain in the German navy.

60. For the texts of the various treaties, see *Treaties, Regulations etc. Between Corea and Other Powers, 1876-1889; Kojong sillok*, 21.5*.4; *TGIG*, 21.5.18, 21.5.19, 21.5*.1, 21.5*.5, 21.5*.6, 21.5*.9, 21.5*.15, 23.5.3; *CSS*, pt. 6, vol. 4, pp. 721, 811; *FRUS*, 1885, No. 238, Foulk to Bayard, October 14, 1885; same to same, October 21, 1885. The French legation was housed in von Moellendorff's former mansion. *North China Herald*, June 18, 1886. The Russian chargé d'affaires, Karl Waeber, took up residence at Seoul in October 1885. *TGIG*, 22.9.7, 22.9.8. Russia had long been interested in getting Korea to regulate the Russian-Korean border trade by treaty. In the 1884 treaty no stipulations for the overland trade were made, and it was not until 1888 that *Regulations For the Frontier Trade* were concluded between Korea and Russia.

Chapter 10

1. *IS-KJ*, 14.8.4 (196:10); *CJHSL*, No. 355, pp. 485–486.

2. *CKHCJ*, 4:34b-35; *CJHSL*, No. 554, p. 912; "Conversations on the US-Korean Treaty in 1882 between the Korean Delegates and the Chinese Envoys," *The Yŏksa Hakpo* 22:131 (January 1964). For a background study on von Moellendorff, see Chapter 9.

3. *IS-KJ*, 19.12.14 (267:41); *CJHSL*, No. 554, p. 910; No. 584, pp. 967–970 (text of the contract); *CKHCJ*, 4:33b; Moellendorff, *Lebensbild*, pp. 50–55; FO46/299, Parkes' 59, April 21, 1883; Ma Chien-chung, *Tung-hsing san-lu*, 1:22–23; 2:48–50; *Korea III*, Pelldram to Bismarck, Tientsin, November 30, 1882; von Brandt to Bismarck, Shanghai, April 12, 1883; Albert Feuerwerker, *China's Early Industrialization*, pp. 158–159. There seems to be no indication that any repayment of the loan took place. It was carried as an asset on the books of the China Merchants' Steam Navigation Company until the Sino-Japanese war, with only a small reduction recorded during 1891. Chang P'ei-lun, in his *Chao-hsien shan-hou liu-shih* of October 27, 1882, vehemently opposed the idea of granting Korea a Chinese government loan, for he feared that Korea would use it for the repayment of the indemnity to Japan, a course which he thought would have a bad effect on China. Li Hung-chang refuted Chang's argumentation and insisted that this loan had no connection with the indemnity and would be paid from non-governmental sources. Tabohashi Kiyoshi, *Kindai Nissen kankei no kenkyū*, I, 863, 866.

4. *Ch'onggwan kongmun*, KH11.11.17; *TGIG*, 22.7.25, 22.8.22, 22.11.17; *Yŏngwŏnan*, August 17, 1885. The customhouse at Inch'ŏn was immediately rebuilt in Western style and was partly functioning again by the end of the year. Pertinent data on the customs administration at Pusan for the last three lunar months of 1883 and for 1885 are contained in vols. 1 and 3 of *Pusanhang ch'urip susei silsu sŏngch'aek*, which was compiled by the treaty port superintendent of Pusan.

5. *TGIG*, 20.8.4, 20.9.16, 20.9.17, 20.9.18, 20.10.10, 20.10.18; 21.5.4; *Tongnaebu kyerok*, KH9.9.7, KH9.10.5; Chŏng Kyo, *Taehan kyenyŏnsa*, p. 25; Moellendorff, *Lebensbild*, p. 54; FO17/900, Grosvenor's 140 (most conf.), November 25, 1882; FO17/923, Grosvenor's 91, June 18, 1883; Jardine Matheseon Correspondence, Jenchuan 21, April 28, 1884; H. F. Merill, *Letterbooks*, to Sir Robert Hart, September 2, 1885; *North China Herald*, February 27, 1884; March 26, 1884. In the summer of 1884, for example, there were eight Westerners, one Chinese, and one Japanese employed in the customs service at Pusan. *CJHSL*, No. 880, p. 1474.

6. *TGIG*, 21.5.4, 21.5*.23, 21.5*.25, 21.5*.27; *Hwasin*, KH10.3.26, KH10.5*.23.

7. *TGIG*, 21.6.25, 21.6.26, 21.6.27, 21.7.6, 21.10.4; *Ku Han'guk oegyo munsŏ, Ilan*, No. 252, p. 128; Nos. 288–292, pp. 144–147; No. 327, p. 161. There was a controversy about this issue because the Korean government demanded that those items which were taxed more lightly in the trade regulations with Japan be adjusted to the British regulations, an undertaking which was vehemently opposed by the Japanese.

8. *TGIG*, 20.10.10, 20.10.20.

9. For the circumstances leading to von Moellendorff's dismissal, see Chapter 11.

10. *IS-KJ*, 22. 9. 7 (301:14); *Kojong sillok*, 22.9.23; *TGIG*, 22.9.13, 22.9.14, 22.9.

18; *CJHSL*, No. 1063, pp. 1943–1945 (Merrill's contract); No. 1086, pp. 1962–1963; *Ch'onggwan naesin*, KH11.10.1, KH11.12.15, KH12.1.7, KH12.1.8, KH12.2.6; H.F. Merrill, *Letterbooks*, letters to Sir Robert Hart, October 26, 1885; November 10, 1885; December 15, 1885; February 15, 1886; FO17/900, Grosvenor's 140 (most conf.), November 25, 1882; H. B. Morse, *The International Relations of the Chinese Empire*, III, 13–14 (Morse quotes letters from Sir Robert Hart to Merrill); Takayanagi Matsuichirō, *Shina kanzei seido ron*, pp. 78–80. Merrill's administration is well documented: his correspondence with the Korean Foreign Office is contained in *Ch'onggwan kongmun* and *Ch'onggwan naesin*. Moreover, his letterbooks are preserved in Houghton Library of Harvard University. For a discussion of the latter, see Pak Pong-sik, "Merrill sŏgan," in *Kim Chae-wŏn paksa hoegap kinyŏm nonch'ong*, pp. 353–377. The returns of the Korean customs were appended to the reports of the Chinese Maritime Customs Service. For a general picture of the activities of the Korean customs, see Appendix II in *Decennial Reports on the Trade, Navigation, Industries, etc. of the Ports Open to Foreign Commerce in China and Corea and on the Condition and Development of the Treaty Port Provinces, 1882-1891*, China Imperial Maritime Customs, 1. Statistical Series: No. 6, Shanghai, 1893. The three new commissioners of customs under Merrill were the German J. F. Schoenicke at Inch'ŏn, Piry at Pusan, and F. E. Creagh at Wŏnsan. Merrill was succeeded by Schoenicke in 1889. The last chief commissioner was the Englishman John McLeavy Brown who took office in 1893 and stayed on until 1905.

11. *Jinsenfu-shi*, pp. 16–17, 38, 116–118; FO17/915, Parkes' 76, July 5, 1882 (inclosures 1 and 2: Memorandum of Considerations bearing on the Selection of a Port to be opened on the West Coast of Corea by W. G. Aston); *Korean Repository*, 4: 377–378 (1897); Villetard de Laguérie, *La Corée*, pp. 57–60; Isabella B. Bishop, *Korea and Her Neighbours*, p. 30; *North China Herald*, January 9, 1884.

12. The question of the ground rent at Wŏnsan was settled in the *Agreement with Japan Regarding the Land Rent of the Settlement at Yuensan* concluded between the Japanese consul general, Maeda Kenkichi, and the prefect of Tŏgwŏn, Kim Ki-su, on August 4, 1881. The rent was fixed at fifty yen per annum, as it was in Pusan. The annual rent for the Japanese cemetery, which lay outside the settlement, was one yen. *Treaties*, pp. 39–49.

13. *TGIG*, 20.8.17, 20.8.30; *Ku Han'guk oegyo munsŏ, Ilan*, Nos. 84 and 85, p. 64; No. 90, p. 66; No. 165, p. 95. Kondō Masuki's successor as consul was Kobayashi Hatachi who took up residence in the port in July 1883; No. 303, p. 152; No. 307, p. 154; *NGB*, vol. 16, No. 113, pp. 296–298; *Jinsenfu-shi*, pp. 118–127; Ch'oe Sŏng-yŏn, *Kaehang kwa yanggwan yŏkchŏng*, pp. 31–33; Harold J. Noble, "The Former Foreign Settlements in Korea," *The American Journal of International Law* 23. 4:766–769 (October 1929); *Treaties*, pp. 126–131; G. James Morrison, "Some Notes of a Trip to Corea, in July and August, 1883," *Journal of the North-China Branch of the Royal Asiatic Society* 18:141–142 (1883).

14. *TGIG*, 20.12.19, 20.12.22, 20.12.24, 21.1.12, 21.1.16, 21.2.22, 21.3.7, 21.3.16, 21.3.22, 21.3.29, 21.4.1, 21.4.14; *Hwasin*, KH9.12.18, KH10.2.7, KH10.2.10, KH10.2.21; *CJHSL*, No. 821, p. 1339; No. 884, p. 1478; *Jinsenfu-shi*, pp. 128–134 (for the complete text of the agreement, pp. 131–133); Ch'oe Sŏng-yŏn, *Kaehang kwa yanggwan yŏkchŏng*, p. 33; Jardine Matheson Correspondence, Jenchuan 11, February 12, 1884.

15. FO46/299, Parkes' 66, April 28, 1883; FO17/927, Parkes' 72, December 31, 1883. For the texts of the various treaties, see *Treaties*.

16. *TGIG*, 21.4.14, 21.4.16, 21.5.17, 21.5.24, 21.5*.13, 21.5*.24, 21.5*.27, 21.8.12; *Yŏngan*, 21.4.14, 21.4.16, 21.5*.24; FO17/950, Parkes' 10, May 31, 1884; *Diplomatic*

Despatches, Korea, Foote's 72, May 1, 1884; Foote's 100, July 30, 1884; *Jardine Matheson Correspondence,* Jenchuan 35, June 17, 1884; Ch'oe Sŏng-yŏn, *Kaehang kwa yanggwan yŏkchŏng,* pp. 33–34; Noble, "The Former Foreign Settlements in Korea," p. 770. The reason the agreement on Inch'ŏn's foreign settlement did not bear a date from the outset was that the foreign representatives did not sign it on the same day. The Korean government notified the foreign powers in a note dated June 12, 1885, that the agreement had been signed, sealed, and had gone into operation on October 3, 1884. *TGIG,* 22.4.30. Parkes sent a revised and signed version of the document to the Korean Foreign Office on September 22, 1884. *TGIG,* 21.8.4, 21.8.15. Takezoe Shinichirō returned a signed version on November 7. *Ku Han'guk oegyo munsŏ, Ilan,* No. 322, p. 159; No. 325, p. 160; *TGIG,* 21.9.20. Kim Hong-jip may have actually signed it on October 3. The German consul general, Captain Zembsch, notified the Foreign Office on October 21, 1884, that he intended to sign the document. *TGIG,* 21.9.3. There does not seem to be an indication when Foote and Yüan Shih-k'ai signed the agreement. For the text of the agreement, see *Treaties,* pp. 308–314.

17. *TGIG,* 21.9.23, 21.9.24, 22.3.27; Jardine Matheson Correspondence, Chemulpo, August 5, 1884; *Korean Repository,* 4: 380 (1907); *Jinsenfu-shi,* pp. 134–136 (contains several maps); Noble, "The Former Foreign Settlements in Korea," pp. 770–771; Yi Hyŏn-jong, "Ku Hanmal oegugin kŏryujinae chojikch'e e taehayŏ," *The Yŏksa Hakpo* 34: 5, 40–41, 46–47 (June 1967). Whereas the Japanese organized a kind of municipal council for their own settlement, the Chinese do not seem to have had such a body.

18. With the appointment of a *kamni* at Inch'ŏn, *kamni* were also appointed at Pusan and Wŏnsan where the prefect of Tŏgwŏn held the position concurrently. The Pusan treaty port superintendent started work in December 1883. On February 27, 1885, this office was given as a concurrent appointment to the prefect of Tongnae. In December 1885, police officers were also sent to Pusan and Wŏnsan. In January 1884, the prefect of Ŭiju was made superintendent for the border trade *(kamni). IS-KJ,* 20.8.19 (275:42b–43), 20. 12.22 (279:35), 21.4.21 (283:40), 22.1.13 (293:30), 22.5.29 (297:57); *Kojong sillok,* 20.8.22, 22.10.29; *TGIG,* 20.8.19, 20.9.14, 20.9.19, 20.11.7, 21.4.1, 21.4.22, 21.7.16, 21. 7.17, 22.1.13, 22.1.16, 22.10.28; *Oeamun ch'ogi, kiil,* 20.8.22, 22.10.28; *Jinsenfu-shi,* pp. 146–147, 262–270; Ch'oe Sŏng-yŏn, *Kaehang kwa yanggwan yŏkchŏng,* pp. 57-59. For a detailed study on the development and the various forms of the office of the treaty port superintendent, see Yi Hyŏn-jong, "Kamnisŏ yŏn'gu," *Asea yŏn'gu* 31: 3–75 (September 1968).

19. *TGIG,* 21.1.15, 21.1.16, 21.1.17, 21.1.30, 21.2.7, 21.6.26; *CJHSL,* No. 837, pp. 1355–1356; No. 983, pp. 1796–1803; No. 1127, pp. 2051–2054; *Ku Han'guk oegyo munsŏ, Ilan,* Nos. 205–206, pp. 108–109; Nos. 215–216, p. 112; *Jinsenfu-shi,* pp. 279–281 (list of the Japanese settlers in 1883); *FRUS,* 1886, No. 79, Bayard to Parkes, April 28, 1886; *Diplomatic Despatches, Korea,* Foulk's 274, January 29, 1886; Dinsmore's 143, November 29, 1888; FO405/34, Parkes' 78, April 16, 1884 (inclosure); *North China Herald,* February 13, 1884. The first Municipal Council was not elected until December 5, 1888. For details of the settlement's later development, see Noble, "The Former Foreign Settlements in Korea," p. 773ff. Also, Yi Hyŏn-jong, "Ku Hanmal oegugin kŏryujinae chojikch'e e taehayŏ," *The Yŏksa Hakpo* 34: 45–46 (June 1967).

20. *TGIG,* 21.4.14, 21.4.15, 21.4.18, 21.5.9, 21.5.11, 21.8.13, 21.8.18, 22.12.19; *Hwasin,* KH10.4.14; *Miwŏnan,* August 18, 1884; *Ku Han'guk oegyo munsŏ, Ilan,* No. 308,

p. 154; *CJHSL*, No. 837, p. 1355; No. 826, p. 1338; No. 854, pp. 1396–1397; No. 983, pp. 1780–1792; No. 1127, pp. 2045–2051 (there was a considerable reduction of the merchant community at Seoul in 1885); FO46/297, Parkes' 7, January 12, 1883 (inclosure: Acting Consul Hall's report on Korea); FO46/300, Parkes' 84, May 26, 1883 (inclosure: Notes on the Capital of Corea); *FRUS*, 1887, Rockhill to Bayard, December 17, 1886; Bayard to Dinsmore, March 14, 1887; Noble, "The Former Foreign Settlements in Korea," pp. 771–772, 777.

21. *TGIG*, 20.10.23, 20.11.15, 20.11.17, 20.11.18, 20.11.19, 20.12.22, 21.4.2, 21.4.6, 21.4.8, 21.4.14, 21.4.18, 21.5.14, 21.5.24, 21.6.14, 21.6.17; *Tongnaebu kyerok*, KH9.11.25, KH9.12.8; *CJHSL*, No. 551, pp. 902–904; No. 793, pp. 1258–1259; No. 834, p. 1349; No. 852, pp. 1370–1371; No. 880, pp. 1474–1475; No. 884, p. 1478; No. 983, pp. 1792–1796; *Ku Han'guk oegyo munsŏ, Ilan*, No. 233, p. 119; No. 234, p. 120; No. 238, p. 121; *Yŏngan*, 21.4.6, May 7, 1884; *Hwasin*, KH9.10.23, KH9.11.14, KH9.11.17, KH9.11.18, KH9.12.18, KH9.12.22, KH10.4.18, KH10.5.18, KH10.6.13; FO17/915, Parkes' 11, September 25, 1882 (inclosure 1: Aston's report on his fact-finding mission to Pusan and Wŏnsan; inclosure 2: Municipal Regulations of the Japanese Settlement of Pusan in Corea); FO17/950, Parkes' 9, May 31, 1884; *Diplomatic Despatches, Korea,* Heard's 237, January 24, 1892; *North China Herald*, April 28, 1882; September 23, 1882; November 15, 1882; July 20, 1883; November 7, 1883; Yi Hyŏn-jong, "Ku Hanmal oegugin kŏryujinae chojikch'e e taehayŏ," *The Yŏksa Hakpo* 34:5 (June 1967); Kim Yong-uk, "Pusan ch'ukhangji," *Hangdo Pusan* 2:127–131 (June 1963); *Pusan yaksa*, pp. 151–159. In April 1885, the Japanese asked for a site to build a coaling station on Chŏlyŏngdo. After some negotiations, an agreement was drafted in September 1885 and finally signed in January 1886. *TGIG*, 22.2.18, 22.3.23, 22.4.17, 22.8.7, 22.12.25, 22.12.27.

22. *IS-KJ*, 20.11.23 (278:52); *Tŏgwŏnbu ŭpchi*; *TGIG*, 21.8.16; *Tŏgwŏnbu kyerok*, 21.7.16, 21.8.10; *Hwasin*, KH10.8.17; *CJHSL*, No. 551, pp. 904–906; No. 834, p. 1349; No. 886, p. 1482; No. 890, pp. 1488–1489; No. 983, pp. 1775–1780; No. 1127, pp. 2060–2066; FO17/915, Parkes'11, September 25, 1882(inclosure 1: Aston's report on his fact-finding mission to Pusan and Wŏnsan); *North China Herald*, January 30, 1884; W. R. Carles, *Life in Corea* (London, 1888), pp. 274–279; *Tō-Chōsen*, pp. 31, 54; Yi Hyŏn-jong, "Ku Hanmal oegugin kŏryujinae chojikch'e e taehayŏ," *The Yŏksa Hakpo* 34:8–9 (June 1967).

23. *Kojong sillok*, 21.10.12; *TGIG*, 20.9.16, 20.11.8, 21.4.9, 21.4.11, 21.4.18, 21.5*.11, 21.7.6, 21.7.12, 21.8.9, 21.10.9, 21.10.11; *Tongnaebu kyerok*, KH10.8.18, KH10.9.3, KH11.1.28; *Hwasin*, KH10.3.18; *CJHSL*, No. 831, pp. 1344–1345; *Yŏngan*, 21.4.6; *Ku Han'guk oegyo munsŏ, Ilan*, Nos. 205–206, pp. 108–109; No. 237, p. 121; No. 333, p. 164; No. 336, p.165; *Treaties*, pp. 120–122 (text of the *Agreement with Japan Regarding the Treaty Port Limits*). The first extension of the treaty limits at Inch'ŏn, for example, opened Ansan and Sihŭng in the east, Kimp'o in the northeast and Kanghwa in the north. The second extension of 1884 opened Namyang, Suwŏn, and Kwangju (Kyŏnggi) in the south, Seoul in the east, T'ongjin in the northwest, and the islands Yŏngjong, Taebu, and Sobu in the southwest. See *Jinsenfushi*, pp. 354–357.

24. *NGB*, vol. 16, No. 112, pp. 292–296; *Jinsenfu-shi*, pp. 287–288, 764–765; FO17/915, Parkes' 11, September 25, 1882(inclosure: Aston's report on Pusan and Wŏnsan).

25. *TGIG*, 20.10.3, 20.10.6, 21.3.7, 21.4.25, 21.5.4, 21.5*.22, 21.7.5; *Hwasin*, KH9.10.2(text of the contract), KH9.12.14, KH10.2.26, KH10.3.24, KH10.5.16; *CJHSL*, No. 837, p. 1355.

26. See footnote No.23.

27. *Kojong sillok*, 20.1.24, 20.1.27; *TGIG*, 21.9.16, 20.11.6, 20.12.1, 21.2.28;*Tongnaebu* kyerok, KH9.10.24, KH9.10.26; *Ku Han' guk oegyo munsŏ, Ilan*, Nos. 113–114, p. 78; Nos. 123–125, pp. 81–82; Nos. 139–140, p. 87; Nos. 152–153, p. 91; *NGB*, vol. 16, No. 111, pp. 289–292; *North China Herald*, November 7, 1883.

28. *Kojong sillok*, 22.6.6(text of the Sino-Korean Telegraph Agreement in eight articles);*TGIG*, 22.8.19, 22.8.21, 22.8.22, 22.9.2, 22.10.15, 22.10.26, 22.11.2; *Chŏnan*, KH11.8.8, KH11.9.1, KH11.10.17; *Hwasin*, KH11.6.11, KH12.1.16. The Koreans had to repay the Chinese loan without interest after five years in such a way that it would be liquidated after twenty years. Within these twenty-five years, Korea was committed not to build other overland telegraphic lines with the help of a third party.

29. *Kojong sillok*, 22.11.16(text of the additional Korean-Japanese agreement), 23.2.19 (additional agreement with China); *TGIG*, 22.8.8, 22.8.12; *Ku Han'guk oegyo munsŏ, Ilan*, No. 550, pp. 262–263; No. 562, pp. 268–269; No. 571, pp. 272–274; No. 581, pp. 279–281; No. 612, pp. 294–295; Nos. 614–616, pp. 295–296.

30. FO46/299, Parkes' 66, April 28, 1883.

31. *TGIG*, 21.3.7; *Daiichi Ginkō shi*, pp.526–533; *Shibusawa Eiichi denki shiryō*, 16: 22–34; *NGB*, vol. 16, pp. 315–324; vol. 17, pp. 367–377. A new agreement was concluded in 1886. An agency was opened at Seoul in 1888. *Daiichi Ginkō shi*, pp. 533–535, 539.

32. *Jinsenfu-shi*, pp.1022–1123; Wŏn Yu-han, "Tangojŏn ko," *The Yŏksa Hakpo* 35/36:330(Dec. 1967).

33. *TGIG*, 21.5.22; *CJHSL*, No. 1148, p. 2117; *Jinsenfu-shi*, pp. 1023–1024; Han U-gŭn, *Han'guk kaehanggi ŭi sangŏp yŏn'gu*, p.89 (gives a list of names of Chinese firms in footnote 187).

34. Many entries in the *TGIG*. Also Han U-gŭn, *Han'guk kaehanggi ŭi sangŏp yŏn'gu*, pp. 81–88.

35. *TGIG*, 22.8.21, 21.8.22, 21.8.26; *Tongnaebu kyerok*, KH11.9.20, KH11.10.5, KH11.11.4.

36. *Oeamun ch'ogi, kii*, 20.6.15; *TGIG*, 20.10.15, 20.10.17, 21.5.1, 21.6.4, 21.6.23, 21.6.25, 21.6.30, 21.7.1, 21.7.21, 21.7.29, 21.8.4; *Yŏngan*, 21.6.24, 21.7.4, 21.8.8, October 1, 1884; *Jardine Matheson Correspondence*, Chemulpo 1, July 21,1883; 4, August 2,1883; 40, June 25,1884; 42, July 12,1884; 57, July 27,1884; Seoul 11, July 18,1883; 13, July 19,1883; Moellendorff, *Lebensbild*, pp. 52–53; *North China Herald*, July 6, 1883. The name of the village where the first mine was opened is transcribed as "Foong Tung." It was situated thirty *ri* southeast of Kimsŏng. Such a place can not be located now. It was perhaps the village Tanghyŏn, thirty *ri* north of Kimsŏng, where in the later 1880s Carl Wolter of Meyer & Company started to mine again. For the losses incurred during mining activities, Jardine Matheson pressed the Korean gvernment for compensation. The negotiations which were held early in 1885 between the British consulate and the Korean Foreign Office were greatly hampered by the British occupation of Port Hamilton. *TGIG*, 21.12.14, 22.3. 2, 22.5.25, 22.6.2.

37. *TGIG*, 22.2.17, 22.7.18; *Yŏngan*, October 1, 1884; 21.12.5, 21.12.14; March 2, 1885. The Korean Foreign Office was willing to reimburse half of the *Nanzing's* losses but could not pay because of the 1884 disturbances. *Jardine Matheson Correspondence*, Chemulpo 5, August 2,1883; 16, April 9,1884; 18, April 26,1884; 20, April 28,1884; 24, May 5,1884; 32, June 2,1884; 105, September 21,1884; 118, October 30,1884; Seoul 16, February

11, 1884; *Diplomatic Despatches, Korea*, Foulk's 212, August 6, 1885.

38. *TGIG*, 22.2.25, 22.7.15, 22.7.20, 22.8.25, 22.9.12, 22.11.28; *Tŏgan*, August 24, 1885; August 29, 1885; October 3, 1885; October 14, 1885; October 15, 1885; December 16, 1885; January 2, 1886. The contract concerning the purchase of minting machinery was renewed on March 31, 1886. *CJHSL*, No.1105, pp. 1999–2000; *Jardine Matheson Correspondence*, Jenchuan 29, May 19,1884; Merrill, *Letterbooks*, January 25, 1886, to Sir Robert Hart; Moellendorff, *Lebensbild*, pp. 64–65; *Korea VI*, Wolter to H.C. Edward Meyer, July 4 and 7, 1885; Wolter to von Brandt, July 10, 1885; Zembsch to Bismarck, August 1, 1885; von Brandt to Bismarck, October 22, 1885; *Korea VII*, Budler to Bismarck, December 9, 1885; Budler to Bismarck, January 2, 1886; Budler to Bismarck, April 3, 1886; *Jinsenfu-shi*, p. 380; Ch'oe Sŏng-yŏn, *Kaehang kwa yanggwan yŏkchŏng*, pp. 92–95. It is likely that the Korean Foreign Office did not grant mining rights to Meyer because the Koreans themselves were starting mining operations in Kyŏngsang and Hamgyŏng during 1885. A mining office was opened in November 1884. *IS-KJ*, 21.9.16 (289:26b-27); *TGIG*, 22.1.16, 22.1. 25, 22.1.30, 22.8.6, 22.10.24. Meyer & Company's European headquarters were in Hamburg, Germany. Its main office in the Far East was in Hongkong, and it had branches in Shanghai, Tientsin, and Kobe. Its Chinese name was Shih-ch'ang yang-hang. This firm still exists, but unfortunately no archives on its Far Eastern activities are preserved.

39. Harold F. Cook, "Kim Ok-kyun and the Background of the 1884 Emeute," pp.245–246.

40. *IS-KJ*, 21.1.11(280:20a-b); *TGIG*, 21.4.8, 21.8.15, 21.10.10, 21.12.21, 21.12.27, 22.1.3, 22.4.4, 22.7.8, 22.7.14, 22.8.16; *Miwŏnan*, Feburary 16, 1885; June 12, 1885; *Diplomatic Despatches, Korea*, Foote's 101, July 31, 1884; Foulk's 175, May 25, 1885; *Jardine Matheson Correspondence*, Jenchuan 43, June 27, 1884; 65, July 30, 1884; *Ku Han'guk oegyo munsŏ, Ilan*, Nos. 202–204, pp. 106–108; Nos. 277–278, pp. 139–140; No. 316, p. 157; Nos. 479–480, pp. 233–234; No. 541, p. 259; Nos. 560–561, pp. 267–268; No. 597, p.287; No. 604, p. 291; Ch'oe Sŏng-wŏn, *Kaehang kwa yanggwan yŏkchŏng*, pp. 96–98; Harold F. Cook, *Korea's 1884 Incident*, pp. 87–91. Cook has made a detailed study of Townsend's career. See his "Walter D. Townsend—Pioneer American Businessman in Korea," *Transactions of the Korea Branch of the Royal Asiatic Society* 48:74–103(Aug. 1973). The dispute between the Korean and Japanese governments concerning the Ullŭngdo timber apparently was settled at the end of 1885 when the Japanese authorities confiscated the illegally cut timber, and the Korean government commissioned a German firm in Japan to sell it on its behalf. Mitchell seems to have cut the timber with a number of workmen he had recruited in Japan.

41. *TGIG*, 21.6.4, 21.10.14; *Miwŏnan*, July 11, 1884; *Mian*, November 14, 1885; *Diplomatic Despatches, Korea*, Foote's 97, July 26, 1884; Foulk's 251,November 17, 1885.

42. *PBTN*, 263: 676a-b.

43. *IS-KJ*, 20.6.23 (273:55a-b). It is not quite clear in what sense the term *togo*, "monopolists," is used here. Presumably it embraced the government-protected merchants (*sijŏn*), although the new government measure may also have had an effect on the authorized merchants (*yugŭijŏn*) who were officially abolished only in 1894. For a discussion of the meaning of the term *togo*, see Kang Man-gil, "Chosŏn hugi sangŏpchabon ŭi sŏngjang," *Han'guksa yŏn'gu* 1:80–81(September 1968).

44. *TGIG*, 21.5*.19, 21.5*.26; *Ku Han'guk oegyo munsŏ, Ilan*, No. 83, pp. 63–64; Nos. 87–88, pp. 65–66; No. 91, pp. 66–67; Han U-gŭn, *Han'guk kaehanggi ŭi sangŏp yŏn'gu*, pp.

189–190.

45. *Ku Han'guk oegyo munsŏ*, Ilan, No. 265, pp. 133–134; Han U-gŭn, *Han'guk kaehanggi ŭi sangŏp yŏn'gu*, pp. 181–184.

46. For a detailed treatment on the establishment of the Office for the Benefit of Trade (Hyesang kongguk), see Han U-gŭn, *Han'guk kaehanggi ŭi sangŏp yŏn'gu*, pp. 151–164.

47. Han U-gŭn, *Han'guk kaehanggi ŭi sangŏp yŏn'gu*, p. 122. Goods which were imported for the government or the royal palace were admitted dutyfree. See, for example, *TGIG*, 21.8.4.

48. *TGIG*, 20.8.15, 20.9.6, 20.9.16, 21.4.22, 21.6.29, 21.7.9, 22.8.22; *P'alto sado samhanggu kwanmun*, 21.10.14, 21.9.10; Kim Yun-sik, *Ŭmch'ŏngsa*, p. 227; *Jinsenfu-shi*, p. 1023; Han U-gŭn, *Han'guk kaehanggi ŭi sangŏp yŏn'gu*, pp. 204–215. There is a list of the names of these companies on pages 214–215.

49. *IS-KJ*, 19.10.14 (265:41a-b).

50. *TGIG*, 21.3.19, 21.4.25, 21.5.14, 21.6.22, 21.7.16, 21.7.27, 22.2.18, 22.2.19, 22.7. 8; *Ku Han'guk oegyo munsŏ*, Ilan, Nos. 446–447, pp. 221–222; *Ch'onggwan naesin*, KH12.8.10, KH12.8.14; *Ch'onggwan kongmun*, KH13 (without date).

51. *IS-KJ*, 20.10.3 (277:3), 20.10.30 (277:50b), 21.1.27 (280:50b), 21.7.6 (287:10a-b); *TGIG*, 21.1.22, 21.1.25, 21.5*.18; *Hwasin*, KH10.1.22,KH10.5.21; *CKHCJ*, 5:18b.

52. *TGIG*, 21.4.13, 21.4.21, 21.4.28, 21.5.4, 21.6.2, 21.6.11, 21.6.24, 21.9.6, 21.9.7, 21.9.8, 21.9.10, 22.2.1, 22.6.23; *Hwasin*, KH10.4.21, KH10.7.7, KH10.7.19, KH10.7.28, KH10.9.18, KH10.9.19, KH10.12.2, KH10.12.8, KH10.12.20; *P'alto sado samhanggu kwanmun*, 21.6.22, 21.9.16, 21.10.6, 22.2.2; the complaints of the Japanese are collected in *P'ia wangbok sŏdŭngnok* and *Ilch'ae pogwallok*.

53. *IS-KJ*, 19.10.7 (265:17b), 19.12.5 (267:12), 20.2.26 (269:26); *TGIG*, 21.9.13; HC36/4778, "Report on the Trade of Corea for the Year 1883," by W.G. Aston to Parkes; *Decennial Reports on the Trade, Navigation, Industries, etc. of the Ports Open to Foreign Commerce in China and Corea and on the Condition and Development of the Treaty Port Provinces, 1882–1891*, Appendix II, Jenchuan, p.XXXIX; *Diplomatic Despatches, Korea*, Foulk's 167, April 30, 1885; *Daiichi Ginkō shi*, p. 536; *Shibusawa Eiichi denki shiryō*, 16: 24–25, 35; *Jinsenfu-shi*, pp. 1205–1209; *Jardine Matheson Correspondence*, Seoul, June 28, 1883; also see Wŏn Yu-han, "Tangojŏn ko," *The Yŏksa Hakpo* 35/36:337(Dec. 1967). Perhaps because of the poor quality of the *tangojŏn*, a great number of counterfeiters were at work. Some Koreans even seem to have had Japanese collaborators. *IS-KJ*, 20.9.13 (276:23), 21.5*.29 (285:47a-b), 21.6.1 (286:1b), 21.6.22 (286:66a-b); *TGIG*, 21.5.28, 21.5*.1, 21.5*.3, 21.5*. 25, 21.6.12, 21.6.16, 21.8.2, 21.8.4, 21.8.16; and numerous documents in *Ku Han'guk oegyo munsŏ*, Ilan.

54. HC36/4778, Aston's "Report on the Trade of Corea for the Year 1883"; *Decennial Reports on the Trade, Navigation, Industries, etc.*, Appendix II; *Kankoku shi*, pp. 124–125, 138–139; *Diplomatic Despatches, Korea*, Foote's 15, July 17, 1883; enclosure in Foulk's 300: C.A. Welch to Foulk, April 23, 1886; *FRUS*, 1884, Foote to Frelinghuysen, April 28, 1884; *North China Herald*, September 28, 1883. For a comparison of Japanese and Chinese shares in the Korean trade from 1885 on, see Kitagawa Osamu, "Nisshin sensō made no Nissen bōeki," *Rekishi Kagaku* 1:72–78 (1932). Yu Kyo-sŏng studied Korea's foreign trade from 1885–1887 using Merrill's regular reports. "Yijo malyŏp ŭi samgwan muyŏk ko," *Sahak yŏn'gu* 18:675–702 (Sept. 1964); Ch'oe Yu-gil, "Yijo kaehang chikhu ŭi Han-Il muyŏk ŭi tonghyang," *Asea yŏn'gu* 47:175–221 (Sept. 1972). Despite the increased maritime trade between Korea and China, the Sino-Korean border trade continued to be quite

significant. For figures for 1881 and 1882, see Ch'oe Yu-gil, p. 178. There seems to be no uniformity of opinion on the outflow of gold. See Han U-gŭn, "Kŭm ŭi kug'oe yuch'ul" in *Han'guk kaehanggi ŭi sangŏp yŏn'gu*, pp. 281–300.

55. *Kankoku shi*, p. 124.

Chapter 11

1. Two recent studies on the enlightenment party are Harold F. Cook, *Korea's 1884 Incident* (Seoul, 1972) and Yi Kwang-rin, *Kaehwadang yŏn'gu* (Seoul, 1973), especially pp. 1–66. For a discussion on background sources which shaped enlightened thought, see Yi Kwang-rin, *Han'guk kaehwasa yŏn'gu*, pp. 19–34.

2. For background information on the reformers, see Tabohashi Kiyoshi, *Kindai Nissen kankei no kenkyū*, I, 898–899; H.F. Cook, "Kim Ok-kyun and the Background of the 1884 Emeute," pp.121–138.

3. On Yi Tong-in, see Yi Yong-hŭi, "Tong-in sŭng ŭi haengjŏk," *Nonmunjip*, 1:7–47 (1973) and Yi Kwang-rin, *Kaehwadang yŏn'gu*, pp.93–110. Kim Ok-kyun's first trip to Japan is described by Cook, *Korea's 1884 Incident*, pp. 39–49.

4. Yi Kwang-rin thinks that the enlightenment party was formed in 1879. *Kaehwadang yŏn'gu*, p.16. Fukuzawa Yukichi and his historical background are described, for example, in G.B. Sansom, *The Western World and Japan* (New York, 1950) and Hilary Conroy, *The Japanese Seizure of Korea: 1868–1910*, pp. 127–133.

5. Quoted from Hilary Conroy, *The Japanese Seizure of Korea: 1868–1910*, p.137.

6. Kim Ok-kyun's second trip to Japan is treated in Cook, *Korea's 1884 Incident*, pp. 51–71; Tabohashi Kiyoshi, *Kindai Nissen kankei no kenkyū*, I, 908–910; Pak Yŏng-hyo, *Sahwa kiryak*, pp. 214,231,250,252,263,264,267. Kim Yun-sik, *Umch'ŏngsa*, p.194, writes that "some ten students" accompanied Pak Yŏng-hyo to Japan. Not all of them can be accounted for. Pak's embassy also included other people who later became prominent. Min Yŏng-ik went to Japan in an unofficial capacity. Pak Che-gyŏng was the author of *Mirror of Korean Politics* (*Chosŏn chŏnggam*), a description of behind-the-scenes events during the period of the Taewŏn'gun, published in Tokyo in 1886. See Yi Kwang-rin, *Han'guk kaehwasa yŏn'gu*, pp. 237–257. Another member was Yi Su-jŏng, who stayed in Japan and was baptized in April 1883. He undertook the first Korean translation of the Gospel of Saint Mark. See Yi Kwang-rin, ibid., pp. 222–236.

7. Kim Ok-kyun's memorial is translated in Harold F. Cook, *Korea's 1884 Incident*, appendix B, pp. 238–244.

8. Pak Yŏng-hyo's memorial entitled *Kaehwa e taehan sangso* (*Memorial on Enlightenment*) can be found in the supplement to *Sindonga* (January 1966), pp. 12–23. Kim Yŏng-ho's article on Yu Kil-chun's thinking is also relevant in this context. See "Yu Kil-chun ŭi kaehwa sasang," *Ch'angjak kwa pip'yŏng* 11:476–492 (fall 1968).

9. The fascinating story of the *Hansŏng sunbo* is told in Yi Kwang-rin, *Han'guk kaehwasa yŏn'gu*, pp. 48–65. The newspaper office which was destroyed by a furious mob in December 1884 was reestablished in May 1885, again under Kim Man-sik's supervision. Renamed *Hansŏng chubo*, its first issue was published on January 25, 1886, and henceforth appeared weekly. Its articles were written in a mixture of *han'gŭl* and Chinese and at times

only in *han'gŭl*. It was abolished on July 7, 1888, due to financial difficulties. See Yi Kwang-rin, *Han'guk kaehwasa yŏn'gu*, pp. 65–75. Prof. Yi also analyzes the contents of this newspaper and its operation. See pp.75–87. Inoue Kakugorō was dismissed from the newspaper staff and had to return to Japan after he was held responsible for an article which criticized the Chinese military. See Tabohashi Kiyoshi, *Kindai Nissen kankei no kenkyū*, I, 892–893.

10. *FRUS*, 1885, No.128, Foote to Frelinghuysen, December 17, 1884(enclosure: Foulk's report of information relative to the revolutionary attempt in Seoul, Corea, December 4–7, 1884). Also in McCune and Harrison, *Korean-American Relations*, I, 101–111. (Hereafter cited only as Foulk, *Report*). FO46/299, Parkes' 65 (conf.), April 28, 1883 (inclosure: Aston's memorandum to Parkes); Yi Sŏn-gŭn, *Han'guksa, ch'oegŭnse-p'yŏn*, pp. 579, 581 (footnote 1).

11. *Kojong sillok*, 20.3.17.

12. Kim Ok-kyun was appointed to the post of councillor in the Foreign office when he was in Japan. Harold F. Cook, *Korea's 1884 Incident*, p.74.

13. Tabohashi Kiyoshi, *Kindai Nissen kankei no kenkyū*, I, 912–913, 918. The exact number of students who were sent to Japan does not seem to be known. Tabohashi speaks of "some forty," whereas Sŏ Chae-p'il writes in his diary that he was one of sixty-one students. See Yi Sŏn-gŭn, *Han'guksa, ch'oegŭnse-p'yŏn*, p. 581 (footnote 2).

14. Pak Yŏng-hyo, *Sahwa kiryak*, pp. 213–214, 250; Harold F. Cook, "Kim Ok-kyun and The Background of the 1884 Emeute," p. 232. It seems that Li Hung-chang, who had received a report by Wu Ch'ang-ch'ing on Pak Yŏng-hyo's employment of Japanese-trained military instructors, was not happy about this. Li urged Wu to arrange with the Korean government for the continued use of Chinese instructors, especially in view of the eventual withdrawal of part of the Chinese troops. *CKHCJ*, 5:14.

15. FO46/300, Parkes'91, May 31, 1883 (inclosure: Memorandum from Aston to Parkes).

16. *IS-KJ*, 20.3.17(270:24b), 20.4.20(271:46); Tabohashi Kiyoshi, *Kindai Nissen kankei no kenkyū*, I, 917. Yi Sŏn-gŭn maintains that Kim Ok-kyun was appointed to the post of development commissioner for the southern and eastern islands and whaling commissioner to remove him from Seoul. This assertion is problematic because there is evidence that he went to Japan with the blessing of the Min. Yi Sŏn-gŭn, *Han'guksa, ch'oegŭnse-p'yŏn*, p. 557. For the details of Kim Ok-kyun's third trip to Japan, see Harold F. Cook, *Korea's 1884 Incident*, pp. 73–100.

17. FO46/288, Parkes' 140,October 2, 1882 (inclosure: Memorandum by Aston); Parkes' 145, October 16, 1882.

18. *IS-KJ*, 20.6.5 (273:15), 20.6.7 (273:23), 20.6.11 (273:32), 20.6.12 (273:34); *Kojong sillok*, 20.11.21, 21.5.9. The dispatch of a Korean mission to the United States was apparently suggested to King Kojong by Minister Foote. Von Moellendorff considered it an intrigue behind his back. *FRUS*, 1883, No.14, Foote to Frelinghuysen, July 13, 1883; Moellendorff, *Lebensbild*, p. 61. For a brief report on the mission's itinerary, see Frelinghuysen to Foote, No.27, October 16, 1883, in McCune and Harrison, *Korean-American Relations*, I, 32–34. One member of Min Yŏng-ik's mission was Yu Kil-chun who stayed on in the United States as a student. For Yi Kwang-rin's article on Yu's stay in the U.S., see *Han'guk kaehwasa yŏn'gu*, pp. 258–274.

19. Quoted from McCune and Harrison, *Korean-American Relations*, I, 7.

20. *IS-KJ*, 21.3.27 (282:60a-b); *Kojong sillok*, 21.5.15, 21.9.11. At least four Japanese came to Seoul to help organize the postal service. Harold F. Cook, *Korea's 1884 Incident*, p. 118.

21. The establishment of the model farm is described in Yi Kwang-rin, *Han'guk kaehwasa yŏn'gu*, pp. 190–205. Ch'oe Kyŏng-sŏk brought back to Korea a variety of agricultural tools and seeds which were given to him by his American hosts. *IS-KJ*, 21.9.12 (289:18).

22. *TGIG*, 21.6.30; *IS-KJ*, 21.8.26 (288:45a-b); Foulk, *Report*, p.108. Min Yŏng-ik held a number of concurrent appointments. On October 16, 1884, he was appointed a vice-president of the Home Office. *IS-KJ*, 21.8.28 (288:54b).

23. *CSS*, pt.6, vol.4, pp. 724, 725; Tabohashi Kiyoshi, *Kindai Nissen kankei no kenkyū*, I, 918; Yi Sŏn-gŭn, *Han'guksa, ch'oegŭnse-p'yŏn*, pp. 597–598; Foulk, *Report*, pp. 108–109.

24. FO46/288, Parkes' 140(conf.), October 2, 1882 and inclosure; FO46/302, Parkes' 114(conf.), July 16, 1883.

25. For documents pertaining to Kojong's request for American military instructors, see part 2 "Securing American Advisers for the Korean Government" in McCune and Harrison, *Korean-American Relations*, I, 51–65. Yi Kwang-rin studies background and employment of the American instructors in *Han'guk kaehwasa yŏn'gu*, pp. 146–189. In September 1884, the king again approached Foote with the request to provide school teachers for the modern school (Yugyŏng kongwŏn). For a thorough discussion of this subject, see Yi Kwang-rin, *Han'guk kaehwasa yŏn'gu*, pp. 90–120.

26. Pak Yŏng-hyo had married King Ch'ŏlchong's only surviving daughter and thus had access to the royal palace even after his retirement from his post at Kwangju. Harold F. Cook, *Korea's 1884 Incident*, pp. 79, 104, 166, 180; Foulk, *Report*, p. 110. The king seems not to have known the full extent of the plot. Cook, ibid., p. 187. Although the Min presented quite a uniform front to the outside world, they seem to have formed at least two rather distinct groups, according to Pak Yŏng-hyo's testimony. One consisted of Cho Yŏng-ha, Min Yŏng-ik, Kim Yun-sik, and Yun T'ae-jun flocking around Min T'ae-ho; the other was made up of Han Kyu-jik, Yi Cho-yŏn, and Min Ŭng-sik, with Min Yŏng-mok as its leader. The differences between these two groups seem to have been personal rather than political. Cook, ibid., p.149.

27. Kim Ok-kyun was made a vice-president of the Foreign Office sometime in late 1884. He served in this capacity right up to the time of the coup. Harold F. Cook, *Korea's 1884 Incident*, p. 91, 103. For the enmity between Min Yŏng-ik and Kim Ok-kyun, see Cook, ibid., pp. 54–55, 111; Chŏng Kyo, *Taehan kyenyŏnsa*, p.24.

28. Harold F. Cook, *Korea's 1884 Incident*, pp. 124, 127, 132, 149–150. Cook devotes a whole chapter to an analysis of this decision. See pp.101–134.

29. Foulk, *Report*, pp. 109–111; FO17/953, Parkes' 38, December 12, 1884(inclosure: Aston's report on the political situation in Korea); *CJHSL*, No. 893, pp. 1491–1492; Harold F. Cook, *Korea's 1884 Incident*, pp.168–169.

30. *Kojong sillok*, 21.9.15; *TGIG*, 21.9.22; Tabohashi Kiyoshi, *Kindai Nissen kankei no kenkyū*, I, 924–925; FO46/317, Plunkett's 231(conf.), December 11, 1884.

31. The story of the coup d'état and its preparations is told in Kim Ok-kyun's *Kapsin Illok* (Journal of 1884). The diary encompasses the period between October 30 and December 6, 1884, inclusive. Since this document was written after the failure of the 1884 incident, it contains inconsistencies and errors. Harold Cook has supplemented Kim's

diary with other pertinent material. Cook, *Korea's 1884 Incident*, pp. 135–136.

32. Harold F. Cook, *Korea's 1884 Incident*, pp. 140–141, 153, 162–163, 195–196. Shimamura Hisashi had acted as chargé d'affaires during Takezoe's absence from Seoul.

33. Harold F. Cook, *Korea's 1884 Incident*, pp. 204–220; for a plan of the seating arrangement at the inaugural party, see appendix E, p. 248; Tabohashi Kiyoshi, *Kindai Nissen kankei no kenkyū*, I, 955–962; Yi Sŏn-gŭn, *Han'guksa, ch'oegŭnse-p'yŏn*, pp. 619–630. There are several eyewitness reports: Moellendorff, *Lebensbild*, pp. 71–74; *Diplomatic Despatches, Korea*, Foote's 127, December 5, 1884; FO17/977, Parkes' 18, January 17, 1885 (inclosure: Memorandum of events connected with Corean Coup d'état of 4th and 5th December by E.L.B. Allen of the British Consulate Journal); Parkes' 27, January 24, 1885 (inclosure: Narrative embodying views of Corean Government on recent events at Sŏul, with marginal notes by W. Aston).

34. Tabohashi Kiyoshi, *Kindai Nissen kankei no kenkyū*, I, 962–963; Yi Sŏn-gŭn, *Han-guksa, ch'oegŭnse-p'yŏn*, pp. 632–633.

35. Tabohashi Kiyoshi, *Kindai Nissen kankei no kenkyū*, I, 964–967; Yi Sŏn-gŭn, *Han-guksa, ch'oegŭnse-p'yŏn*, pp. 637–639. The fourteen-point program of the reform government is translated in Harold F. Cook, *Korea's 1884 Incident*, appendix D, p. 247.

36. *Diplomatic Despatches, Korea*, Foote's 128, December 17, 1884 in McCune and Harrison, *Korean-American Relations*, I, 98.

37. Foote's 128 in McCune and Harrison, *Korean-American Relations*, I, 98; *CKHCJ*, 5:30, 6:16–20(Yüan Shih-k'ai's report); Tabohashi Kiyoshi, *Kindai Nissen kankei no kenkyū*, I, 973–982; Yi Sŏn-gŭn, *Han'guksa, ch'oegŭnse-p'yŏn*, pp. 642–655.

38. Tabohashi Kiyoshi, *Kindai Nissen kankei no kenkyū*, I, 981–986; Yi Sŏn-gŭn, *Han'guksa, ch'oegŭnse-p'yŏn*, pp. 655–658. As both Aston and von Moellendorff later reported, the anger of the Korean populace was not directed against the Western foreigners. Moellendorff, *Lebensbild*, p. 76; FO17/953, Parkes' 38, December 12, 1884 (inclosure: Aston's Report on the Political Situation in Korea). The Korean coup had a Japanese aftermath, the Osaka Incident, which was the Japanese liberals' answer to their government's refusal to help Korea. See Conroy, *The Japanese Seizure of Korea, 1868–1910*, pp. 162–168.

39. *IS-KJ*, 21.10.21 (290:34); *CSS*, pt.6, vol.4, p. 739; *TGIG*, 21.10.20; Tabohashi Kiyoshi, *Kindai Nissen kankei no kenkyū*, I, 987–988; Yi Sŏn-gŭn, *Han'guksa, ch'oegŭnse-p'yŏn*, pp. 658–660.

40. *IS-KJ*, 21.10.21 (290:32), 21.10.27 (290:52b); *Ku Han'guk oegyo munsŏ, Ilan*, No. 341, pp. 167–168; No. 353, pp. 174–175; No. 367, pp. 181–182; *Diplomatic Despatches, Korea*, Foote's 128, December 17, 1884; Foote's 131, December 19, 1884; Tabohashi Kiyoshi, *Kindai Nissen kankei no kenkyū*, I, 992–1011.

41. FO46/317, Plunkett's 244 (conf.), December 21, 1884; Plunkett's 247 (conf.), December 22, 1884; Tabohashi Kiyoshi, *Kindai Nissen kankei no kenkyū*, I, 1014–1024, 1027–1039; Yi Sŏn-gŭn, *Han'guksa, ch'oegŭnse-p'yŏn*, pp. 672–673.

42. *CKHCJ*, 5:25, 30; *CJHSL*, No. 938, pp. 1610–1611; Tabohashi Kiyoshi, *Kindai Nissen kankei no kenkyū*, I, 1024–1025; Yi Sŏn-gŭn, *Han'guksa, ch'oegŭnse-p'yŏn*, pp. 673–674.

43. *IS-KJ*, 21.11.20(291:32), 21.11.21(291:33a-b). Inoue Kaoru was received by the king on January 6, 1885. *TGIG*, 21.11.16, 21.11.22, 21.11.23, 21.11.24, 21.11.25; *Kojong sillok*, 21.11.24; *Ku Han'guk oegyo munsŏ, Ilan*, No. 400, pp. 198–200; No. 402, pp. 200–201; No. 403, pp. 201–204; No. 408, pp. 205–206; No. 411, p. 207; *CJHSL*, No. 938, pp. 1611–

1612; FO46/327, Plunkett's No.31(conf.), January 24, 1885; Tabohashi Kiyoshi, *Kindai Nissen kankei no kenkyū*, I, 1039–1062. Two separate clauses were appended to the treaty text. The first stipulated that the sums of money mentioned in articles 2 and 4 were stated in Japanese currency and had to be paid at Inch'ŏn within three months; the second provided that article 3 had to be fulfilled within thirty days after the conclusion of the treaty.

44. Yi Sŏn-gŭn, *Han'guksa, ch'oegŭnse-p'yŏn*, p. 682.

45. *TGIG*, 21.12.21; Moellendorff, *Lebensbild*, pp. 77–79. It was during this stay in Tokyo that von Moellendorff conducted unauthorized negotiations with the secretary of the Russian legation, von Speyer, about the hiring of Russian army instructors. For details, see Yi Sŏn-gŭn, *Han'guksa, ch'oegŭnse-p'yŏn*, pp. 791ff.

46. FO46/328, Plunkett's 73 (very conf.), March 2, 1882 (inclosure: extract of a private report made [by Kim Ok-kyun] to Mr. Plunkett).

47. Minister Bingham stated that the terms of the Seoul treaty were "most creditable to Japan and most liberal to Corea."*Diplomatic Despatches,Japan*,Bingham's 1991,January 14, 1885.

48. FO46/328, Plunkett's 32 (secret), January 24, 1885; Tabohashi Kiyoshi, *Kindai Nissen kankei no kenkyū*, I, 1066–1067; Hilary Conroy, *The Japanese Seizure of Korea: 1868–1910*, pp. 170–171.

49. FO46/328, Plunkett's 54 (conf.), February 18, 1885; Plunkett's 66 (secret), February 27, 1885; Plunkett's 70, March 1, 1885; Plunkett's 71 (secret), March 1, 1885; Tabohashi Kiyoshi, *Kindai Nissen kankei no kenkyū*, I, 1074-1086.

50. *CWCSL*, 54:8a-b; Tabohashi Kiyoshi, *Kindai Nissen kankei no kenkyū*, I, 1087–1093. The Chinese government did not allow the negotiations to take place in Peking, and Itō Hirobumi had to present his credentials to the Tsungli Yamen ministers instead of to the boy emperor.

51. In an attached communication of the same date, which was sent to Itō, Li Hungchung pledged that he would send officials to Korea to investigate Japanese allegations of outrages committed by Chinese soldiers against Japanese nationals. If evidence were found, the culprits would be punished according to Chinese military law. Tabohashi Kiyoshi, *Kindai Nissen kankei no kenkyū*, I, 1097–1126; Yi Sŏn-gŭn, *Han'guksa, ch'oegŭnse-p'yŏn*, pp. 682–693; FO46/331, Plunkett's154, June 3, 1885; Plunkett's 162 (secret), June 7, 1885. The Chinese and the Japanese versions of article three seem to have differed slightly. The Peking version read:" . . . must first reciprocally give *notice* of the fact in writing . . .," whereas the Tokyo version read:" . . . shall give, each to the other, *previous notice* in writing . . ."

52. Tabohashi Kiyoshi, *Kindai Nissen kankei no kenkyū*, I, 1126–1128.

53. *TGIG*, 22.6.14.

54. FO46/328, Plunkett's 54(conf.), February 7, 1885; Foulk to Bayard, No. 172, May 19, 1885 in McCune and Harrison, *Korean-American Relations*, I, 75. For brief discussions of the British occupation of Port Hamilton, see Yi Sŏn-gŭn, *Han'guksa, ch'oegŭnse-p'yŏn*, pp. 775–781.

55. FO46/33, Plunkett's 176 (very conf.), July 3, 1885; Foulk to Bayard, No. 172, May 19, 1885 in McCune and Harrison, *Korean-American Relations*, I, 73–7 4;Yi Sŏn-gŭn, *Han'guksa, ch'oegŭnse-p'yŏn*, p. 694. Just before the negotiations between Li Hung-chang and Itō Hirobumi started, Li received a proposal for the neutralization of the Korean peninsula under Big Power guarantee. The proposal came from the German vice-consul

in Korea, Hermann Budler. See Yi Sŏn-gŭn, ibid., pp. 699–703.

56. FO46/331, Plunkett's 156, June 4, 1885; Plunkett's 162 (secret), June 7, 1885; Plunkett's 173 (very conf.), June 23, 1885; FO46/332, Plunkett's 182 (very conf.), July 14, 1885; Foulk to Bayard, No. 180, June 16, 1885 in McCune and Harrison, *Korean-American Relations*, I, 77–78.

57. FO46/332, Plunkett's 187 (secret), July 20, 1885; Foulk to Bayard, No. 187 (conf.), June 26, 1885; No. 189, June 29, 1885; No. 192 (conf.), July 5, 1885 in McCune and Harrison, *Korean-American Relations*, I, 78–82. The Korean call for US mediation was withdrawn by the Korean government, presumably on British insistance, a few days later. Foulk to Bayard, No. 196, ibid., p. 83.

58. FO46/332, Plunkett's 176 (very conf.), July 3, 1885; Foulk to Bayard, No. 223 (conf.), September 1, 1885; No. 238, October 14, 1885 in McCune and Harrison, *Korean-American Relations*, I, 84–86.

59. *TGIG*, 22.8.26, 22.9.13, 22.10.10; Foote to Bayard, No. 214, August 16, 1885; No. 237, October 14, 1885; No. 240, October 15, 1885; No. 255 (conf.), November 25, 1885 in McCune and Harrison, *Korean-American Relations*, I, 125, 133–135, 137–138; Yi Sŏn-gŭn, *Han'guksa, ch'oegŭnse-p'yŏn*, pp. 800–813. The king had begun working for his father's return almost immediately after his abduction to China in 1882. The Min greeted the news of his return with the execution of three persons who were charged of having conspired with the Taewŏn'gun in 1882.

BIBLIOGRAPHY

Allen, Horace N. *Korea: Facts and Fancy.* Seoul, 1904.
——— *Things Korean.* New York. 1908.
Appenzeller, Henry G. "The Opening of Korea: Admiral Shufeldt's Account of It," *Korean Repository* 1:57–62 (1892).
Ariga Nagao 有賀長雄. "Jinsen kaikō shimatsu" 仁川開港始末 (History of the opening of Inch'ŏn), *Gaikō jiho* 外交時報 (Revue diplomatique) 151:95–102 (Juin 1910).
Asien (German diplomatic documents). Bonn, Auswärtiges Amt.

Banno, Masataka. *China and the West, 1858–1861: The Origins of the Tsungli Yamen.* Harvard East Asian Series, No. 15. Cambridge, Harvard University Press, 1964.
Bee, Minge C. "Origins of German Far Eastern Policy," *Chinese Social and Political Science Review* 21:65–97 (April 1937).
Bishop, Isabella B. *Korea and Her Neighbours: A Narrative of Travel with an Account of the Recent Vicissitudes and Present Condition of the Country.* New York, 1898.
Broughton, William Robert. *A Voyage of Discovery to the North Pacific Ocean, performed in His Majesty's Sloop Providence and her Tender in the Years 1795, 1796, 1797, 1798.* London, 1804.
Buckingham, B. H., Foulk, George C. and McLean, Walter. *Observations upon the Korean Coast, Japanese-Korean Ports, and Siberia, made during a Journey from the Asiatic Station to the United States through Siberia and Europe, June 3 to September 8, 1882.* Washington, 1883.

Carles, W. R. *Life in Corea.* London, 1888.
Chang Chien 張謇. *Chang Chi-tzu chiu-lu* 張季子九錄 (Collected writings of Chang Chien). 1931.
Chang Hsiao-jo 張孝若. *Nan-t'ung Chang Chi-chih hsien-sheng ch'uan-chi, fu nien-p'u nien-piao* 南通張季直先生傳記, 附年譜年表 (A biography of Mr. Chang Chi-chih, Chang Chien of Nantung; with an appended chronological sketch of life and events of Chang Chi-chih). Shanghai, 1931.
Chang P'ei-lun 張佩綸. *Chien-yü chi, tsou-i* 澗于集, 奏議 (Collected memorials). 6 chüan. 1918.
Chang Tsun-wu 張存武. *Ch'ing-tai Chung-Han pien-wu wen-t'i t'an-yüan* 清代中韓邊務問題探源 (Investigation of Sino-Korean border problems during the Ch'ing period), Academia Sinica Publications, No. 2. Taipei, 1971.
———"Ch'ing-Han feng-kung kuan-hsi chih chih-tu-hsing fen-shi," 清韓封貢關係之制度性分析 (An institutional analysis of Sino-Korean tributary relations, 1637–1894), *Shih-huo Monthly* 食貨 1.4:201–207 (July 1971).
Chien, Frederick Foo. *The Opening of Korea: A Study of Chinese Diplomacy, 1876–1885.* The Shoe String Press, 1967.
Ch'ing-chi Chung-Jih-Han kuan-hsi shih-liao 清季中日韓關係史料 (Historical materials pertaining to the relations between China, Japan, and Korea at the end of the Ch'ing dynasty). 3 vols. Academia Sinica, Institute of Modern History. Taipei, 1970.

Ch'ing-chi wai-chiao shih-liao 清季外交史料 (Documents on foreign relations of the late Ch'ing dynasty). Compiled by Wang Yen-wei 王彦威. 1932–1935.

Ch'ing Kuang-hsü ch'ao Chung-Jih chiao-she shih-liao 清光緒朝中日交涉史料 (Documents on Sino-Japanese relations during the Kuang-hsü period). Palace Museum, Peiping, 1932.

Cho Ki-jun 趙璣濬 and O Tŏg-yŏng 吳德永. *Han'guk kyŏngje sa* 韓國經濟史 (Korean economic history). Seoul, 1962.

Choe Ching Young. "Yüan Shih-k'ai: His Role in Korea, 1882–1894," Seminar paper, Harvard University, 1956–1957.

———"The Decade of the Taewŏn'gun: Reform, Seclusion, and Disaster." 2 vols. Ph.D. thesis, Harvard University, 1960.

———"Kim Yuk (1580–1658) and the Taedongbŏp Reform," *The Journal of Asian Studies* 23.4:21–35 (Nov. 1963).

———*The Rule of the Taewŏn'gun, 1864-1873:Restoration in Yi Korea*. Cambridge, Mass., Harvard East Asian Research Center, Harvard University, 1972.

Ch'oe Ho-jin 崔虎鎭. *Han'guk kyŏngje sa kaeron* 韓國經濟史概論 (Outline of the economic history of Korea). Seoul, 1962.

Ch'oe Sŏk-u 崔奭祐. "Han-Pul choyak kwa sin'gyo chayu" 韓佛條約과信敎自由 (The Korean-French treaty and religious freedom), *Sahak yŏn'gu* 21:209–229 (Sept. 1969).

Ch'oe Sŏng-yŏn 崔聖淵. *Kaehang kwa yanggwan yŏkchŏng* 開港과 洋館歷程 (History of the opening of the port of Inch'ŏn and its Western buildings). Inch'ŏn, 1959.

Ch'oe Yu-gil 崔柳吉. "Yijo kaehang chikhu ŭi Han-Il muyŏk ŭi tonghyang" 李朝開港 直後의 韓日貿易의 動向 (Trade between Korea and Japan after the opening of the ports), *Asea yŏn'gu* 47:175–221 (Sept. 1972).

Chŏn Hae-jong 全海宗. "T'ongni kimu Amun sŏlch'i ŭi kyŏngwi e taehayŏ" 統理機務 衙門設置의 經緯에 대하여 (On the establishment of the T'ongnigimu Amun), *The Yŏksa Hakpo* 17/18:687–702 (June 1962).

———*Han'guk kŭnse taeoe kwan'gye munhŏn piyo* 韓國近世對外關係文獻備要 (Manual of Korean foreign relations, 1876–1910). Studies on the Kyujang-gak Archives, No. 1. Seoul, 1966.

———"Han-Chung chogong kwan'gye ko—Han-Chung kwan'gyesa ŭi chogam ŭl wihan toron" 韓中朝貢關係考—韓中關係史의 鳥瞰을 위한 導論 (A historical survey of Sino-Korean tributary relations), *Tongyang sahak yŏn'gu* 東洋史學研究 (Journal of Asian historical studies) 1:10–41 (October 1966).

———"Ch'ŏngdae Han-Chung chogong kwan'gye chonggo" 清代韓中朝貢關係綜考 (A study on the Sino-Korean tributary relations), *Chindan hakpo* 震檀學報 (The Chindan Journal) 29/30:239–284 (1967).

———*Han-Chung kwan'gyesa yŏn'gu* 韓中關係史研究 (A study on the history of Sino-Korean relations). Seoul, 1970.

Chŏnan 電案 (Documents concerning telegraphic matters). 3 vols.

Chŏng Kyo 鄭喬. *Taehan kyenyŏnsa* 大韓季年史 (Chronological record of the later part of the Yi dynasty). Han'guk saryo ch'ongsŏ, No. 5. Seoul, 1957.

Ch'onggwan kongmun 總關公文 (Communications from the Foreign Office to Henry F. Merrill). vol. 1.

Ch'onggwan naesin 總關來申 (Communications from Henry F. Merrill to the Foreign Office). vols. 1 and 2.

Ch'ŏngsang saan 清商事案 (Sino-Korean correspondence).

Chōsen jimu shimatsu satsuyō 朝鮮事務始末撮要 (Documents pertaining to Japanese-Korean relations). vol. 3. 1879.

Chōsen jimu sho 朝鮮事務書 (Documents pertaining to Korean affairs). vols. 25 and 26.

Chōsen shi 朝鮮史 (Chronological abstracts of historical documents on Korea), comp. Chōsen sōtokufu. Pt. 6, vol. 4. Keijo, 1938.

Chosŏn'guk such'urip pannyŏnp'yo 朝鮮國輸出入半年表 (Half-yearly tables of Korea's imports and exports). 1880.

Chou Fu 周馥. *Chou Ch'ueh-shen kung ch'üan-chi* 周愨愼公全集 (Collected works of Chou Fu). 1922.

Ch'ou-pan i-wu shih-mo 籌辦夷務始末 (The complete account of our management of barbarian affairs). Photolithograph of the original ed. Peiping, 1930. T'ung-chih period, 1862–1874, 100 chüan.

Chronicle and Directory for China, Corea, Japan, The Philippines, Cochin-China, Annam, Tonquin, Siam, Borneo, Straits Settlements, Malay States, &c. For the year 1889. Hongkong.

Chung-Jih chan-cheng 中日戰爭 (Documents relating to the Sino-Japanese war). 7 vols. Shanghai, 1961.

Chungjong sillok 中宗實錄 (The annals of King Chungjong).

Chung Ok-ja (Chŏng Ok-cha) 鄭玉子. "Sinsa yuramdan ko" 紳士遊覽團考 (A study on the "gentlemen touring corps"), *The Yŏksa Hakpo* 27:105–142 (April 1965).

Chŭngbo munhŏnbigo 增補文獻備考 (The enlarged and supplemented encyclopedia). Reprint. Seoul, 1957.

Conroy, Hilary. *The Japanese Seizure of Korea: 1868-1910*. University of Pennsylvania Press, 1960.

"Conversations on the US-Korean Treaty in 1882 between the Korean Delegates and the Chinese Envoys" 清國問答 *The Yŏksa Hakpo* 22:121–132 (Jan. 1964).

Cook, Harold F. "Kim Ok-kyun and the Background of the 1884 Emeute." Ph.D. thesis, Harvard University, 1968.

———*Korea's 1884 Incident: Its Background and Kim Ok-kyun's Elusive Dream.* Royal Asiatic Society, Korea Branch. Seoul, 1972.

———"Walter D. Townsend, Pioneer American Businessman in Korea," *Transactions of the Royal Asiatic Society* 48:74–103 (Aug. 1973).

Daiichi Ginkō shi 第一銀行史 (History of the First National Bank of Japan). Comp. by Daiichi Ginkō hachijūnenshi hensanshitsu, vol. 1. Tokyo, 1957–1958.

Decennial Reports on the Trade, Navigation, Industries, etc. of the Ports Open to Foreign Commerce in China and Corea and on the Condition and Development of the Treaty Port Provinces, 1882–1891. China Imperial Maritime Customs, 1. Statistical Series: no. 6. Shanghai, 1893.

Dennett, Tyler. *Americans in Eastern Asia: A Critical Study of the Policy of the United States with Regard to China, Japan and Korea in the 19th Century.* New York, 1922.

———"Early American Policy in Korea, 1883–1887," *Political Science Quarterly* 38. 1:82–103 (March 1923).

Denny, O. N. *China and Korea.* Seoul, 1888.

Deuchler, Martina. "The Opening of Korea, 1875-1884." Ph.D. thesis, Harvard University, 1967.

Dore, R. P. *Aspects of Social Change in Modern Japan*. Princeton University Press, 1967.

Fairbank, John K. *Trade and Diplomacy on the China Coast: The Opening of the Treaty Ports, 1842-1854*. Harvard Historical Studies, No. 62. Cambridge, Mass., Harvard University Press, 1953.

Fairbank, John K. and Teng S. Y. "On the Ch'ing Tributary System," in *Ch'ing Administration, Three Studies*. Harvard-Yenching Institute Studies, No. 19. Cambridge, Mass. 1960.

Fairbank, John K., ed. *The Chinese World Order: Traditional China's Foreign Relations*. Harvard East Asian Series, No. 32. Cambridge, Mass., 1968.

Feuerwerker, Albert. *China's Early Industrialization*. Harvard East Asian Series, No. 1. Cambridge, Mass., 1958.

FO17. Foreign Office Records, China correspondence, Public Record Office, London.

FO46. Foreign Office Records, Japan correspondence, Public Record Office, London.

Foulk, George C. "Foulk Papers" 3 boxes (Manuscript Room, New York Public Library).

Gilmore, George W. *Korea from Its Capital: with a Chapter on Missions*. Philadelphia, 1892.

Gompertz, G. St. G. M. "Some Notes on the Earliest Western Contacts with Korea," *Transactions of the Korea Branch of the Royal Asiatic Society* 33:41–54 (1957).

Griffis, William E. *Corea, the Hermit Nation*. New York, 1882.

Gutzlaff, Charles. *Journal of Three Voyages along the Coast of China in 1831, 1832 and 1833*. London, 1834.

Hahm Pyong-Choon. *The Korean Political Tradition and Law: Essays in Korean Law and Legal History*. Royal Asiatic Society, Korea Branch. Seoul, 1967.

Hall, Captain B. *Account of a Voyage of Discovery to the West Coast of Corea and the Great Loo-choo Island*. London, 1818.

Hamel, H. *An Account of the Shipwreck of a Dutch Vessel on the Coast of the Isle of Quelpart, together with the Description of the Kingdom of Corea*. Amsterdam, 1668.

Han U-gun 韓㳓劤. *Han'guk kyŏngje kwan'gye munhŏn chipsŏng* 韓國經濟關係文獻集成 (Annotated bibliography of Korean economic history, 1570–1910). Studies on the Kyujang-gak Archives, No. 2. Seoul, 1966.

——"Kaehang tangsi ŭi wigiŭisik kwa kaehwa sasang" 開港當時의 危機意識과 開化思想 (The transformation of thought in the late 19th century: crisis-conscious versus modernization), *Han'guksa yŏn'gu* 韓國史研究 (The Journal of Korean History) 2:105–139 (Dec. 1968).

——*Han'guk kaehanggi ŭi sangŏp yŏn'gu* 韓國開港期의 商業研究 (A study of trade during the period of the opening of the ports). Seoul, 1970.

——*Han'guk t'ongsa* 韓國通史 (General history of Korea). Seoul, 1970.

Han Young-kook (Han Yŏng-guk) 韓榮國 "Hosŏ e silsi toen Taedongbŏp" 湖西에 實施된 大同法 (On the great harmony system in Chung-cheng province), *The Yŏksa Hakpo* 13:77–107 (Oct. 1960) and 14:77–132 (April 1961).

Han'guk inmyŏng taesajŏn 韓國人名大事典 (Korean biographical dictionary). Seoul, 1967.

Han'guksa sidae kubullon 韓國史時代區分論 (Discussions on the periodization of Korean history) ed. by Han'guk kyŏngje sahakhoe. Seoul, 1970.

Hansŏng sunbo 漢城旬報 (Seoul newspaper). Reprint. Seoul, 1969.

Harrington, Fred H. *God, Mammon, and the Japanese: Dr. Horace N. Allen and Korean-American Relations, 1884-1905*, Madison, University of Wisconsin Press, 1944.

Hashima Hanjirō 羽島半次郎. "Kōka jōyaku teiketsu tōji no tsuioku" 江華條約締結當時の追憶 (Recollection of the conclusion of the Kanghwa treaty), *Seikyū gakusō* 靑丘學叢 5:171–179 (1931).

Henderson, Gregory. *Korea: The Politics of the Vortex*. Cambridge, Mass., Harvard University Press, 1968.

Henthorn, William E. *A History of Korea*. New York, The Free Press, 1971.

Hirschmeier, Johannes. *The Origins of Enterpreneurship in Meiji Japan*. Harvard East Asian Series, No. 17. Cambridge, Mass., 1964.

Hong I-sŏp 洪以燮. "Han'guk oegyosa—sipkusegi huban ihu ŭi kukche kwan'gye rŭl chungsim hayŏ" 韓國外交史—十九世紀後半以後의 國際關係를 中心하여 (Diplomatic history of Korea of the second half of the 19th century), in *Han'guk munhwasa taegye* 韓國文化史大系 (Outline of the cultural history of Korea), II, 389–534. Seoul, 1965.

Hsü, C. Y. *China's Entrance into the Family of Nations: The Diplomatic Phase, 1858-1880*. Harvard East Asian Series, No. 5. Cambridge, Mass., 1960.

Hsüeh Fu-ch'eng 薛福成. *Yung-an ch'üan-chi* 庸盦全集 (Collected works). 1884–1898.

Hwaan (Hwasin) 華案 (華信) (Sino-Korean correspondence). vols. 1–11.

Hwang Hyŏn 黃玹. *Maech'ŏn yarok* 梅泉野錄 (Collected works). Han'guk saryo ch'ongsŏ, No. 1. Seoul, 1955.

Hyŏn Sang-yun 玄相允. *Chosŏn yuhaksa* 朝鮮儒學史 (A history of Korean Confucianism). Seoul, 1954.

Ike Nobutaka. *The Beginnings of Political Democracy in Japan*. The Johns Hopkins Press, 1950.

Ilbonin mundap chamnok 日本人問答雜錄 (Documents pertaining to the negotiations with the Japanese).

Ilch'ae pogwallok 日債報關錄 (Reports on debts to Japanese). 1885.

Ilsa munja 日使文字 (Documents concerning the Japanese envoys). 2 vols.

Ilsŏngnok 日省錄 (Royal annals). vols. 146–316.

Inch'ŏn sŏkkŭm 仁川昔今 (Inch'ŏn past and present). Inch'ŏn, 1955.

Inch'ŏnbu ŭpchi 仁川府邑誌 (Local gazetteer of Inch'ŏn prefecture).

Injo sillok 仁祖實錄 (The annals of King Injo).

Ishihata Tadashi 石幡貞. *Chōsen kikō yoroku* 朝鮮歸好餘錄 (Miscellaneous writings on Korea). 1878.

Jardine, Matheson & Company papers. Preserved in the University Library, Cambridge University, Cambridge, England.

Jinsenfu-shi 仁川府史 (A history of Inch'ŏn). Jinsen, 1933.

Jones, G. H. "Chemulpo," *The Korean Repository* 6:374–384 (1897).

Kang Man-gil 姜萬吉. "Chosŏn chŏn'gi kongjang ko" 朝鮮前期工匠考 (A study of artisans in the first half of the Lee dynasty), *Sahak yŏn'gu* 12:1–72 (Sept. 1961).

———"Chosŏn hugi sangŏpchabon ŭi sŏngjang" 朝鮮後期商業資本의 成長 (Growth of commercial capital during 18-19th century Korea: with emphasis on wholesale trade in the capital and Songdo area), *Han'guksa yŏn'gu* 1:79–107 (Sept. 1968).

——— "Kaesŏng sangin yŏn'gu—Chosŏn hugi sangŏpchabon ŭi sŏngjang" 開城商人研究 ―朝鮮後期商業資本의 成長 (The Kaesŏng merchants: the growth of commercial capitalism during the late Yi dynasty), *Han'guksa yŏn'gu* 8:1–24 (Sept. 1972).

——— *Chosŏn hugi sangŏpchabon ŭi paltal* 朝鮮後期商業資本의 發達 (The development of commercial capitalism in late Chosŏn). Seoul, 1973.

Kikuchi Kenjō 菊池謙讓. *Kindai Chōsen shi* 近代朝鮮史 (A history of modern Korea). 2 vols. Tokyo, 1940.

Kim Byung-ha (Kim Pyŏng-ha) 金柄夏. *Yijo chŏn'gi tae-Il muyŏk yŏn'gu* 李朝前期對日貿易研究 (A study of the trade between Korea and Japan during the early Yi dynasty). The Korean Studies Series, no. 26. Seoul, 1969.

Kim Chong-wŏn 金鍾圓. "Cho-Chung sangmin suryungmuyŏk changjŏng e taehayŏ" 朝・中商民水陸貿易章程에對하여 (A study on the regulations for maritime and overland trade between Chinese and Corean subjects in 1882), *The Yŏksa Hakpo* 32: 120–169 (Dec. 1966).

Kim Hong-jip 金弘集. *Susinsa ilgi* 修信使日記 (Diary of an envoy), in *Susinsa kirok* 修信使記錄 (Collection of records of envoys). Han'guk saryo ch'ongsŏ, No. 9 韓國史料叢書. Seoul, 1958.

Kim Ki-su 金綺秀. *Iltong kiyu* 日東記游 (The record of a trip to Japan) and *Susinsa ilgi* 修信使日記 (The diary of an envoy), in *Susinsa kirok* 修信使記錄 (Collection of records of envoys). Han'guk saryo ch'ongsŏ, No. 9 韓國史料叢書. Seoul, 1958.

Kim Kyŏng-t'ae 金敬泰. "Kaehang chikhu ŭi kwanse'gwŏn hoebok munje" 開港直後의 關稅權回復問題 (The restoration of tariff-rights in the late 19th century: the case of "Pusan tariff incident"). *Han'guksa yŏn'gu* 8:81–111 (Sept. 1972).

Kim Pyŏng-dŏk 金炳德. *Chonghwan ilgi* 從宦日記 (Diary). 2 vols. 1883–1884.

Kim Sŏng-ch'il 金聖七. "Yŏnhaeng sogo" 燕行小攷 (A study on the Korean missions to China), *The Yŏksa Hakpo* 12:1–79 (May 1960).

Kim Tae-sang 金大商. "Kaehang chikhu Pusan ŭi sahoe-munhwa" 開港直後釜山의 社會文化 (Society and culture of Pusan after the opening of the port), *Hangdo Pusan* 港都釜山 (The port of Pusan) 6:163–200 (June 1967).

Kim Ŭi-hwan 金義煥. "Pusan kaehang ŭi yŏn'gu" 釜山開港의 研究 (A study on the opening of Pusan), *Hangdo Pusan* 港都釜山 (The port of Pusan) 3:7–101 (Dec. 1963).

——— *Pusan ŭi kojŏk kwa yumul* 釜山의 古蹟과 遺物 (Historical remains of Pusan). Pusan, 1969.

Kim Yŏng-ho 金泳鎬. "Hanmal sŏyang kisul ŭi suyong" 韓末西洋技術의 收容 (The acculturation of Western techniques in the late period of the Yi dynasty), *Asea yŏn'gu* 31:295–343 (Sept. 1968).

——— "Yu Kil-chun ŭi kaehwa sasang" 兪吉濬의 開化思想 (The enlightened thought of Yu Kil-chun), *Ch'angjak kwa pip'yŏng* 創作과 批評 (Creativity and criticism) 11: 476–492 (fall 1968).

——— "Chosŏn hugi e issŏsŏ ŭi tosisangŏp ŭi saeroun chŏn'gae" 朝鮮後期에있어서의 都市商業의 새로운展開 (A new development of Seoul merchants' activities during the late Yi dynasty), *Hanguksa yŏn'gu* 2:25–52 (Dec. 1968).

——— "Han'guk chabonjuŭi ŭi hyŏngsŏng munje" 韓國資本主義의 形成問題 (Problems concerning the formation of Korean capitalism), in *Han'guksa ŭi pansŏng* 韓國史의 反省 (Reflections on Korean history). Seoul, 1969.

Kim Yong-uk 金容旭. "Pusan ch'ukhangji" 釜山築港誌 (On the construction of Pusan harbor), *Hangdo Pusan* 港都釜山 (The port of Pusan) 2:121–292 (June 1963).

Kim Yun-sik 金允植. *Ŭmch'ŏngsa* 陰晴史 (Diary). Han'guk saryo ch'ongsŏ, No. 6. Seoul, 1958.

King, Paul. *In the Chinese Customs Service*. Rev. ed. London, 1930.

Kirosup'il 騎驢隨筆 (Biographical essays), comp. by Song Sang-do 宋相燾. Han'guk saryo ch'ongsŏ, No. 2. Seoul, 1955.

Kitagwa Osamu 北川修. "Nisshin sensō made no Nissen bōeki" 日清戰爭までの日鮮易貿 (Japanese-Korean trade to the Sino-Japanese war), *Rekishi kagaku* 歷史科學 (Historical Science) 1:64–79 (1932).

Ko Pyŏng-ik 高柄翊. "Mok In-dŏk ŭi sugi" 穆麟德의 手記 (Moellendorff's diary), *Chindan hakpo* 24:149–196 (Aug. 1963).

———"Mok In-dŏk ŭi kobing kwa kŭ paegyŏng" 穆麟德의 雇聘과그背景 (Moellendorff's employment and its background), *Chindan hakpo* 25–27: 225–244 (Dec. 1964).

———"Chosŏn hae'gwan kwa Ch'ŏngguk hae'gwan kwa ŭi kwan'gye—Merrill kwa Hart rŭl chungsim ŭro" 朝鮮海關과 清國海關과의 關係—「메릴」과「하트」를 中心으로 (The relationship between the Korean and Chinese Customs Service: Merrill and Hart), *Tong-a munhwa* 東亞文化 (Journal of the Institute of Asian Studies) 4:1–30 (Oct. 1965).

Kojong sillok 高宗實錄 (The annals of King Kojong).

Kondō Masuki 近藤眞鋤. *Keijō zokuto ikken temmatsu sho* 京城賊徒一件顚末書 (Complete account on the rebels of Keijō). 1882.

Korea, German diplomatic documents, Korea. Bonn, Auswärtiges Amt.

Krasnyi Arkhiv, "First steps of Russian imperialism in the Far East, 1888–1903," *Chinese Social and Political Science Review* 18.2:236–281 (July 1934).

Ku Han'guk oegyo munsŏ, Ilan 舊韓國外交文書, 日案 (Documents relating to the foreign relations of old Korea). Vol. 1 (1876–1889). Koryŏ taehakkyo Asea munje yŏn-guso 高麗大學校亞細亞問題研究所 comp. Seoul, 1965.

Ku Hanmal komunsŏ haeje mongnok 舊韓末古文書解題目錄 (Annotated bibliography of the late Yi dynasty archives, 1871–1912). Seoul, 1970.

Ku Pŏm-mo 具範謨. "Kaehang chŏn Yijo chŏngch'i chilsŏ ŭi hwan'gyŏngjŏk yŏgŏn e kwanhan koch'al" 開港前李朝政治秩序의 環境的與件에 關한 考察 (A study on the environmental factors of the political order in Yi dynasty prior to the opening of the ports), *Tong-a munhwa* 東亞文化 (Journal of the Institute of Asian Studies) 10:233–293 (Sept. 1971).

Kuksa taesajŏn 國史大事典 (A dictionary of Korean history), comp. by Yi Hong-jik 李弘稙. 2 vols. Seoul, 1962–1963.

Kwon Sok-bong (Kwŏn Sŏk-pong) 權錫奉. "Yŏngsŏn sahaeng e taehan ilgoch'al" 領選使行에 對한 一考察 (A study of *yŏngsŏnsa*), *The Yŏksa Hakpo* 17/18:277–312 (June 1962).

———"Li Hung-chang ŭi tae Chosŏn yŏlguk ibyak kwŏndoch'aek e taehayŏ" 李鴻章의 對朝鮮列國立約勸導策에 대하여 (Li Hung-chang's recommendations on Korean foreign policy, 1879–1880), *The Yŏksa Hakpo* 21:101–130 (Aug. 1963).

———"Kukki chejŏng ŭi yurae e taehan kwan'gyŏn" 國旗制定의 由來에 대한 管見 (A brief history of the Korean national flag), *The Yŏksa Hakpo* 23:41–54 (April 1964).

Kyeha chamunch'aek 啓下咨文冊 (Documents pertaining to Sino-Korean relations). 2 vols.

1881–1882.

Kyŏngguk taejŏn 經國大典 (The great code of administration). Collated and repr. by Chōsen sōtokufu chūsūin. Keijo, 1934.

Kyŏngsang namdo Tongnaebu ŭpchi 慶尙南道東萊府邑誌 (Local gazetteer of Tongnae prefecture). 1 vol.

Kyujanggak tosŏ, Han'gukpon ch'ongmongnok 奎章閣圖書, 韓國本總目錄 (Catalogue of Korean books and manuscripts in the Kyujanggak collection). The Institute of Asian Studies, Seoul National University. Seoul, 1965.

Laguérie, R. Villetard de. *La Corée, Independente, Russe ou Japonaise.* Paris, 1898.

Ledyard, Gari. *The Dutch Come to Korea: An Account of the Life of the First Westerners in Korea, 1653–1666.* Royal Asiatic Society, Korea Branch. Seoul, 1971.

Lew Young Ick. "Kabo Reform Movement: The First Modern Reform Movement under the Japanese Control, 1894," Ph.D. thesis, Harvard University, 1971.

Li Hung-chang 李鴻章. *Li-wen-chung-kung ch'üan-chi* 李文忠公全集 (Li Hung-chang's works). Comp. by Wu Ju-lun 吳汝綸. Nanking, 1908.

Lin, T.C. "Li Hung-chang: His Korea Policies, 1870–1885," *Chinese Social and Political Science Review* 19.2:202–233 (July 1935).

Lowell, Percival. *Choson: The Land of the Morning Calm: A Sketch of Korea.* Boston, 1886.

Ma Chien-chung 馬建忠. *Tung-hsing san-lu* 東行三錄 (Records of three trips to Korea). Repr. Taipei, 1964.

Malozemoff, Andrew. *Russian Far Eastern Policy, 1881–1904.* Berkeley, University of California Press, 1958.

Man'gi yoram chaeyongp'yŏn 萬機要覽財用篇 (Guide to royal administration, section of finance), Collated and repr. by Chōsen sōtokufu. Keijo, 1937.

Mayo, Marlene J. "The Korean Crisis and Early Meiji Foreign Policy," *Journal of Asian Studies* 31.4:793–819 (Aug. 1972).

McCune, George M. "The Exchange of Envoys between Korea and Japan during the Tokugawa Period," *Far Eastern Quarterly* 5.3:308–325 (May 1946).

McCune, George M. and Harrison, John A. *Korean-American Relations.* Documents Pertaining to the Far Eastern Diplomacy of the United States. Vol. 1: The Initial Period. University of California Press, 1951.

Merrill, Henry F. "Letterbooks" (Manuscripts) in Houghton Library, Harvard University.

Mian 美案 (Documents pertaining to Korean-American relations). vols. 1–3.

Min T'ae-wŏn 閔泰瑗. *Kapsin chŏngbyŏn kwa Kim Ok-kyun* 甲申政變과 金玉均 (The 1884 incident and Kim Ok-kyun). Seoul, 1947.

Miwŏn'an 美原案 (Documents pertaining to Korean-American relations). vols. 1–3.

Moellendorff, Rosalie von. *P. G. von Moellendorff. Ein Lebensbild.* Leipzig, 1930.

Morrison, G. James. "Some Notes of a Trip to Corea, in July and August, 1883," *Journal of the North-China Branch of the Royal Asiatic Society* 18:141–157 (1883).

Morse, H. B. *The International Relations of the Chinese Empire.* 3 vols. London, 1910–1918.

Nakamura Hidetaka 中村榮孝. *Nissen kankei-shi no kenkyū* 日鮮關係史の研究 (Studies on the history of Korean-Japanese relations). 3 vols. Tokyo, 1965–1969.

Nelson, M. Frederick. *Korea and the Old Orders in Eastern Asia*. Baton Rouge, Louisiana State University Press, 1946.

Nichinichi shimbun.

Nippon gaikō bunsho 日本外交文書 (Diplomatic documents of Japan), comp. Gaimushō chōsabu 外務省調査部 (Research division of the Foreign Ministry). 16 vols. (1875–1890). Tokyo, 1936-.

Noble, Harold J. "The Korean Mission to the United States in 1883, the First Embassy sent by Korea to an Occidental Nation," *Transactions of the Korea Branch of the Royal Asiatic Society* 18:1–21 (1929).

———"The Former Foreign Settlements in Korea," *The American Journal of International Law* 23.4:766–782 (October 1929).

———"The United States and Sino-Korean Relations, 1885–1887," *Pacific Historical Review* 2.3:292–304 (Sept. 1933).

North China Herald, Shanghai, 1875–1885.

Ŏ Yun-jung 魚允中. *Chongjŏng yŏnp'yo* 從政年表 (Chronology of political events). Han'guk saryŏ ch'ongsŏ, No.6. Seoul, 1958.

Oeamun ch'ogi, kiil 外衙門草記其一 (Draft documents of the Foreign Office, first series). 2 vols.

Oeamun ch'ogi, kii 外衙門草記其二 (Draft documents of the Foreign Office, second series). vol. 1.

Ŏje ch'ŏksa yunŭm 御製斥耶綸音 (Royal message concerning the rejection of heresy). 1881.

Okudaira Takehiko 奥平武彦. *Chōsen kaikoku kōshō shimatsu* 朝鮮開國交渉始末 (A complete history of the opening of Korea). Tokyo, 1935.

Pak Il-gŭn 朴日槿. *Kŭndae Han-Mi oegyosa* 近代韓美外交史 (History of modern Korean-American relations). Seoul, 1968.

Pak Kyu-su 朴珪壽. *Hwanjae sŏnsaeng chip* 瓛齋先生集 (Collected works), with a preface by Kim Yun-sik 金允植. 11 *kwŏn*. 1911.

Pak Pong-sik 朴奉植. "Merrill sŏgan" 「메릴」書簡 (Merrill's letterbooks), in *Kim Chae-wŏn paksa hoegap kinyŏm nonch'ong* 金載元博士回甲紀念論叢 pp. 353–377. Seoul, 1969.

Pak Wŏn-p'yo 朴元杓. *Pusan ŭi ko'gŭm* 釜山의 古今 (Pusan past and present). Pusan, 1965.

———*Kaehang kusimnyŏn* 開港九十年 (Ninety years opening of Pusan). Pusan, 1966.

———*Hyangt'o Pusan* 鄉土釜山 (Pusan). Pusan, 1967.

Pak Wŏn-sŏn 朴元善. *Pobusang* 負褓商 (A study on Korean native merchants). The Korean Studies Series No. 16. Seoul, 1965.

Pak Yŏng-hyo 朴泳孝. *Sahwa kiryak* 使和記略 (Diary of a mission to Japan), in *Susinsa kirok* 修信使記錄 (Collection of records of envoys). Han'guk saryo ch'ongsŏ No. 9. Seoul, 1958.

———"Kaehwa e taehan sangso" 開化에 대한 上疏 (Memorial on enlightenment). Supplement of *Sindonga* 新東亞, pp. 12–23 (Jan. 1966).

Palais, James B. "Korea on the Eve of the Kanghwa Treaty, 1873–1876." Ph.D. thesis, Harvard University, 1968.

———*Politics and Policy in Traditional Korea*. Cambridge, Harvard University Press, 1975.

Palmer, Spencer J. *Korea and Christianity: The Problem of Identification with Tradition*. Royal Asiatic Society Monograph No. 2. Seoul, 1967.

P'alto sado samhanggu kwanmun 八道四都三港口關文 (Documents pertaining to the eight provinces, four cities and three ports). 2 vols.

Paullin, Charles O. *Diplomatic Negotiations of American Naval Officers, 1778–1883*. Baltimore, 1912.

P'ia wangbok sŏdŭngnok 彼我往復書謄錄 (Documents exchanged between the Japanese and the Koreans). 1 vol.

Pibyŏnsa tŭngnok 備邊司謄錄 (The records of the Pibyŏnsa). Repr. vols. 26–28. Seoul, 1959–1960.

Pollard, Robert T. "American Relations with Korea, 1882–1895," *Chinese Social and Political Science Review* 16.3:425–471 (Oct. 1932).

Pusan yaksa 釜山略史 (Short history of Pusan). Second ed. Pusan, 1968.

Pusanhang ch'uripku susei silsu sŏngch'aek 釜山港出入口收稅實數成冊 (Exact figures of the customs income at Pusan). vol. 3. 1883.

Reischauer, Edwin O. and Fairbank, John K. *East Asia: The Great Tradition*. Boston, Houghton Mifflin Company, 1958/1960.

Rokuku Ōkurashō Kankoku shi 露國大藏省韓國誌 (Russian Finance Ministry Report in Japanese translation). 1905.

Samhanggu kwanch'o 三港口關草 (Draft documents pertaining to the three ports). 2 vols.

Sansom, George B. *The Western World and Japan*. Alfred A. Knopf, New York, 1950.

Shibusawa Eiichi 澁澤榮一. *Shibusawa Eiichi denki shiryō* 澁澤榮一傳記資料 (Biographical materials). vol. 16. Tokyo, 1957.

Shikata Hiroshi 四方博. "Chōsen ni okeru kindai shihonshugi no seiritsu katei" 朝鮮に於ける近代資本主義の成立過程(The development of modern capitalism in Korea). *Chōsen shakai keizai shi kenkyū* 朝鮮社會經濟史研究 (Studies on the socio-economic history of Korea), pp. 1–211. Tokyo, 1933.

Sinjŭng Tongguk yŏji sŭngnam 新增東國輿地勝覽 (The new and enlarged gazetteer of Korea). Repr. Seoul, 1958.

Sinyak hu kanrikan yŏ Tongnae pusa yakchoch'o 新約後管理官與東萊府使約條草 (Draft agreements negotiated by Kondō Masuki and Hong U-ch'ang after 1876).

Sohn Pow-key. "The Opening of Korea: A Conflict of Traditions," *Transactions of the Korea Branch of the Royal Asiatic Society* 36:101–128 (April 1960).

———"Social History of the Early Yi Dynasty, 1392–1592." Ph.D. thesis, University of California, Berkeley, 1963.

Sok taejŏn 續大典 (Supplementary great code). Collated and repr. by Chōsen sōtokufu chūsūin. Keijo, 1938.

Song Pyŏng-gi 宋炳基. "Killin-Chosŏn sangmin susimuyŏk changjŏng yŏkchu," 「吉林・朝鮮商民隨時貿易章程」譯註 (Translation and commentary of Korean-Kirin treaty), *Sahak yŏn'gu* 21:193–207 (Sept. 1969).

Tabohashi Kiyoshi 田保橋潔. *Kindai Nissen kankei no kenkyū* 近代日鮮關係の研究 (A study on modern Korean-Japanese relations). 2 vols. Keijo, 1940.

Taehan minguk chido 大韓民國地圖 (The standard atlas of Korea). Seoul, 1960.

T'aejo sillok 太祖實錄 (The annals of King T'aejo).

T'aejong sillok 太宗實錄 (The annals of King T'aejong).

Tagawa Kōzo 田川孝三. *Richō kōnōsei no kenkyū* 李朝貢納制の研究 (A study on the tribute system of the Yi dynasty). The Toyo Bunko Publications Series A, No. 47. Tokyo, 1964.

Takayanagi Matsuichirō 高柳松一郎. *Shina kanzei seido ron* 支那關稅制度論 (A study of the Chinese maritime customs administration). Rev. and enlarged ed. Kyoto, 1926.

The Tokyo Times.

Tō-Chōsen 東朝鮮 (Eastern Korea). Wŏnsan, 1910.

Tŏgan 德案 (Korean-German correspondence). vols. 1–4.

Tŏgwŏnan 德原案 (Korean-German correspondence). vols. 1–2.

Tŏgwŏnbu kyerok 德源府啓錄 (Documents pertaining to Tŏgwŏn prefecture). 2 vols.

Tŏgwŏnbu ŭpchi 德源府邑誌 (Local gazetteer of Tŏgwŏn prefecture). 1 vol.

Tongnaebu kyerok 東萊府啓錄 (Documents concerning Tongnae prefecture). vol. 9.

T'ongmun kwanji 通文館志 (Records of the Bureau of Interpreters). Repr. Chōsen sōtokufu, Keijo, 1944.

T'ongni kyosŏp-t'ongsangsamu Amun ilgi 統理交涉通商事務衙門日記 (Diary of the Foreign Office). vols. 1–11.

T'ongni kyosŏp-t'ongsangsamu Amun sonap yŏmse chŏlmok 統理交涉通商事務衙門所納鹽稅節目 (Rules for the collection of the salt tax for the Foreign Office). 1885.

Treat, Payson J. "China and Korea, 1885–1894," *Political Science Quarterly* 49.4:506–543 (Dec. 1934).

Treaties, Regulations etc. Between Corea and Other Powers, 1876–1889. China, Imperial Maritime Customs III. Miscellaneous Series, No. 19. Shanghai, 1891.

Tsiang, T. F. "Sino-Japanese Diplomatic Relations, 1870–1894," *Chinese Social and Political Science Review* 17.1:1–106 (April 1933).

Tsiang (Chiang) T'ing-fu 蔣廷黻. *Chin-tai Chung-kuo wai-chiao-shih tzu-liao chi-yao* 近代中國外交史資料輯要 (Selected documents on modern Chinese diplomatic history). vol. 2. Repr. Taipei, 1959.

U.S. Department of State. *Despatches from United States Ministers to China.* (File microcopies of records in the National Archives, No. 92).

———*Despatches from United States Ministers to Japan.* (File microcopies of records in the National Archives, No. 133).

———*Despatches from United States Ministers to Korea.* (File microcopies of records in the National Archives, No. 134).

———*Diplomatic Instructions, Korea.* (File Microcopies of records in the National Archives, No. 77).

———*Papers Relating to Foreign Relations, 1875–1885.*

Waesa ilgi 倭使日記 (Diary of the negotiations with the Japanese). 14 vols.

Waesa mundap 倭使問答 (Conversations with the Japanese envoys). 3 vols.

Wang Yün-sheng 王芸生. *Liu-shih-nien-lai Chung-kuo yü Jih-pen* 六十年來中國與日本 (China and Japan during the last sixty years). Tientsin, 1932–1933. 6 vols.

Watanabe Katsumi 渡邊勝美. *Chōsen kaikoku gaikō shi kenkyū* 朝鮮開國外交史研究 (Diplomatic history of the opening of Korea). Keijo, 1937.

Won You-han (Wŏn Yu-han) 元裕漢. "Tangojŏn ko" 當五錢攷 (A study on the *tangojŏn*), *The Yŏksa Hakpo* 35/36:313–339 (Dec. 1967).

————"Chŏnhwan'guk ko" 典圜局攷 (A study on the Chŏnhwan'guk or the first modern Korean government mint), *The Yŏksa Hakpo* 37:49–100 (June 1968).

Wright, Mary C. "The Adaptability of Ch'ing Diplomacy, the Case of Korea," *The Journal of Asian Studies* 17.3:363–381 (May 1958).

Wright, S. F. *Hart and the Chinese Customs*. Belfast, 1950.

Yamabe Kentarō 山邊健太郎 "Jingo gunran ni tsuite" 壬午軍亂について (Concerning the rebellion of 1882), *Rekishigaku kenkyū* 歷史學研究 (Historical Studies) 257:13–26 (Sept. 1961)

Yi Chong-yŏng 李鍾英. "Chosŏnch'o hwap'yeje ŭi pyŏnch'ŏn" 朝鮮初貨幣制의 變遷 (Attempts to establish a currency by the Yi dynasty), *Inmun kwahak* 人文科學 (Journal of the humanities) 7:295–338 (June 1962).

Yi Hyŏn-jong 李鉉淙. *Chosŏn chŏn'gi tae-Il kyosŏpsa yŏn'gu* 朝鮮前期對日交涉史研究 (A study of Korean-Japanese relations in the early Yi dynasty). The Korean Studies Series, No. 10. Seoul, 1964.

————"Ku Hanmal oegugin kŏryujinae chojikch'e e taehayŏ" 舊韓末外國人居留地內 組織體에 대하여 (On the organizations in the foreign settlements of later Yi dynasty), *The Yŏksa Hakpo* 34:1–66 (June 1967).

————"Kamnisŏ yŏn'gu" 監理署研究 (A study of *kamnisŏ*), *Asea yŏn'gu* 31:3–75 (Sept. 1968).

————"Kojong ttae Kamsaengch'ŏng sŏlch'i e taehayŏ" 高宗때 減省廳設置에 대하여 (On the establishment of the Kamsaengch'ŏng), in *Kim Chae-wŏn paksa hoegap kinyŏm nonch'ong* 金載元博士回甲紀念論叢 pp. 311–330. Seoul, 1969.

————"Ku Hanmal oegugin kobing ko" 舊韓末外國人雇聘考 (Invitation of foreign advisers during the late 19th century), *Han'guksa yŏn'gu* 8:113–148 (Sept. 1972).

Yi Ki-baek 李基白. *Han'guksa sillon* 韓國史新論 (Korean history), Seoul, 1967.

————*Minjok kwa yŏksa* 民族과 歷史 (Nation and history). Seoul, 1971.

Yi Kwang-rin 李光麟. *Han'guk kaehwasa yŏn'gu* 韓國開化史研究 (Studies on Korea's enlightenment movement). Seoul, 1969.

————*Kaehwadang yŏn'gu* 開化黨研究 (The progressive party: 1879–1884). Seoul, 1973.

Yi Nŭng-hwa 李能和. *Chosŏn kidokkyo kŭp oegyosa* 朝鮮基督教及外交史 (Christianity and diplomacy in Korea). Repr. Seoul, 1968.

Yi Po-hyŏng 李普珩. "Shufeldt chedok kwa 1880nyŏn ŭi Cho-Mi kyosŏp" Shufeldt 提督과 1880年의 朝‧美交涉 (Commodore Shufeldt and the attempt to open Korea in 1880), *The Yŏksa Hakpo* 15:61–91 (Sept. 1961).

Yi Pyŏng-do 李丙燾. *Han'guksa, kodae-p'yŏn* 韓國史古代篇 (History of Korea; the ancient period). Seoul, 1959.

————*Han'guksa taegwan* 韓國史大觀 (Survey history of Korea). Seoul, 1960.

————*Han'guksa, chungse-p'yŏn* 韓國史中世篇 (History of Korea; the medieval period). Seoul, 1962.

Yi Sang-baek 李相佰. *Han'guksa, kŭnse chŏn'gi-p'yŏn* 韓國史近世前期篇 (History of Korea; the early modern period). Seoul, 1962.

————*Han'guksa, kŭnse hu'gi-p'yŏn* 韓國史近世後期篇 (History of Korea; the late modern period). Seoul, 1965.

Yi Sŏn-gŭn 李瑄根. *Han'guksa, ch'oegŭnse-p'yŏn* 韓國史最近世篇 (History of Korea; the modern period). Seoul, 1961.

Yi Wan-yŏng 李完永. "Tongnaebu mit Waegwan ŭi haengjŏng sogo" 東萊府 및 倭舘의 行政小考 (Study on the administration of the Japan House and Tongnae prefecture), *Hangdo Pusan* 港都釜山 (The port of Pusan) 2:11–75 (1963).

Yi Yong-hŭi 李用熙. "Tong-in sŭng ŭi haengjŏk—Kim Ok-kyun p'a kaehwadang ŭi hyŏngsŏng e yŏnhayŏ" 東仁僧의 行蹟(上)金玉均派開化黨의 形成에 沿하여 (On the activities of Yi Tong-in), *Nonmunjip* 論文集 (The Journal of International Studies) 1:7–47 (1973), part I.

Yi Yu-wŏn 李裕元. *Kao koryak* 嘉梧稿略 (Collected works). vols. 1, 4, 5, and 11 (approx. 1880).

Yŏngan 英案 (Documents pertaining to Korean-British relations). vols. 1–3.

Yongho hallok 龍湖閒錄 (Documents pertaining to Korea's foreign relations). vols. 22 and 23.

Yŏngsin 英信 (Korean-British correspondence).

Yŏngwŏnan 英原案 (Korean-British correspondence). vol. 1.

Yoo Won-dong (Yu Wŏn-dong) 劉元東. *Yijo hugi sanggongŏpsa yŏn'gu* 李朝後期商工業史研究 (History of commerce and industry in the latter period of the Yi dynasty). The Korean Studies Series, No. 25. Seoul, 1968.

———"18segi huban'gi ŭi sugongŏp palchŏn kwa sangŏp" 18世紀後半期의 手工業發展과商業 (The development of handicrafts in the second half of the 18th century and trade), *Kim Chae-wŏn paksa hoegap kinyŏm nonch'ong* 金載元博士回甲紀念論叢 pp. 227–267. Seoul, 1969.

———"19segi ch'ogi ŭi ponggŏn sangŏp ŭi punggoe kwajŏng" 19世紀初期의 封建商業의 崩壞過程 (The crumbling process of the feudalistic commerce in the 19th century), *The Yŏksa Hakpo* 48:1–48 (Dec. 1970).

Yu Kyo-sŏng 劉教聖. "Sŏul yugŭijŏn yŏn'gu" 서울六矣廛研究 (A study on ryuk-i-chun in Seoul), *The Yŏksa Hakpo* 8:377–434 (Sept. 1955).

———"Yijo malyŏp ŭi sam'gwan muyŏk ko" 李朝末葉의 三關貿易考 (On trade at the three ports in the late Yi dynasty), *Sahak yŏn'gu* 18:675–702 (Sept. 1964).

———"Han'guk sanggongŏp sa" 韓國商工業史 (A history of industry and commerce), in *Han'guksa munhwasa taegye* 韓國文化史大系 (Outline of Korean cultural history), II:967–1156. Seoul, 1965.

Note: Yu Wŏn-dong and Yu Kyo-sŏng are two different names of the same author.

INDEX

Peking

Tientsin

Paotingfu

Gulf of Chihli

Gulf of
Liaotung

Newchwan

K'aip'ing

Chefoo

Shantung Peninsula

Ching-tao

YELLOW

To Shanghai

Mattielli